Everyday Life in the
North Korean Revolution,
1945–1950

Everyday Life in the North Korean Revolution, 1945–1950

Suzy Kim

Cornell University Press
Ithaca and London

Cornell University Press gratefully acknowledges receipt of a grant
from the Association of Asian Studies First Book Subvention
Program, which aided in the publication of this book.

First published 2013 by Cornell University Press
Printed in the United States of America

Library of Congress Cataloging-in-Publication Data

Kim, Suzy, 1972– author.
    Everyday life in the North Korean revolution, 1945–1950 / Suzy
Kim.
        pages cm
    Includes bibliographical references and index.
    ISBN 978-0-8014-5213-0 (cloth : alk. paper)
    1. Revolutions—Social aspects—Korea (North)—History—20th
century. 2. Korea (North)—History—20th century. 3. Korea
(North)—Social life and customs—20th century. I. Title.
    DS935.55.K567   2013
    951.9304—dc23   2013004294

Cornell University Press strives to use environmentally responsible
suppliers and materials to the fullest extent possible in the publishing
of its books. Such materials include vegetable-based, low-VOC inks
and acid-free papers that are recycled, totally chlorine-free, or partly
composed of nonwood fibers. For further information, visit our
website at www.cornellpress.cornell.edu.

Cloth printing   10 9 8 7 6 5 4 3 2 1

Contents

Illustrations

Tables

Acknowledgments

Academic and intellectual work can be an intensely solitary endeavor, but this book is the result of a genuinely collaborative journey that began at the University of Chicago. My greatest thanks go to Bruce Cumings, whose scholarship has been an inspiration for its rigorous pursuit of truth and justice while he remains a compassionate historian above all. He has been there from the very inception of the project to the last draft of the manuscript. I am also grateful to Kyeong-Hee Choi, who injected the renewed significance of women's studies into my academic training, opening up a whole new world of inquiry. William Sewell and Friedrich Katz were valuable guides in comparative studies of revolutions and communisms, respectively.

A close community of cohorts continued to provide encouragement and support throughout the past ten years. Henry Em, Albert Park, Saul Thomas, and Yoon Sun Yang have unstintingly shared their time amid their own busy schedules to read the manuscript in whole or in part and to comment on and critique it at various stages. I thank them for their genuine friendship. Chong-myong Im, Namhee Lee, Mike Shin, and Jun Yoo have also provided support in many ways, from offering opportunities to present my work to furnishing countless research and teaching materials.

My home department of Asian Languages and Cultures at Rutgers University gave me much needed time to finish the book, and I am particularly grateful for my senior colleague, Young-mee Yu Cho, for her generosity. A fellowship at Seoul National University's Kyujanggak Institute for Korean Studies accommodated my sabbatical leave in the last year of finalizing the book, and I thank Professors Pak T'ae-kyun and Sem Vermeersch for their hospitality. I also thank Professor Chŏng Yong-uk, his modern Korean history graduate students, and the Korean History Department for hosting a colloquium where I benefited from comments about my work. In addition,

Professors Kim Myŏng-hwan and Chŏng Kŭn-sik were vital mentors on an otherwise unfamiliar campus. Likewise, opportunities to present my work at Yonsei University, hosted by Professors Paek Mun-im and Sin Hyŏng-ki, and at Chonnam University, hosted by Professor Im Chong-myŏng, were much appreciated. At a much earlier stage, Professors Pang Ki-jung and Kim Sŏng-bo at Yonsei University were generous guides during my research, and I learned a great deal in their seminars.

Various stages of research and writing have been supported by funds from the Korea Foundation Postdoctoral Fellowship at the University of Michigan, the University of Chicago Center for East Asian Studies Dissertation Writing Fellowship, the University of Chicago Gender Studies Fellowship, Foreign Language and Area Studies Fellowship (Title VI) from the U.S. Department of Education, Fulbright IIE Dissertation Research Fellowship, and a graduate studies fellowship and a travel grant from the Northeast Asia Council of the Association for Asian Studies.

An earlier version of chapter 6 was published in *Comparative Studies in Society and History* (October 2010) and I acknowledge Cambridge University Press for permission to publish an expanded version here. Roger Haydon at Cornell University Press has been a steadfast steward throughout the arduous process of getting the manuscript to press, and I am grateful for his guidance and the helpful comments offered in the anonymous reviews he commissioned. I had the great fortune to have John Raymond as my copyeditor, who went beyond the call of duty to lend a sympathetic and careful reading of the manuscript, not only to improve its readability but also to make it more coherent. In that regard, I must also thank Susan Specter for putting the manuscript in John's care and for meticulously going through the edits one last time.

The whole winding journey would not have started or continued without two communities outside academe. First, my family deserves much of the credit for the tenacity the project required, especially my mother, Jaehi Kim, and my partner, Isaac Trapkus. Their perseverance and patience will always put me to shame. More than anyone, I owe my mother for teaching me true grit. And second, I learned much from the families and staff at Minkahyup, a human rights group based in Seoul, who opened my eyes to the social and political world. Sadly, one of them passed away as I finished the book. It has been almost twenty years since I worked there, but the experience has stayed with me, reminding me what it means to live in this world and not just study it.

Note on Usage

I have used the McCune-Reischauer system for the romanization of Korean names and terms, except in quoting original North Korean publications in English and in cases where the spelling has become common usage, such as in Pyongyang or Kim Il Sung. I have kept the last name first in referring to Korean historical figures in the text and to Korean authors in the notes, as is the standard practice in Korean unless they have their own romanized names. For the romanization of foreign terms other than Korean, I have simply duplicated the system used in the source consulted. In the discussion of the colonial period in chapter 2, I have indicated Japanese terms with a "J" where it was unclear whether the transliterated term was Korean or Japanese.

The two Koreas were officially named the Democratic People's Republic of Korea (DPRK) in the north and the Republic of Korea (ROK) in the south with the founding of separate states in 1948, but following general convention I refer to them in shorthand as North Korea and South Korea. For consistency, I also use these terms with the beginning of the two separate occupation zones in 1945 despite the fact that they were not two separate states until 1948.

All translations are mine unless otherwise indicated.

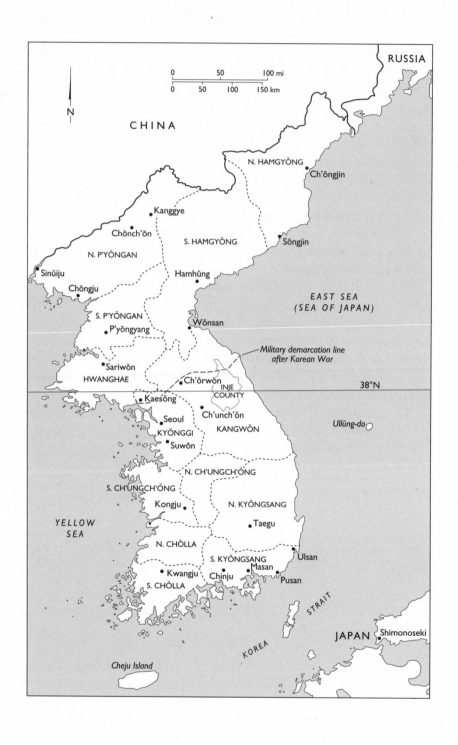

RUSSIA

CHINA

N

0   50   100 mi
0   50   100   150 km

N. HAMGYŎNG

Ch'ŏngjin

Kanggye

Chŏnch'ŏn

S. HAMGYŎNG

Sŏngjin

N. P'YŎNGAN

Sinŭiju

Hamhŭng

Chŏngju

EAST SEA
(SEA OF JAPAN)

S. P'YŎNGAN

Wŏnsan

P'yŏngyang

Military demarcation line
after Korean War

Sariwŏn

HWANGHAE

Ch'ŏrwŏn

38°N

INJE
COUNTY

Kaesŏng

Ch'unch'ŏn

Seoul

Ullŭng-do

KYŎNGGI

KANGWŎN

Suwŏn

N. CH'UNGCH'ŎNG

S. CH'UNGCH'ŎNG

Kongju

N. KYŎNGSANG

YELLOW
SEA

Taegu

N. CHŎLLA

Ulsan

S. KYŎNGSANG

Masan

Kwangju

Chinju

Pusan

S. CHŎLLA

KOREA
STRAIT

JAPAN

Shimonoseki

Cheju Island

Everyday Life in the
North Korean Revolution,
1945–1950

Introduction

A satellite image of the Korean Peninsula at night shows South Korea and the surrounding regions bathed in light while North Korea seems engulfed in darkness except for the capital city of Pyongyang. The image has symbolized North Korea's "backwardness" since U.S. Secretary of Defense Donald Rumsfeld referred to it during a news briefing on December 23, 2002: "If you look at a picture from the sky of the Korean Peninsula at night, South Korea is filled with lights and energy and vitality and a booming economy; North Korea is dark."[1] From this description, he concludes matter-of-factly, "It is a tragedy what's being done in that country." To be sure, North Korea has serious problems, but what is the precise nature of the tragedy?

A closer look at the process of creating the image reveals a more complicated picture. A product of modern technology, it is a composite of multiple images from repeated orbits around the earth—236 to be exact—with sophisticated algorithms to adjust for anomalies such as fires and lightning.[2] In other words, it is not an image that the naked eye could see from the sky, nor an image that speaks for itself, as Rumsfeld would have us believe. It is a constructed image, made possible only through sophisticated engineering. It is worth pondering to what extent other images of North Korea are deployed to fit certain premises.

Rumsfeld's conclusion linking light and energy with "a booming economy" implies that economic growth is an inherent good, and without it there is only tragedy. However, as unrestrained consumption of energy comes under growing scrutiny, it is no longer clear how desirable it is for so much light to flood such uneven patches of the globe. North Korea is not the only place in the world without as much light as South Korea or Japan. Vast inhabited stretches of Africa, South and Southeast Asia, and China do not come close to the amount of electricity consumed per capita in the United States and Europe.[3] Rather than split the world into simplistic binaries of light and dark as markers of good and evil, in this book I start from the premise that the world is integrated, particularly with the acceleration of modernity that, beginning in the nineteenth century, compressed time and space, creating a world that is highly uneven, with some places modernizing at the expense of others.

North Korea is a part of that world, and I begin with this common image in order to deconstruct widespread perceptions that it is "backward" and therefore outside of modernity. Even those who trace North Korea's predicament to the trauma of the Korean War (1950–53) and American responsibility for carpet bombing much of the country still characterize it as "a country suspended in time, one that exists off modernity's grid . . . a place where the cold war never ended, where the heirloom paranoia is taken down and polished daily."[4] It is true that the Cold War has not ended in Korea—the North and South remain divided—but North Korea was a different place before the Korean War.

Indeed, northern Korea was more modern than many other parts of East Asia, witnessing substantial industrialization under Japanese colonial rule (1910–45), especially during the 1930s when mobilization for war required industries from steel to chemical factories. The capital, Pyongyang, was known as the "Jerusalem of the East," the largest center of Christian activity in East Asia with the attendant importation of Western culture. Despite the acknowledged importance of history, however, North Korea is seldom thought to have a history worth examining; through the lens of the Cold War, it is consigned to the dustbin of history as an anachronistic relic of a Stalinist state. This book is an attempt to restore North Korea's historicity and its place within the history of modernity, an inconvenient truth perhaps better left ignored for fear that North Korea's problems may not be its alone. There is enough responsibility to go around, including that of the United States, for modernity's discontents. Rather than recognize the shared heritage, however, Western media coverage of North Korea paints it as a vast network of gulags ruled over by an omnipotent dictator, a realization of George Orwell's dystopia in *1984* where modern technology is used to police both thought and action. Through repeated stock images, modernity's worst excesses are displaced onto North Korea as a singular anomaly rather than the common by-product of modernity. Consequently, North Korea has become a place where "Dr. Evil" rules over one corner of the "axis of evil" in the last "outpost of tyranny," in the words, respectively, of *Newsweek*, President George W. Bush, and Secretary of State Condoleezza Rice.[5]

Scholars have not done much better. After acknowledging that politics in North Korea is far more complicated than it is usually made out to be, one specialist declared, "Of course, the simplified historiography of North Korea is not totally without merit, for the political history of North Korea is essentially a history of the rise of one man. Kim Il-song [*sic*] is the sole winner, the hero, the omnipotent one."[6] But North Korea emerged out of a complicated and neglected history, and this book opens at the beginning. Without an understanding of its origins, North Korea will forever remain the Other, potentially taking us to the brink of another tragic war on the Korean Peninsula. North Korea's history is not simply the history of one man or the party, but part and parcel of the history of modernity, not "suspended in time" but part of the global history of decolonization. This is a story of peasants and villagers during North Korea's social revolution from 1945, when Korea was liberated from Japanese colonial rule, to 1950, before the start of the Korean War.[7] North Korea embarked on an alternative path to modernity, opposing both colonial and capitalist modernity.

Generally, modernity has been linked with a wide variety of developments in the modern age, from rationality, science, and technology to bureaucracy, social stratification, market systems, legal jurisprudence, and democratic institutions. From the perspective of modernization theory, modernity was the natural outcome of a universal linear development of mankind from traditional agrarian societies to modern industrialized ones, aided by technological innovation that led to increased production and mass consumption. However, a broad survey shows that different forms of technologies, markets, laws, bureaucracies, and social differentiation have existed in different parts of the world throughout much of human history.[8] What set the modern era apart from previous history to define the main characteristics of modernity was industrialization and the impetus for it—namely, capitalism. As Immanuel Wallerstein has stated succinctly, "We do not live in a modernizing world but in a capitalist world."[9]

Although the Enlightenment is often touted as the beginning of modernity, its faith in science as the source of universal laws was not too far a leap from faith in the divine as the source of absolute truth, as demonstrated by the deep religiosity of such key Enlightenment figures as Isaac Newton and René Descartes.[10] Not until the Industrial Revolution was the power of human design made visible through revolutionary advances in transportation and manufacturing, changing the fabric of everyday life. Despite a growing sense of human agency, however, the mechanization of labor that replaced the tradition of skilled craftsmanship subjected increasing numbers of workers and their families to the "laws" of the market.

Regulated by the "invisible hand," the status of capitalism as "scientific" marginalized human agency just when it seemed historically most substantive. The publication of Adam Smith's *The Wealth of Nations* (1776), the first major treatise on modern economics and capitalism, was followed emblematically by the French Revolution in 1789. The revolution declared man master of himself with the Declaration of the Rights of Man and of the Citizen, invoking natural law rather than a higher being as the basis for inviolable rights. This was the birth of modern subjectivity. The modern subject was to remain largely bourgeois, defined by those privileged enough to own property and participate in public life in the exercise of their economic and political rights. Socialist modernity was a direct response to the limits of capitalist modernity. It attempted to realize more fully the emancipatory potential of modernity, not by faith in the "invisible hand" of capitalism but by purposeful planning in service of collective social need over individual profit.[11]

The problem with defining modernity as the rise of bureaucracy and rationality is, from Max Weber to Michel Foucault, the conflation of modernity's form common to all modern societies with its varied substance, quite deliberately blurring the boundaries between different political systems. Yet it matters whether modernity is colonial, capitalist, or socialist. Critique of modern methods of discipline and control should not preclude a rigorous analysis of differences *within* modernity, so as to restore its potential for human emancipation. Admittedly, much violence has been perpetrated in the name of freedom, but the present as a stage toward a better future is not the monopoly of the modern era. What is central to modernity is not the notion of liberation per se, but the idea that the efforts of men (and more recently also women) will bring about change—that is, Man as Creator. As Agnes Heller aptly described it, "None of our predecessors could consciously create history, prepare the future, or plan it. Only the moderns are able to do these things."[12] The revolutionary and emancipatory potential of Marxist thought that differentiates it from the liberal variety is precisely the elevation of the most downtrodden and exploited to the position of privileged subjects—the ones to bring about a better future for all of humanity. Invoking the term *heroic modernism*, I mark socialist modernity as distinct from either capitalist or colonial modernity in its belief in the emancipatory potential of history through new forms of community. Socialist modernity embodied the capacity of people to boldly step out as political agents to make history, even if the conditions were not of their choosing and the outcomes were not what they intended. It is the very definition of heroism: the courage to try even at risk of failure.

With the Japanese surrender at the end of World War II, Korea gained its independence from Japan's thirty-five-year colonial rule not on its own terms, but by default. Still, years of colonial discrimination and political oppression had created a fiercely nationalistic people with a desire for self-government and independence. These desires found expression through numerous self-governing organizations spontaneously formed throughout the peninsula in the void left by the dissolution of the Japanese colonial apparatus after August 15, 1945. They were called "people's committees" (PCs, *inmin wiwŏnhoe*), among other names, and they quickly spread across the country, organizing people at every level down to the villages. The PCs were organs of self-government with local autonomy, providing a basis for an independent Korean government. But Korea became the first victim of the Cold War. Liberation was marred by the division of the country into two separate occupation zones—the Soviets in the north, the Americans in the south. As the two spheres solidified, the northern PCs, supported by the Soviets, became organs for social change albeit centrally directed, whereas the southern PCs were quickly suppressed by the American occupation, which perceived them as left-wing and as challenging the power of the United States military government. By 1948 the increasingly centralized regimes on both sides declared two separate states—the Republic of Korea in the south on the third-year anniversary of liberation, and the Democratic People's Republic of Korea in the north the following month. Participatory grassroots organs of self-government, unprecedented on such a scale in Korea, had by then been purged in the south and centralized in the north.

The colonial experience weighed heavily on the resurgence of centralized state power, which fused the ethnic nation and the political state to create the first modern republic in Korea in the north and the south. However, the process of state formation was complicated by the division of the country, which exacerbated colonial cleavages mapped onto Cold War conflicts. Those who had sided with the colonial government, either to survive or to get ahead, believing in its imperial project for modernizing Korea, were now considered useful by the American occupation for setting up an anticommunist bulwark on the peninsula. Colonial collaborators were given a new lease on life by joining with the United States in the coming Cold War. On the other hand, the vast majority of peasants who made up Korean society were ready for radical change; they had been relegated to the margins under colonial rule with few to no opportunities offered by modernity, whether in the form of education or consumerism. Peasants demanded land reform and political autonomy through the people's committees—all programs supported by the Soviets—which automatically branded them as communists whether they had any understanding of its actual tenets. Under these circumstances, the division of Korea decreased room for maneuvering on both sides. Nonetheless, North Korea attempted to sketch out its own path, instituting sweeping changes that sought to eradicate both its painful colonial past and its traditional hierarchical relations of gender, class, and social status. Although older forms of inequality and exploitation were eliminated only to be replaced by different forms of hierarchy and domination, changes in North Korea in this period were revolutionary and unprecedented in Korean history.

The Russians hardly show up in the coming pages precisely because they were not present at the local level. Koreans were running the show the further away one got from Pyongyang. Local documents—many of them scribbled in newly learned handwritten letters—reveal token acknowledgment of the Soviet Union but overall show people preoccupied with reconstructing a new nation and governing themselves. As the only American reporter to travel through North Korea in 1947, Anna Louise Strong was struck by how "naïvely" insistent "Koreans seemed to think that they were running things."[13] She observed that the "only concentration of Russians was in the capital, Pyongyang, and they were not very conspicuous even there." A local Korean informed her that only ten to twelve Russians were in his provincial capital and three to four in his county seat "just to give advice." A committed admirer of Soviet Russia, Strong was openly condescending, seeing North Koreans as "adolescents in politics who still have to learn some international facts of life," but she was also keen to note that "their attitude showed an awakened sense of their own political power . . . [as a] furiously active political life went on."[14]

Of course, in looking at Soviet documents it is clear that the Soviets were attempting to mold the newly emerging North Korean state, and successfully so.[15] They were particularly influential in the drafting of the constitution and reform measures, as well as the formation of foreign policy, military organizations, and the training of party cadres. However, as Erik van Ree documented from Soviet sources, the Soviets pursued the same interests as the Russian Empire in the nineteenth century—access to warm water ports and a friendly government in Korea as a bulwark against Japanese threats.[16] Soviet military maps at the end of the Asia-Pacific War indicated plans only down to the 38th parallel, honoring the agreement with the United States for a divided occupation zone; the units to be deployed for the occupation of North Korea were not finalized until August 25, 1945, five days *after* fighting had ended with the Japanese in Korea.[17]

Moreover, a decree by the Soviet occupation dated September 27, 1945, announced the abolition of all Japanese colonial institutions and the confiscation of all lands owned by Japanese and pro-Japanese elements.[18] Such a decree was in stark contrast to orders issued by the American occupation, which in effect instructed that the colonial structure be left intact and made English the official language in the south.[19] Although both occupation powers were unprepared for their mission, the Soviets clearly understood the political stakes of decolonization, whereas the Americans did not.

What is missing from Soviet documents, and indeed from most studies on North Korea, is the everyday life of local villages undergoing a major transformation, instituting hands-on the radical changes in a revolution that no Soviet official could have orchestrated. Andrei Lankov, another scholar who has looked at the role of the Soviet Union in early North Korea, concludes from Soviet sources that there was limited coordination between the Soviets and Koreans: "Most decisions were made on the spot, and the military reported to Moscow only some problems and plans. . . . Sometimes, local Communists were 'more Catholic than the Pope himself,' copying the Moscow pattern with a zeal that even their Soviet patrons occasionally found a bit excessive."[20]

However, attention solely to local politics has its own pitfalls. Paradoxically, a postcolonial history that purports to go beyond the "nation" to emphasize local developments combines powerfully with a nationalist history that wants to find domestic origins for historical change to erase the truly transnational character of Korea's socialist and nationalist movements. This combination has had unfortunate results in the historiography of socialist movements in Korea by sidelining the internationalism inherent in the socialist program (despite "socialism in one country"), particularly with respect to socialism in North Korea.[21] Partly, this was necessary to move beyond Cold War binaries while also deflecting charges of an international communist conspiracy.[22] North Korea itself has increasingly deemphasized the role of the Soviet Union and the international communist movement in its history. Still, local developments in North Korea need to be situated within a transnational context.

Local people's committees, party chapters, and mass organizations served as forums through which transnational ideologies and competing visions for the ideal nation-state were played out in the immediate postliberation period. What distinguished these competing visions were not lofty political ideas—principles of independence, democracy, and equality were touted by all—but the minute details of how everyday life should be organized. Everyday life, whether public or private, came under scrutiny as the primary arena for social change. This move was solidly within the current of discourses and practices of modernity in the first half of the twentieth century, as the opening chapter shows.

Rather than take the everyday for granted as a natural unit of time, however, chapter 1 historicizes the everyday as a distinctly modern concept that emerged from the experience of industrial capitalism. Although everyday life is often conflated with the ordinary—the common, repetitive elements that make up daily life, such as food, fashion, home, work, and recreation—the everyday is a modern phenomenon and there is nothing ordinary about it.[23] It is a distinctly modern temporal category whereas the ordinary is a normative concept, making the latter that much more arbitrary and ambiguous since what is deemed normal is specific to place and time. A particular everyday may certainly be ordinary, but not every day is ordinary. During revolutions the everyday is quite purposefully the site of social change, making it extraordinary. Indeed, an alternative everyday was envisioned within socialist modernity during the heyday of revolution in the Soviet Union. Adding Chinese examples to the discussion, the North Korean Revolution is located within these currents of everyday socialist modernity in the first chapter.

I want to make clear that my focus on the everyday differs from studies of everyday life that take the everyday as the "authentic" and the "real," offering a potential for resistance against metanarratives and hegemonic structures. I do not take the everyday as an authentic space of agency *outside* of or *against* structure, but as a site of conjuncture in which different forms of agency are articulated *within* and *through* various structural formations. Chapter 1 presents the everyday as a site of such articulations in order to show how the socialist everyday articulated a specific kind of agency quite different from, and in opposition to, the one under capitalist modernity. Although the everyday served to maintain the status quo under capitalist modernity, it became the most visibly radical site of social change during the North Korean Revolution.

After having laid out the everyday as the theoretical framework for the book, chapter 2 looks back at Korea's colonial period to show how North Korea's socialist modernity was a direct response to colonial and capitalist modernity, which together had introduced a form of modernity without the concomitant recognition of modern subjects. Although Japan's colonial modernization brought rationalized production and public education to Korea as two hallmarks of modernity, its treatment of colonial subjects and "imperialization" policies stripped colonial modernity of a full-fledged sense of modern subjectivity. In reaction, North Korea would develop an alternative collective subject based on the idea of self-reliance that was to become one of the most distinct aspects of North Korea's socialist modernity.

Describing the formation of this alternative collective subject, chapters 3 and 4 hone in on one particular county in North Korea—Inje County—for a detailed view of how everyday life was transformed during the revolution to produce a new modern subject. Not only is the county situated along the 38th parallel but the archives offer the most abundant material on the county of any county in North Korea, facilitating its close study. Chapter 3 highlights three events—a radical land reform that restructured social relations, the first mass election in Korea's history, and a literacy campaign that brought educational opportunity to the most remote villages—as particularly significant in forging a new basis for social relations, political participation, and cultural life.

No matter how groundbreaking they may be, landmark events have to be sustained by permanent organizations and ongoing practices that institutionalize the essential tenets of those events into the everyday. Chapter 4 focuses on organizations through which the revolution was institutionalized, defining one of the primary changes in everyday life as the emergence of a collective life through participation in organizations, especially in the ubiquitous meetings and study groups that structured daily habits.

Organizational practices are brought together with discursive ones in chapter 5, showing how specific identities such as "worker," "peasant," and ambiguous terms such as "*samuwŏn*" (office worker, or clerk) were constructed as revolutionary subjects through the practice of writing autobiographies and filling out resumes. In the process of narrating their personal lives within the larger history of the revolution, individuals came to identify themselves as part of a collective, and abstract categories like worker and peasant came to have concrete meaning. To show the process of narrative construction, one particular dossier—that of Kim Ho-ch'ŏl—is examined in depth, comparing three different versions of his autobiography.

Although women are part of the story throughout the chapters, chapter 6 examines more specifically the treatment of the "woman question" during the revolution and the gendered discourse of revolutionary subjectivity through a close reading of *Chosŏn yŏsŏng* (Korean Woman), the only women's journal published in North Korea after liberation. Contrary to pervasive images of masculine revolutionary brotherhood in communist iconography, revolutionary motherhood became the quintessential symbol of revolutionary subjectivity, melding the old and the new, as a model for all of North Korean society.

Finally, chapter 7 bridges past and present by looking at how the revolution is remembered within the broader frame of "liberated space," as the immediate postliberation period is often described. Incorporating oral histories and memoirs from both the north and the south, the chapter points out differences between men's and women's narratives of liberation, signaling the importance of organizations and collectives by which experiences take on meaning and memories live on. Indeed, collective memories are powerful sources of individual identity, but collective memories cannot be sustained without institutional support. In that sense, this final chapter reaffirms the significance of a collective life, particularly for marginalized groups such as women.

Whereas North Korea's focus on the collective has been explained through corporatist models, there has been little effort to explain what such a collective orientation means in terms of concrete practices and how it might be understood within the socialist project. Past legacies such as Korea's commitment to neo-Confucianism or the colonial experience of the Japanese emperor system fail to account for the development of a collective society in North Korea that drew specifically on Soviet socialist practices. After all, socialism is grounded in the idea of the collective, not only in its faith in the collective power of the working class but also in its utopian vision of society organized on the basis of collective social needs. Illustrating everyday practices that generated a sense of collectivity during North Korea's formative years, each of the following chapters paints a picture of how particular collectives began to take on meaning and the extent to which they resonated with those living through the revolution. This book will have achieved its purpose if it succeeds in explaining why and how the everyday was defined by "social practice" in North Korea, which sought to create a "socially productive life" that challenged both colonial and capitalist notions about modernity.

Historiography and Sources

Although the idea that North Korea was a satellite state of the Soviet Union has lost credibility since the fall of the Soviet bloc, many continue to emphasize the Stalinist roots of North Korean state formation, using the opening of Soviet archives to support such analysis without taking into consideration North Korean reactions to Soviet policies.[24] Even among those that acknowledge domestic and internal dynamics, the focus remains on state building, the political leadership, party politics, and the policies of the Soviet Union, emphasizing the top-down state-led aspect of the North Korean Revolution.[25] Although a handful of pathbreaking works, beginning with *The Origins of the Korean War* by Bruce Cumings, went beyond this top-down focus to include social conditions, covering statistical data on tenancy rates, political disturbances, and affiliations of the people's committee leadership, studies on the inner workings of the people's committees and village life have remained major lacunae. Although the people's committees in the south have been studied by South Korean historians, the people's committees in the north have received scant attention.[26] There are only a handful of monographs in Korean, and none in English, that focus on the people's committees in North Korea.[27] Even though, starting in the mid-1990s, scholars in South Korea have begun to look at the relationship between national and local developments in North Korea, the focus remains on political history.

The reasons are many. The study of North Korea, whether historical or contemporary, has been shrouded in the continuing legacy of the Cold War. Much too often, events in Korea are seen as extensions of the growing conflict between the Soviet Union and the United States, with Koreans acting as pawns rather than as historical actors in their own right. To this day, the various aspects of a socialist system are simplistically lumped together as a "one-party" state or a "totalitarian" state, without defining what socialism meant in concrete terms for people's lives.[28] One-party states can take on many different forms, and the simple fact of one-party rule has little explanatory power in itself. Meanwhile, totalitarianism, a term that gained popular currency during the Cold War to refer to the Soviet Union, has been polemically driven, defined either too narrowly and thus unrealistic—focusing overwhelmingly on the state as a monolithic political system, in which absolute obedience is effectively enforced by dogmatic ideology and terror—or encompassing so many different characteristics that its usefulness as a theoretical category is compromised.[29]

By contrast, I frame the history of North Korea as part of socialist modernity. Some might question whether such variants of "actually existing socialism" are genuinely socialist.[30] The point here is not to engage in a theoretical debate about the essential tenets of socialism but to historicize what socialism meant for postcolonial, predominantly agrarian societies like North Korea, and how they went about putting what they considered to be socialism into practice through mass participation. I take socialist modernity to encompass the general impulse to liberate people from the adverse effects of capitalism toward the full achievement of human potential and emancipation through new forms of community. It is in this emphasis on a socialist collective (not necessarily a "workers' state") that the North Korean Revolution was fully within the frame of socialist modernity, however broadly defined. This line of argument also challenges Eurocentric histories of socialist modernity that relegate socialism in the Third World to top-down Soviet manipulation, as if they were mere puppets, discounting their variant of socialism as "parochial" and "instrumental," as if their motivations for economic development and national sovereignty had nothing to do with social equality or political freedom.[31]

Nonetheless, the dominance of the state in the politics of a divided country such as Korea have led conventional histories in both Koreas to emphasize the role of the state in history-making and the extent of state penetration in social life, dichotomizing state and society. The approach I take in this book challenges the strict separation of state and society, examining the degree to which state-society relations are actually fluid and interdependent. The newly forming state was not simply expanding into remote villages as an oppressive force. It had to be sensitive to everyday life concerns, public opinion, and demands, particularly at a time of competing hegemony between north and south.

This book is thus a social history, focusing on the practices of everyday life in North Korea—to date the only work of its kind—moving away from an emphasis on political leaders and central urban institutions toward those less prominent, such as women, peasants, the local, the rural, and the everyday. These populations and locales are difficult to trace historically because they do not have access to conduits through which history has usually been passed down. Personal memoirs and other writings were limited to the elite by disparities in education and positions of power and status. Official documents serve a particular purpose, and areas outside their purview were neglected and ignored. Compounding the problem in the case of North Korea is the lack of access to North Korean archives.

The best source for North Korea's early history is, ironically, in the United States, just a few miles outside Washington, D.C. The collection commonly referred to as the North Korean Captured Documents contains 1,608,000 pages of "Records Seized by the US Military Forces in Korea" during the Korean War (1950–53). Declassified in 1977, the collection is housed at the National Archives II in College Park, Maryland, under Record Group 242.[32] It includes an amazing collection of materials including letters, diaries, personnel files, minutes of meetings of various organizations, educational materials, newspapers, magazines, court documents, and photographs.[33] The collection offers an excellent window into early North Korea, but only a handful of scholars have used it, and no one to date has used the materials for a microhistory of everyday life.[34] Parts of this collection have been reproduced in a continuing series of volumes entitled *Historical Materials Related to North Korea* (*Pukhan kwan'gye saryojip*) published by the National History Compilation Committee (NHCC, *Kuksa p'yŏnch'an wiwŏnhoe*), a government research institution in South Korea. As of 2011, sixty-seven volumes in this series have been published.[35]

The vast majority of the captured documents are government documents and official publications. Nonetheless, combing through the pages reveals multiple voices and competing interests underneath the official line that come through *despite* attempts to centralize and homogenize what was actually a complicated revolutionary process involving conflict, negotiation, and compromise. The story of the North Korean Revolution is not a triumphant story of the heroic coming together of revolutionary leaders and masses for a social revolution, nor a tragic story of a revolution betrayed by the revolutionary leaders who had forsaken the masses in their own rise to power. Neither the top-down model of revolution that views the North Korean Revolution as Kim Il Sung's singular project nor the bottom-up model that views it as entirely spontaneous is accurate. People are never automatons simply doing what they are told, and neither are they completely spontaneous, without histories or trajectories. The spontaneity under such circumstances was similar to what Pierre Bourdieu, in describing the *habitus*, called "regulated improvisations" or "spontaneity without consciousness."[36] Spontaneity within the flow of time can never be something that arises out of nothing, but strictly speaking must be revisions and transformations based on the historical past. Looking at North Korean peasants as historical actors, I bring together individual subjectivity and agency with collective interests and identities as a process of negotiation between the larger revolutionary agenda and the individual's place in it.

1. Revolutions in the Everyday

Even in a crowd, they know how to express their opinions, clap and raise their hands, and exclaim with bursting sincerity that women also need to learn. This must be the noble lesson taught to them by the era. In everyday life from liberation until today, they have personally experienced that without learning one cannot be useful as a person. They have become the valiant women of Korea supporting the radical development of a new Korea.
SOYŎN, *CHOSŎN YŎSŎNG*, MAY 1947

Figure 1.1. Korean–Soviet friendship (n.p., n.d.). RG 242, SA 2012, box 5, item 139. Courtesy of the National Archives and Records Administration.

During the North Korean Revolution, everyday life became at once the primary site of political struggle and the single most important arena for experiencing the revolution in progress. Publications were peppered with expressions that emphasized a particular aspect of everyday life, from more recognizable terms such as family life (*kajŏng saenghwal*) and social life (*sahoejŏk saenghwal*) to less familiar ones such as party life (*tang saengh-wal*), organizational life (*chojik saenghwal*), collective life (*tanch'e saenghwal*), ideological life (*sasang saenghwal*), scientific life (*kwahakchŏk saenghwal*), life reform (*saenghwal kaesŏn*), and life skill (*saenghwal kisul*). Life after liberation was variously described as a new life (*sinsaenghwal*), a happy life (*haengbokhan saenghwal*), and ultimately a total "revolution in life" (*saenghwal hyŏngmyŏng*). Composed of two Chinese characters for life and living, *saenghwal* (生活) denotes life in the act of living. Thus, the repeated references to *saenghwal* in these phrases refer more accurately to a way of living, a lifestyle for everyday life.

Indeed, an article calling on women to revolutionize their *saenghwal* advocated the following:[1]

1. Let's work and learn.
2. Let's overthrow superstition.
3. Let's eliminate extravagance and gossip.
4. Let's have a plan in daily life.
5. Let's reform old habits and customs of the past (simplify the traditional rituals for capping, marriage, funeral, and ancestor worship).
6. Let's have a scientific dietary life (maximize nutrition; shorten cooking time).
7. Let's reform our clothes to suit productive activities (dark clothes; appropriate fabric).
8. Let's fix our home so that we can work comfortably and live well (ventilation; heating).
9. Let's strengthen our sense of hygiene in daily life.

No aspect of the everyday was left untouched, from undesirable habits to the appropriate housing, clothing, diet, and hygiene. Topping the list were the two most important elements to incorporate anew into one's everyday life—work and education.

At first glance, however, such slogans and appeals may seem rather mundane and banal, reminiscent of other modernization projects, particularly under colonial Korea when various attempts had been made to mobilize peasants as well as women. Cultural reformers had advanced remarkably similar advice about leaving behind "traditional" customs, such as extended families, and "bad" habits, such as white clothing (which required extra laundering), as part of the life reform movement among urban intellectuals.[2] Likewise, agrarian reformers in the 1920s and early 1930s from the Ch'ŏndogyo, an eclectic Korean religion founded in the mid-nineteenth century, and Christian organizations including the Young Men's Christian Association (YMCA) had attempted, with limited success, to modernize the countryside through peasant participation in rural development projects that included literacy and other educational programs.[3] In the 1930s and 1940s, the colonial government organized groups at the local level, including Councils for Rural Revitalization (*nongch'on chinhŭng wiwŏnhoe*), financial co-ops (*kŭmyung chohap*), and mutual-aid production associations (*siksan'gye*), to foster agricultural production and elevate the standard of living in the countryside.[4] After the Japanese invasion of mainland China in 1937, Patriotic Units (*aegukpan*) and Village Leagues (*purak yŏnmaeng*) were organized all across Korea; they controlled the entire process of production and distribution of goods in order to increase productivity and extract resources for the war effort.[5] All of these programs attempted to rid Korea of traditional customs that were thought to hinder its development, replacing them with a new set of practices defined by rational ordering, productivity, and hygiene that bore a striking similarity to the above list of advice for women in postliberation North Korea.

Some might question whether anything new was going on in North Korea, not only due to ostensible parallels with the colonial period but also because North Korea was seen as a Soviet satellite throughout much of the Cold War.[6] Although colonial and Soviet legacies were certainly instrumental after liberation, exactly how they were influential is either not made clear or the reputed influence is off the mark. The colonial period, for example, can hardly be lumped into one uniform experience: the more liberal 1920s operated in a mood substantially different from the 1930s and 1940s war mobilization, which curbed the already limited gains. In short, the colonial antecedent and Soviet influence help situate the North Korean Revolution within the history of modernity by highlighting the North Korean Revolution as a simultaneous critique of colonial modernity and capitalist modernity. The dual critique allowed a repudiation of Korea's colonial past while also rejecting a capitalist modernity for Korea's future, pointing toward an alternative modernity modeled on the Soviet Union. The North Korean Revolution sought to bring a new kind of everyday life, free of colonial and capitalist subjugation. But how was everyday life experienced differently as something new?

Those living through the colonial to the postcolonial period articulated what was felt to be so different. In September 1948, some three years after liberation, a poor peasant named Sŏ Yŏng-jun from Sŏnch'ŏn County in North P'yŏngan Province, wrote a short autobiography attached to his resume as required for his admission into the Youth League.[7] The full text read:

As a poor peasant family since before my grandparents, we lived (*saenghwal*) as tenant farmers to Mr. Kim Un-pu in Sŏkhwadong for 13 years and in 1925 lived (*saenghwal*) as Mr. Pak Pyŏng-ŭp's farmhand in Sŏkhodong, not only oppressed and exploited but also bitterly suffering a wretched life (*pich'amhan saenghwal*), not able to go to school, caring for my younger siblings until I was 12, and then in order to support my siblings, I started farming at 13 until liberation when we were allotted land, and I was able to farm freely and live a life of freedom (*chayusŭrŏun saenghwal*). Before liberation, I couldn't even read, but after liberation in 1946, I started attending Korean School until 1947, learning to read and participate in organizational life (*chojik saenghwal*) and beginning a collective life (*tanch'e saenghwal*), joining the Youth League on May 26, 1946 and the Peasant League on February 10, 1946, and then I took charge of physical education for the Youth League in our village, training the league members every morning and having fun with this work, and then I wanted to have an organizational life (*chojik saenghwal*) and joined the Workers Party in January 1947, beginning my organizational life (*chojik saenghwal*) and taking charge of the party cell on January 6, 1948 and carrying on the cell life (*sep'o saenghwal*) to this day.[8]

Born on December 15, 1926, Sŏ Yŏng-jun had not learned to read and write until 1946, when he was twenty years old. This fact was inscribed into the very pages of his handwritten autobiography, which was composed only a couple of years after he became literate, as indicated in the repeated spelling errors and lack of punctuation that are lost in translation. Nonetheless, the differences in his work life and educational life before and after liberation are quite clearly marked throughout the short autobiography: he uses the term *saenghwal* nine times within a text no longer than a paragraph. His "wretched life" of tenancy and suffering had turned into a "life of freedom" supported by the seven thousand *p'yŏng* (just over two hectares or almost six acres) of land he had received in the land reform of 1946, an important detail noted in his resume. Moreover, he was eager to embrace a collective lifestyle, joining one organization after another in quick succession. This changed his daily routine, as signaled by the morning exercises he notes in his autobiography. The two most important components of everyday life—work and education—had fundamentally changed for this poor peasant, who was no longer destitute and illiterate but now tilled his own land, living a full collective life.

Making a similar distinction in women's lives before and after liberation, an editorial in a women's journal, dated August 13, 1947, argued that Korean women in the past had been relegated to the private realm solely to live a "family life," whereas men lived "social lives," dominating the public realm.[9] Admittedly, the number of women finding work outside the home had been increasing throughout the colonial period. However, the editorial claimed that this kind of work did not constitute an authentic social life because women worked to support their families, rather than to foster an "independent productive life." The social life, thus entered through work, was an extension of family life to aid the social life of men. Moreover, responding to the claim that women had increasingly become consumers, participating in public life in the process of consumption if not production, the editorial argued that their consumption of fashion and cosmetics was not for their own sake but in order to fulfill the desires and tastes of men. Thus, the editorial reasoned, "Korean women did not have a life of their own, and could not have an independent life as a human being, living subjugated under men. A life of domination, always being dragged around, this was the totality of the life of past Korean women." However, after liberation, North Korean women now had the right to vote and be elected to public office; they could participate in the full range of public life: political, economic, and cultural. The editorial triumphantly concluded, "The life of a North Korean woman today has been completely freed from subordination, domination, subservience and exploitation so that she can live a social life of her own, an economic life of her own, for a socially productive life from a position of equality with men." Although the editorial was intended for women readers, a "socially productive life" was expected of everyone as part of the general reconstitution of everyday life.

The everyday, thus, became the chief arena for revolutionary change in North Korea, situating it broadly within the history of modernity and more specifically within the history of socialist modernity.

What Is the Everyday?

The everyday as a privileged site for theorists of social change gained prominence mostly through such postwar European thinkers as Fernand Braudel, Henri Lefebvre, and Michel de Certeau.[10] Less studied but no less important were the intellectuals outside Western Europe at the beginning of the twentieth century who were preoccupied with the everyday as they attempted to come to terms with the modern. Harry Harootunian's study of Tosaka Jun is just one example, showing how everydayness became "a philosophic concept in order to understand the 'modern life' of the present" in Japan.[11] Indeed, modernity may be defined by the birth of the everyday as an experiential and temporal category. There was no everyday as such before modernity precisely because each day lacked the objective continuity of clockwork. Time was attached to space, unique to each locality, and each day had yet to be encompassed within a universal homogeneous temporality. Greenwich Mean Time (GMT) became a means to standardize time worldwide only in the late nineteenth century.

As Japan became the first nation to modernize in East Asia, its formal colonization of Korea in 1910 happened to coincide with the beginnings of a qualitative shift in the way people experienced the world, which was evidenced by paradigmatic changes in fields as varied as music and physics.[12] The debut of Igor Stravinsky's *The Rite of Spring* in 1913 resulted in riots as people reacted to the unsettling sound of atonal music. Ferdinand de Saussure's structuralism threw out the idea that the meaning of words had anything to do with the objects they represented. At the pinnacle of this paradigm shift was Albert Einstein's theory of relativity, which signaled the end to any sense of fixity in time and space. Such cultural and intellectual transformations in Europe were accompanied by concrete technological changes in everyday life across the globe. The expansion of railway networks, together with the telegraph, radio communication, steamships, and automobiles, led to dramatic time-space compressions, while advances in photography and motion pictures further revolutionized the way people experienced space and time. The practices of listening to music, looking at images, traveling to distant places, and hearing the latest news had fundamentally changed daily life.

Likewise, Korea witnessed a boom in road construction between 1907 and 1912, and by the end of 1938 over twenty-eight thousand kilometers of road had been laid under the supervision of Japanese colonial authorities.[13] Moreover, the expansion of railways, with 5,411 kilometers of rail laid by 1939, not only connected Korea domestically but with China and Russia on the South Manchurian Railway. Streetcars rattled on the streets of Seoul, which were lined with modern shops and department stores. Increasing numbers of urban residents were drawn to the novelties of modern life with "talkies and taxies, modern girls and modern boys . . . mini-skirts and bell-bottomed trousers, as well as revue girls, jazz and radio."[14] If, as Raymond Williams argues, "the key cultural factor of the modernist shift is the character of the metropolis," which brings together individuals, "lonely and isolated," in the "crowd of strangers" as part of the seemingly "impenetrable city," then the changes in Seoul brought about by colonial modernity certainly marked the beginnings of that shift.[15]

Rather than taking such changes as a sign of "progress," however, it is worth asking what was driving such titanic shifts. The dynamic engine of capitalism itself made "efficiency" and "productivity" cornerstones of everyday life, making it necessary to compress time and space in order to maximize profit. Walter Benjamin elegantly formulated the way in which capitalist logic compressed time in the rationalization of labor so that time became "homogeneous empty time." Time was detached from socially meaningful activities and events, making each day equivalent to another and thus emptied of singular significance. Partha Chatterjee elaborates:

> Empty homogeneous time is the time of capital. Within its domain, capital allows for no resistance to its free movement. When it encounters an impediment, it thinks it has encountered another time—something out of pre-capital, something that belongs to the pre-modern. Such resistances to capital (or to modernity) are therefore understood as coming out of humanity's past, something people should have left behind but somehow haven't. But by imagining capital (or modernity) as an attribute of time itself, this view succeeds not only in branding the resistances to it as archaic and backward, but also securing for capital and modernity their ultimate triumph, regardless of what some people may believe or hope, because after all, as everyone knows, time does not stand still.[16]

The everyday, then, functioned not as a duration of actual lived time, but as a concept, a commodified form of time in the age of capital. In other words, time equaled money. This idea of the everyday as mundane and repetitious, tied to the rhythm of production, existed side by side with the spectacle and novelty of consumption, which gave modernity its dazzling image. The deadening, monotonous routine of industrial work had to be mitigated by leisure time. For the first time in history, leisure as part of private life was available to large numbers of people as a time of "rest and relaxation" away from the daily grind of urban life and industrial work. It is no wonder that the everyday came to be identified with private life and conflated with "authentic" experience set against the discipline of work. But the everyday must be understood as a distinctly modern idea, a product of capitalist modernity in the juxtaposition of the mundane and the eventful.

It is therefore no accident that social revolutions have focused on the everyday as both a stage on which the extraordinary eventfulness of the revolution itself is fully displayed and as the very fabric of old structures that must be transformed into new ones, representing the radical departure of the revolution from the past. Some theorists, represented by de Certeau and Mikhail Bakhtin, have imbued the everyday with far-reaching potentials for resistance, looking into facets of life that are spontaneous, sensuous, heterogeneous, playful, and effervescent. Others, such as Lefebvre and Braudel, who focus on the material conditions, have viewed everyday life as the oppressive temporal fabric to which we have been subjugated. For the latter, the everyday set modern life apart from traditional life, which had encompassed a unity and creativity of daily experience. By contrast, modern life "deprived everyday life of its power, disregarding its productive and creative potentialities," leading Lefebvre to conclude that "in the modern world everyday life had ceased to be a 'subject' rich in potential subjectivity; it had become an 'object' of social organization."[17]

In light of two different characterizations of the everyday, is everyday life "a realm of submission to relations of power or the space in which those relations are contested (or at least negotiated in relatively interesting ways)?"[18] The simple answer is that it is both. The materiality of things and the subjectivity of individuals dialectically constitute the everyday in concrete terms. The everyday is both the product of capitalist modernity and the site of its resistance. It brings together the material conditions within which subjects maneuver and by which subjects are negotiated, simultaneously enabling various subjectivities to emerge through those interactions. In other words, the everyday is where choice and constraint meet. What makes it subversive is the possibility for unintended consequences at the intersection between structural mechanisms and individual contingencies.

Although the regimentation and regularization of everyday life reproduces itself most of the time, revolutions represent rare historical moments when old structures are shaky, adding momentum for individual and collective action in the destruction of the old and the construction of something new. In this sense, revolutions explicitly target transformations in everyday life as a reflection of deep structural changes, involving social relations in both the public (class relations) and private (family relations) spheres as new social roles are adopted and new identities are created. The distinction between public and private becomes ambiguous at best. As Maurice Blanchot suggested in reflecting on the French Revolution, it becomes a "question of opening the everyday onto history, or even, of reducing its privileged sector: private life. This is what happens in moments of effervescence—those we call revolution—when existence is *public through and through*."[19] Revolution can thus be characterized by radical changes in

everyday life in a short span of time. As a corollary, the heyday of the revolutionary period can be said to have come to an end when such changes in
everyday life are habitualized and become once again mundane.

The imagery of violence and chaos that is commonly associated with
revolutions is misleading and one-sided. Although revolutions have been
memorialized much more for their destructive qualities through dramatic
images of the guillotine and political purges, they are as much times of
creativity in which everyday life is transformed. Hannah Arendt, arguably one of the few political theorists to have truly appreciated the creative rather than the destructive potential of revolutions, thus defined it
as a "new beginning . . . to bring about the formation of a new body
politic."[20] This book, like Arendt, emphasizes the constitutive qualities,
particularly the revolutionary institutions that became the forum for the
everyday practices of empowerment. Revolutions are a time when much
more seems possible, a rupture in history with all the uncertainties and
contingencies that today we forget as we look back without the burden of
making history.

In the remainder of the chapter, examples from the Soviet Union
and China together with North Korea illustrate how the everyday became quite deliberately the object of revolutionary socialist transformation, beginning with the Soviet Union in the aftermath of the October
Revolution.

Novyi Byt (New Everyday Life)

Walter Benjamin kept a diary while visiting Moscow in the 1920s, describing firsthand what the experience of the everyday was like in revolutionary Russia. He was particularly struck by the lack of private space,
people's proximity in the streets, the sparse furnishings in the communal
apartments, and people's total absorption in political work.[21] On January 8,
1927, he wrote:

> It is precisely this transformation of an entire power structure that
> makes life here so extraordinarily meaningful. It is as insular and as
> eventful, as impoverished and yet in the same breath as full of possibili-
> ties as gold rush life in the Klondike. The dig for power goes on from
> early morning to late at night. The entire scheme of existence of the
> Western European intelligentsia is utterly impoverished in comparison
> to the countless constellations that offer themselves to an individual

here in the space of a month. Admittedly this can lead to a certain state of inebriation in which it becomes almost impossible to conceive of a life without meetings and committees, debates, resolutions, and ballotings (all of which are the wars or at least *maneuvers of the will to power*).[22]

Throughout his two-month stay, Benjamin repeatedly emphasized the dramatic change in daily life, observing how people were no longer tied to domestic pursuits, as evidenced by the "withering away of private life," because "there is simply not time enough for it" and "because their way of life has so alienated them from domestic existence" now that the "place in which they live is the office, the club, the street."[23] Benjamin was not alone in his observations. Maxim Gorky, the founding father of socialist realist literature, remarked during travels across the country in 1928 that people were engrossed in politics, and "political consciousness" was becoming "an everyday phenomenon."[24]

Russia on the eve of revolution, much like Korea at the turn of the century, had confronted a host of political and economic problems, heightened by defeat in the 1904–05 Russo-Japanese War. Russia was the first Western power to be defeated at the hands of the "yellow race." The news made headlines throughout the world, exposing the weakness of the Russian Empire and opening the way for Japan to establish a protectorate over Korea. Subsequent events in Russia, culminating in the 1917 October Revolution, had ripple effects far beyond its own borders, providing many so-called backward societies, such as colonial Korea, a way to envision a dramatic revolutionary leap into an alternative modernity that would overcome the problems of colonialism and capitalism. In fact, the Korean representative to the executive committee of the Communist International in 1919 attributed the Russian Revolution with having "woke[n] up the Korean masses . . . inspir[ing] them with aspirations for a new life."[25] Reporting on the founding of the Korean Socialist Party, he spoke of the party's program, which sought to "free Korea from the yoke of Japanese imperialism and capitalistic exploitation." For those under colonial rule, the alternative offered by the revolution in Russia was compelling particularly for its anti-imperialist program. As reflected in Benjamin's diary entries, this alternative imbued the everyday with spontaneity and meaning through the popular participation of the masses in the politics of day-to-day life. It was qualitatively different from the submission to capitalist drudgery, with respite promised only by consumerism, an option left out of reach for the majority working class. By contrast, the revolutionary spontaneity in the participatory politics of the socialist everyday, even if materially inadequate, was experienced through the various councils, or *soviets*, that formed in the early stages of the revolution.

A tradition of peasant communes with customs of deliberation and self-governance in village meetings facilitated the rise of the councils.[26] Massive strikes in the first two months of 1905 led to the organization of workers councils, sparking off the first Russian Revolution.[27] What started out in St. Petersburg eventually swept throughout the larger and smaller industrial cities in the last months of 1905 with the greatest number of soviets in Moscow's industrial region. The soviets were often headed by an executive committee, consisting of several members who were responsible for taking care of day-to-day business. Sessions of the soviets were "public through and through," proceeding in a heated atmosphere with voting by a show of hands. Some soviets formed special commissions to establish strike funds, assist the unemployed, acquire weapons, and issue propaganda materials.

Soldiers and peasants councils were eventually formed, although the soldiers' councils were not to become a major force until 1917, when Russia's military defeats in World War I, combined with an economic crisis, resulted in mass desertions. In 1917, peasants, lagging behind the workers, were instigated to rebel by the rural intelligentsia of teachers and reformers. Ousting former local authorities, the rural soviets were called by a wide variety of labels, such as peasants committees, rural committees, and committees for people's rule.[28] Although the provisional government saw them as mere instruments for governance, the rural committees increasingly became the basis for a peasant revolution, taking radical measures against estate owners by appropriating land and forests.

With the task of seizing power complete, attention shifted to "cultural work" during the 1920s. Trotsky's tract on the *Problems of Everyday Life*, published in 1923, opened a passionate debate about what the new everyday life (*novyi byt*) after the revolution was supposed to entail, "whether in terms of living arrangements, family and sexual relationships, friendships, personal appearance, leisure activities, or consumer practices."[29] Not only the "scientific organization of labor" but the "scientific organization of life" was sought as Trotsky recommended the division of the day into three eight-hour segments of sleep, work, and leisure in order to achieve a rationally organized lifestyle.[30] His prescriptions were very much in tune with the Constructivist movement, which emerged in the early 1920s in Moscow, dominating Soviet architecture, photography, film, set design, and literature throughout the decade with lasting effects. Constructivists believed that a new man and new consciousness could be formed by applying scientific laws to man's behavior at work and at home "so that in his every movement he might live the maximally rationalized and simultaneously collectivized and aestheticized existence," with a focus on "hygiene, regularity, efficiency, and utility."[31] Habits, morals, and culture were considered important arenas of social change as a way of instituting socialist hegemony.

In targeting everyday objects, Russian constructivism sought to counter the affective power of the "commodity fetish" that endlessly organized and gave form to material desires by creating socialist objects that would in effect be "object-as-comrade," or "comradely object," that would be "an active, almost animate participant in social life" as a "coworker" rather than dead commodities that dull the senses.[32] In other words, people did not have to renounce material possession as mere commodities but could begin to appreciate them for their materiality, which could be used in socially meaningful ways. Passive capitalist commodities would be transformed into active socialist objects. Thus artists began focusing on such everyday objects as pots and pans and the design of fabrics, advertisements, and theater sets with the belief that artists should go into industrial production and use their artistic expertise to produce useful objects for the new socialist collective. The goal of art was to be useful, functional, and convenient. Art would be the result of the very materiality of everyday life. Consequently, sculpture and other forms of public art also took on renewed significance as revolutionary history was written into the physical urban space for the masses to see and experience on a daily basis. Constructivists challenged not only the formal conventions of art but also the institutional structures upholding art under capitalism in order to "reintegrate art in the life process and so to regain a social use value for art."[33]

Although debates about *novyi byt* among public and intellectual circles varied widely, a detailed theoretical exposé about everyday life published in 1925 by Boris Arvatov (1896–1940)—an art historian and critic who championed the Constructivist avant-garde—best explains why the everyday had taken on the significance that it had, and what was at stake in transforming the everyday as part of the revolutionary project.[34] He conceptualized the everyday in the following way:

> The concept of the everyday was formed in opposition to the concept of labor, just as the concept of consumer activity was formed in opposition to that of productive activity, and the concept of social stasis was formed in opposition to the concept of social dynamism. Such divisions were possible only on the basis of the class-technical differentiation

that characterized the capitalist system, with its administrative top brass standing above production. . . . In proletariat society, and even more in socialist society, where production will directly form all aspects of human activity, the static everyday life of consumption will become impossible. Furthering this evolution is the real task of the builders of proletarian culture. The resolution of this historical problem can proceed only from the forms of material *byt*.[35]

Not only did Arvatov explicitly connect the genesis of the everyday with capitalism, but he presented the real task for the builders of socialism as that of reinventing and reconfiguring the everyday in a postcapitalist world by bringing together the domains of production and consumption, public and private, which had been torn asunder under capitalism. He reasoned that Marxists had privileged the technological domain (base) over the everyday (superstructure) because, under capitalism, social relations were defined by one's relation to the means of production. But now with the triumph of socialism, consumption, as expressed in everyday practices, the artistic realm, and social-organizational forms, was equally, if not more, important. Under socialism, the task was to bridge the rupture between things (commodities) and people that had characterized bourgeois society in order to form a new social order that is ideologically imbued with the deepest sense of the material totality, which Arvatov calls the Thing.[36]

The task for socialism was formulated precisely on what was perceived to be problematic about capitalism. Under capitalism, the bourgeoisie had no direct physical contact with the production of material values, but only with those forms that things take when they make up the sphere of consumption. Thus, private everyday life—the everyday life of consumption—was thoroughly permeated by the market and was entirely dependent on it, so that the bourgeoisie dealt with the Thing first and foremost in its guise as a commodity, as an object bought and sold. The Thing became an abstraction, appearing merely in its capacity as exchange value and means of accumulation. Thus the everyday was commodified, as Arvatov concludes: "The commodity nature of bourgeois material *byt* constitutes the fundamental basis for its relation to the thing. The Thing as an a-material category, as a category of pure consumption, the thing outside its creative genesis, outside its material dynamics, outside its social process of production, the Thing as something completed, fixed, static, and, consequently, dead—this is what characterizes bourgeois material culture."[37]

Here, of course, Arvatov is talking about the Marxist concept of commodity fetish, except that by focusing on the materiality of the everyday he is able to bring together the simultaneous process of commodity fetishization with the alienation of the labor process, which only sharpens his critical edge. The implication is that human beings have been relegated to mere thing or commodity under capitalism because the social reality of the relations of production and consumption remains hidden:

> For the bourgeois the Thing exists only to the extent that he can extract profit from it or use it to organize his everyday life. This determines his methods of forming his material *byt*. "A richly appointed apartment"; "humble surroundings"; "sparsely decorated"; "expensively furnished"—these are the typical everyday conceptions, formulated in casual speech, that have developed among the bourgeoisie. But there is a more important, even fundamental, characteristic of the bourgeois *byt* of things: private property, the private-property relation to the world of Things. For the bourgeois there exist "my" things and "someone else's" things. "My" things appear primarily not only as material blessings, but also as social-ideological categories. . . . In all of this the objective social meaning of the Thing, its utilitarian-technical purpose and its productive qualification, are definitively lost. . . . Production works for the market and therefore cannot take into account the *concrete* particularities of consumption and proceed from them. . . . The Thing thus takes on the character of something that is passive by its very nature. The Thing as the fulfillment of the organism's physical capacity for labor, as a force for social labor, as an instrument and as a co-worker, does not exist in the everyday life of the bourgeoisie.[38]

By pointing out aspects of daily life that are taken for granted, from the home to the language used in referring to the commodities surrounding everyday life, Arvatov pulls apart the ideological curtain occluding our perceptions, laying bare the emptiness in bourgeois everyday life that lacks creativity and social meaning.

If this is the state of things under capitalism, then it becomes clear what must be done under socialism in order to reclaim the Thing and restore the totality of the material world. Arvatov hones in on the collectivization of labor in Soviet Russia to conclude that everyday life no longer consisted of commodified private life in individual apartments. It had qualitatively shifted to a "new type" of "everyday life of enormous offices, department stores, factory laboratories, research institutes," that is, in the collective sphere connected with material production. He praises, for example, the collectivization in the material functions of city life through public transport, heating, lighting, plumbing, and communal buildings, which "led to the sphere of private everyday life being narrowed to the minimum and reformed under the influence of progressive technology." Rather than the extraction of profit, Arvatov concludes, "Other criteria of value now took pride of place: convenience, portability, comfort, flexibility, expedience, hygiene, and so on—in a word, everything that they call the adaptability of the thing, its suitability in terms of positioning and assembling for the *needs of social practice*."[39] Much of this is strikingly similar to Benjamin's observations while in Moscow about the blurring of the boundaries between public and private, the proximity of people, and the focus on the collective. Arvatov goes further than simple observation, however, to generate a theoretical prescription for how the everyday must proceed to change based on standards of social need as opposed to capital accumulation.

The profound dilemma with the turn toward social need, however, was how to define or come to a consensus about what these social needs were. The "woman question" was a case in point—was free love and divorce a social need, or was a stable family a more urgent social imperative? In the context of the 1920s New Economic Policy, rampant liberalism and individualism stoked fears of bourgeois contamination of party and society, with fingers pointed at the rise of free love, divorce, and suicide.[40] Reflecting this quandary, discussion of everyday life abounded in the 1920s Soviet press. In 1923, *Pravda* published a series of articles entitled "Pictures of Daily Life" (*Kartinki byta*), dealing with how to emancipate women workers and peasants, and the proper relationship of male party members to their wives and female citizens.[41] Much of the discussion exposed fears and anxieties about the changing nature of gender relations in the wake of the revolution: if women were to participate in productive labor, how were they to combine work and family; who was to take care of domestic duties if both husband and wife worked; should women now leave their husbands since they had their own income; and so on.

Subsequently, the discussion turned to how women might ruin the revolution with their traditional habits and bourgeois customs, dragging down the morale and political consciousness of their husbands, rather than on how daily domestic chores continued to oppress women.[42] For example, the "Down with Domestic Trash" campaign, launched in 1928 by the newspaper *Komsomol Truth*, proposed to "burn the little idols of things" and create a new revolutionary home free of bourgeois sensibilities represented by such items as gramophones, lace curtains, rubber plants, porcelain elephants, and yellow canaries.[43] The campaign called for the eradication of the "dictatorship of the workshop of faience figurines" and its replacement by the "dictatorship of revolutionary taste," which included a new promotion of physical health, fitness, and sports. This attack on domesticity occurred within the context of communist identification of the private home with the bourgeoisie.

As a result, the state focused on the twin goals of modernization and collectivization in everyday life by targeting women through the health and cooperative sectors. The purpose was to modernize the peasantry and its households, promoting modern forms of personal and domestic hygiene through reforms in childcare, cooking, and laundry practices. In the process, the revolution was normalized, combining so-called high revolutionary tasks with everyday deeds.[44] By the 1930s, the discussion of *novyi byt* so prevalent throughout the 1920s was replaced by an emphasis on *kul'turnost* or "cultured life," which stressed private life and individual consumption as the path to a modern, rational, cultured Soviet everyday life.[45] Marking this shift, the International Women's Day celebrations in 1929 included a campaign for the cultural reconstruction of daily life (*kul'turno-bytovoi pokhod*), setting the agenda for the state's policy toward women in the 1930s. Subsequently, the state began providing social services to enable women's participation in the five-year economic plan, and waged an all-out assault on former "backward lifestyles" (*staryi byt'*), targeting the sexual exploitation and physical abuse of women and children, drunkenness, hooliganism, and the unsanitary conditions of working class quarters, including facilities such as public baths, laundries, and dining halls.[46]

Whereas much has been made in traditional Soviet historiography of the transition from the 1920s to the 1930s as a "revolution betrayed," the sustained focus on hygiene, utility, and the rational ordering of life highlights the continuity in the Constructivist avant-garde that was now inflected toward the affirmation of socialism as true and authentic rather than toward the demystification of capitalism (as Arvatov had attempted to do in the 1920s).[47] The 1930s did not so much kill the avant-garde radical spirit as focus singularly on the act of affirmation, ritualized through everyday practices, for the purposes of consolidation of the new Soviet order under an increasingly hostile international environment with the rise of European fascism and Japanese aggression.[48] This affirmative strain of constructivism was to be duplicated in North Korea at a time of national foundation that was all the more pressing under conditions of national division and foreign occupation.

Cultural Revolution

An element that facilitated the continuity from the 1920s to the 1930s was the lack of critique of a state-centric model. Arvatov's heroic formulations of the everyday as the site of creative social transformation toward an alternative socialist modernity still retained the statist framework of modernity, paralleling fascist movements in the 1930s. Formal similarities between state socialism and fascism were the result of the state's common preoccupation with purging what was considered the decadence of capitalist modernity through "life reform" movements that advocated a healthy life-style. These movements popularized diverse forms of bodily discipline throughout the first decades of the twentieth century, from gymnastics, body building, and calisthenics to utopian communes, homeopathic remedies, and nudism.[49]

The New Life Movement in China was one such example. Launched by the Kuomintang under Chiang Kai-shek in 1934, the goal was to build a modern, disciplined nation-state by reorganizing the way people used time and space. Almost a hundred rules would govern the habits of everyday life, from being on time and keeping regular meal hours to "buttoning clothes, lacing shoes, maintaining straight posture . . . not eating noisily, not spitting in public, washing faces in cold water, urinating only in toilets, and removing dirt and vermin from living quarters."[50] China's modernization efforts implied being aware of homogeneous empty time that could be rationally broken down and organized according to specific schedules toward "nationalization" (*guojiahua*), "militarization" (*junshihua*), and "productivization" (*shengchanhua*), all slogans used during the New Life Movement. Synchronizing everyone's sense of time was necessary not only for a regimented military but also for a disciplined workforce. Likewise, the emphasis on cleanliness and hygiene, while reflecting a concern for public health, was also an attempt at redefining space so as to differentiate between public and private spaces. It was part and parcel of a Foucauldian microtechnique of power that sought to instill a sense of proper conduct—a sense that there is a time and place for everything.

The movement, which had begun to wane by 1936 even before the Japanese invasion of 1937, ultimately failed due to lack of cohesion. But the particular focus on changing the daily habits of thought and behavior remained; they continued to influence cultural politics under Mao Zedong and would be taken up with full force during the Cultural Revolution some three decades later. Everyday items such as "high heels, houseplants, goldfish, classical literature and paintings" were derided as "feudal" and "bourgeois" while new "revolutionary" lifestyles such as "tattered dark-colored clothing, simple diets, and daily recitations of Mao's quotations, self-examination/confession, and manual labor" were exalted as exemplary.[51]

Despite some superficial similarities, the two movements were different at their core. The New Life Movement sought to expand the power of the state and was instituted from the top down for the purposes of mobilizing people around its own agenda as a form of "controlled popular mobilization," whereas the Cultural Revolution was a bottom-up movement that periodically escaped the control of the state, ultimately founded on the Marxist philosophy that class struggle and social conflict lay at the root of social change.[52] Irrespective of the ultimate assessment of the Cultural Revolution, "the masses" themselves became the agents of social change, leading to the violent excesses that have tainted its history. It was this bottom-up process that radically transformed the experience of the everyday during the Cultural Revolution. The model for this transformation was sought in the example of the nineteenth century Paris Commune as a representation of antibureaucratic and egalitarian politics.

With the deterioration in Sino-Soviet relations over the issue of "peaceful coexistence" and the loss of revolutionary zeal among the Chinese Communist Party elite in the 1960s, Mao began to reconsider the experience of the Paris Commune.[53] Earlier, the Commune had been used as an example of what *not* to do as the CCP declared, "The working class cannot simply lay hold of the ready-made state machinery and wield it for its own purpose."[54] In other words, no compromise can be made with the old regime, and previous structures must be destroyed. However, by 1966, a reevaluation of the experience of the Paris Commune singled out three characteristics applicable to the Chinese context: first, new political structures directly responsible to the people through elections and recalls; second, the combination of legislative and executive functions in a single nonparliamentary body; and third, the prevention of the emergence of a privileged class of bureaucrats by pegging the wages of officials to those of average workers.[55]

An article in *Hongqi* published in March 1966 in commemoration of the 95th anniversary of the Paris Commune hailed it in glowing terms:

The masses were the real masters in the Paris Commune. While the Commune was in being, the masses were organized on a wide scale and they discussed important state matters within their respective organizations. Each day around 20,000 activists attended club meetings where they made proposals or advanced critical opinions on social and political matters great and small. They also made their wishes and demands known through articles and letters to the revolutionary newspapers and journals. This revolutionary enthusiasm and initiative of the masses was the source of the Commune's strength.[56]

The article had started off by claiming that "the most fundamental principle of the Paris Commune is the use of revolutionary violence to seize power, smash the state machine of the bourgeoisie and practice the dictatorship of the proletariat," reiterating China's opposition to Khrushchev's revisionism and its earlier attitude toward the Commune. However, by the end of the article, detailed descriptions of the spontaneous mass movement during the Commune, with its emphasis on the daily practices of attending meetings and debating through newspapers, became a rallying cry for the Cultural Revolution.

Students at Beijing University spearheaded the mass movement when Nie Yuanzi and six others put up a big-character poster criticizing the university's party leadership on May 25, 1966.[57] Such written criticisms soon expanded to struggle sessions, denunciation meetings, and mass demonstrations. Verbal and physical attacks on figures of authority spread like wildfire, denouncing them as corrupt and counterrevolutionary. Violent beatings, parading "capitalist roaders" in the streets, renaming stores and streets with revolutionary names, raiding temples and churches, burning books, and ransacking "class enemy" homes became daily rituals.[58] Such brutal and vicious incidents have understandably left a negative impression of the Cultural Revolution, but there were other aspects to the revolution as well.

Taking elements of the Paris Commune to heart, the commune model was implemented in February 1967 in China's two largest cities, Beijing and Shanghai.[59] Revolutionary committees replaced the party apparatus throughout the country, and workers took up positions of power like never before, especially in places such as Shanghai.[60] Factory-level study groups, called Workers' Theory Troops (*gongren lilun duiwu*), attempted to distill proletarian practice into theoretical writing as an example of "workers occupying the superstructure" (even if most of them were Red Guard students-turned-workers).[61] Substantial numbers of workers also entered the leadership of Shanghai's municipal government, especially with the establishment of the Frontline Command Post to Grasp Revolution and Promote Production in January 1967. When transportation was disrupted by revolutionary turmoil, with railways and wharves blocked with unloaded cargo, the Frontline deftly took over administration, restoring transportation and communication lines, promoting and coordinating production by convening meetings and mobilizing Red Guard students to move the cargo, relieving the bottleneck at the train stations and wharves.[62] Departments of industry, transportation, research, finance, health, and others were organized by the Frontline, serving as the de facto municipal government, until the Shanghai Revolutionary Committee took over the following month. The day the Shanghai commune was officially founded on February 5, 1967, leaflets hailed the birth of the Shanghai People's Commune as "a joyous event in the political life of the Shanghai revolutionary people . . . open[ing] a new chapter in the Shanghai laboring people's control of our own fate."[63]

Instead of the Marxist-Leninist emphasis on the party vanguard and their careful orchestration, it was the spontaneity of everyday life and the mass political participation during the Paris Commune that became the lessons to be learned. The sixteen-point "Decision of the Central Committee of the Chinese Communist Party concerning the Great Proletarian Cultural Revolution," adopted on August 8, 1966, concluded: "Large numbers of revolutionary young people previously unknown, have become courageous and daring pathbreakers. . . . Through the media of big-character posters and great debates, they argue things out, expose and criticize thoroughly, and launch resolute attacks on the open and hidden representatives of the bourgeoisie."[64] In a strong affirmation of Mao's mass line, the party decision went on to assert:

> In the great proletarian cultural revolution, the only method is for the masses to liberate themselves. . . . Trust the masses, rely on them and respect their initiative. Cast out fear. Don't be afraid of disorder. . . . It is normal for the masses to hold different views. Contention between different views is unavoidable, necessary and beneficial. . . . The cultural revolutionary groups, committees and other organizational forms created by the masses in many schools and units are something new and of great historic importance. . . . It is necessary to institute a system of general elections, like that of the Paris Commune, for electing members to the cultural revolutionary groups and committees and delegates to the cultural revolutionary congresses.

Despite such initial approbation, however, the Commune movement was soon curtailed by the government, alarmed at the loss of control. By the spring of 1967, there was no longer any mention of the Paris Commune in the official press.[65]

Nonetheless, radical changes had taken place in the power structure of local municipalities and villages as ordinary workers and peasants rose to positions of power, "infus[ing] the government with a group of women and workers who, unlike their predecessors, looked, talked, and thought like the people they represented."[66] Trade unions were no longer totally subservient to the party as before and workers made up the bulk of those inducted into the party. Although the Cultural Revolution barely lasted a decade, the experience of self-rule and local autonomy in everyday practices of debates and meetings would long be remembered by those who had taken part.[67] Even those who were highly critical of the way the masses were manipulated by the leadership in their own power struggle conceded that "the Cultural Revolution played an invaluable role in enlightening the people," by giving them the "opportunity to exercise their democratic rights . . . for the first time since the founding of the People's Republic."[68] Writing secretly in the early 1970s as a participant and witness to the revolution, Liu Guokai is unambiguously derisive of Mao, who is seen as using the mass movement for an "unprecedented purge."[69] But he is equally clear in his assessment: "During the Cultural Revolution, the people broke down the highly bureaucratic and undemocratic social order that previously existed. The mass movement dealt a deserved blow at bureaucrats and broke down the spiritual shackles imposed upon the people. . . . People actually exercised their democratic rights such as freedom of speech, publication, assembly, and demonstration. This was unprecedented."[70] The "massive and solemn demonstrations, emotional mass rallies, deafening shouting, and writings sparkling with new ideas" had left a lasting impression, which Liu took as the essential legacy of the Cultural Revolution: it "widened people's horizons" who were no longer "shackled" by government bureaucrats and party cadres.[71]

In an attempt to counter bureaucracy and government corruption, Mao had given free rein to the students, workers, peasants, and soldiers who became the primary agents of the Cultural Revolution, decentralizing state power and reviving the revolutionary fervor that had dissipated in the process of consolidation twenty years after the founding of the People's Republic of China in 1949. To bridge the gap between manual and mental labor, officials and intellectuals were compelled to participate in physical labor while peasants and workers were given the opportunity to go to school and participate in politics as elected officials. Centralized control was also lifted from agricultural production as local self-sufficiency was promoted through cooperatives and communes. Whereas the winter slack season had been traditionally used for private enterprise, peasants were now engaged in collective projects such as digging reservoirs and leveling fields as a "regular part of the rhythm of peasant life," creating "a psychological interdependence and spirit of mutual assistance and concern among neighboring villages and rural inhabitants that would replace marketing and other forms of commercial interaction."[72] Factories were encouraged to be self-reliant, and local governments were given autonomy with oversight over local industries. Despite the violent excesses, the Cultural Revolution fostered "a spirit of independent judgment and self-reliance" among the people, initiating a renewed everyday life that was communal and participatory.[73]

Saenghwal Hyŏngmyŏng (Revolution in Life)

The Chinese and Russian experiences, while not contemporaneous, offer a sense of continuity in the revolutionary project of transforming the everyday as part of instituting socialist modernity. Korea was situated within this historical milieu when the "revolution in life" was waged in North Korea. Under colonial rule, everyday life had already offered an opportunity for a materialist critique. Writers such as Yu Hang-rim and Kim Nam-ch'ŏn "quotidianized Marxist theory and politicized the everyday," criticizing not only capitalist modernity but also colonial modernity at a time when freedom of expression was increasingly curtailed beginning in the 1930s.[74] Much like Benjamin, they understood everyday life as the sphere of daily occurrences that could shed light on the deeper fundamental structures for a Marxist critique of modern society. The everyday became the object of analysis while offering a surreptitious methodology grounded in a materialist critique. Contemporary to the rise of the Frankfurt School, colonial-era Marxists in Korea also began to see the significance of culture as an autonomous force shaping society; culture was no longer simply relegated to ancillary status but was considered constitutive of the very material base. Part of a global reconfiguration of Marxism in the interwar years, this turn toward cultural forces and the everyday took on particular resonance in colonial Korea where everyday life (ilsang saenghwal) came under colonial domination through ordinances that directed almost all aspects of life. In a program of forced assimilation, Korean colonial subjects were prohibited from speaking the Korean language in schools (1934), forced to worship at Shinto shrines (1935), coerced to adopt Japanese names (1939), and conscripted as soldiers, laborers, and military sex slaves euphemistically called "comfort women" (1940).[75] Moreover, the traditional Korean white *hanbok* was discouraged and dark work clothes encouraged in its place to reduce laundry.

Capitalist modernity is disruptive and invasive no matter where it penetrates, eroding local roots and cultural distinctiveness.[76] Colonial modernity compounded these effects in a highly visible way because of its unevenness and discriminatory practices. Whereas capitalist modernity counterbalanced its most acerbic qualities with the lure of consumption, colonial modernity could not operate in the same manner due to the very function the colony held for the metropole. Despite expansion of mass consumption during the relatively liberal period of the 1920s Cultural Rule, during which the colonial government relaxed regulations on publications, organizations, and businesses, by the time Japan pushed ahead with its imperial ambitions beyond Korea and Taiwan in the 1930s, Korea had to be squeezed for maximum efficacy in the drive toward further empire-building, curtailing both cultural production and consumption.

With increasing political repression in the 1930s, anticolonial struggles moved underground, making coordination difficult, but elements of resistance in the northern regions of the peninsula bordering Manchuria had never been entirely stamped out due to its remoteness. Traditionally, the north had been isolated from the centralized bureaucracy in Seoul with the majority of landed elites based in southern Korea. Furthermore, people in the northern regions had a transnational history of intermingling with Mongolian and Jurchen tribes along the northern border. As a result, the north was much less attached to traditional Confucian hierarchies based on status and wealth. Mobile slash-and-burn farmers in these areas were radicalized through Red Peasant Unions as the region became the geographical base for radical movements among peasants and workers.[77] Anticolonial resentment created fertile ground for both professional revolutionaries and newly politicized peasants, who almost immediately filled the power vacuum left in the wake of Japan's surrender in World War II on August 15, 1945. Peasant unions throughout Korea served as a prelude to the people's committees as those who had been active in the unions were often elected to head the PCs.[78] As Japanese troops retreated to their barracks and colonial officials nervously awaited the occupation forces, villagers banded together to preserve peace and organize local self-governing committees throughout the country.

By the end of 1945, the entire peninsula was covered with people's committees at all levels down to the villages.[79] Showing a variety of forms and political leanings across different regions, they were spontaneously organized to carry out revolutionary justice. They set up people's courts to punish those who had collaborated with the Japanese as "national traitors," and took over local government offices to distribute land and preserve local security. They showed enormous capacity for organization. Most of them had sections for propaganda, peacekeeping and security, food, finances, welfare relief, consumer affairs, labor relations, and tenancy rates, among others.[80] An American official in Korea at the time observed that "all [colonial] government agencies became powerless" and that people's committees "preserved the peace and collected necessary taxes," preventing "looting, bloodshed, and rioting."[81] People's committees were supplemented by peasant unions, worker unions, peacekeeping groups, and organizations of students, youth, and women. In the immediate aftermath of liberation, local people's committees had substantial autonomy and space for self-governance, transforming the nature of the everyday into one reminiscent of Benjamin's reflections about Moscow, and China's enactment of the commune model.

Interestingly, the assistant chief of the North Korean Provincial Peace Section also made references to revolutionary France during a press conference on March 3, 1946:

> Our sovereign power has been established since Korea was liberated. . . . The actions of the peace section are, so to speak, something similar to a garrison which serves to protect laborers, farmers, small citizens, students, intellectual classes, and the life of [sic] property of others. . . . In tracing the origin of the People's Peace Police, we find that there was a system of public police for maintaining peace and order temporarily in the days of the French Revolution from 1789 to 1870. . . . Now we will devote ourselves for the task of strengthening ourselves for self-protection. I hope that all the people will cooperate with us whole heartedly.[82]

Despite the years that separate the revolutions, modern revolutions shared attempts to refashion politics for a different kind of everyday life that is "public through and through" and imbued with the deepest sense of social meaning, free from commodification.

Major reforms in the northern half of the peninsula within the first year after liberation came to constitute the North Korean Revolution. A sweeping land reform that confiscated land without compensation in a land-to-the-tiller program was officially promulgated on March 5, 1946, to formalize much of the ad hoc confiscations. In June, the Labor Law was instituted, calling for an eight-hour work day, a standardized wage scale, two weeks of paid annual vacation, the right to collective bargaining, and the elimination of child labor in hazardous industries. The Law of Equal Rights for Men and Women was passed in July to liberate women from the "triple subordination" of family, society, and politics. It nullified all previous Korean and Japanese laws regarding women, provided women with equal rights to political participation, economic and educational opportunities, and freedom of choice in marriage and divorce, outlawing polygamy and the sale of women as wives and concubines. Finally, major industries, banks, and transportation services were nationalized, many of which had been owned by the Japanese, facilitating the process of nationalization while giving satisfaction to nationalist impulses. The traditional social hierarchy, the status of peasants and women, forms of political and social organizations, and the role of the state had changed overnight.

In many instances, the socialist experiment in the Soviet Union was seen as providing a "profound lesson" and "roadmap" for North Korea, according to Paek Nam-un, the minister of education. Paek had visited the Soviet Union between February 22 and April 7, 1949, as part of the North Korean delegation to sign the Treaty on Economic and Cultural Cooperation with the Soviet Union.[83] During a visit to a chocolate factory, Paek noted how the packaging of consumer products in Soviet society preserved the use value—that is, the function and form—of the product.[84] The materiality of the product—its use value and social significance—rather than its exchange value as something to be bought and sold for profit determined the way the product was designed and made. Moreover, Paek saw the mechanization of the production line in the Soviet Union not as enslaving the worker, as in capitalist societies, but as freeing workers from tedious work. They became masters over the machines, monitoring and directing the production process, with time left over to pursue a cultural life. Touring the various sites from factories and educational facilities to museums and art galleries, Paek was struck by the collective forms of entertainment in the various "circles" (ssŏk'ŭl) and the extent to which everyday life was connected to the arts through music, dance, sculpture, and architecture: "All the recreation and pastime is directed toward collective circles, developing the cultural standard of socialist life to a new level . . . everyday life is connected to the arts, and it is the highest civilizational life and the happiest in the world in terms of making life artistic."[85] Paek's travelogue was filled with precise and meticulous descriptions, including full lists of memorable museum pieces and detailed features of building interiors and public spaces. He explained that such diligence was needed because the "timeliness . . . must be grasped historically for a scientific worldview, which is a necessary condition to recognize Soviet society that has created a new history for humanity."[86]

No doubt, Paek and his delegation were shown nothing but the pinnacle of Soviet achievement, and spared evidence of the devastating toll that the recent war had taken on Soviet society. The delegation was made up of worldly intellectuals and politicians, however, and one must assume they were astute enough to observe aspects of the country that their hosts did not intend for them to see during their six-week tour, which involved long train rides through the countryside. As the following observations of another delegation member show, it is not the expected generic praise of their hosts that stands out but the specific everyday details that impressed the North Korean delegates, each in their own specialized fields, as examples of socialist modernity to take back home.

As the minister of commerce, Chang Si-u noted store operations in detail, from the uniforms the sales clerks wore to how the merchandise was displayed. He particularly noticed the pragmatic construction of the sales counter.[87] Comparing the glass cases back home, which he deemed more expensive and fragile, Chang praised the wooden counters as being sturdy and easy to make while providing more room to attend to customers. He concluded that the Soviet counter was practical as opposed to showy, assisting customers rather than displaying commodities. Moreover, he observed how the development of machines had transformed artistic form in the Soviet Union, making art more accessible to people through mass production. He pointed out how architecture, craftwork, and other works of art were no longer produced by hand but mechanized, reiterating Benjamin's point in "The Work of Art in the Age of Mechanical Reproduction" (1936) in uncanny similarity.[88] He concluded that art had not only become part of everyday life but that life itself had become artistic: "The Soviets have absolutely made art part of one's everyday life. As a smoker who cannot go without a cigarette, they become restless when they go to a dance hall [because they want to dance]. Even in the making of a door lock or frame, they must have some kind of engraving."[89] Finishing his essay, Chang lamented the fact that Korea could not be like the Soviet Union soon enough, urging the workers in his department to learn from the Soviets. Many of the sites that the delegation visited, including the subway, the kolkhoz (collective farm), the Kremlin, the National Pediatrics Hospital, Lenin's Mausoleum, and the Leningrad Palace of Young Pioneers eventually became prototypes for similar sites in North Korea. However, such modeling of the Soviet Union as the vanguard of socialism was not seen to contravene the principle of autonomy and independence that the North Korean leadership advanced as the primary condition for a Korean nation-state. Indeed, Paek saw mutual aid and cooperation with the Soviet Union as the basis for a strong independent Korea with *chuch'esŏng* (subjectivity), invoking a variation of the term Juche (self-reliance) that Kim Il Sung was to use in 1955 as the centerpiece of North Korean political ideology.[90]

Despite the political liberation of Korea from Japanese rule, observations made by the North Korean delegation point to the importance of transforming everyday life to fully overcome the experience of colonialism and capitalism. Just as cultural work became of primary importance in the Soviet Union of the 1920s, a similar agenda was recognized by the Korean leftist writer, Im Hwa. He astutely remarked that whereas the effects of political domination by the Japanese might be easy enough to eradicate, the lasting effects in everyday life would take much longer: "It is easy to liquidate the cultural effects of political domination by Japanese imperialism, but the cultural remnants of cultural domination will take a long time to be eradicated . . . in such invisible effects remaining in the sphere of language, custom, taste, and style."[91] The seizure of political power was only the beginning; a thorough cultural revolution had to be waged to overcome the colonized everyday.

Differentiated from the universal or high modernism of the interwar and postwar period, which settled into a comfortable relationship with the dominant power structures of capitalism, *heroic* modernism was at the core of North Korea's social and cultural revolution by which peasants, workers, and women took center stage as revolutionary heroes sketching out a new path in Korean history. As David Harvey and Raymond Williams point out, modernist impulses in the twentieth century were varied to the point of being contradictory. The Enlightenment project of controlling and rationalizing the world in the name of science and progress was not only deeply flawed in theory but extremely destructive in practice, particularly visible in the two world wars. Multiple modernisms responded in various ways. *Reactionary* modernists, or "modernists against modernity," as Williams describes them, attempted to redeploy the use of science and rational order for expedient goals in the pursuit of state power, turning back the clock for a mythical sense of coherence as the ticket to greater stability.[92] In East Asia, this trend was best exemplified by Japanese discourses and policies in the 1930s and 1940s that wanted to "overcome modernity" through a singular emphasis on the deification of the Japanese emperor and subsequent policies of "imperialization" of colonized subjects in the construction of the Greater East Asia Co-Prosperity Sphere.[93]

Others sought to build what Harvey terms *heroic* modernism in the form of politically committed movements such as surrealism, constructivism, and socialist realism that dared to critique the present *and* the past while offering alternatives for an altogether different future grounded in a belief in historical progress.[94] The collective embodied in these movements was defined by concrete material interests brought together for social ends as opposed to ambiguous collectives relying on a fabled past for militarist expansion. Modernity did not only produce isolated individuals in crowds of strangers but made possible "new kinds of human solidarity" based on the "liberating diversity and mobility of the city."[95] The socialist project grabbed hold of this possibility presented by modernity, critiquing the effects of capitalist modernity by putting society above the logic of capital. The superficial similarities in form between the different strains of modernism that stress efficiency and rationality should not be mistaken for substantive differences in content. Movements such as constructivism sought to create a life of social meaning toward a better future as opposed to the pursuit of profit in the here and now or the glory of a transcendental past.

It is within this history of modernity that we must situate North Korean history—as a critique of capitalist colonial modernity rather than a failed modernist project from the vantage point of postmodernity. The North Korean Revolution was an attempt at a heroic socialist modernity through the creation and maintenance of a revolutionary society, and it is the task of the rest of this book to show how North Korea attempted to institutionalize the revolutionary practices of everyday life.

2. Legacies

Fomenting the Revolution

I feel as though my mind is suffering from a kind of psychological
split. . . . From the outer to the inner room and back again from the
inner to the outer room, I go back and forth aimlessly, mumbling to
myself. A happy day has come. You and I, we must all be happy. . . .
I grin and shake hands with everyone I meet as if to embrace them. But,
for some reason, I feel empty as if there is a gaping hole in one corner.
Japan is now completely bankrupt. But is Japan the only one?
O YŎNG-JIN, AUGUST 15, 1945

Processions continue in many regions. Assemblies and unique meetings
planned instantaneously, they happen all the time, all of a sudden spontaneously. . . . The old, the young, workers, teachers, lawyers, students,
and merchants speak. Everyone speaks their mind, breaking the long
years of forced silence, closure, and subjugation.
PANYA SHAVSHYNA, AUGUST 22, 1945

Figure 2.1. North Hamgyŏng Province People's Committee first-year
anniversary of liberation (1946). RG 242, SA 2005, box 7, item 5.
Courtesy of the National Archives and Records Administration.

By many accounts, August 15, 1945 was a quiet day in Korea when the voice of Japanese Emperor Hirohito was broadcast on radio acknowledging defeat in the Asia-Pacific War.[1] Many people had not yet heard the news and others who had were apprehensive about what would happen next. However, by the next day the streets were filled with celebration as people paraded and congregated in huge numbers. Panya Shavshyna, a member of the Soviet consulate stationed in Seoul between 1940 and 1946, was there to bear witness. She wrote in her diary for August 16, 1945, that "every two or three hundred meters, there were spontaneous assemblies" of people making impassioned speeches, singing, crying, and embracing.[2] In villages throughout the peninsula, people began organizing almost immediately, creating peacekeeping and self-governing organizations to take over the colonial administration.

Japanese intelligence reports intercepted by Americans described the electric situation in the north:

> Soviet Forces and Korean Committees are taking charge of public security. All policemen have been disarmed. . . . All Japanese are in a state of extreme terror. . . . Though the city is generally quiet and calm, Koreans are demonstrating with Soviet and Korean flags and pasting posters everywhere. Though no trouble has yet developed between Japanese and Korean people, it is feared among the Japanese that robbery, crime and violence may develop. Though there have been no changes in government, financial organizations, companies and factories, the chiefs of police stations have been changed to Koreans. . . . The local government office and administrative powers were taken over immediately by the advancing forces and turned over to the Committee for the Reconstruction of Korea. The weapons at the Police Station were turned over to the Hoan Tai [sic] (Guardians of the Peace Organization), a branch of the above mentioned Committee, and the Korean policemen, wearing civilian clothes, are assisting the Hoan Tai [sic] in maintaining the public peace.[3]

Much of the mobilization was facilitated by those who had been politically active during the colonial period. Some twenty thousand political prisoners were released on August 16 across the country, and the young men who had been forcibly conscripted into the Japanese Imperial Army began returning to their homes. In Seoul, one thousand "patriots" were released from Sŏdaemun Prison beginning at ten in the morning with spontaneous speeches and the singing of the Korean anthem and the "Internationale" while rickshaw drivers jostled to be the first ones to take the prisoners home.[4] The released prisoners played key roles when they returned to their hometowns, taking up leadership positions.[5] Local elders were often touted as the leader while the actual work was carried out by younger activists with political experience in the anticolonial movement. Maintaining peace and security was the primary goal in the early days, and a variety of organizational names were in circulation—among others, security force (*ch'iandae*), peacekeeping force (*poandae* or *hoandae*), self-governing committee (*chach'i wiwŏnhoe*), political committee (*chŏngch'i wiwonhoe*), and people's committee (*inmin wiwŏnhoe*).

Meanwhile, in the capital, Yŏ Un-hyŏng, veteran of the independence movement and a moderate leftist, had been approached by the Japanese colonial government for help in maintaining peace and security. Yŏ spearheaded the formation of the Committee for the Preparation of Korean Independence (CPKI, *Chosŏn kŏn'guk chunbi wiwŏnhoe*) to begin preparing for an independent Korea, organizing security forces and arranging emergency food aid. Almost overnight, 145 branches had popped up across the peninsula.[6] News of the CPKI's founding prompted villages to create their own CPKI branches, which was often as simple as replacing the signboard over the office of the existing local security force or people's committee.[7] Although local groups were brought under the umbrella of the CPKI in this fashion, the relationship was tenuous at best. More often than not, the leadership in Seoul lagged behind the mass movement.[8] Under Yŏ's leadership, the People's Republic of Korea (*Chosŏn inmin konghwaguk*) was declared on September 6, 1945, two days before the American occupation forces landed in Inch'ŏn, as an expression of Korea's capacity for self-government and desire for independence lest the Americans should have other designs. CPKI branches throughout the country followed suit by renaming themselves people's committees (PCs, *inmin wiwŏnhoe*). Although other names persisted at the village level, most groups, especially those at the provincial level, were organized into people's committees throughout Korea in the month of September.

Through these committees, revolutionary justice was meted out to colonial authorities and their collaborators, at times violently. The "enemies" were defined in terms of their association with the colonial government: landlords who had been protected by the colonial government to control the countryside, local government officials and the police, and rice collection agents carrying out the orders of the colonial administration.[9] Regardless of political affiliation, the primary targets were all those organs that had constituted the colonial machinery. People's committees took

Table 2.1. Organization of People's Committees, November 1945

National total		South of 38th Parallel			North of 38th Parallel		
		Total	Organized	Unorganized	Total	Organized	Unorganized
Township	2,244	1,680	1,667	13	564	564	–
Town (*ŭp*)	103	75	75	–	28	28	–
Island	2	2	2	–	–	–	–
County	218	148	148	–	70	70	–
City	21	12	12	–	9	9	–
Province[a]	13	9	7	2	7	6	1

Source: RG 242, SA 2006, box 13, item 65, *Minutes of the National Congress of People's Committee Representatives* (November 1946). There are also copies in *Collection of Modern Korean History Materials*, vol. 12 (Seoul: Tolbaege, 1986), 470, and NHCC, vol. 6, 618, with slight variations.
[a] The provinces of the north and south add up to sixteen rather than thirteen because three provinces were divided by the 38th parallel, creating southern and northern Kyŏnggi, Kangwŏn, and Hwanghae Provinces. The three provinces without organized PCs were northern Kyŏnggi Province, southern Kangwŏn Province, and southern Hwanghae Province.

over local governance in the vacuum left by the collapse of the Japanese colonial government, punishing "national traitors" and criminals in people's courts, distributing grain, and maintaining local security.[10] Peasants, who made up the vast majority of the population, dominated the PCs.[11] It was reported that peasants, refusing the orders of district officials, obeyed only the people's committees, and that peasants controlled most police stations.[12]

In the south, this period of autonomy did not last. The PCs were seen to threaten the power of the American occupation forces, which refused in principle to acknowledge any preexisting Korean authority. To make matters worse, PCs took on a reputation as left leaning when they advocated land reform and the nationalization of major industries owned by the Japanese. The beginning of the United States Army Military Government in Korea (USAMGIK) thus spelled eventual doom for the southern committees, although this was by no means a forgone conclusion.[13] Depending on the relationship between the local American occupation forces and the committees, many PCs lasted into the fall of 1946, especially in the villages, because the occupation forces were not able to penetrate very far below the provincial level.[14]

By contrast, the people's committees in the north were aided by the Soviet occupation, which largely consigned the administration of its occupation zone to the institutions set up by Koreans. Through information culled from the press and informants, an American intelligence report described how "when Soviets entered north Korea in late August 1945 they found that after surrender of Japs, Koreans had formed local 'self rule councils' in many places. . . . A council of 27 members was formed in each of the five northern provinces."[15] As in the south, northern committees were formed through village assemblies, or at the initiative of village leaders. Rather than seeing them as threats, however, the Soviets supported and fostered the PCs. They became structures on which to build a government that had popular support and was friendly toward the Soviet Union, which was ensured by Soviet backing of leftist political figures. Soviet influence notwithstanding, there was no Soviet military government set up in the north comparable to the U.S. military government in the south. The primary Soviet objective was not to occupy Korea, but to set up a buffer against Japan and retrieve the Sakhalin region that had been lost after the Russo–Japanese War of 1905.[16]

The irony of Korea's division was that Pyongyang was home to one of the largest concentrations of Christians in East Asia, known as the "Jerusalem of the East," whereas the south harbored the majority of domestic communists that had been active throughout the colonial period.[17] In Pyongyang, Cho Man-sik, a renowned moderate nationalist Christian educator, formed the South P'yŏngan Province CPKI branch on August 17, 1945.[18] With the coming of the Soviets the following week, this moderate branch was reorganized into the South P'yŏngan People's Political Committee on August 27 with the addition of leftist figures who had recently been released from prison. This prompted Cho to form his own party, the Korean Democratic Party, which was composed mostly of Christians, merchants, and former landlords. Still, Cho remained as head of the South P'yŏngan People's Political Committee and he formally set up office with Soviet support, relocating from a small primary school classroom to a large office with a reception area including a desk, sofa, carpet, and all.[19] This was to become the tried-and-true method for the Soviet occupation of the north, in which PCs were supplemented by leftists where they were lacking, as in the P'yŏngan Provinces. Han Kŭn-cho, the mayor of Pyongyang from August 26 until November 2, 1945, confirmed this in a report furnished to the American authorities, stating that "there is no central government in N Korea. Each province has established its own government." He added that the South P'yŏngan Province People's Committee had more "democrats" (those affiliated with Cho's Democratic Party) than any other province, with eighteen communists and fourteen democrats, whereas other provinces had about three democrats only in each committee.[20] In any case, the "democrats" had

Table 2.2. Overview of provincial People's Committees in North Korea, 1945

Province	Development of PCs	Political orientation	Date of Soviet entry
North Hamgyŏng	8.16~8.17 Formation of city level people's committees in Najin, Unggi, Ch'ŏngjin, and elsewhere Late September, North Hamgyŏng People's Committee (North Korean sources cite 10.26, a later date likely attributed to when communists took control of PC)	Leftist stronghold with active Red Peasant Union movement during colonial period	August 10-12
South Hamgyŏng	8.16 South Hamgyŏng People's Committee Left Split between South Hamgyŏng Communist Association and South Hamgyŏng CPKI 8.25 South Hamgyŏng Executive Committee 9.1 South Hamgyŏng People's Committee	Leftist stronghold since colonial period with largest concentration of industrial workers	August 21
North P'yŏngan	8.16 Sinŭiju City Provisional Self-Governing Committee, followed by other city level committees 8.26 North P'yŏngan Self-Governing Committee 8.31 North P'yŏngan Provisional People's Political Committee	Right-Left Coalition Largest number of tenant conflicts in the northern half during the colonial period Sinŭiju student protest against PC in Nov. 1945 Stronghold of New People's Party	August 22
South P'yŏngan	8.15 South P'yŏngan Peace Preservation Committee => 8.16 South P'yŏngan CPKI 8.17 Korean Communist South P'yŏngan Committee 8.27 South P'yŏngan People's Political Committee (coalition of CPKI and communists) 11.24 South P'yŏngan People's Committee (left)	Conservative due to large concentration of Christians in Pyongyang	Aug. 24
Hwanghae	8.17 Korean Communist Haeju Committee, Haeju Security Corps, etc. 8.20 CPKI Hwanghae Branch 8.25 Hwanghae People's Political Committee (conservative) 9.2 Hwanghae People's Committee (coalition) 9.13 Hwanghae People's Committee (left)	Strong class conflict Largest agricultural region in the north Borders 38th parallel	Aug. 25

(Continued)

Table 2.2 (*Continued*)

Province	Development of PCs	Political orientation	Date of Soviet entry
Kangwŏn	10.18 Kangwŏn People's Committee (8.16 Kangwŏn Self-Governing Committee => Kangwŏn CPKI formed south of the 38th parallel in Ch'unch'ŏn)	Left Divided by 38th parallel	Aug. 25

Sources: RG 242, SA 2009, box 3, item 103, "Survey of Two Years of Work in Each of the Provincial People's Committees," (1947.9); Kim Kwang-un, "Formation of the Power-Structure and the Recruitment of Cadre in North Korea (August 1945~March 1947)" (PhD diss., Hanyang University, 1999), 44; Kim Yong-bok, "Organization and Activities of the North Korean People's Committees in the Immediate Postliberation Period," in *Haebang chŏnhusa ŭi insik* [Understanding pre- and postliberation history], ed. Kim Nam-sik (Seoul: Han'gilsa, 1989); Ryu Kil-chae, "Study of the People's Committees in State Building in North Korea, 1945–1947" (PhD diss., Korea University, 1995), chapter 3; Ryu Chae-in, *Kangwŏndo pisa* [Hidden history of Kangwŏn Province] (Seoul: Kangwŏn ilbosa, 1974), 19, 29; Bruce Cumings, *The Origins of the Korean War: Liberation and the Emergence of Separate Regimes, 1945–1947*, vol. 1 (Princeton: Princeton University Press, 1981), chapter 11.

Table 2.3. Population figures in North Korea, 1947

	Pyong-yang	South P'yŏngan	North P'yŏngan	Hwanghae	Kangwŏn	North Hamgyŏng	South Hamgyŏng	Total
Korean	352,101	1,489,193	1,950,718	1,718,006	1,162,308	943,582	1,555,185	9,171,093
Chinese	3,921	3,736	20,093	3,546	1,344	5,470	2,753	40,863
Japanese	163	191	28	107	70	84	245	888
German	0	0	0	0	62	2	8	72
Total								9,212,938

Source: RG 242, SA 2005, box 6, item 1, Department of Interior and Security documents (1946–48).
Note: The total number is off by twenty-two in the original. The German presence consisted mostly of missionaries.

reason to work with the communists, not only because of Soviet pressure but also because of the pragmatic need to work within a broad coalition. Besides, many of the Christian nationalists embraced a degree of socialism for the future of Korea, having participated in anti-imperialist movements during the colonial period.[21] By November 1945, people's committees had been organized in all the cities, townships, and villages of the six northern provinces.[22]

To facilitate the occupation of northern Korea, Soviet authorities set up what they called a "Civil Administration" (Grazhdanskia Administratsiia) on October 3, 1945.[23] Relying on Korean initiatives, the Soviets made sure to institute a pro-Soviet leadership as shown in the turn toward the left in the composition of committee members in the more conservative regions of Hwanghae and P'yongan Provinces. With the consolidation of key political figures in Pyongyang, including Kim Il Sung, who had returned to North Korea in September from leading anti-Japanese partisans in Manchuria (1932–41) and in the Russian Maritime Province (1941–45), the Soviet occupation actively pushed a national meeting of the provincial PCs. This facilitated the establishment of the Five Provinces Administrative Bureau (*Pukchosŏn 5-to haengjŏngguk*) on October 8, 1945, with 110 people's committee representatives, fifty-one of whom were members of the Korean Communist Party. They were joined by thirty-nine representatives of workers, peasants, and intellectuals from other parties, and twenty Soviet personnel.[24] Representatives from each of the provinces and parties met in Pyongyang to form a central administration with ten departments: industry, transportation, communication, agriculture, commerce, finance, education, health, justice, and security.[25] Consequently, the various regional administrative organizations came to be uniformly called people's committees and took on a semblance of central authority while the local committees still maintained power and control over regional affairs.

Early next year, on February 8, 1946, the Administrative Bureau was reorganized to become the North Korean Provisional People's Committee (PPC, *Pukchosŏn imsi inmin wiwŏnhoe*) with three more departments—planning, publicity, and general affairs—added to the previous ten.[26] Consisting of twenty-three members, including the chair, vice-chair, secretary, and two members who made up the five-person Standing Committee, the Provisional People's Committee announced an eleven-point plan, laying out the main tasks for the emerging government. The first two dealt with the two most pressing issues: a purge of pro-Japanese elements and antidemocratic forces, and a land reform that would distribute land to the tillers. The next five included steps to revive the economy, focusing on emergency measures to deal with the serious food shortage; development of industries for daily necessities; restoration of railways, electricity, communications, and transport; organization of financial institutions to facilitate trade and commerce; and the promotion of medium-sized industries to foster initiative among merchants and entrepreneurs. The last four points focused on social reforms, calling for the institution of factory committees; the expansion of mass education; increases in the number of teachers and schools; and the eradication of the Japanese "slave ideology" for a "true democratic spirit" through the implementation of broad cultural enlightenment projects.[27] The formation of the Provisional People's Committee was thus the first attempt to institutionalize the people's committees that had spontaneously formed in the immediate postliberation period as *the* legitimate form of government in Korea.

To offer itself as a model of genuine people's democracy, the next logical step for the PPC was to organize the election of PC representatives to create not only a provisional but a permanent democratic government in Korea. Indeed, the first election in Korea's history was organized in November 1946. After the election, over the course of four days beginning on February 17, 1947, 1,158 representatives from the provincial, city, and county PCs met for a congress to elect a 237-member North Korean People's Assembly (*Pukchosŏn inmin hoeŭi*) from among them, with 86 percent in favor of the entire slate of nominated candidates.[28] The PC representatives at the congress and the Central Committee of the North Korean Democratic National United Front had the right to nominate candidates. A ballot with all the names of the nominees was then distributed to each of the representatives at the congress. They could write in additional nominees, cross off anyone not to their liking, and leave alone those they supported. The secrecy of each vote was guaranteed by collecting the ballots in a box before proceeding to the count. The candidates with the largest number of votes to fill the first 237 seats were declared the winners. The number of seats in the People's Assembly was determined by allocating one seat for every five congress representatives. Predictably, the ranks of the representatives elected to the first People's Assembly were filled with illustrious names that stretched back to the colonial period: intellectuals such as Kim Tu-bong and Han Sŏr-ya; women activists such as Hŏ Chŏng-suk and Pak Chŏng-ae; artists such as Yi Ki-yŏng (writer) and Ch'oe Sŭng-hŭi (dancer); revolutionaries such as Chang Si-u, O Ki-sŏp, Ch'oe Ch'ang-ik, Mu Chŏng, Kim Ch'aek; and, of course, Kim Il Sung. The famed and celebrated were not the only ones to be elected to the assembly, however, as the next chapter shows. The People's Assembly encompassed a wide variety of people that included merchants, entrepreneurs, clergy, and intellectuals, who were usually cast out in other socialist revolutions. The only groups that went unrepresented were landlords and Japanese collaborators. The formation of the People's Assembly as the supreme legislative body gave it the authority to elect the chair of the North Korean People's Committee, the highest executive body, which reorganized and added more departments to the previous thirteen under the PPC. The publicity department was changed to the culture and publicity department, and five new departments were added: national audit, internal affairs, foreign affairs, labor, and city management.[29]

With the official founding of the Democratic People's Republic of Korea (DPRK) in September 1948 and the promulgation of the constitution, the duties of the local people's committees were officially outlined in Article 74 of the new constitution:[30]

1. Protection of citizens' rights, including the right to property
2. Protection of national property in its jurisdiction
3. Maintenance of social order
4. Guaranteed implementation of laws, edicts, decisions, and orders decreed by higher organs
5. Revitalization and development of local industries in its jurisdiction
6. Revitalization and development of local transportation facilities
7. Construction and repair of roads
8. Formation and implementation of the local budget and the collection of taxes
9. Direction of educational and cultural programs
10. Organization of hospitals for health care, medical assistance for the people, and direction of other health care programs
11. Formulation and implementation of plans for city/rural development; direction of housing construction, waterworks facilities, and sanitation projects
12. Investigation of arable land and direction of their rational usage
13. Collection of agricultural tax-in-kind
14. Establishment of a strategy for natural disasters and infectious diseases

Topping the list was the protection of individual rights, including the right to personal property, with the remainder highlighting the central role that PCs played in local administration, from transportation, education, health care, and housing to the collection of taxes, signaling the extent to which local autonomy was written into the constitution itself. Nonetheless, item four connected the local PC to national policy by requiring all local PCs to follow the decisions reached by higher levels of government. All things considered, the organization of people's committees and their consolidation into a central government took place at breakneck speed, traditionally explained as the result of Soviet planning. The Soviets were certainly influential, providing an inspirational model for emulation, as shown in the last chapter. However, the swiftness with which a centralized government was organized, with a concrete program adopted by the Provisional People's Committee, points to deeper legacies that go back to the colonial period, not only in providing a ready-made infrastructure for mobilization but also a blueprint for reform.

Colonial Modernity

As O Yŏng-jin's diary entry in the opening epigraph shows, the end of colonial rule was met with a psychic split, on the one hand with a sense of ecstasy but on the other hand with feelings of emptiness and powerlessness.[31] He took his own ambivalent response as a symptom of the long years of colonial rule that had penetrated and seeped into his consciousness, internalizing his colonial subjecthood despite his outward anticolonial stance. He concluded that his "political consciousness had been completely paralyzed from the weight of colonial oppression, eliminating any sense of autonomy." What awakens him from this "sense of deep slumber and surreality" is the sight of a Shinto shrine burning on the night of August 15, which signaled to him the dawn of a new era. Modernity may be unsettling on the whole, but the acute contradictions of colonial modernity splintered the psychic core of its colonized subjects.

Whereas modernity has more often been defined by the qualitative shifts in the organization of time and space, with the expansion of transportation networks and communication systems in the process of industrialization, the formation of modern subjectivity defined by the emergence of autonomous rights–bearing individuals, even if illusory, is no less integral a component to modernity. But the full sense of modern subjectivity was limited in colonial Korea, whether as "free" laborers bound by nothing but the "objective" relations of market exchange, as Marx had envisioned, or as rational subjects with a "self-confidence nurtured by self-discipline," in Weberian fashion.[32] To be sure, there was a steady stream of workers joining the ranks of the proletariat. Peasants, pushed out by desperate conditions in the countryside and pulled into the city in search of new opportunities, found factory jobs, particularly in the textile industry that sought out young women for their nimble fingers.[33] Others migrated as far as Japan to fill dangerous and difficult jobs in construction and mining.[34] The number of Koreans in Japan peaked at two million by 1945. However, half of them were forcibly conscripted during World War II due to wartime labor shortages.[35] Thus, the contractual relationship between the propertied and working classes, as well as between landlords and peasants, was rendered moot once total war mobilization after 1937 removed any semblance of autonomy from colonial subjects.

In other words, colonial modernity was not always as modern as the term implies, often leading to a kind of modernity without modern subjects.[36] Its logic proclaimed itself to be a modernizing influence by engendering industrial development with the attendant urbanization and the beginnings of consumer culture through the efficient operation of a highly centralized state; however, demands for political rights and self-determination as expressions of modern subjectivity were suppressed, at times ruthlessly, as in the crackdown on the March First Movement in 1919, in which thousands of Koreans demanding independence were slaughtered.[37] Although nationalism as one form of modern subjectivity may have intensified as a result of colonialism, despite the colonizer's intentions, the consolidation of the modern subject as a self-empowered agent with certain inalienable rights was not to be part of Japan's "civilizing" mission in Korea. To be sure, the creation of modern subjects in the latter sense was never Japan's goal despite its official rhetoric nor was it the goal of any colonial power in the twentieth century. The nationalist response went much further in facilitating the emergence of modern subjectivity through numerous publications and social movements promoting Korean language and culture. These included rural cooperatives and literacy programs to modernize the Korean countryside, which was aided by colonial modernization in the form of railways, radios, and print media.[38] The point is not to make light of these efforts at modernization, but to emphasize their limits.

Despite the best efforts of nationalist reformers and colonial modernization projects, literacy rates were still exorbitantly high and the limited expansion in political rights by the end of colonial rule left Koreans the equal right to die for the imperial cause when they were allowed to join the Imperial Army. Rather than a survey of the colonial period, the following sections stress the limits to colonial modernity, particularly in the 1930s and 1940s, which was the more significant antecedent to the immediate postliberation period. Indeed, as colonial-era writers were keen to observe through a proliferation of stories with disabled characters, the trope of disability was used as a metaphor to denote "uneven and unequal access to modernity," linking the disabled figure, hampered both physically and mentally, with the Korean nation subjugated by colonial rule.[39] The kind of internal subjectification that was necessary to imagine colonized Korea as a "community of the impaired" already required a self-reflexive modern subject who could pinpoint the limits of colonial modernity in its failure to recognize Koreans as modern subjects with political self-determination. Colonial modernity thus signified the dramatic expansion in technologies of discipline and governmentality without an accompanying political emancipation that would engender full modern subjects.[40]

Various policies were implemented toward this end, beginning with the concentration of power in the hands of the governor-general. The Law concerning Laws and Regulations to be Enforced in Korea gave the Japanese governor-general the power to issue ordinances with the same effect as legislation passed by the Diet in Japan.[41] The Office of the Governor-General had sweeping powers in colonial Korea that incorporated executive, legislative, and judiciary functions in one body, facilitating control over the colony. The official pretext for withholding political representation from Koreans was the lack of requisite conditions, including their low level of political and cultural development and the logistics necessary for the registration of voters.[42] Parliamentary oversight would have challenged imperial sovereignty, which was codified in Japan with the promulgation of the Meiji Constitution in 1889. It designated the emperor as "sacred and inviolable," "combining in Himself the rights of sovereignty" to rule over the empire with power over the cabinet and the military even while granting a limited number of civil rights to Japanese subjects.[43]

In colonial Korea, there was no comparable sense of social pact between state and society, whether in the form of protection from arbitrary exercises of state power in exchange for acquiescence, or social security from the excesses of the market in return for hard work. Summary judgments were made on a wide variety of minor offenses, and offenders were punished without trial, often through corporal punishment. Although flogging was abolished in Japan in 1882, the 1912 Flogging Ordinance institutionalized flogging as the primary method of punishment in Korea, affecting almost half of all offenders, until it was abolished in 1920 after the March First Movement.[44] The ideological rationale for maintaining "traditional" practices against the tide of modernization was that the "uncivilized" would not be deterred by mere detention and had to be controlled by harsh physical pain.[45] Pragmatically there was not enough capacity to imprison the increasing numbers of Koreans held for offenses from petty crimes to all-out insurgency against colonial rule by bands of "righteous armies." Japanese arguments that colonial rule was necessary to bring modern reforms to Korea turned out to be a blatant contradiction in this case, overturning the 1894 Kabo Reforms by the Korean government that had already banned flogging before Japanese colonization.

Moreover, Japanese capital was given preferential access to colonial Korea, affording little protection for Korean workers. Although the 1916 Factory Law limited working hours and regulated working conditions for Japanese workers and the 1931 Major Industries Law restricted trusts and cartels in Japan, neither of these applied to colonial Korea in order to allow Japanese capital unfettered access to the colony.[46] Colonial policy disregarded capital's own requirement for the reproduction of labor—whether by providing a living wage capable of sustaining the workers' livelihood or a public education system capable of socializing the future generation of workers—in the short-term interest of maximizing the extraction of resources from the colonies for the benefit of the metropole. A more detailed account of working conditions and the role of education in colonial Korea will show how the unevenness of colonial modernity manifested itself in the lives of the colonized.

Despite the expansion of industrial infrastructure in cities and port towns such as Hamhŭng, Hŭngnam, Ch'ŏngjin, Inch'ŏn, Seoul, and Pusan, Korea remained overwhelmingly agricultural throughout the colonial period. Even with the large-scale migration of peasants into industrial work, 71 percent of people were still engaged in agricultural work and the urban population only made up 14 percent of the total population by the end of colonial rule.[47] Understanding the agrarian economy and changes in rural social relations is, therefore, critical in discerning the nature of colonial modernity in Korea. Ironically, a Japanese administrative official in the colonial government offered instructive insight into how coloniality inflected modernity in rural Korea.[48] Working as a tenancy officer for almost fifteen years between 1930 and 1944, Hisama Kenichi interacted with landlords, managers, and tenants, observing Korean rural life and publishing several treatises on Korean agrarian development. His official position was the result of a new rural pacification program devised by the colonial government to deal with the increasing number of tenancy disputes throughout the 1920s. Colonial records show disputes rising sharply from only one reported case in 1920 to over seven hundred cases by 1930 involving over ten thousand tenants.[49] The rapid increase can be attributed to the more liberal Cultural Rule of the 1920s—a change in colonial policy ushered in by reaction to the March First Movement—but more instrumental was the spread of socialist and communist ideas in the aftermath of the October Revolution.[50] Radical Red Peasant Unions proliferated throughout the Hamgyŏng regions beginning in the late 1920s. Between 1928 and 1933, 1,575 people were arrested for Red Peasant Union activities in the region, which made up 56 percent of such arrests for the whole country.[51] The colonial government feared that such class conflict fueled nationalist and other political movements with a potential to turn into outright rebellion to overthrow colonial rule itself.[52]

Consequently, a new system of tenancy administration was set up by the colonial government. Tenancy officers were stationed in each county to investigate problems, and prevent and mediate disputes by promoting written contracts with regular contract periods and reforms in the most deleterious practices, including abuse by tenant managers. Although the increasing conflict in the countryside signaled a crisis of landlordism in Korea, colonial rule institutionalized tenancy, not only prolonging it but systematizing its very operation in order to tap both landlords and tenants as partners in agrarian development. In addition to administrative reforms, legislation on tenancy disputes and farmland through the 1932 Tenancy Arbitration Ordinance and 1934 Agricultural Lands Ordinance created a legal framework by which disputes could be settled, thereby providing an outlet for peasant discontent and absorbing any potential political pressure. The Rural Revitalization Campaign (1932–40) also provided low-interest loans, in principle to both peasants and landlords, through financial co-ops (kŭmyung chohap) and mutual-aid production associations (siksan'gye) to ameliorate rural conditions.[53]

Working within this system, Hisama Kenichi was acutely sensitive to the way colonial modernization was coercive and exploitative, viewing it as a "misfortune" rather than a blessing, contrary to so many others in his position. His perspective reveals the intricate ways in which colonial modernity was indeed *colonial*, and not just modern:

> The other side of development is paved with the history of surprising levels of coercive control by the authorities. Plots that do not follow the righteous rules given by the authorities are crushed and destroyed, and seedlings that have not been planted in checkered rows are uprooted and forced to be planted again. . . . Cultivation of unapproved seeds is prohibited, proceeding forcefully regardless of peasant desires. . . . Obeying official orders, peasants plant the distributed seeds in the designated plots according to checkered rows, sowing fertilizer and herbicide on the assigned day, weeding on the appointed day, and preparing to harvest according to authorized method. Here there is only surveillance and command.[54]

No decision-making power was left in the hands of the tillers, who were relegated to sheer robotic movements, much like industrial workers in a factory, following the minutiae of the plans and orders laid out by colonial officials. It was an entirely different kind of mobilization from those in which participants are encouraged to offer up models to be emulated by others and to propose new ideas for the implementation of goals (even if those goals might already be set, as was to be the case in postliberation North Korea). Reflecting peasant desire for autonomy more than material gain, the vast majority of tenancy disputes throughout the 1930s revolved around tenant rights rather than tenant rents.[55] Peasants drew on the more amenable landlord–tenant relations before colonial modernization when rent was adjusted according to harvest conditions and tenants controlled their labor time and labor conditions.

The loss of self-sufficiency and exposure to the whims of the market were poignantly depicted in novels produced during the colonial period as former spaces of autonomy were replaced by newly emerging symbols of modernization: railroad stations, irrigation levees and dikes, land reclamation projects, factory buildings, police stations, and banks.[56] These institutions marked the penetration of Japanese capital into the Korean countryside; more and more people had to purchase foodstuffs, clothes, and shoes on the market rather than producing them for themselves. Labor power increasingly became the only commodity left for peasants to sell as they were unable to live off the land. This did not translate into industrial jobs for the vast majority, however, and most were relegated to becoming hired hands doing odd jobs whether in the cities as day laborers and domestic workers or in the countryside as landless agricultural workers.[57]

Hisama concluded that the methods of rural development were much more coercive in Korea than in Japan proper in order to supply food to the growing Japanese population. He saw the strong hand of the state in agricultural production as being in perfect alignment with Japanese capital, which was looking for profit at a time when the worldwide market crash of 1929 left few places for capital to continue reaping profits. Korean landlords also began to take advantage of the greater profitability of exporting rice and other commercial crops to Japan by embracing modern methods of agricultural production. They utilized Japanese seeds and chemical fertilizers, which tenants had no choice but to use, even at the risk of accruing yet larger amounts of debt, for fear of losing their tenant contracts. Whereas peasants in the past could weather market fluctuations by subsisting on edible crops, now they were forced to grow commercial crops, such as cotton to be sold to textile factories, that were of little use as a source of either income or food when cotton prices plummeted.[58] Moreover, the colonial government began regulating the production of alcohol and tobacco so that peasant households, which were accustomed to planting and producing them for their own consumption, now had no choice but to buy them on the market at prices beyond their means. As a result, increased agricultural production through modern methods coincided with, and indeed caused, increases in landless peasants and food shortages. Under such dire conditions, competition between tenants destroyed traditional communal support systems such as *ture* (labor collective) and *kye* (mutual aid group) that had pooled labor and shared resources in times of need, dismantling long-established institutions throughout the peninsula.[59]

Hisama was unequivocal in his assessment of colonial agrarian policies; any attempt at rural revitalization under conditions that left 70 percent of farmers with less than one *chŏngbo* (2.45 acres) of land was doomed to fail: "When 75 percent of farmers are tenant farmers, and 60 percent of land is tenant land, any plan for revitalization must deal with the problem of tenancy. . . . Any revitalization movement under such conditions only serves to maintain tenant rents, improving the landlords' ability to receive rent payments."[60] It is no surprise that he advocated a land reform that would give land to the tillers as the way to true rural revitalization. This never happened under colonial rule, but it is precisely what happened in North Korea after liberation, as we shall see in the next chapter.

Along with agrarian development, mass education under colonial rule was often touted as another shining example of colonial modernity, but it was only after the beginning of the second Sino-Japanese War that there was a sharp increase in primary school enrollment, to over 30 percent, with the promulgation of the 1938 Education Ordinance.[61] The expansion of education was closely tied to military mobilization and the need to recruit disciplined youth into the ranks of the military. Still, as of 1942 enrollment of school-aged children hovered below 50 percent—66.1 percent of boys and 29.1 percent of girls.[62]

The difficulty of recruiting students to attend school during the early years of colonial rule partly had to do with resistance from parents. The "normal schools" (*pot'ong hakkyo*) set up by the Japanese focused on Japanese language acquisition at the expense of training in classical Chinese, which was regarded as the most legitimate form of education, especially among the former literati and *yangban* elites that had been the backbone of the landed bureaucracy before colonization under the Confucian order of the Chosŏn Dynasty.[63] Some parents astutely observed that Japanese language training was designed to eradicate Korean identity and turn their children into soldiers, workers, or "slaves" of Japan. In response, colonial officials stressed the necessity of learning Japanese in an era when there were increasing interactions between Korea and Japan.[64] In other words, learning Japanese would determine whether one advanced up the social ladder in colonial Korea. Consequently, attitudes toward the schools began to change, but there was another problem. Basic education was limited to four years of Japanese language and job training, reflecting colonial objectives in extending public education. The few privileged enough to have acquired basic schooling were not content to give up their continued education once the four years were over. However, the colonizers were anxious about extending higher education to colonial subjects, especially when opportunities for social advancement after graduation were limited. The program of mass education under colonial rule was a stunted one that focused on disciplining and training students to work hard to provide for one's family as "law-abiding people" (yangmin).[65]

The colonial education system was thus founded on an inherent contradiction: it sought to foster mass education without the opportunity for higher education or social advancement when social advancement was precisely the rationale given from the beginning by colonial authorities for recruiting students. Colonial authorities had initially blamed Korean "stupidity" and "narrow-mindedness" for problems in enrolling Korean students in the schools. Yet when Korean graduates sought to enroll in middle schools to continue their education, they were deemed "frivolous and lazy," steeped in the vices of Korean tradition, which avoided manual labor.[66] As a result, only 10 to 15 percent of Korean students went on to middle school, and total enrollment never exceeded 1 percent of school-aged children throughout the colonial period.[67]

"Tradition" thus served multiple purposes, more often denounced as an impediment to "civilization and enlightenment," but also exploited when it served colonial interests. For example, traditional academies called sŏdang had been the main venues for education in Korea prior to colonization, proliferating during the latter half of the Chosŏn Dynasty. They competed with the public schools set up by the Japanese in the early years of colonial rule, and were roundly regarded by modernizers as useless for their focus on the memorization of Confucian texts. The private academies were accused of spreading "traditional vices," using education as a means to cultivate bureaucrats rather than workers, conflating education with politics.[68] Meanwhile, Confucian ethics were embraced by the colonizers in promoting hierarchy and obedience to authority, citing "good Korean traditions" such as close relationships between teachers and students, complete deference to parents, respect for elders, and worship of ancestors.[69] In reaction, Korean educators retorted that the purpose of education was to develop active citizens who vigorously participate in national affairs with a sense of patriotism and national consciousness.[70] The private academies had in effect pinpointed what made colonial modernity indeed colonial— the development of cultural and economic forces without parallel *political* development. Any advancements made during the 1920s and early 1930s would in any case be shelved with the total mobilization for war that had already begun with the Japanese expansion into Manchuria in 1931, and accelerated with general war between China and Japan starting in 1937.

Total War Mobilization

The onset of the second Sino-Japanese War and the beginning of the Asia-Pacific War in the late 1930s saw a definitive shift in colonial policy because the integration of colonial subjects was required for total war mobilization. Mobilization was facilitated by the social pacification policies of the 1930s that had organized over two-thirds of all rural households as members of financial co-ops and mutual-aid production associations.[71] But this time, mobilization required nothing short of total devotion both in material *and* spiritual terms. As part of the National Spirit Total Mobilization Movement (*Kungmin chŏngsin ch'ongdongwŏn undong*) that was organized in Japan shortly after the invasion of China in 1937, village branches were set up throughout the Korean Peninsula with every ten households grouped together into Patriotic Units (*aegukpan*). They were to embody the Japanese slogan *naisen ittai*, which literally meant "Japan and Korea as one body" united through the imperial spirit. As part of the movement, it became everyone's duty to serve the empire through one's labor in support of the war front while maintaining defense on the home front.[72] As more and more able-bodied men were drafted into the military, the patriotic units were in charge of almost all forms of labor, from agricultural work to road and bridge repair, sanitation, and firefighting.[73]

Active participation was difficult to obtain from colonized subjects. They had to be induced through material incentives, such as monetary aid when there was a death or a birth in the family.[74] Women made up the overwhelming majority of the patriotic units despite official demand for the attendance of male heads of household.[75] The decisive change came in 1941 when the patriotic units were put in charge of distributing rations and other daily necessities, including rice. People had no choice but to participate in order to survive. By 1944, 370,000 patriotic units were organized, encompassing over 4.6 million of the 4.9 million households in Korea.[76]

The numbers, however, indicated nothing about the actual level of allegiance held by colonial subjects toward the empire. Consequently, the colonial government turned to spiritual integration as one of the defining elements of Japanese colonial modernity. It is no wonder that socialist and communist thought was perceived to be so threatening: any materialist analysis would have jeopardized the very integrity of an essentialist ideology emanating from the Japanese emperor as the spiritual core of the empire.[77] Daily rituals enacting the spiritual integration of the colony with the empire were thus paramount. The rituals, which were scheduled periodically throughout the day in both public and private spaces, embodied outward expressions of colonial assimilation that could be enforced and monitored for proper compliance. Bowing toward the imperial palace and observing silence at noon were two of the most important rituals forced on colonial subjects. The noontime silence, when all pedestrians and cyclists had to stop at the sound of a siren and observe a minute of silence in honor of the imperial soldiers and the war dead, was practiced only in colonial Korea, and was not practiced in Japan.[78] Despite discourses of *naisen ittai*, defining Japan and Korea as one body, colonial difference was already marked onto the everyday as unequal and asymmetrical.

Colonial difference also required detailed instructions on daily life that would replace previous practices. Everyone's day was now mandated to begin with a bow toward the imperial palace: one had to rise early in the morning before sunrise, cleansing oneself thoroughly, before gathering with one's family members and bowing toward the imperial palace at sunrise with a grateful mind, reciting the oath of the imperial subject.[79] Additional precepts advised frugality, restricting elaborate traditional weddings, funerals, and banquets past 11 o'clock at night, and curbing the consumption of liquor and tobacco out of respect for the sacrifices made by imperial soldiers.[80]

Such physical manifestations of spiritual integration were accompanied by ideological purification campaigns in order to "rehabilitate" (*kyohwa*) colonial subjects in their hearts and minds through proper "guidance" (*sŏndo*).[81] Less intrusive methods included lectures and roundtable discussions, but more overt means involved surveillance, especially of those who had served prison terms for anticolonial activities, and the organization of self-defense units (*chawidan*) to assist the police in suppressing anticolonial resistance. Those deemed ideologically "dangerous" were often sequestered from the village and forced to undergo "training," including saluting the imperial flag, taking Japanese language classes, and renouncing communism. Lectures preached the futility of Korean independence, the righteousness of *naisen ittai*, and conviction of ultimate Japanese triumph in the war. Guidelines for proper guidance and instruction denied Korea was ever historically independent, emphasizing its "confused state in foreign relations and in internal affairs, driving people's livelihood into impoverishment."[82] Japanese annexation of Korea was regarded as "nothing but the relinquishment of sovereignty by the Korean emperor and his officials to Japan," in order to be "included within the powerful Japanese civilization, forever enjoying a secure life." Colonial rule was justified by the "close ethnic-national ancestry" between Korea and Japan, which "have enjoyed close relations since ancient times" and are thus inseparable. This kind of indoctrination was supposed to convince colonial subjects that "there is no greater glory and happiness for Koreans than to be part of the Japanese nation-state," since "*naisen ittai* leads to ten thousand good things."

However, the very process of explaining Korean and Japanese congruity delineated Koreans as different, in need of (re)definition as historically *not* independent, requiring conversion to the belief that Korea, and Koreans, were indeed part of the Japanese empire. The term *naisen ittai* (內鮮一體) itself demonstrates the point. It uses the character *nai* (interior) to refer to Japan, as was customary in referring to the metropole as *naiji* (內地)—that is, interior land as opposed to exterior lands (外地) made up of its colonies. Meanwhile, the second character from Chosŏn (朝鮮), the name of the last Korean dynasty, was used to refer to Korea. Thus, the ideological term to denote Japanese-Korean oneness contained within itself its own contradiction, whereby Japan was inscribed as the agent, naming and defining Korea unilaterally from the dominant position. Moreover, thought purification sessions and all official activities were carried out in the Japanese language as yet another way to "imperialize" (J: *kominka*) Koreans as Japanese imperial subjects. However, as of 1943, only 16.6 percent of Koreans were proficient in Japanese.[83] Thus, the very activities instructing Koreans to be part of the Japanese empire inscribed ethnic difference through language differences. The promise of equality was even less convincing for the older generation whose ethnic and cultural identities were already marked through language and customs that had to be expunged to make room for imperial subjecthood.

Beset by anxiety about the efficacy of spiritual integration, colonial authorities often worked at cross-purposes with *naisen ittai*. Not only was spiritual integration continuously policed through daily rituals but fears were particularly acute about the potential influence of those convicted of antistate activities. Imprisonment was not enough—they had to be converted (J: *tenkō*) and reintegrated into the national body (J: *kokutai*), not just physically but ideologically, in order to maintain the integrity of the empire.[84] National subjects, or citizens (J: *kokumin*), in body and soul thus constructed, had to submit their individual happiness to that of the nation and to sacrifice themselves and their private interests for the welfare of the empire. There are certain similarities here with any nationalist rhetoric, but the confusion was in the ambiguity of the national collective in colonial discourse. Who was a national subject? And what was the basis for the national collective to which one should submit?

The nation that represented the empire was none other than Japan, contrary to official rhetoric that called for a pan-Asian multiethnic empire under the slogan of the Greater East Asia Co-Prosperity Sphere. Beginning in 1941, primary schools were called "national schools" (*kungmin hakkyo*) through the National School Ordinance, which ordained that schools should cultivate imperial subjects through primary education that included the following subjects: "national language" (*kugŏ*), which actually meant the Japanese language; "national history" (*kuksa*), which in reality referred to Japanese history; and "national lands" (*kukt'o*), which in fact designated Japanese geography.[85] A Japan-centered "national history" that relegated Korean history to the periphery, either as part of Chinese history in the textbooks of the 1930s or as part of Japanese history in the textbooks of the 1940s, ultimately painted the union of Korea with Japan through *naisen ittai* as a predestined outcome that had been in the making since time immemorial.[86] It may have been easier for children without a coherent sense of identity to identify as part of this new collective that brought Japan and Korea together under the umbrella of imperial subjecthood; for those already speaking the Korean language, however, "imperialization" required a total erasure of one's previous identity, which was already shaped by one's language, name, dress, habits, and customs. The "imperial subject" was an ideological construct, like any other national identity, that attempted to make room for Koreans within the imperial collective, but the collective was defined by Japanese-ness to which Koreans had to submit by giving up their former selves. Still, with more than half of school-aged children not enrolled in school and thus outside the purview of colonial educators, the minister of education under the governor-general was justifiably concerned that "the over one million children being educated as imperial subjects do not make up even half of the 23 million Koreans. Combining other organizations such as the youth groups, women's associations, and rural revitalization committees . . . still does not exceed five million people. The remaining 17 million are all outside the scope of cultivation, out of reach of rehabilitation."[87]

Additional attempts at "rehabilitation" by print media, as well as by lectures, workshops, and traveling film presentations confronted substantial difficulty reaching the remote countryside due to the lack of facilities, frequent power outages, and gaps in Japanese language comprehension.[88] Due to language problems, recitations of the oath of the imperial subject had to be replaced by radio lectures, particularly in rural villages, while the noon minute of silence was considered too long and cumbersome in an urbanized city like Seoul and was reduced to thirty seconds.[89] Thus, spiritual devotion and the integration sought in colonial subjects through the performance of daily rituals was in reality difficult to foster, and the increasing restrictions in daily life, from limiting the consumption of cosmetics, permed hairstyles, expensive clothing, jewelry, and fancy cuisine to limits on elaborate traditional wedding and funeral rites, served only to increase resentment.[90] As much as they tried, without any way to scrutinize the hearts and minds of the masses, colonial officials had recourse only to outward assurances of compliance rather than true spiritual integration. The outward appearance of the devout imperial subject—an emulation of neither Western consumer culture nor traditional Eastern culture—was to be a man with a shaved head and wearing the "national uniform" (kungminbok), a simplified version of the Japanese army uniform, or a woman in a simple hairstyle with a loose-fitting trouser narrowed at the ankle to facilitate work (momppe, the standard pants imposed by wartime policy), which pervaded the late colonial landscape as it drew to a close.[91] One of the first reversals witnessed after liberation was the ubiquity of people in hanbok, with Koreans back in their traditional attire and the Japanese now slipping into it in order to avoid persecution by the formerly colonized.[92]

The forms of mobilization through lectures, study sessions, and collective labor projects might appear to be the same in postliberation North Korea, but the content was substantially different. Lectures and study sessions no longer preached naisen ittai, but focused on teaching Korean language and history. Labor was no longer mobilized for the empire, but solicited by distributing land to the tillers and placing the management of local industries in the hands of factory committees. As a result, a sense of consensus was forged between the emerging government and the people that promised the fulfillment of social needs, cultural reform, and political empowerment, not simply in exchange for their acquiescence, but through their own identification with the revolutionary cause. In postliberation North Korea, the experience of wartime mobilization was harnessed to facilitate the rapid mobilization of society, but this time in a way that combined the social, cultural, and political emancipation of Koreans toward a socialist modernity—a modernity *with* modern subjects. Although the colonial period had the unintended consequence of laying down the institutional foundation (form) for the rapid mobilization and centralization of society in the postliberation period, the purpose of mobilization (content) would be very different. Much of that content was drawn from the other important legacy from the colonial period: the experience of anticolonial struggle waged by Kim Il Sung and his partisans in Manchuria.

Manchuria

The formation of a highly centralized state in North Korea has often been attributed to Kim Il Sung's partisan experience in Manchuria. Wada Haruki famously coined the term the "guerrilla state" to refer to North Korea while Han Hongkoo more specifically pointed to the Minsaengdan Incident, in which upward of two thousand Korean communists were purged from the Chinese Communist Party (CCP) as pro-Japanese spies between late 1932 and early 1935. Kim Il Sung himself came under accusation, only narrowly escaping death, which thus, argues Han, made the experience a defining one for the North Korean leadership in forming a "guerrilla state haunted by a siege psychology" to this day.[93] The guerrilla experience, however, was more than that, particularly in the way it served as a platform for envisioning what socialist modernity might entail.

To understand the guerrilla experience as a formative one, not only traumatic but also constructive, we must first turn our attention to eastern Manchuria, a peripheral part of China bordering northern Korea that was better known as Kando (present day Yanbian Korean Autonomous Prefecture) among Koreans at the time. It had been a major destination for Korean peasants in search of a new life since the late nineteenth century, attracting yet more immigrants during the colonial period not only among those looking for work but also among revolutionaries fleeing colonial oppression. As a result, Koreans made up between 70 to 80 percent of the entire Kando population throughout the colonial period.[94] The active Red Peasant Union movement in the Hamgyŏng Provinces partly had to do with its close proximity to this region.[95] After Japanese encroachment into Manchuria in September 1931, Japanese troops were sent into Kando to wage a brutal campaign to wipe out Korean and Chinese revolutionaries. Thousands were killed, including local residents. Terrified Korean peasants

fled to nearby mountains under the leadership of Korean communist organizations, setting up guerrilla bases and soviet communes. At times known
as "communist utopias," these base areas served as the first experiments in
building socialism for Koreans, becoming a "source of inspiration for the
development of the revolutionary movement in Korea proper."[96]

Indeed, policies carried out in the soviets—confiscating all properties
owned by landlords and Japanese collaborators; distributing land to the
tillers; stripping political rights from wealthy peasants; and electing poor
peasants into leadership posts—would be reproduced during the North
Korean Revolution. But the more radical impulse to create a utopian
commune by confiscating lands owned by middle peasants and even the
meager possessions owned by poor peasants, such as cooking utensils to
form a communal kitchen, eventually alienated peasants, thwarting the
soviet experiment. The more moderate united front policy adopted during the North Korean Revolution, while moving ahead with the successful elements of the previous socialist experiment, such as the land reform,
should be understood within the historical experience of the colonial
period—both the forms imposed by colonial rule and the struggles waged
in reaction to it, especially in Manchuria. Before the purge, Kando had
been the seat of radical experimentation in self-rule through the formation of soviets, often overshadowed by the devastation and tragedy of the
Minsaengdan Incident.

The Minsaengdan Incident was, in part, the result of the unique ethnic makeup of the Kando region combined with decisions made by the
Communist International under the leadership of the Soviet Union. The
1928 Comintern decision for "One Country One Party" mandated one
national party structure for each country, obliging Korean communists
in Manchuria to join the Chinese Communist Party. As a result, Koreans
made up over 90 percent of CCP membership in Manchuria in the early
1930s.[97] Even before the policy, Korean communists had eagerly joined the
revolution in China with a strong sense of proletarian internationalism.
However, the 1931 Japanese incursion into Manchuria led to the founding
of competing pro-Japanese and nationalist Korean organizations, such as
the Minsaengdan, which advocated Korean self-rule in Kando. Although it
disbanded in a mere six months due to communist assault, subsequent Japanese intervention led to scores of arrests, sparking fears that Minsaengdan
spies had infiltrated the communist movement. Such fears were aggravated
by the class composition of the Chinese and Koreans in Kando: 92.9 percent
of tenants were Koreans, whereas 51.1 percent of landlords were Chinese.[98]
Japanese authorities were able to manipulate class and ethnic antagonisms

to pit the Chinese against the Koreans, as well as the communists against the nationalists. Japan justified its intervention in Manchuria by the need to "protect its imperial subjects" (Koreans), which branded Koreans as collaborators, weakening the anti-Japanese coalition of Chinese and Koreans, as well as a potential united front of communists and nationalists.

The results were disastrous. In early 1932, the eastern Manchuria branch of the CCP launched an anti-Minsaengdan campaign that consisted of mass riots, arson, and assassinations. Amid widespread accusations against Koreans for inviting Japanese intervention in Manchuria, Korean communists, in order to prove their loyalty, went after those suspected of being Japanese collaborators with particular vengeance. As suspicion spread to frenzied proportions, any association with someone suspected of having ties to Minsaengdan came under attack, including communists. By late 1932, the Chinese leaders of the eastern Manchuria branch of the CCP began to interrogate, torture, and execute any rank-and-file party member, the vast majority of whom were Koreans, suspected of ties to Minsaengdan.

The madness of the purge can be gleaned from the trivial ways in which people were suspected of being members of Minsaengdan, such as spilling a few grains of rice during meals, under- or overcooking rice for the guerrillas, and complaining of headaches, indigestion, or overwork. Even advocating independence for Korea was seen as a breach of communist internationalism, siding with reactionary nationalist organizations like the Minsaengdan.[99] At the height of absurdity, the Korean soviets were accused of emulating the Minsaengdan's advocacy for Korean self-rule.[100] The purge devastated the Kando region as a base for guerrilla operations, killing more Korean revolutionaries and their supporters than the extermination campaign waged by Japanese troops. The lasting impact on the partisans, who were to become leaders of North Korea after liberation, was a solid unbreakable bond with Kim Il Sung. Kim Il Sung's memoir and those of his partisans point to the dramatic moment when Kim burned all the files of the suspects compiled by the Purge Committee as key in solidifying Kim's leadership, not only for the bold move but also for his compassion.[101] As news of the burning of the files and the rehabilitation of suspects spread, those that had fled to escape the purge now rallied around Kim Il Sung. He emerged from the purge as a definitive leader, capable of overcoming the mistrust and suspicion plaguing the communists to create an immutable bond between himself and his partisans.

As the remaining communists and partisans in Manchuria regrouped to form the Northeast Anti-Japanese United Army under Chinese command,

Kim became commander of the Third Division of the Second Army and was instrumental in rehabilitating many of the accused Koreans for the formation of his own guerrilla unit. Soon after, he gained notoriety among the Japanese for waging the "largest and most successful" guerrilla campaign along the Sino-Korean border in eastern Manchuria.[102] The most famous of his exploits was the raid on Poch'onbo, a Korean town just across the border in Manchuria. Kim led almost two hundred guerrillas on June 4, 1937, attacking the town and destroying local government offices, setting fire to the Japanese police station and post office. Although it offered clear evidence of Kim's talents as a military leader, the raid was more important for the political organization and coordination that went on for nearly half a year beforehand between the guerrillas and the Korean Fatherland Restoration Association (*Hanin choguk kwangbokhoe*), an anti-Japanese united front organization based in Manchuria.[103] Perhaps taking the cue from Mao, Kim embraced the importance of the mass line, making sure that the guerrillas were in close contact with the people.

Indeed, the ten-point platform of the Association shows striking parallels to reforms implemented in postliberation North Korea, whether in calling for a united front against the Japanese and their collaborators or in the specific programs that called for the confiscation of Japanese property (including land), the development of collective farms, and the replacement of the "slave education of the Japanese" with free education that enhances "our national culture."[104] Points that called for the abolition of Japanese policies on taxes, military conscription, and white terror were quite explicit; others that advocated freedoms of speech, assembly, and organization to ally against the Japanese and to "reform the daily life of laborers, peasants, soldiers, youth, women, and all working masses" were rather general, making it difficult to fully trace how they were implemented, if in fact the Association had occasion to do so amid guerrilla warfare. Nonetheless, the reforms carried out in postliberation North Korea, from the land reform to the beginnings of a free universal education with a heavy emphasis on Korean language and history, signal the way the changes in everyday life of "all working masses" took their inspirational blueprint from the Manchurian experience during the colonial period, but now with the resources and the space to become fully effective.

The Declaration of the Korean Fatherland Restoration Association in Manchuria, issued on June 10, 1936, summoned "all Koreans, regardless of class, sex, position, faction, age, and religious belief" to "unite and fight the Japanese to restore our fatherland."[105] It renounced discrimination against anyone, beckoning "the old and the young, the rich with their wealth, those who have food with their food, those who have skills with their skills, all twenty-three million Koreans" to unite and mobilize against Japanese imperialism. Consistent with this inclusion of "all working masses" for a united front that would bring together almost all Koreans with the exception of "national traitors," a broad social category called *samuwŏn* was incorporated into the classification system in postliberation North Korea. Although the term literally means office worker or clerk, it was used as a catch-all social class distinct from the peasants and the workers in order to incorporate intellectuals and professionals into the revolution. This class was represented by the writing brush, which was added to the hammer and the sickle in the Korean Workers' Party emblem, when the communists came to power in North Korea. The ambiguity of the category enabled those with questionable class backgrounds to join the revolution, continuing the legacy of the united anti-Japanese front.

It is within this context of the anticolonial guerrilla struggle in Manchuria and the trauma of the Minsaengdan Incident that Han Hongkoo claims we must understand the development of Juche ideology and Kim Il Sung's repeated emphasis on independence as the "lifeblood of the nation"—that the "master of the Korean revolution is the Korean people."[106] As the only communist leader in history to have been imprisoned by both Chinese and Soviet communists, Kim Il Sung was keenly aware of how expendable revolutions in small countries such as Korea could become when weighed against the national interests of larger powers such as China and the Soviet Union despite communist principles of internationalism.[107] Eschewing big-power chauvinism, Kim Il Sung understood proletarian internationalism as inseparable from patriotism: "He who does not love his own country cannot be loyal to internationalism, and he who is unfaithful to internationalism cannot be faithful to his own country and people. A true patriot is precisely an internationalist and vice versa."[108] This combination of internationalism with nationalism in the form of self-reliance, or Juche, was to become a defining feature of North Korean socialist modernity.

Although much has been made of colonial modernity in the historiography of colonial Korea, much of this historiography remains a description of modernization during the colonial period without theorizing the singularity of this experience. In the face of the difficulty in identifying what is specifically *colonial* about colonial modernity at a time when the postmodern critique of modernity seems to relegate all of modernity as necessarily and always colonial, studies of colonial modernity have focused on what was modern about it at the expense of critiquing its coloniality. But the question persists: What makes colonial modernity not just modern but colonial? A theoretically relevant answer demands more than its description simply as modernity that happens to take place under colonialism. As this chapter has shown, signs of modernity in the *universalizing* drive toward the rationalization of production, the expansion of capital, and the socialization of mass education was inflected by an altogether different logic of colonialism as *particularizing* that delineated difference, working at cross-purposes with the universalizing aims of modernity.[109] Certain forms of traditional practices such as flogging and tenancy were redeployed, ascribing difference through the legalization of physical punishment and the codification of social stratification. Ultimately, imperial subjectivity was defined by resorting to a primordial past traced through the lineage of the Japanese emperor—the very antithesis of the modern subject—rendering Korea's colonial modernity deeply antimodern by its end.

Japan's preoccupation with "overcoming" modernity led to the revival of "traditions" such as the emperor system, through which the Japanese "essence" was displayed and the Japanese nation was spiritually united, much like the Nazis sought to transcend class divisions and political tensions through a "myth of transcendent unity" in the ideal of *Volksgemeinschaft*.[110] Whether a national essence that was traced to time immemorial through the Japanese emperor, or a superior Aryan race that united German society against class and party divisions, both ideologies were outside of time, meant to overcome the chaos of the modern present. In that sense, both systems were quite deliberately antimodern. By contrast, modern social revolutions have attempted to overturn the past by delineating an abrupt rupture from tradition toward a radically different future. North Korea was no different in this respect from other modern social revolutions.

In the next chapter, we look at the social, political, and cultural practices that made socialist modernity an everyday reality in North Korea, transforming the very fabric of that everyday as distinctly modern, this time very purposely peopled by modern subjects. Although the idea of Juche was not to become part of a systematic ideology until after the Korean War, it is no wonder that it has come to occupy such a central position in postcolonial North Korea, where the recuperation of the modern subject was to become its crowning achievement.[111] Three main events facilitated the articulation of modern subjectivity—a radical land reform that liberated peasants from their centuries-old submission to landlords, an unprecedented election that reshaped mass politics, and a national literacy campaign that rewrote the rules of cultural and educational accessibility. It is now time to see up close the changes in everyday life within the North Korean Revolution by looking at one particular county, Inje.

3. Three Reforms

Initiating the Revolution

Illiteracy is the enemy of civilization and enlightenment. . . . After realizing the need to learn to read and write, today I have come to gain the ability to compose the minutes with my own hand as a result of diligent self-study.

INJE COUNTY PARTY MEETING MINUTES, MARCH 26, 1948

Figure 3.1. "Let's learn even while we work" (n.p., n.d.). RG 242, SA 2005, box 7, item 9. Courtesy of the National Archives and Records Administration.

At the end of colonial rule, Korea consisted of thirteen administrative provinces (*to*) that were divided into counties (*kun*), townships (*myŏn*), and villages (*ri*).[1] Inje County was located in the middle of Kangwŏn Province, a province situated in the center of the peninsula along the 38th parallel that divided Korea in half into the two separate occupation zones in 1945. With the partition, five and a half provinces out of the thirteen fell into the northern half, and Kangwŏn Province was split almost exactly in half, as was Inje County. The upper half of the county fell above the 38th parallel, including four townships—Puk, Inje, Sŏhwa, and the upper tip of Nam—with an estimated population of just over thirty thousand people. The total adult population in the county in December 1948 was reported to be 18,359.[2] The province, along with the county, has since become part of South Korea after the redrawing of the boundary at the end of the Korean War in 1953.[3] Today, geographically a bit larger than Los Angeles County, the county's population has remained stable at just over thirty-two thousand and thrives on the many tourists that visit the region for its scenic mountains, the most famous of which is Mount Sŏrak.[4]

Divided as it was, Inje County offers a microcosm of the overall situation in North Korea as a median point that was neither dominated by conservatives nor communists, in contrast to such places as South Hamgyŏng Province, traditionally a leftist stronghold, or South P'yŏngan Province, longtime center of Christian activity.[5] Despite regional differences in the political orientation of local people's committees in the aftermath of liberation, local variations during the revolution were muted by the push toward centralization and by broad peasant support of the measures adopted by the revolutionary government. Comparisons with other counties and provinces in North Korea show remarkable similarities across the sorts of projects implemented, making the study of Inje suitable as a microhistory of North Korea. In practical terms, Inje also offers the richest and most complete set of archival records, facilitating the reconstruction of its history in detail.[6]

As shown in table 2.2 in the previous chapter, Kangwŏn Province was the last to organize a provincial PC, on October 18, 1945, due to its location along the 38th parallel.[7] Despite the late official date, the province had been governing itself quite effectively by the time the National Congress of People's Committee Representatives convened in November 1945. The provincial representative reported to the Congress on the situation in Kangwŏn, providing a glimpse of the enthusiasm and capacity for self-rule at the local level only three months after liberation:

> The administration and the application of justice are being carried out at the hands of the people's committee. Our province has 140,000 unemployed people, and is in the process of constructing a hydroelectric dam by raising 85 million *won*. . . . The people's committee decides the price [of commodities]. . . . Security has been very favorable, and people's courts have convened multiple times. . . . We strictly observe the 3–7 rent system [whereby the landlord keeps 30 percent and the tiller

keeps 70 percent of the harvest]. . . . All land owned by the Japanese and national traitors have been confiscated, and the confiscated land are tilled by peasants according to the same 3–7 rent system, submitting the rent as tax to the people's committee.[8]

Despite such dynamism in the province, Inje County was isolated from urban centers and difficult to reach due to the lack of adequate transportation as 90 percent of the county territory consisted of forests and mountain ranges. Newspapers took almost two weeks to reach the area.[9]

Like much of the country, Inje was also overwhelmingly rural, with most of the 6,388 households engaged in full-time farming in 1945.[10] However, unlike the south, traditionally known as the "rice bowl" of the peninsula with its rich rice paddies, Inje was similar to most other parts of the north with limited wet paddy fields. It relied on the less fertile dry fields instead, which produced wheat, barley, and potatoes, yielding as little as half that of the irrigated lands.[11] As a result, it was considered one of the most "backward" areas in terms of living conditions, with few cultural and educational opportunities. Eighty percent of the county's economy relied on farming, which made livestock, especially oxen, an important resource.[12] The ox is still common throughout rural Korea, north and south, dotted as it is with small plots nestled in the valleys surrounded by mountains, making large tractors difficult to operate in many areas. Some studies have estimated that as much as a third of all arable land in North Korea is unsuitable for tractors.[13] Heavily agricultural, the county had few industries except for some ceramic factories, but forests provided opportunities for logging.[14] Most industries came to a standstill after liberation because the majority of skilled workers and engineers were Japanese, whose exodus left the factories without personnel. The scant number of skilled workers in the county can be gleaned from a list of such workers compiled by the North Korean Workers' Party in 1946. It included 175 people with military skills, most of whom were forcibly conscripted in the last year of colonial rule, and a handful of additional skilled workers: seven ceramic workers, two carpenters, four mechanics, seven automobile drivers, one electric car operator, one generator operator, one telephone repairman, and one doctor for a county population of some thirty thousand.[15]

A 1947 survey of peasant conditions in Inje found that the overwhelming majority were still in the "poor peasant" (pinnong) category, which designated those suffering from chronic food shortages regardless of harvest conditions. In contrast to categories of social class used before liberation—such as landlord, self-cultivator, and tenant farmer (sharecropper)—new

Table 3.1. Class breakdown of peasants in Inje County by township, July 1947

	Employed peasants				Poor peasants				Middle peasants				Rich peasants				Total			
	H	M	F	T	H	M	F	T	H	M	F	T	H	M	F	T	H	M	F	T
Inje	19	28	22	50	1,478	4,100	3,694	7,794	292	1,008	881	1,899	4	11	7	18	1,793	5,147	4,604	9,751
Nam	6	9	5	14	480	1,576	1,392	2,968	151	386	403	789	–	–	–	–	637	1,971	1,800	3,771
Puk	6	6	–	6	1,117	2,964	2,746	5,710	138	361	329	690	–	–	–	–	1,261	3,331	3,075	6,406
Sŏhwa	10	14	3	17	1,581	4,535	4,083	8,618	304	1,309	1,334	2,643	10	44	40	84	1,905	5,902	5,460	11,362
Total	41	57	30	87	4,656	13,175	11,915	25,090	885	3,064	2,947	6,011	14	55	47	102	5,596	16,351	14,939	31,290

Source: RG 242, SA 2007, box 6, item 9, "Various Documents" (1947).
Note: H: Households; M: Male; F: Female; T: Total

categories after liberation were not simply defined by land ownership but emphasized living conditions in order to differentiate *among* the peasantry, which made up the overwhelming majority of the population. "Middle peasants" (*chungnong*) were defined as those who were dependent on the quality of the harvest, having enough food with a good harvest but difficulty sustaining themselves during a bad year. "Rich peasants" (*punong*) referred to those who had more than enough food irrespective of harvest conditions, so that they could sell or loan out their surplus. At the bottom of the rung were "employed peasants" (*konong*), or agricultural workers, who had to find work as hired help on other people's farms. A mammoth 80 percent of peasants in Inje were still in the poor peasant category in 1947, as shown in table 3.1, before the effects of the 1946 land reform could be fully felt.

Under such circumstances, revolution for peasants meant three things—redistribution of land, political representation, and educational opportunity—each of which created unprecedented economic, political, and cultural prospects of advancement for peasants in North Korea. Each of these will be dealt with in turn in the following sections.

Land Reform

For the peasants who made up 80 percent of the Korean population, there was nothing more pressing than the resolution of the land issue. It became the first and the most significant way by which peasants participated in the revolutionary process. The founding of the Provisional People's Committee in February 1946 occasioned several days of festivities and celebrations throughout northern Korea, drawing crowds of one hundred thousand in Pyongyang. Peasants used the occasion to demand a thorough land reform before the spring planting with many sending letters of appeal directly to the newly formed provisional government.[16] Between February 23 and March 2, the Second Congress of the North Korean Peasant League was held in Pyongyang with 150 peasant delegates, ninety-three of whom were poor peasants, demanding "Land to the tillers!"[17] They demanded that the land come from the Japanese, pro-Japanese collaborators, and national traitors, confiscated without compensation and distributed for free to agricultural workers and peasants with little to no land. All debts owed by tenants would also be canceled, abolishing the tenancy system for good. Over three hundred peasants converged on the PPC office to demand that it settle the agrarian problem, and the anniversary of the March First

Movement instigated over three million peasants to demonstrate and hold rallies in different parts of North Korea on March 1, 1946, calling out "We want agrarian reform!"[18]

Such explosiveness was to be expected. Japanese colonization of Korea had exacerbated an already difficult situation, with private ownership, unequal land distribution, and tenancy all increasing throughout the colonial period.[19] When the cadastral land survey was completed in the first decade of colonial rule, officially recognizing the private ownership of land and thereby its commodification, a whopping 77.2 percent of the rural population was reported to lease part or all of their cultivated land.[20] Most tenants had to hand over 50 to 70 percent of the harvest in rent, leaving the vast majority of peasants near the point of starvation.[21] With the collapse of the world market after 1929, living conditions deteriorated rapidly and the polarization of the rural classes intensified. Landlord households making up 4 percent of all rural households owned 50 percent of all agricultural land.[22] A newspaper article described the desperate situation:

> Despite the sowing season ahead, countless impoverished peasants are drifting away from their villages. . . . Conditions are none other than a living hell. . . . Peasants have been depending on grass roots and tree bark for their sustenance, but even such stuffs have now been exhausted. . . . There is no other way for them than to go out and beg. They live because they cannot die.[23]

With worsening conditions, the 1930s saw the rise of radical and often violent protests by Red Peasant Unions until the highly repressive colonial machinery crushed almost all forms of dissent within Korea by the 1940s. Until then, Red Peasant Unions were active in the northeastern region of the peninsula with the participation not only of tenant farmers but of owner-cultivators, who became the central actors with slogans and demands that went beyond the traditional emphasis on economic interests. In addition to rent reduction and secure tenancy contracts, political issues such as the abolition of oppressive laws and national liberation took center stage.[24] These ideas became the basis for an agrarian revolution in North Korea in the postliberation period.

In order to meet peasant demands while solidifying the legitimacy of the revolutionary government, the Land Reform Law was proclaimed on March 5, 1946, confiscating land owned by the Japanese government, Japanese nationals and organizations, as well as "traitors to the Korean nation who collaborated with Japanese enslavers."[25] Land belonging to

Korean landlords in excess of five *chŏngbo* (roughly twelve acres) was also confiscated without compensation, as was land rented out by landlords permanently irrespective of size.[26] Land owned by those who left the north after liberation; land owned by absentee landlords; and land owned by churches, monasteries, and other religious organizations in excess of five *chŏngbo* were likewise confiscated without compensation. The confiscated land was distributed among peasants for free under the principle of "land to the tiller" with hired and poor peasants designated as most entitled to receive land. Although land could be inherited, the law strictly prohibited the purchase, sale, and mortgage of land, thereby preventing its commercialization and commodification. The hiring of farmhands was also prohibited. Debts owed to landlords whose lands were subject to confiscation were canceled; cattle, agricultural implements, and houses formerly owned by landlords were confiscated, as were orchards, forests, and irrigation facilities.

In addition to Soviet influence on drafts of the reform legislation, discussions about land reform in Korea date back to the Chosŏn Dynasty, as shown by Kim Seong-bo's detailed study of the historical origins of different models of agrarian reform. The more immediate precursor to North Korea's land reform were proposals by socialists during the colonial period, from nationalization of all land to more moderate programs that advocated distribution of land to the tillers.[27] Notwithstanding the role of the Soviet occupation, which facilitated the swift implementation of the reform, it is undeniable that Korean peasants were at the center of the agrarian revolution, ultimately resulting in "one of the most rapid and radical land reforms in world history."[28] Indeed, initial proposals put forth in September 1945 by Korean communists limited the confiscation of land to that owned by the Japanese and pro-Japanese collaborators. This was radicalized by demands from peasants that all lands owned by landlords—irrespective of nationality—be confiscated without compensation and distributed for free to the tillers.[29]

More than half of the 1,860,000 *chŏngbo* of arable land in North Korea was confiscated by the reform. Over 60 percent of the confiscated land came from households with medium-sized holdings that had owned no more than five *chŏngbo* but had rented out part or all of their land. Nearly all of the confiscated land was redistributed, with less than 2 percent kept under state ownership. By the end, a total of 1,050,000 *chŏngbo* of land had been confiscated and 980,000 *chŏngbo* of it was distributed to 710,000 peasant households for free—all within twenty-five days.[30] In short, 99 percent of rented land was confiscated without compensation, benefiting over 70 percent of all peasant households in North Korea.[31] The land reform broke the power of the landowners, many of whom were tainted as Japanese collaborators, while gaining popular support for the new regime from the large stratum of landless and poor peasants. For landlords, it was a difficult pill to swallow, as one former landlord remembered years later:

> The new Communist government took away all our land overnight and gave it to the tenant farmers. They called it Land Reform Number One, saying the land should belong to the people. . . . Overnight we lost all our ancestral land. They did let us keep the Big House and three rice paddies that lay between our house and the church. For the first time in my life, we had to do some work. . . . That is the first time I ever put my foot right into the rice beds—leech beds, I called them.[32]

In effect, the land reform had legitimized what already had been under way at the initiative of local people's committees and peasant unions shortly after liberation. It reinforced the revolutionary nature of the reform, which not only satisfied peasant demand for land but more important brought down landlord power that had held sway for centuries. A relatively fixed elite status, which combined landed wealth with official government positions going back for generations, had been sustained under colonial rule. Landlords collaborated with the Japanese to maintain their power and

Table 3.2. Results of the land reform: Confiscated land, 1946

Owners of land	Total area (in *chŏngbo*)	Number of cases[a]	Average area per case
Japanese government and nationals	111,561	12,919	8.63
National traitors and deserters	12,518	1,366	9.09
Landlords with over 5 *chŏngbo*	231,716	29,683	7.80
Those who rent all of their land	259,150	145,688	1.77
Those who continuously rent their land	354,093	228,866	1.54
Churches, monasteries, and religious groups	14,916	4,124	3.54
Total	**983,954**	**422,646**	**2.32**

Sources for tables 3.2 and 3.3: Mun Woong Lee, "Rural North Korea under Communism: A Study of Sociocultural Change," *Rice University Studies* 62, no. 1 (1976): 21; *The Historical Experience of Agrarian Reform in Our Country* (Pyongyang: Foreign Language Publishing House, 1974), 95. There are some discrepancies between the two sources and North Korean documents from 1949, but the numbers are in similar ranges. Here I have followed the information in Lee (1976).

Notes: All land areas are in *chŏngbo*. Orchards are excluded.

[a] These may include households, corporations, or other social units.

Table 3.3. Results of the land reform: Redistribution of confiscated land, 1946

Recipients	Area	Number of households	Average allotment (in *chŏngbo*)
Agricultural laborers	21,960	17,137	1.28
Tenants without land	589,377	442,973	1.33
Peasants with little land	344,134	260,501	1.32
Landlords who relocated	9,598	3,911	2.45[a]
Subtotal	**965,069**	**724,522**	**1.33**
Land reserved by the PC	18,885		
Total	**983,954**		

Sources: See sources for table 3.2
Note: All land areas are in *chŏngbo*.
[a] The greater amount allotted to landlords who relocated may be due to possible differences in the average size of landlord households since land was distributed based on a point system tabulated by the age and sex of the members of each household. Landlords generally had larger households. Another reason may be due to differences in the quality and productivity of the land distributed to landlords. See Mun Woong Lee, "Rural North Korea under Communism: A Study of Sociocultural Change," *Rice University Studies* 62, no. 1 (1976): 22.

wealth while colonial authorities found landlords useful in administering the countryside. The basis for an elite status that had lasted the five hundred years under the Chosŏn Dynasty into the colonial period had thereby finally come to an end.

Guided by the PCs, the land reform was implemented under the leadership of local rural committees. As beneficiaries and administrators of reform, the peasants turned into revolutionary agents. Poor peasants and agricultural workers were organized into rural committees, consisting of five to nine people nominated through a general assembly of all the poor peasants and agricultural workers in the village.[33] The role of rural committees as revolutionary organs that institutionalized and gave structural form to peasant participation was key. Throughout North Korea, 12,001 rural committees were organized with 90,697 peasant league members and almost eight hundred thousand peasants participated in the process as "peasants became protagonists of the countryside, becoming masters of rural administration."[34] As a result, landlords were not only stripped of their land and wealth but were also eliminated from institutions of political power.[35] By September 1946, six months after the law was passed, in Inje County thirty-one landlord houses had been confiscated; twenty-four landlords had been relocated to another county; and twenty landlords had already left for the south in 1945.[36] These numbers pale in comparison to the overall county population of over thirty thousand, foretelling the

Table 3.4. Land confiscated according to Land Reform Law in Inje County

	Article 2			Article 3					Total
	A. Japanese owned land	B. Land owned by "national traitors"	Subtotal	A. Land in excess of 5 chŏngbo	B. Tenant land	C. Land continuously leased regardless of size[a]	D. Land of religious groups in excess of 5 chŏngbo	Subtotal	
Amount of land (in chŏngbo)	21.11	1.05	22.16	787.05	560.27	1,825.98	20.59	1,825.98	3,216.05 (53% of total land in county)
Number of people	20	1	21	72	321	424	3	820	841

Source: "1946 Inje County Land Reform Statistics" (January 21, 1947), in *Compilation of Materials on the North Korean Economy between 1945 and 1950* (Japan: Asia Economic Research Institute, 2001), vol. 7, 619, cited in Monica Hahn, "Transformation of System in the 'Re-taken Areas' during the Korean War—Focused on Inje-gun in Gangwon-do" (PhD diss., Catholic University of Korea, August 2009), 36.

[a] Article 3.C with the word "continuously" was added in order to exclude those who had temporarily rented out their land at the end of the colonial period due to forced conscription for labor or military service.

Table 3.5. Land distributed according to Land Reform Law in Inje County

| | Land distributed according to Article 6.1 acknowledging right to ownership | | | |
	To agricultural workers	To landless and tenant farmers	To farmers with insufficient land	Total
Amount of land (in *chŏngbo*)	62.17	1,336.55	1,712.83	3,111.57
Number of households	35.0	2,614.0	2,324.0	4,973.0
Average amount of land acquired per household	1.77	0.511	0.73	0.625
Points[a]	88.7	9,155.0	8,262.0	17,505.7

Source: "1946 Inje County Land Reform Statistics" (January 21, 1947), in *Compilation of Materials on the North Korean Economy between 1945 and 1950* (Japan: Asia Economic Research Institute, 2001), vol. 7, 620–21, cited in Monica Hahn, "Transformation of System in the 'Re-taken Areas' during the Korean War—Focused on Inje-gun in Gangwon-do" (PhD diss., Catholic University of Korea, August 2009), 41.

[a] The exact amount of land to be distributed to each household was calculated according to a point system in which members of the household were assigned points. Men between eighteen and sixty years old were given one point; women between eighteen and fifty were also given a point; youth between fifteen and seventeen were given 0.7 point; children between ten and fourteen were given 0.4 point; children below the age of nine were given 0.1 point; men over sixty-one and women over fifty-one were given 0.3 point.

scarcity of land for distribution. Indeed, the average size of landholding per household after the land reform was about one *chŏngbo* (2.45 acres) in Inje County whereas the national average was 1.33 *chŏngbo*.

As with any reform of such magnitude, clarification was necessary and the Provisional People's Committee issued directives, including the Law on Temporary Measures for the Enforcement of the Land Reform and Regulations Relative to the Application of the Land Reform Law.[37] Punishment was mandated in cases of hiding, destroying, purchasing, or otherwise disposing of materials slated to be confiscated. Landlords were also allotted plots if they chose to work the land themselves, although they were given land in other counties in order to sever the traditional ties between them and the villagers, isolating them from their former base of power. True to the slogan "land to the tillers," those who owned more than five *chŏngbo* of land were allowed to keep it if they had worked all of it themselves. The drafters of the reform law were strategic "on the question of with whom to ally, whom to oppose, and whom to isolate."[38]

In order to ensure the broadest support for the reform while isolating the minority of landlords, the law was applied so as not to alienate the middle or rich peasants.[39]

The process was not without challenges, however, as there were "ultra-leftist" and "ultra-rightist" deviations that indicated discontent on both sides of the political spectrum. Although the reform targeted landlords who owned more than five *chŏngbo* of land, "ultra-leftist" excesses designated rich peasants with less than five *chŏngbo* as landlords in South Hamgyŏng and South P'yŏngan Provinces. Such tendencies led to the seizure of land and property that went beyond the bounds of the law. In North P'yŏngan and South Hamgyŏng Provinces, owner-cultivator lands were also confiscated while former low-ranking colonial officials were mistakenly categorized as national traitors and thus subject to confiscation.[40] Official documents reporting on the results of the land reform lamented not being able to stop some of the more vengeful acts by peasants, which breached the broad coalition meant to wage a united front peasant revolution against the small minority of landlords.

On the other hand, "ultra-rightist" tendencies resulted in incidents of armed rebellion against the reform. The rebels called for the protection of property rights as sacrosanct and refused to acknowledge the legality of a law passed by a provisional government.[41] Peasants also continued to display their submission to paternalism, sympathizing with landlords by hiding their tenant status, concealing the landlords' surplus grain, and attempting to prevent their expulsion from the village. One resident of Inje recalled that former tenants continued to secretly submit a sack of rice to their former landlord as rent, and some landlords were able to remain in their homes when the house had technically been confiscated as part of the reform.[42] At times, peasants seemed to act against their own interests, creating cause for concern that "although peasants with a strong desire for ownership are leftist at the moment of gaining land, there is abundant possibility to sympathize with the landlords after they have gained the land. . . . There is much potential for the remnants of feudal ideology still remaining in peasant consciousness to bring in the danger of rightist [tendencies] into the party."[43]

Despite such challenges, the reform was hugely popular and successful by all measures. It was reported that "meetings were held at which Korean peasants . . . expressed their warm thanks to the Provisional People's Committee for enacting the law . . . [which] received 30,000 letters of thanks in the first month after the law had been enacted."[44] Another telling example of peasant approval was the dramatic increase in membership in the North Korean Communist Party (forerunner to the North Korean Workers' Party), which doubled from 4,560 in December 1945 to 9,058 in March 1946, almost tripling to 26,000 by the next month. There was a steady increase thereafter to 105,000 members in July, 276,000 in August, and 750,000 members by March 1948, initiating the transformation of the North Korean Communist Party from a vanguard party of experienced revolutionaries to a mass party of peasants.[45] With the enthusiasm generated by land ownership, agricultural production increased by as much as 50 percent in some provinces; for example, in South Hamgyŏng Province grain production increased from 1,260,790 sacks in 1945 to 1,885,200 sacks in 1946.[46]

In the face of severe food shortages, which were exacerbated by separation from the large grain-producing regions of the south, such increased production was still insufficient, however. It was imperative for the provisional government to begin the systematic collection of grain for distribution to nonagricultural areas. Just a few months after completion of the land reform, regulations on an agricultural-tax-in-kind were passed on June 27, 1946, assessing 25 percent of the harvest for collection, far below the 50 to 70 percent that used to be submitted to landlords in rent.[47] Still, there were wide regional variances in the rate of compliance, from 100 percent to as low as 30 percent.[48] When penalties were imposed for failing to submit the requisite tax, however, the average rate of submission quickly jumped to 90 percent.[49] The change did not signify evidence of enthusiastic compliance, however, as members in the Korean Democratic Party were particularly prone to complain. When harvests were bad in 1949, one member sarcastically commented, "If they collect all the taxes today, then are we all supposed to die tomorrow?"[50] Concerned that people were likening the collection of taxes with the expropriation of grain during the colonial period, internal documents were careful to instruct local people's committee officials to educate the public about the local budget in detail in order to show how the taxes were being used.[51] Moreover, in order to increase not only the tax base but overall agricultural output, the project of greatest priority for the countryside was to increase the amount of land under cultivation through land reclamation projects. Local government and party records show heavy emphasis on the planning and mobilization of labor for such endeavors.

Although production could have been increased by taking advantage of economies of scale through the introduction of state farms, official policy, issued in 1947, explicitly banned any form of collectivization in order to foster "individual creativity":[52]

1. It is forbidden to use any name suggestive of collectivization under the pretext of rationalizing agricultural work either by organizing production teams or changing the names of traditional work groups in disregard of individual ownership and management.
2. The organization of traditional work groups (*p'umasi*) should be voluntary, and should not be placed under the authority of the peasant league or the people's committee reminiscent of control by the colonial government.
3. Production teams that have been organized despite there being no history of traditional work groups in the area should be disbanded immediately.[53]

Responding to peasant desire for ownership, care was taken to make sure peasants retained control over the management of their own plots; any hint of outside control was prohibited, including the use of names that might be reminiscent of colonial-era labor mobilization. The confiscated land was not taken over by the state and nationalized, but distributed to the peasants in order to satisfy "their centuries-old hunger for land."[54] By leaving agricultural management and production in the hands of the peasants, the emerging North Korean state not only satisfied peasant hunger for land but in that very process enabled peasants to identify themselves as revolutionary agents whose productive activities were seen to serve a social purpose. This view was reinforced by leaving 75 percent of the harvest under peasant control, entrusting them with the management of both production and consumption. The land reform effectively eliminated the landlords, who had fled to the south in record numbers by the following month, from posing the staunchest opposition to the revolution.[55] Most important, it signaled the decommodification of land and the empowerment of the rural majority, bringing together production and consumption as part of a "socially productive life" in the peasants' everyday lives.[56]

People's Committee Elections

With the explosive land issue effectively marshaled through the mobilization of peasants to overturn the foundation of rural social relations, the next groundbreaking event was to institutionalize the transformation of the political landscape that had already begun with the ad hoc formation of local people's committees. Elections became an occasion to nominate those who had proven to be good neighbors and peers, in contrast to the village chief who had been appointed by the colonial government. As one peasant women commented, "I thought elections would be useless because higher officials used to appoint the village chief in the olden days, but now that elections are used to bring out good people, how can politics go wrong. This time we must nominate Mr. Kong, who lives in the village yonder. He'll be able to sympathize with other people's situation because he's been through a lot himself."[57]

Voting for representatives of the people's committees began with the election of provincial, city, and county representatives on November 3, 1946, moving on to village elections on February 24–25, 1947, and township elections on March 5, 1947.[58] Differentiating between indirect and direct elections, a party document contrasted these elections with the system under colonial rule when only men over twenty-five years of age who paid over five *won* in taxes (hardly any) could vote for the provincial governor. In the upcoming elections, the document explained, one would vote directly for one's representatives based on the principle of equality—one person, one vote—cast secretly. One representative was to be elected for every three thousand residents, with the right of recall should the elected person fail to carry out his or her duties.[59] These elections were meant to replace the indirect system that had been temporarily put in place at the October 1945 meeting of the provincial people's committee representatives.[60] Each of the villages had elected one village leader (*ch'onjang*), who then gathered with other village leaders to elect a seven- to nine-member township people's committee. These township leaders had then met to vote for a thirteen- or fourteen-member county people's committee, who finally elected a nineteen-member provincial people's committee for each of the six provinces in North Korea. Under this system, none of the representatives beyond the village leaders had been directly accountable to a constituency.

The process of selecting a slate of candidates with broad popular support was facilitated by the creation, on July 22, 1946, of the North Korean Democratic National United Front (*Pukchosŏn minjujuŭi minjok t'ongil chŏnsŏn*), a coalition of three political parties and thirty-five social organizations in North Korea with a total membership of some six million (including children) by 1947.[61] The election was an unprecedented event, and official documents did not shy away from self-congratulatory praise for the many accomplishments in conducting the first democratic election in Korea's history. Although these may be easy to dismiss as mere propaganda, it is worth quoting at length a detailed firsthand account by

Lieutenant Colonel Walter F. Choinski, who was stationed in Pyongyang as part of the XXIV Corps Liaison Section of the U.S. Army Military Government in Korea:

Election day was as noisy as a charivari with band laden trucks moving up and down the streets, its occupants exhorting the people to turn out to vote; street corners and by-ways presented a chautauqua scene with dancers and singers lauding candidates for their virtues and abilities; radio and public address speakers blasted encomium from vital street intersections throughout the day. The early morning crowd (0700) attended the polls eagerly. They comprised the eager people who were fascinated by their first experience in casting a democratic vote; towards noon the crowds thinned out to a mere trickle at the polls and thereafter until dark the people wandered listlessly along the streets like small boys with nothing to do. Since shops were closed there was nothing to distract the people from performing their 'bounden' [sic] duty. Polling places were conspicuously designated by evergreen boughs arches decorating entrances, signs, colored streamers and above all large colored pictures of KIM IL SEUNG [sic] and Joe Stalin. No other 'portraits' were on display in the vicinity of the polling places. Photographs of the 41 chosen candidates were on exhibit at principal thoroughfare intersections. These are still on display. Many of the candidates are entirely unknown to inhabitants of the Pyongyang area. Individuals wishing to cast votes presented a small identification card which had been given him on registration day. The poll official, upon receiving the identification card, checked the name off the voter's list and presented the elector with a ballot. (It has been verified that ballots were not marked by number or name or voter). The voter then retired to a table in another room, where he indicated his choice, folded the ballot and deposited the ballot in one of two boxes—one white, the other black. A slot was out in the top of each box into which the ballots were dropped. Those who voted for the 'chosen' candidates placed their ballot in the white box; those against the chosen candidate placed their ballot in the black box. In order to guarantee secrecy and protect the voter many polls placed low fences in front of the two boxes and cut an arm-size hole in the fence midway between the two boxes. This permitted the voter to stick his arm into the hole, over the two slits of the ballot boxes and observe, without being observed, the hole into which he was casting his lot. In the villages, no attempts were made to protect the voter. A 'worker' or 'official' stood at the white and black box to protect them from pilfering and observed each voter casting his ballot. A reliable source reports that all inhabitants of villages were required to vote. Those who did not make a voluntary appearance by the noon hour were visited by the local constabulary and escorted to the polls to cast their vote. The homes of the Presbyterian ministers were under observation twenty four hours preceeding [sic] the casting of votes and continued throughout the election day. The Catholic school was one of the polling places in Pyongyang.

Addenda:

Election places are brightly decorated with Korean, Red Banner, North Korean colors and bright lanterns and evergreen. Groups of small girls travel from place to place to sing songs and dance folk dances. Trucks are traveling the streets carrying brass bands. An aircraft of the low-wing, radical engine type (silver colored) and bearing the TAE Duk [sic] or national emblem of Korea has been flying low all morning (roof-top) scattering small handbills one of which is attached. The prevailing westerly wind carries most of the bills in the TAEDONG River. The people are listlessly and aimlessly walking along the streets—like small boys who have nothing to do—all business houses are closed—except a few of the braver ones. The voting places are all well guarded by Communist police, Soviet Army troops are scarce—Russians are not at any of the booths seen.

Methods to whip up an interest in the elections were reminiscent of the 1900's in the United States. Street cars filled with a brass band blared the virtues of the 41 candidates as did the radio and press. Trucks laden with noisy party members shouted their wares to the people from street corners and along their route of march. At night specially decorated street cars moved up and down the streets each brilliantly lighted by three tiers of electric bulbs.[62]

Barring the condescending reference to North Korean voters as "small boys with nothing to do," the description captures the excitement and energy of the day, evocative of the "withering away of private life" and the life of the offices, clubs, and streets that Benjamin and Arvatov described in the first chapter. Russians are not observed to be part of the process, duly noted no doubt with surprise because of emerging Cold War fears that a Soviet puppet regime was being installed in the north. Not only did the election prove such perceptions to be utterly mistaken but the results were by no means guaranteed, eliciting a massive mobilization effort with months of intense preparation both logistically and politically. Lists of voters were compiled; propaganda workers, election officials, and

Figure 3.2. Campaigning for election (n.p., n.d.). RG 242, SA 2010, box 3, item 50. Courtesy of the National Archives and Records Administration.

polling stations were organized; voters were educated on the significance and importance of voting; and voters were urged to cast their ballot for the slate of candidates endorsed by the United Front.

Whereas provincial, city, county, and township candidates could be nominated only by registered political parties and social organizations, candidates for village elections were nominated at a public meeting of all the voters in the village, in a true demonstration of participatory democracy.[63] With the consensus of all the villagers, five to seven candidates were nominated for each village, depending on the size of the village. Although competitive elections were not prohibited, the number of candidates usually matched the number of seats available.[64] Propaganda workers urged voters that "as long as seven have been chosen during the public assembly, everyone should put the seven ballots in the white box."[65] The strategy for getting consensus on acceptable candidates was relatively simple. During the village meeting, a party member nominated the chosen slate of candidates, voicing all the worthwhile reasons, and another party member clapped in support.[66] With a convincing argument in favor of the nominees, who were already familiar to villagers due to their merits, villagers were easily won over to supporting the slate of candidates. In fact, the village meetings served to vet candidates who were popular and respected among the villagers even before the election itself.

Anna Louise Strong, the lone American journalist that reported on the country in 1947, debated a North Korean woman about the efficacy of such a system in comparison to the competitive process in the West: "What was the use of voting, I argued, if there was only one candidate. Her vote could change nothing. It would be a great shame for the candidate, she replied, if the people did not turn out in large numbers to vote for him. He would even fail of election unless at least half of the people turned out."[67] The woman went on to explain: "We all knew the candidate. We all liked him, we all discussed him. . . . The political parties held meetings in our mines and factories and found the people's choices. Then they got together and combined on the best one, and the people went out and chose him. I don't see what's wrong with this or why the Americans don't like it. . . . I don't see what the Americans have to say about it, anyway!"

Step by step, village by village, the election process mobilized all segments of North Korean society to participate in the political process. Local PCs put together five-member election committees to compile the list of voters for registration. Local police made rounds to make sure that every house had signs posted about the upcoming election and that there were no conspiracies to sabotage the election. Social organizations of women, peasants, and youth mobilized their members to publicize the election, visiting remote villages, holding rallies, and going door to door.[68]

One creative method of voter education was a game called the "People's Committee Election Contest," the objective of which was to see which team could finish "voting" first.[69] Two teams of approximately thirty people were organized with each team designating its members to be one of the following: an election committee member, a poor peasant, a rich peasant, a worker, a *samuwŏn*, a female Buddhist monk, a priest, a Confucian scholar, a sick elderly woman, a disabled elderly man, a college student, and a traveler with a bicycle or a cart. The game was designed to take place in a large hall or a field at least fifty meters long set up like a voting station with two sets of voting booths, each with a black box and a white box and a pair of election committee members. The game in effect emulated the voting process with the teams competing against each other in order to teach villagers how to vote.

Rackets and batons were used in place of identification cards and the two teams were lined up fifty meters away from each voting booth. Once the signal was given, the first "voter" ran to the voting booth with his baton, used it to receive his voting card by checking his name off the voters list at the election committee table, voted, and quickly returned to his team, handing the baton to the next "voter." The different roles that were

Figure 3.3. Woman casting vote in ballot box behind screen (n.p., n.d.). RG 242, SA 2010, box 3, item 50. Courtesy of the National Archives and Records Administration.

given to each team member illustrated the special attention intended for the sick and the disabled in the exercise of their right to vote. When it was time for the "sick" person to vote, she was to yell out "sick person" and the election committee member at the booth had to come to the voter with the boxes. When it was time for the "disabled" person to vote, the next voter in line had to carry him on his back to the voting booth and they voted together before returning to the team. Such methods of voter education imparted the significance of the election process while increasing the level of excitement and anticipation in participating in a novel political process.

On the actual election day, those who knew how to read received all seven ballots for each of the candidates, which they placed in either the black or the white box. Those who were illiterate were given one ballot at a time and told the name on the ballot before going up to place it in the desired box.[70] The high rates of illiteracy in the countryside required special accommodations for illiterate voters. Several methods were used to maintain voter secrecy. One involved putting up a screen in front of the boxes, as mentioned in Choinski's description, while

Figure 3.4. For figures 3.4 and 3.5: People celebrating the elections in diverse attire, including a costume imitating Charlie Chaplin (Kangwŏn Province, Kimhwa County, Kimsŏng Township mass rally of 6,565 residents, November 1946). RG 242, SA 2010, box 3, item 11. Courtesy of the National Archives and Records Administration.

Figure 3.5.

another instructed voters to insert the folded hand with the ballot hidden inside into both boxes, dropping the ballot secretly into the desired box.[71] As indicated by Strong, elections did not generally involve direct competition among different candidates seeking a majority vote but was a process of expressing agreement or disagreement with the nominations made by the United Front. Still, 4.5 million North Koreans, or 99.6 percent of all eligible voters, took part in the first ever mass election held in Korea and 97 percent of them expressed approval of the United Front candidates.[72] Indeed, people's excessive enthusiasm came under criticism for "wasting too much time decorating the poll stations" and holding up the election process![73]

As people became acquainted with electoral procedures and the attendant political process, excitement waned among some who were no longer intrigued by the novelty of it all, while others became politically savvy, maneuvering within the system to mount a challenge by fielding competing candidates or engaging in outright sabotage against the elections. A top-secret government document detailed numerous problems with the second set of elections for village and township representatives in 1947.[74] Election committees failed to keep regular work hours or to provide adequate voter information in the required format; former landlords in South Hamgyŏng Province spread false rumors about an impending repeal of the land reform, demanding rent from their former tenants; and election officers in North P'yŏngan Province wasted public funds by making unnecessary phone calls and trips.[75] Kangwŏn Province, which was divided by the 38th parallel, saw attempts from the south to lure voters away from the polls by tempting them with free food, while "reactionary terrorist groups" set fire to three election offices in North P'yŏngan Province. Election officers were repeatedly admonished for neglecting the second set of elections and failing to publicize the United Front candidates sufficiently to deter the counterpropaganda that urged people to cast their vote in the black box.[76] In fact, more than 55 percent of the voters of West Village in T'ongch'on Township, Kangwŏn Province, cast their votes in the black box, rejecting the candidates.[77] Consequently, United Front workers came under criticism for choosing candidates without popular support. In other counties, former colonial officials and police officers, as well as those who had acquired land illegally through forged documents during the land reform in Sinch'ŏn County, North P'yŏngan Province, were nominated as candidates, while several counties in Hwanghae Province saw the election of merchants and entrepreneurs as representatives, rather than peasants or workers. Some places, such as Ch'ŏrwŏn County in Kangwŏn

Province and Ŭiju County in North P'yŏngan Province, saw competition surface between the various parties despite the best efforts to nominate a United Front candidate.[78]

Christians posed a particularly strenuous challenge by refusing to attend events on Sundays, including the elections scheduled for that day.[79] An article published just before the 1947 elections in the journal *Kŏnsŏl* (Construction), the organ of the North Korean Literature and Arts League, urged Christians to vote, arguing that the Sabbath was there for the benefit of the people, and not the other way around, quoting the Gospel of Mark (2:23–28).[80] Responding to criticisms from Christians asking, "Why is a national event held on Sunday? This is surely to exclude Christians from voting!," the *Kŏnsŏl* article retorted that only 5 percent of the population was Christian and yet Sunday was observed as a day of rest fifty-two days out of the year. Moreover, the article argued that voting was "not working nor selling anything, and certainly not desecrating God, but rather the small act of voting is to enable the people to live a better life in complete independence."[81] The article asked pointedly whether Christian moneylenders refused to charge interest or whether Christian landlords refused to charge rent on Sundays, slamming them for their willingness to stand in line for the distribution of shoes whether it was Sunday or not while refusing to vote because it was Sunday. Despite such arguments, some Christian communities boycotted the elections, such as in Chŏngju, North P'yŏngan Province, where rumors circulated that ballots had secret marks to identify dissenters who would be sent away to Siberian labor camps.[82] Fearful about the truth behind such rumors, Christians in the area gathered at church for a prayer meeting on Saturday night and stayed through Sunday to boycott the vote collectively. In the end, nothing happened to them, but most of them fled to the south anyway. Ironically, South Korea also scheduled its first election on May 10, 1948, a Sunday, facing opposition from Christians, especially those from the north.[83]

On the whole, people were most discontented with local party officials, reflected in the number of negative votes for them in the second set of elections—hardly a surprise since party leaders were at the forefront of mobilizing villagers to pay taxes and to volunteer for local projects. Voters were likely to be much more critical of local officials they knew firsthand; only 86.6 percent of the coalition candidates were elected, still a large majority but not quite as high as in the November 1946 election.[84] Food shortages resulting from bad harvests in 1946 compounded negative public opinion and did not help garner support. Propaganda workers were called on to remind people about the harsh conditions under colonial rule,

appealing for their understanding during a difficult time: "We are fighting to build a new country under terrible conditions. We have to create
something out of nothing despite all the deficiencies, and we can survive
and build a new, strong and wealthy country only if we clench our teeth
and go forth past all the barriers and obstacles."[85]

In Inje County, 18,176 people out of a total population of 37,776 were
registered to vote, while seventeen people were stripped of the right to
vote due to mental illness and court rulings that deemed them unfit to
vote (likely designated as national traitors).[86] Inje had its fair share of complications in the second set of elections as the nominated candidates did
not receive everyone's support, and competing candidates were proposed
instead. According to the minutes of one township party cell meeting, the
members decided not to support the candidate nominated by the upper
ranks of the party. Although acknowledging the importance of democratic procedures, the party official sent to review the work of the cell
pointed out that it was against party rules to fail to pass the nominee
recommended by higher levels. Rather than taking disagreement as an
indication of genuine discontent, it was thought that the lack of "correct
understanding" had led to mistaken notions about what was truly in the
interest of the people: "Should Kim Ku [nationalist independence leader]
or Syngman Rhee [first president of South Korea] be nominated if people
approve of them? As leaders, we should in such instances give people the
correct understanding, and only by putting forth those that will serve the
public in the interest of the people will we have completed our mission."[87]
Ultimately, responsibility for the lack of support by the cell members was
attributed to the cell leader for failing to unite the membership around the
chosen candidate.

To be fair, discrepancies between choices fielded by the party leadership and those preferred by the membership were not a simple matter of
strong-arm politics. In many instances, the party leadership was trying to
forestall discontent while pursuing a form of affirmative action by calling for a more diverse and fair distribution of candidates. For example, in
Inje Township, 40 percent of the candidates were to be chosen from the
Workers' Party, 10 percent from the Democratic Party, and 50 percent
from unaffiliated independents.[88] In the case of Nam Township, three
candidates out of the five to seven nominees from each village were replaced by women, independents, and Democratic Party members so as to
ensure a diverse representation.[89] Indeed, as shown in tables 3.6 through
3.9, unaffiliated peasants made up the overwhelming majority of newly
elected people's committee representatives, particularly at the village level.

All in all, 46,245 peasants were elected as village representatives, making up 86.7 percent of all village representatives, and 7,795 peasants were elected as township representatives, making up 58 percent of the total. The greater percentage of Workers' Party candidates elected at the village level (60%) in contrast to the provincial level (32%) could be interpreted as the direct result of the land reform, which won many peasants over to the Workers' Party. Moreover, 7,049 women (13.2%) were elected as village representatives and 1,986 (14.7%) women were elected as township representatives, incorporating an unprecedented number of women into positions of political power.

With the institutionalization of the PCs through the elections, a 237-member North Korean People's Assembly was elected from among the provincial representatives as the highest legislative organ, from which the North Korean People's Committee was constituted as the national executive body.[90] By the time the Democratic People's Republic of Korea was founded in September 1948, references to North Korea (*pukchosŏn*) were dropped in favor of the Republic (*konghwaguk*), and the North Korean People's Committee was referred to as the Standing Committee of the Supreme People's Assembly. The People's Assembly included one representative for every fifty thousand people, who served a term of three years. The Assembly had authority over the executive and judiciary branches through its power to appoint the cabinet and the Supreme Court.[91]

Thus, paradoxically, the institutionalization of local PCs through the elections of 1946 and 1947 effectively began the process of centralizing North Korea's political structure, establishing central control down to the villages. Until then, village PCs had been staffed by people who had come to occupy those positions based on their own prestige and status in their hometowns; the central government or political parties did not play a role. Many village leaders had reportedly been in power since liberation in August 1945, taking up leadership positions without formal elections in the vacuum left by the collapse of the colonial government.[92] Their autonomous source of power based in local politics had hindered central control.

One of the major reasons given for the township and village PC elections in a top-secret document was the challenge posed by the collection of the agricultural tax-in-kind, which proved that the township and village PCs were ineffective in implementing national policies.[93] The elections served a dual purpose: displaying democracy in action to mollify discontent among villagers about the way grain procurement was handled by local officials while making sure that candidates acceptable to both the

Table 3.6. Class background of representatives elected in the elections of 1946 and 1947

	Peasant	Worker	Samuwŏn	Merchant	Intellectual	Entrepreneur	Former landlord	Clergy	Total
People's Assembly	62 (26%)	52 (22%)	56 (24%)	10 (4%)	36 (15%)	11 (including 4 artisans) (5%)	–	10 (4%)	237
Province, city, county	1,256 (36.3%)	510 (14.8%)	1,056 (30.5%)	143 (4.1%)	311 (9.1%)	73 (2.1%)	14 (0.4%)	94 (2.7%)	3,457
Township	7,795 (58%)	1,121 (8.3%)	3,901 (29%)	228 (1.7%)	310 (2.3%)	48 (0.4%)	1	40 (0.3%)	13,444
Village	46,245 (86.74%)	2,508 (4.7%)	3,681 (6.9%)	493 (0.92%)	174 (0.34%)	129 (0.24%)	17 (0.03%)	67 (0.13%)	53,314

Sources: RG 242, SA 2005, box 5, item 43, "Overview of the North Korean Township and Village People's Committee Elections (Top Secret)," Central Election Committee (1947), 195, 197; RG 242, SA 2005, box 2, item 89, "Minutes of the North Korean Province, City and County People's Committee Congress," (April 1947), Day 4, 49, 57.

Table 3.7. Party affiliation of provincial, city, and county People's Committee representatives elected in 1946

	North Korean Workers' Party	Democratic Party	Ch'ŏndogyo Young Friends Party	Independent	Total
National total	1,102 (31.8%)	351 (10%)	253 (8.1%)	1,753 (50.1%)	3,459
South P'yŏngan	154 (27.5%)	68 (12.1%)	71 (12.7%)	263 (47.7%)	561
North P'yŏngan	214 (28.8%)	77 (10.3%)	61 (8.2%)	392 (52.7%)	744
South Hamgyŏng	223 (36.4%)	39 (6.4%)	44 (7.2%)	307 (50%)	613
North Hamgyŏng	125 (33.3%)	27 (7.2%)	21 (5.6%)	202 (53.9%)	375
Hwanghae	213 (32.6%)	32 (4.9%)	34 (5.2%)	320 (57.3%)	653
Kangwŏn	162 (34.7%)	52 (11.1%)	17 (3.6%)	235 (50.6%)	467
Pyongyang	10 (24.4%)	6 (14.6%)	5 (12.2%)	20 (48.8%)	41

Source: RG 242, SA 2009, box 2, item 198, Chosŏn chungang yŏn'gam [North Korea yearbook] (Pyongyang: Korean Central News Agency, 1949), 84.

Table 3.8. Party affiliation of township and village People's Committee representatives elected in 1947

	North Korean Workers' Party	Democratic Party	Ch'ŏndogyo Young Friends Party	Independent
Township (*myŏn*)	7,501 (55.8%)	1,122 (8.3%)	900 (6.8%)	3,921 (29.1%)
Village (*ri*)	32,011 (60.05%)	3,962 (7.43%)	2,577 (4.83%)	14,764 (27.69%)

Source: RG 242, SA 2005, box 5, item 43, "Overview of the North Korean Township and Village People's Committee Elections (Top Secret)," Central Election Committee (1947), 195, 197.

Table 3.9. Party affiliation of People's Assembly members in 1947

	North Korean Workers' Party	Democratic Party	Ch'ŏndogyo Young Friends Party	Independent
People's Assembly	86 (36%)	30 (13%)	30 (13%)	91 (38%)

Source: RG 242, SA 2005, box 2, item 89, "Minutes of the North Korean Province, City and County People's Committee Congress," (April 1947), Day 4, 57.

central government and the villagers were elected in order to facilitate coordination in the future. To ensure that public opinion was incorporated into the process of nominating candidates, a directive to the village and township election workers in the United Front urged them to consider for candidacy even those who had no party affiliation if the person worked on behalf of his or her constituents. This would enable local governments to work in close cooperation, "living and breathing along with the villagers."[94] Although most of those elected as provincial, city, and county representatives were independent candidates, the process of centralization was now firmly in place. The electoral process itself required central coordination at all levels, from the issuance of citizen identification cards (*kongminjŭng*) and the registration of voters to surveys of local political conditions for the nomination of United Front candidates who could work effectively with the central government. For one, this meant making sure that no landlords would continue to hold positions of power in the local government while aiming to secure that at least 15 percent of those elected were women.[95] Local autonomy may have been curtailed by this process, but central coordination also facilitated many of the reforms and movements to restructure society from top to bottom.

Literacy Campaign

One such movement was a nationwide literacy campaign launched to educate peasants and to elevate the overall standard of intellectual life. The campaign mobilized vast numbers of people and resources to build schools, libraries, and other educational facilities to educate the staggering number of illiterates, especially in the countryside and particularly among women. As shown in table 3.10, as of 1944 almost twenty million Koreans out of a population of twenty-five million had had no formal schooling of any kind. Despite the expansion of public education during the colonial period, the vast majority of the population, especially in rural areas, had never had the opportunity to attend school. Moreover, even the educated were only versed in Japanese while illiterate in vernacular Korean, thus requiring a massive overhaul of the education system.

In the aftermath of liberation, illiteracy posed problems not only in the promotion of education and technical skills for the developing economy but also in political education and administrative tasks, which uniformly required reading and writing skills. Party recruitment brought large numbers of peasants into the Workers' Party, many of whom were illiterate. They could not keep proper records, including minutes of meetings, which explains the difficulty in finding local records from the first year after liberation. The handwritten minutes speak volumes about the educational

Table 3.10. Level of schooling among Koreans before liberation, May 1944

Level of schooling	Male	Female	Total
College graduate	7,272	102	7,374
Technical school graduate	18,555	3,509	22,064
High school graduate	162,111	37,531	199,642
Middle school graduate	40,702	9,240	49,942
Primary school graduate	1,281,490	355,552	1,637,042
Some primary school	190,250	64,555	254,805
Basic schooling (two years)	864,308	115,814	980,122
No schooling	8,430,940	11,211,835	19,642,775

Source: Minjujuŭi minjok chŏnsŏn, *Chosŏn haebang yŏnbo* [Korean liberation yearbook] (Seoul: Munuinsŏgwan, 1946), 347, cited in Kim Kwang-un, "Formation of the Power-Structure and the Recruitment of Cadre in North Korea (August 1945~March 1947)" (PhD diss., Hanyang University, 1999), 177.

level of the various groups at the different levels of the political structure. Predictably, the minutes are much more elementary in both content and form, including spelling and penmanship, at the village level. But PCs were also criticized for writing their minutes in Chinese script—the lingua franca of East Asian civilization that had traditionally been limited to the elite—attesting to the fact that the PCs were initially run by more educated people. These were often the local notable, perhaps a landlord or merchant, who may not have been from the appropriate "revolutionary" class but was nonetheless reputable among local residents.[96] The party had less control over such figures, and this was often a source of tension as the PCs and the party competed for local hegemony.

The literacy campaign was facilitated by the retention of election campaign offices (*sŏn'gŏ sŏnjŏnsil*) as local meeting places after the elections were over, institutionalizing them as "socially productive" spaces in everyday life. By July 1947, some 11,595 halls dotted the landscape throughout North Korea.[97] They were renamed the "democratic publicity halls" (*minju sŏnjŏnsil*) and came to function much like cultural centers that would elevate the cultural life of the people, fostering communal participation, educational programs, and the dissemination of information.[98] They were often decorated with portraits of Kim Il Sung and Joseph Stalin, posters, current news, and graphs showing increases in the rate of agricultural and industrial production, tax collection, and literacy. They became gathering places for local meetings, were used as classrooms for literacy schools, and at times became senior centers for the village elders.[99] Depending on the resources of the village, some of them were equipped with sports equipment, musical instruments, libraries, public bathhouses, barbershops, and health clinics.[100]

The publicity hall at Nambuk Village in Inje County was named a model hall. It was furnished with a workroom, study room, barbershop, bathhouse, and an entertainment room, the walls of which were decorated with graphs, cartoons, news, and announcements.[101] There were over 160 newspapers and books in the library collection, as well as a record player and board games such as *changgi* and *paduk* (different kinds of Korean chess games). Some forty women and men gathered there every day, some playing games, others working on projects, and still others reading. It came to have a reputation as a place "where one must go to hear the latest news" so that people gathered there at all hours of the day, women bringing their needlework and men bringing straw to make straw shoes and other handicrafts, and the propagandists used this time to organize discussions and talks.

Illiteracy posed a particularly daunting problem for women since as much as 90 percent of women were illiterate in 1945.[102] The campaign benefited women overwhelmingly, and the majority of students were women—three or four times the number of men, as shown in the number of graduates in Inje County in 1948 (see table 3.11).

All illiterate residents in Inje were enrolled in literacy schools, and the great majority of them passed the final test after the four-month program. An article in a women's magazine illustrated how one woman, the chairwoman of a women's league in a rural village, experienced the whole process. She had grown up in a strict household that did not teach girls how to read. When she first started attending the literacy school, she "couldn't attend very diligently with all the housework and the women's league work." As she explained, "In the beginning and for some time, I couldn't understand what they were saying. But then, after I listened again and again, gathering my wits, practicing the writing at home, I don't know when I learned but I had learned."[103] The article concluded that women were now able to express their opinions in public, courageously stepping out into the public arena as never before.

To motivate villagers to attend literacy schools, illiteracy eradication teams (*munmaeng t'oech'iban*) were organized in each village.[104] The village PC chairperson took on the position of team leader (*panjang*), assisted by a secretary (*ch'ongmu*) from one of the political parties. Each of the teams compiled the number of illiterates in their village and the number of potential teachers, rallying publicity and support from among the members of social organizations, school teachers, and students. Classes were usually conducted every day for three hours for a period of four months, focusing

Table 3.11. First literacy campaign graduation test results for Inje County, 1948

	Number of illiterates			Those tested			Average score	Pass	Percentage passed	Remaining illiterates
	Male	Female	Total	Male	Female	Total				
Inje	449	1,246	1,695	449	1,163	1,612	75	1,308	78	387
Nam	132	457	589	132	457	589	82	542	90	47
Puk	376	1,105	1,481	376	1,105	1,481	86	1,403	94	78
Sŏhwa	556	1,483	2,039	507	1,433	1,940	73	1,753	85	286
Total	1,513	4,291	5,804	1,464	4,158	5,622	78	5,006	86	798

Source: North Korean Workers' Party Kangwŏn Province Inje County Standing Committee Meeting Minutes No. 7 (1948.4.6), NHCC, vol. 2, 176. Also in RG 242, SA 2007, box 6, item 1.67.

on Korean language and mathematics. They were divided by age between the young and old, and by sex between men and women. Those between the ages of twelve and fifty attended literacy schools whereas those over fifty attended "adult re-education schools."[105] Older generations posed a particularly difficult group to mobilize and resocialize in the making of a new society, and the peasant league sought them out where they were gathered socially to give lessons on the spot.[106]

The campaign prescribed at least two literacy schools per village, and a personal instructor was to be sent directly to those who could not make it to school because of family circumstances.[107] As women's enrollment posed the greatest challenge, if a woman failed to attend school regularly, members of the women's league were called on to look into her family situation to see whether her husband or parents-in-law were prohibiting her from attending school. In October 1948, it was discovered that there were still 1,454 illiterate women in Inje who had been unable to attend school because it was too far away or they had infants to nurse and were busy with household chores. The women's league took responsibility for these women, placing one member in charge of each illiterate woman to give them one-on-one instruction in her own home.[108] By March 1949, when the final national literacy test took place, illiteracy in the county had reportedly been eradicated, with the exception of 309 people who were considered too old or mentally ill.

Unfortunately, even those who had passed the test often reverted to being illiterate when they stopped going to school since most people had learned to read but not to write.[109] At the end of 1948, the Inje County Women's League was still struggling with nine hundred illiterate women within their own ranks. To get the remaining women to learn to read, bulletin boards were put up at public places where women were likely to gather, such as around the communal well, with basic reading lessons they could recite while doing laundry. Signs were also posted on the doors of the homes of illiterate people as a way to exert peer pressure and public shame, adding extra incentive to learn.[110] To sustain the results of the literacy campaign, a decision approved on December 18, 1946, standardized the public education system to mandate a year of kindergarten beginning at age six, followed by five years of elementary education, three years of middle school or technical school, and three years of high school or specialty school.[111] Students could pursue higher education thereafter in four to five years of college or two years of teachers college, followed by postgraduate research. Such formal schooling was supplemented by various programs targeting adults and workers for vocational training.

Table 3.12. Results of the three-year literacy campaign in Inje County

	Dates	Number of schools	Number of teachers	Number of illiterates	Number of literates	Percentage literate
Literacy schools	1946.12.1–1947.11.30	155	155	8,323	3,157	28
	1947.12.1–1948.11.30	130	130	6,115	5,950	87
	1948.12.1–1949.3.30	48	50	273	273	100
Short-course adult schools	1948.4.1–1948.11.30	201	201	6,964	1,817	26
	1948.12.1–1949.3.30	259	259	3,924	3,481	89

Source: RG 242, SA 2007, box 6, item 12.6, Inje County PC Standing Committee Decision no. 3 (1949.5.10). Also in NHCC, vol. 18, 194–95.

In Inje County by the end of 1948 there were eighty-five publicity halls, a theater, a library, two medical clinics, twenty-five elementary schools with over one hundred teachers and almost six thousand students, three middle schools with twenty-two teachers and over six hundred students, a high school, an adult middle school, nine adult schools, and 191 short-course adult schools with approximately five thousand students.[112] Whereas primary school enrollment had hovered below 50 percent at the end of colonial rule, there were now 1,317,630 children of peasant families enrolled in schools throughout North Korea—an increase of 204 percent.[113] Moreover, 92 percent of illiterate peasants in North Korea had learned to read and write by March 1948, about halfway through the three-year literacy campaign. A financial report for Inje in 1948 showed that more than half of the county's expenses were spent on social and cultural projects, most of which went toward education.[114]

The fervor for education ran deep among peasants, who had had little opportunity for education before. Internal party documents, not meant for public consumption and therefore of limited propaganda value, are replete with stories about people who gave the little they had to make education possible: donating materials they were saving up to build their own homes for the construction of a new school, peasants donating their prized animals, children donating the savings from their piggy banks, and elderly women boarding carpenters and workers in their homes during the construction of local schools. Illiteracy was considered the "enemy of civilization," and as peasants learned to read and write, taking up positions in the local administration of the people's committees, party branches, and social organizations, they were inspired by their newfound abilities. As one party member commented exuberantly, "Realizing the need to learn to read and write, today I have come to gain the ability to compose the minutes with my own hand as a result of diligent self-study."[115] Those just learning to read and write were now becoming leaders, writing up reports and party records. Indeed, empowerment was to be found in the routine, everyday practices that were newly adopted by the previously dispossessed members of society who were now in positions of leadership.

North Korea's revolution in the everyday began with the transformation of the basic foundation of social relations through one of the most rapid and radical land reforms in history as peasants took to the streets to demand a new relationship to land. Once completed, the decommodification of land imbued the process of agricultural production with social meaning as peasants collectively managed the production and distribution of their harvests. The momentum was sustained through the institutionalization of the people's committees, creating an everyday that was "public through and through," lived in the streets, publicity halls, and people's committee offices. Empowerment required both the initial spontaneous thrust of the peasants striking out into the public arena and the tools that came later in the form of political representation and education, through which they learned to participate in a sustained revolutionary process. Increasingly empowered and confident, large numbers of peasants, women, and youth took up leadership positions. In fact, peasants, women, and youth, who together represented the vast majority of the population, created the three largest social organizations for a collective life that was integral to instilling a sense of social purpose. The next chapter details the everyday practices of organizational life and the negotiations that were necessary to navigate one's relationship within the various collectivities.

4. The Collective

Enacting the Revolution

> Complete freedom is not gained by juxtaposing the individual self to
> the collective, but can only be found by way of the collective. . . . Every
> individual guarantees one's individuality by acting as part of a collective.
> We struggle actively against individualism. . . . Democratic virtue does
> not undermine the happiness and well-being of the individual, but is
> achieved only when everyone enjoys happiness and well-being together
> as a collective.
>
> T'AE SŎNG-JU, 1949

Figure 4.1. Children's league meeting (n.p., n.d.). RG 242, SA 2012,
box 5, item 139. Courtesy of the National Archives and Records
Administration.

The text for educators quoted above defined the relationship between
the individual and the collective, not as one of conflict, but as constitutive
of one another, whereby the collective defined the very basis for individual
identity and welfare. In the aftermath of colonial rule, a renewed sense of
national collectivity was to be expected, but this was to be more than a simple fomentation of nationalism. It was a call for a different kind of politics
that would give concrete form to the principle all-for-one and one-for-all.
The last chapter looked at three pivotal events that set the stage: the land

reform that restructured social relations, the elections that institutionalized the people's committees, and the literacy campaign that opened new cultural horizons. This chapter describes the quotidian practices that emanated from these events and became part of daily life by the organization of people into every imaginable collective by occupation, gender, and age group. As shown in the opening epigraph, the happiness and well-being of the individual was to be found through the collective, and this meant living an "organizational life" (*chojik saenghwal*). According to the text, capitalism fostered competition between individuals and social alienation by valuing profit over social need. Only through a collective life under communism would the true nature of social relations be revealed, in which "the new person holds dear the struggle for the general welfare of the people and values the ability to labor."[1] A new kind of social life with different forms of social relations was to emerge from a collective organizational life.

To "enact" the revolution through the collective has multiple meanings in this context—at the most basic level to endorse it, but more specifically to ordain it into being by representing and acting it out, and in that process of performing the revolution to become its very embodiment. Revolution in North Korea certainly included the overturning of previous social relations as the very definition of what a social revolution is, but what this meant in concrete terms for everyday life was a new collective life that had its own distinctive qualities, with its own set of identities and practices, irreducible to its parts. Not simply the aggregate effect of individuals, organizational life created different forms of agency that were represented in new forms of discourse and different configurations of time and space. Daily schedules and the pace of work changed as meetings and study sessions had priority over the production line. Communal spaces took on novel significance as Japanese mansions were turned into kindergartens and Shinto shrines became public parks.[2] People now addressed each other as "comrade" rather than with the familial hierarchical terms of appellation. Thus, to be part of a collective and to live an organizational life was to enact the revolution into concrete reality, making the revolution visible through everyday practices. With multiple organizations, it was not always easy juggling and navigating the many responsibilities and duties. But, the relationships between the different organizations, particularly in the early years as they were being defined, show the extent to which these relationships had to be negotiated. The purpose of this chapter is to show that dynamic, beginning with the most central organization of them all, the North Korean Workers' Party, before moving on to discuss the vital role played by social organizations as "transmission belts" between the party and the people.

The Party

Despite factionalism and political suppression, which had hindered its growth during the colonial period, the Korean Communist Party was the best organized group after liberation, with a history that went back to the 1920s. Communists across the country had begun to regroup after liberation, with a large concentration in Seoul, but a centralized party in North Korea formed quickly from the Conference of Korean Communist Party Members and Enthusiasts in the Five Northwestern Provinces held in Pyongyang in October 1945 and attended by about one thousand members.[3] There were two other contending parties in the north that reflected regional characteristics. The Korean Democratic Party, which formed on November 3, 1945, was led by Cho Man-sik with a membership largely of Christian intellectuals and landowners from the vicinity of Pyongyang. The Ch'ŏndogyo Young Friends Party, which was founded on February 8, 1946, had a peasant membership of adherents to the indigenous Ch'ŏndogyo religion.[4] When the Koreans who had been fighting in the Chinese Revolution in Yenan, led by Kim Tu-bong, returned to Korea they formed the New People's Party on February 26, 1946. This gave the communists an opportunity to overtake the strength of the Democrats and the Ch'ŏndogyo.[5]

The New People's Party and the North Korean Communist Party merged on August 28, 1946, to form the North Korean Workers' Party, creating a membership base of 366,000. Merging the 90,000 members of the New People's Party with the North Korean Communist Party's 276,000 members brought together over 10 percent of the total adult population that was eligible for party membership, most of them from the younger generation. More than 80 percent of the members were between twenty and forty.[6] By 1948, in less than two years, membership had grown to 750,000, with the number of workers doubling, from 73,000 to 143,000, and the number of poor peasants tripling, from 105,000 to 374,000.[7]

Party members were required to become model citizens, actively participating in the revolution and paying membership dues that ranged from 1 percent to 3 percent of one's income, in addition to special fees for extra projects.[8] Members were quite diligent about paying their dues, with 80 to almost 100 percent of members doing so, fluctuating according to different regions and times of year, likely dependent on harvest conditions.[9] The platform of the party was broad-based, emphasizing the construction of a democratic independent state with sovereignty resting on the people's committees. It underscored the importance of the land reform, the nationalization of industries, the labor law guaranteeing an eight-hour workday, and political and civil rights including the right to vote and be elected. Moreover, the full gamut of a socialist program called for equal political and economic rights for women, the protection of mothers and children, the right to an education, an equal and fair tax system, obligatory military service, and solidarity with other nations struggling for world peace.[10]

By the time party membership stabilized in 1948, Inje County had some five thousand members. Poor peasants made up a full 80 percent of the members, with the remainder comprising 10 percent middle peasants, 5 percent workers, 5 percent samuwŏn, and just a handful of merchants and other classes.[11] Women, most of them housewives, made up between 25 and 30 percent of the party. Whereas most of the members were peasants, it took some time before they took up leadership positions within the party. In 1946, 70 percent of the party leaders in the county were samuwŏn, of whom 60 percent had worked under the Japanese colonial government, but by the end of 1948, 47 percent were workers, 33.3 percent were poor peasants, and 19.7 percent were samuwŏn, reversing the party composition in two years. As shown in table 4.1, the concentration of poor peasants among county party officials increased over time from 19 percent in 1946 to 57.2 percent in 1949, reflecting the party's efforts to recruit peasants into its ranks. As we saw in the last chapter, the elections in 1946 and 1947 were instrumental in bringing peasants into leadership positions within the government. Not surprisingly, poor peasants were represented in much greater numbers at the local level, making up almost 94 percent of the leaders of party cells, the most basic unit of the party structure. Even the vast majority of the increasing numbers of workers had until recently been peasants, since 93.9 percent of them had less than one year of work experience and 46 percent of them were under the age of twenty-six.[12]

As the party expanded too quickly, however, the quality of its membership began to suffer, and most candidates in Inje, as much as 87.8 percent, were being turned down for inadequate preparation. Local party branches were criticized for recruiting members simply for their class backgrounds rather than checking their qualifications, leading to "ultra-leftist" deviations.[13] On the other hand, the rapid expansion had also resulted in the "infiltration of the party by the exploitative classes." The party carried out a two-month purge between December 1946 and February 1947 of capitalists, industrialists, merchants, colonial collaborators, landlords, religious leaders, and any member "debasing democratic reforms and the work of the people's committee through factionalism and improper conduct in

Table 4.1. Class background of party officials at various levels over time in Inje County (%)

	Workers	Poor peasants	*Samuwŏn*	Middle peasants
1946 county committee	8.0	19.0	70.0	20.0
Early 1948 county committee	26.3	21.4	41.4	0.63
November 1948 county committee	47.0	33.3	19.7	–
Township committees	18.2	63.6	18.2	–
Cell chairs	6.85	83.15	10.0	–
Cell committees	3.3	93.8	2.6	–
September 1949 county committee	42.8	57.2	4.5	

Source: RG 242, SA 2007, box 6, item 1.62, North Korean Workers' Party Kangwŏn Province Inje County Standing Committee Meeting Minutes No. 69 (1949.11.13). Also in NHCC, vol. 3, 813.

private and public life."[14] Despite the strong language, the majority of those expelled from the party—89.5 percent in the case of Inje County—were purged because they were missing, which usually meant that they had left for the south, facilitated by the county's location along the 38th parallel. Even those spared from expulsion did not escape reproach in the campaign to strengthen ideological unity and organizational life. The most common causes for reprimand among Inje party members were negligence of party work (70.7%) and the careless keeping of party membership cards (34%).

As shown in the fluctuations in the class composition of party leaders and struggles over who was to be admitted and retained as members, the party's constituencies and personalities were in flux as members struggled to define what was appropriate conduct for a party member. The most basic organizational unit at which these new forms of collective practices were to be negotiated and learned was the party cell, established in all workplaces where there were five or more party members, and much effort was put into their development and edification.[15] In April 1948, there were 143 cells in Inje County alone, with fifty in Inje Township, sixteen in Nam Township, thirty-two in Puk Township, and forty-five in Sŏhwa Township.[16] Despite the increasing participation of women in politics, there were still twenty-three cells without any female members in 1948. Made up of some thirty to forty members, cells were led by the cell committee composed of a chair, vice-chair, and three committee members.[17] The chair was in charge of vertically linking the cell to the upper ranks of the party and horizontally linking it to other organizations in the area, as well as delegating tasks to members of the committee in order to prepare for the general meeting, during which party decisions and resolutions were discussed.

From the very inception of considering new members, the significance of joining the party and beginning a new collective life was made abundantly clear through a meticulous process. Cell leaders were alerted about a potential candidate, including information on class background, level of education, and current employment.[18] Then a formal application for membership was submitted with one's resume and a short autobiography (a central topic to be explored in the next chapter). The contents focused on disavowing any connection to the colonial regime before liberation. If the application was approved by the cell, it was then taken to the township level for final approval. The number of recommendations from party members required for each applicant varied according to class. Workers and poor peasants required only one recommendation, whereas merchants, entrepreneurs, and intellectuals required two. The most stringent requirements were placed on people switching parties. They had to obtain recommendations from three Workers' Party members who had been members of the party for longer than a year. This was no easy task since the majority of party members had joined recently. Moreover, their application required the final approval of the provincial level or the approval of the Central Committee in Pyongyang if they had held leadership positions in other parties.

Compared to the painstaking examination process, the induction ceremony itself was rather simple, done without fanfare. During the new members' first cell meeting, they took the following pledge:

1. To fight for the propertyless class
2. To fight for the complete independence and liberation of Korea
3. To place the interest of the party above all others
4. To abide by party rules
5. To endeavor to accomplish party tasks without fearing difficulties
6. To be a model for the masses
7. To keep party secrets
8. To trust the party
9. To never betray the party[19]

The pledge was followed by a short welcome speech from the cell leader and a brief reiteration of the responsibilities and rules of party membership. The ceremony was meant to be pedagogical "rather than imitate religious ceremonies or shamanistic practices," as the instructions on party life forewarned.

In Inje County, the party cell in Nam Township was considered a model cell.[20] Meetings generally lasted for one to two hours with most members in attendance. The cell committee met three days before the general meeting to prepare and decide on the direction of the discussion. Discussants were organized in advance by the committee, although spontaneous discussions during the meeting were also encouraged.[21] Study groups differentiated by level met every Tuesday and Friday for about two-and-a-half hours. Everyone had their own notebook, a fact noted with considerable pride since limited resources were a constant challenge. The first thirty minutes were spent reviewing to make sure everyone understood before moving on to the next topic. At the end of each month, two or three special study sessions were organized to review the month's lessons and announce the evaluations of the students, in which the group with the best grades received notebooks and pencils as prizes. The attendance rate was excellent at 95 percent, and the publicity hall was well run, with reading groups holding their meetings there. At least twenty to thirty people used the hall every day thanks to the efforts of the party cell.

Such examples of model cells did not preclude continued criticisms about improper organizational conduct, ranging from corruption and factionalism to how people should be addressing each other. Internal party documents repeatedly pointed out that local party branches were guilty of "tail-endism" by following the people rather than leading them; that the work of the local leaders was formalistic, bureaucratic, unplanned, chaotic, and superficial; that they failed to go directly to the people to solve their problems and gave orders mechanically from their desks; that not enough effort was spent on learning and teaching study materials; and that "familism" was pervasive, with everyone calling each other brother (*hyŏng*) and sister (*ŏnni*), unable to criticize each other properly.[22] There were concerns that the tradition of calling each other by familial terms could result in factionalism.[23] The party vehemently guarded against factions within the party, looking on with suspicion whenever there were tendencies for party members to form cliques according to their region of origin, family, or other competing collective groupings.[24] This did not signal that the party wanted to dissolve the nuclear family, however, as the constitution designated the family as the basic unit of society. Nor did the party ignore the importance of local institutions, such as the village PCs, which were seen as key representative organs of the people. As we will see later in the chapter, the party competed externally with other institutions such as the PCs for hegemony, but division *within* party ranks was to be strictly prohibited.

Party cells were also chided for not properly filing reports and minutes of meetings, ignoring superior decisions, and failing to wait for higher level approval on party membership.[25] On the other hand, local party officials were also criticized for relying on higher officials in their work.[26] During one local meeting, a party cell was told to stop "simply passing on the orders and decisions from higher ranks" and simultaneously told to "immediately activate the party members as soon as orders are given to carry out the task."[27] Although such remarks may seem contradictory, party officials explained that decisions and orders should be "discussed concretely in order to carry out the task according to local conditions." Thus, a delicate balance was required to uphold higher decisions while also maintaining a level of independence and autonomy in order to solve local problems by adapting higher decisions to conditions on the ground. Local officials were told to stop imitating bureaucratic officials under colonial rule, who "feared rather than embraced critique" by higher officials. This kind of relationship between the upper and lower ranks of the party reflected the principle of "democratic centralism," which required lower levels to submit to higher levels, not blindly, but through a process of debate.[28] As a document on party life explained:

> When there is disagreement with the orders and resolutions of the higher level, one can speak one's opinion freely, but until there is a new order or resolution, one must unconditionally carry it out, and one cannot freely change it or avoid it. The individual's submission to the organization, that is, the party member's submission to the party is absolute.[29]

This principle of democratic centralism was to be replicated in other organizations as the general framework that defined the relationship between the individual and the collective.

Social Organizations

With a relatively strict standard for party admission, the more mass-based social organizations (*sahoe tanch'e*) provided a new collective life for the great majority of people. The party considered these organizations as "transmission belts" connecting the party with the masses, pathways to transmit party policies while acting as reservoirs from which exemplary members could be recruited to join the party.[30] Indeed, many of the organizational procedures and practices in the mass organizations and the party were similar, effectively initiating members into a collective life even before they could come up for party membership. The mass organizations conducted meetings, study sessions, and discussions using democratic procedures, holding internal elections to nominate their own leaders by majority vote with a show of hands.[31] Each level of the organization, from the provinces down to the counties, townships, and villages, elected their own leadership committee, composed of up to twenty-seven members at the provincial level and five members in the villages. Nominations could be made by any member present at the general meeting, but members could also decide to have the outgoing committee nominate the incoming slate. Membership was not automatic and applications along with recommendations had to be submitted in order to join, analogous to the process of joining the Workers' Party.[32] Like membership in the party, it was considered a privilege and an honor to become a member of social organizations, and one had to prove one's dedication to the revolution by diligent effort in all spheres of life. Duties included paying membership dues, regularly attending meetings, and implementing the decisions of the organization, while membership granted the right to vote and be elected in organizational elections, participate in discussions, and launch critiques.[33] Like party cells, local groups (ch'ogŭp tanch'e) were the most basic organizational unit; they could be established when there were more than five members in any workplace.[34]

The party tried to exert influence over social organizations through the formation of party groups (tangjo) within the organization, often facilitated by their leadership positions within them. A party group was organized when there were three or more party members in any given institution, such as factories, schools, social organizations, or government organs. But, as shown in the last chapter, the party was not able to penetrate down to the village level until the 1947 elections. Indeed, Inje County records show that the party groups in the local branches of social organizations were not formed until a year after the branches had been established.[35] The party would have tenuous control until then, but the objective of all organizations was essentially the same—the institution of a collective life—and the practices that would bring it to fruition was replicated throughout, from the writing of minutes and autobiographies to the meetings and study sessions. The three largest organizations were those for peasants, women, and youth, and we shall look at each of them in turn.[36]

The **North Korean Peasant League** (Pukchosŏn nongmin tongmaeng) was founded on January 31, 1946, at a mass rally of some 130 peasant representatives from the provinces and three hundred participants from

Table 4.2. Membership in political parties and social organizations, 1948–1949

Name of organization / party	National membership (February 1948)	Inje County membership
North Korean Workers' Party	771,306	**4,984 (Feb. 1949)**
North Korean Democratic Party	184,357	
Ch'ŏndogyo Young Friends Party	282,743	
North Korean Democratic Youth League	1,052,449	**5,121 (Sept. 1948)**
North Korean Peasant League	2,448,520	**12,726 (Jan. 1949)**
North Korean Democratic Women's League	1,369,188	**5,805 (Mar. 1949)**
North Korean Occupation League	458,436	130 (Sept. 1947)
North Korean Consumers Cooperative[a]	5,180,000	13,167 (Nov. 1949)
Patriotic Fighters Support Group[a]	1,068,997	4,625 (May 1948)
Korea Red Cross Society	787,773	3,836 (May 1948)
Korea-Soviet Cultural Association	756,352	**5,182 (Dec. 1949)**
North Korean Buddhist Alliance	375,478	
North Korean Protestant Society	82,118	
Navy Development Cooperation Society	73,251	
North Korean Technicians Society	41,130	
Agricultural Scientists Society	4,923	
Health Workers Society	4,287	
North Korean Literature and Arts League	1,026	

Sources: "Soviet Civil Administration Three Year Activity Report: August 1945–November 1948," Russian Federation Foreign Ministry Archives, Record Group 0480, Index 4, box 14, folder 46, cited in Kim Kwang-un, "Formation of the Power-Structure and the Recruitment of Cadre in North Korea (August 1945~March 1947)" (PhD diss., Hanyang University, 1999), 136. Membership in various social organizations in Inje County is from Kim Chae-ung, "Rural Governing System in Postliberation North Korea: Focusing on Kangwŏn Province, Inje County, 1946–1949," History and Reality [*Yŏksa wa hyŏnsil*] 60 (2006): 38.

[a] The Consumers Cooperative and the Patriotic Fighters Support Group were utilitarian organizations for the distribution of goods and services rather than politically oriented social organizations.

political parties and other social organizations.[37] The successful implementation of the land reform strengthened the status of the peasant league as peasants witnessed their collective power when their demand for land was met with government support, thereby establishing the peasant league as a firm institution among peasants. Although membership was open to anyone over eighteen, the league was made up mostly of peasants older than twenty-eight years of age because younger peasants joined the youth league.[38] Out of approximately six million peasants in North Korea, 2,493,713 were reportedly members of the league by January 1949, bringing together more than a third of all peasants.[39] In Inje County, there were 12,924 league members in November 1948, almost 75 percent of the county's adult population.[40] Predictably, poor peasants made up the overwhelming proportion of leadership at all levels.

The peasant league empowered poor peasants to become a social force, not only as an economic collective through cooperative agricultural projects but also as a political collective, providing a platform for their leadership. It was instrumental in agricultural planning and in the collective life of rural communities, organizing elections, setting up village self-defense forces, and running educational programs. The peasant league mobilized peasants to participate in memorial celebrations and political rallies; awarded prizes to model peasants as a way to boost morale; organized tax collections and the production of handicrafts; maintained local security and prevented forest fires; arranged educational and entertainment programs, especially during the slack winter season; and fostered innovation in farming techniques. Naturally, much of their activities focused on improving agricultural production, from the development of superior seeds and fertilizers to the raising of livestock.

The minutes of peasant league meetings were filled with discussions about the logistics of agricultural production—target dates, work schedules, mobilization numbers, crop varieties, and productivity rates—which was tedious on paper but a source of social significance for rural collective life, sustaining the rural economy as a whole. The minutes show increasing levels of coordination among villages as large-scale irrigation and land reclamation projects were undertaken that required the cooperation of several villages. Such projects were managed through

Table 4.3. Inje County Peasant League representatives, 1949 (%)

Level (number of representatives)	Worker	Poor peasant	Samuwŏn	North Korean Workers' Party	Democratic Party	Independent
County representatives (19)	10.6	**84.5**	5.0	89.4	5.3	5.3
Township representatives (41)	2.5	**95.0**	2.5	80.0	7.5	12.5
Village representatives (199)	–	**100**	–	83.0	–	17.0

Sources: North Korean Workers' Party Kangwŏn Province Inje County Standing Committee Minutes No. 73 (1949.12.27), NHCC, vol. 3, 923–24; Inje County Peasant League Party Cell Minutes No. 37 (1949.1.19), NHCC, vol. 4, 371.

the township committee of the league, which met first to discuss the task at hand. Each member of the committee then went out to the villages, where each village league discussed how they would handle the project. With the majority of villagers organized as members of the league, it was common for the residents of the entire village to decide on a plan together and organize appropriate work groups. After the work was completed, villagers met again to review the work, bringing up areas in need of improvement. Finally, reports from the villages were submitted to the township committee, ultimately to be compiled for the league's county and provincial leadership.[41]

Most peasant league meetings were entirely devoted to agricultural planning, which was in their collective interest and what they knew best. Political discussions were rare as far as records show, no doubt due to limited political education in the early years. In fact, the party had to provide specific instructions, directing party members in the peasant league to include political discussions during meetings by "expressing hatred of American imperialists and national traitors bent on colonizing the Republic's southern zone by recalling the past oppression and inhuman exploitation of peasants by landlords."[42] The party also urged them to organize staged productions with music and dance that would show the contrast in peasants' lives before and after liberation, accentuating the accomplishments of the land reform. Such instructions left little to the imagination, reflecting the challenges involved in fostering political discussion among peasants. To inspire peasants to discuss the benefits of reform in overcoming the separation between town and country by modernizing the countryside, exemplary peasants were sent to Pyongyang on field trips to observe all the advances being made in the capital. They reported back to their villages, providing a glimpse of the promised future in peasant lives.[43] Without doubt, one of the major changes observed especially in the capital would have been the expanded role of women.

Women were among the first to be organized, with the founding of the **North Korean Democratic Women's League** (*Pukchosŏn minju yŏsŏng tongmaeng*) on November 18, 1945. Much like the people's committees that had spontaneously formed at the village level before being centralized, women's groups had organized in scattered form throughout the country until they were brought together under the umbrella of the women's league.[44] By the time they held their first congress on May 10, 1946, they had branches in twelve cities, eighty-nine counties, and 616 townships with a total of eight hundred thousand members.[45] By the end of 1946, the league membership had expanded to 1,030,000, organizing a third of the adult female population between the ages of eighteen and sixty-one (the age of retirement).[46] By the end of 1947, the league had 1.5 million members, of which peasants made up 73 percent. Workers made up 5.3 percent and *samuwŏn* less than 1 percent, with the remaining 20 percent categorized as "others," most likely referring to housewives.[47]

In Inje County, almost two-thirds of the women had become members of the league by November 1948. Out of 8,749 women who were of eligible age, 5,749 had joined.[48] By April 1949, every village in the county had been organized with a total of 5,805 members and 112 local groups.[49] One of the earliest tasks for members was "enlightening" rural families so that every child would be sent to school. There were 6,885 school-aged children in the county in 1948, and women were asked to make sure that all children were enrolled because there were still many families that neglected education as a result of "feudal remnants." In reality, practical reasons were usually to blame: many women referred to the lack of adequate clothes and the necessity of keeping older children at home to watch younger siblings while the parents went out to the fields.[50]

Some activities clearly reproduced traditional gender roles, requiring women to entertain and help others. The women's league was put in charge of receiving guests visiting the county and collecting gifts for the local security forces. Women were responsible for organizing "comfort units" (*wiandae*) that would provide food and other necessities such as handkerchiefs and socks for the security forces and also launder and mend their clothes. Women were called on to provide drinks and snacks to those who came to submit their tax-in-kind at the collection sites. Moreover, to address shortages of staples women were the ones exhorted to conserve the consumption of rice at home and to donate "patriotic rice" (*aegungmi*) to the government.[51]

Even such relatively mild forms of participation, however, were a source of tension, reflecting the conservatism that dominated the countryside. Women's entry into the public arena clashed with women's traditional roles and their confinement to domestic space. Women were criticized not only for their transgression of the boundaries between the public and private but for the way they behaved in those spaces. During party meetings, women denounced each other for failing to live up to certain standards of propriety, "forgetting the importance of proper service, and laying out cold water thoughtlessly" rather than hot drinking water, offending the peasants that came to submit their taxes. The party members within the women's league concluded that "our cooperation was chaotic with stop-and-go measures."[52]

Women also came under attack for misunderstanding the Gender Equality Law by making their husbands take on what was traditionally considered women's work. In one instance, the publicity director of a local women's league was criticized for "incorrectly understanding the Gender Equality Law and having her husband cook breakfast and dinner while she went about primped up under the pretext of struggling for national construction."[53] In another example, the publicity director of a local people's committee was expelled from the party for making her husband cook and fetch her bath water. It is hardly a coincidence that both of the censured women were publicity workers. Their jobs must have required long hours, meeting and talking with the public with hardly any time left to attend to matters at home. Despite what must have been their tireless efforts to complete their work, their acts were thought to have contributed to the bad reputation that the Gender Equality Law had garnered in the south at a time when the two sides were urgently competing for hegemony over the entire peninsula.[54]

On the other hand, men were not exempt from criticism as women pushed back, lambasting them for failing to live up to the standards of gender equality that they advocated for others. During one party meeting, a female member, Yi Pil-yŏ, excoriated her male comrades for not recruiting their own wives into the party:

> She ruthlessly criticized the low absorption of female members into the party, especially calling out the cell leaders as bureaucratic, who neglect to recruit their own wives and yet talk about absorbing female party members, failing to liberate women from feudal remnants. When she sharply criticized such party members as having led a crippled party life despite having worked enthusiastically, the comrades with wives who were not in the party were heartbroken and the men, thus stimulated, criticized themselves and pledged to recruit their wives into the party and to put all their effort into increasing female members in the party henceforth.[55]

Despite their earnest self-criticism, the resulting phenomenon of recruiting the wives of party leaders also came under attack as being elitist, alienating the masses. The party criticized the women's league for recruiting school teachers, housewives, and wives of men with official positions in the county instead of picking the most enthusiastic and model female workers and peasants as leaders of the league.[56] "Housewives with arrogant faces" (*ppŏnppŏnhan ŏlgul ŭl kajin kajŏng puin*) that made up 75 percent of the league's county leadership were blamed for taking no interest in the conditions of working women, leading to the poor quality of their work. It was said that due to their poor leadership, women from the lower branches of the league still did not know how to hold a general meeting or write minutes of the meetings, and men from the youth league or the party cells were writing the minutes for them.

The conflict was not simply between men and women, however, as women themselves were reluctant to change their priorities. Some women wanted to withdraw their membership from the league because they could not afford their membership dues, and others thought that "women need not participate in the work of society but only work on household chores and agricultural production."[57] Even young women showed signs of "feudal ideology," refusing to be active participants in the youth league, saying "what can women do?"[58] Superstition and "feudal customs" continued to be a problem. Some peasant league members referred to the Confucian precept segregating girls and boys over seven years of age (男女七歲不同席) to say that women and men in the security forces were inappropriately training together all night. What all these examples of conflict reflect, however, were the changes that were taking place, radical enough to make some people uneasy and others indignant.

In addition to the emergence of women as a visible collective, another source of irritation for some was the rising influence of young people, arguably the most profound change in postliberation North Korea. On January 17, 1946, the **North Korean Democratic Youth League** (*Pukchosŏn minju ch'ŏngnyŏn tongmaeng*) was founded, bringing together 250,000 youth between the ages of sixteen and twenty-six for cadre training, political education, and cultural development.[59] Under the slogan "Let's learn and learn again! The youth are the heroes of future society," youth league branches were organized in workplaces, schools, and villages throughout North Korea. By May, in a mere four months, the league had tripled its membership to eight hundred thousand.[60] The youth comprised the most active and organized segment of society, and had great potential for mobilization since the population was relatively young. In Puk Township, almost half of the population was under eighteen years old, and in all of Inje County almost a third of the population was under eighteen.[61]

By July 1948, 91 percent of those eligible in the county had been recruited into the league. There were over five thousand members, almost all of whom were peasants (90.9%). The remaining members included workers (1.4%), engineers (0.2%), and *samuwŏn* (3.2%), a tiny minority by comparison to peasants. Women and men were more or less equally represented, with 57 percent male and 43 percent female members. Most members were unaffiliated with any party with about a third in the Workers' Party and less than 1 percent in the Democratic Party.[62] Nationally, 80 percent of those eligible had joined the league by the end of 1948, comprising some 24,212 local groups and thirty-five thousand study groups.[63] Attesting to the broad appeal and mass base of the league, 65 percent of Christian youth and 80 percent of Ch'ŏndogyo youth were also members of the league. Although initially there had been problems recruiting women, 72 percent of women under the age of twenty-six were members of the league by 1949, pointing to the rapid shift in gender relations among the youth, unlike the slow pace of change among older peasants.[64]

Less tainted by traditional values, the youth became the symbol of the new age, and great care was put into their education as the next generation of workers to carry on the task of the revolution. A pamphlet for educators described the new principle of democracy that was to define the relationship between the younger and older generations:

Of course, respect is also necessary as part of democratic virtue. But, it is not the kind of formal respect that requires one to drop to one's knees without being able to breathe properly because one is in front of an elder as in feudal societies. Even now at gatherings and meetings in the countryside, one can at times point out the incorrect tendency of placing elders before the young, yielding to the words of the village elders even when they are mistaken. Such feudal virtues must be eradicated immediately. We must foster a courageous rearguard that will succeed our generation by struggling against such rotten unequal virtues that deprive the rights of young people, ignoring the young simply because they are younger in age.[65]

With large numbers of youth taking leadership positions, local youth league records show evidence of the youth disregarding the older generation to such an extent that their abuse of power came under criticism as impolite and insulting, damaging the league's reputation. For example, one member was expelled from the league for insulting her parents-in-law and beating them, while another member was expelled for eating chicken with his wife in secret without sharing with his parents, thereby damaging the authority and dignity of the league.[66]

As a testament to the radical nature of the youth, the Communist Youth League (*Kongsanjuŭi ch'ŏngnyŏn tongmaeng*) had been the earliest organization to form, on October 6, 1945, at a meeting of some two hundred representatives from across the northern half of the peninsula. It was only after some months of challenges from other youth groups, particularly those associated with churches and the Democratic Party, that the transition was made to the Democratic Youth League in order to forge a broader appeal.[67] The transition was not always smooth as some radical youth regarded the change as watering down their revolutionary zeal.[68] For example, Chŏng Kyun-su, a high school teacher from a middle peasant family of North Hamgyŏng Province, wrote a detailed description of conflicts among the youth during his student days in his autobiography submitted with his resume.[69] The local youth in his hometown had begun organizing three days before liberation when the Soviets had entered the area, battling the Japanese on August 12.

On August 13, a communist party organization with uncle at the head was formed, and on August 16, upon the joyful news of liberation, the Ŏrang Township People's Committee formed on August 17. On August 18, Soviet troops landed in the port of Ŏdaejin, passing through the village. Father's second cousin (*och'on*) became the chairman of the township people's committee, and uncle (*samch'on*) was the head of security. I was somewhat sad at Japan's defeat, but I was able to taste the thrill of liberation when I could freely use the Korean language, building our own homeland with our own hands. I joined the peace preservation corps, and studied social science with uncle. When I criticized the behavior of some Soviet troops, he instructed me to see the problem from a larger perspective. On September 10, I went back to school, but disputes broke out every day, and liberalism was rampant. When my sister's husband Ch'oe Sang-ku became the general director of Ŏrang Middle School (he was also chairman of the *Komsomol*), the pro-American faction and middle-of-the-roaders among some of the students demanded his expulsion from the school. I was a leading member of the student council, reading *Capitalist Deception* at Ch'oe Sang-ku's instruction in order to educate my classmates, but standing in front of the classroom, sparks would fly. As a result, I could not educate them. I was afraid of their brute force. It seemed as if they had conspired with the reactionary history teacher Chŏn Tong-sŏp, newly appointed to the post, to fight against the trusteeship, threatening many students and forcing them to compose leaflets. I also composed a leaflet. In this fashion, they attempted to enlist all the students under them. In March 1946, the leaflet problem increased and eight instigators were arrested. I was also detained for five days on March 25. My father's cousin, Chǒng Sǒk-hwa, enlightened me with great effort, at which I felt like I had awoken from a dream, regretting what I had done. I thus came to know completely the position I needed to take, joining the Democratic Youth League on May 30 and working as a leading member of the youth league at school until graduating on July 7.

The narrative is patchy and not always coherent, but several important points stand out. Despite having older relatives who appear to be communists, the author was embroiled in antitrusteeship campaigns along with other students, landing him in jail. The Moscow Agreement, reached in December 1945 between the United States and the Soviet Union, proposed a trusteeship over Korea for up to five years that would be administered jointly by the Allied powers as a way to end the separate occupation zones and unify Korea.[70] Despite official support for the proposal in North Korea, there was organized opposition to the Moscow Agreement even in communist strongholds such as North Hamgyǒng Province. In the aftermath of colonial rule, the idea of falling under tutelage yet again, no matter by whom and for how long, faced bitter opposition. Although Chǒng ultimately joined the youth league, it took nearly five months for him to do so in the context of such complexities. Young people vacillated between different poles even where communists had the upper hand as in North Hamgyǒng as evidenced by the formation of the *Komsomol*, using the original Russian acronym for the Young Communist League of the Soviet Union. However, as the year drew to a close and the first elections were held in November 1946, the youth emerged as the strongest bulwark of the revolution.

The youth league was particularly active during the elections. During the 1947 election, 76 percent of all publicity workers were from the league, and young people comprised 27 percent of all those elected to township PCs and 34 percent of all those elected to the village PCs, as well as making up half the members of the Workers' Party.[71] Like other social organizations, the league's regular activities included organizing study groups and lectures; propaganda work through posters, slogans, and bulletin boards; and planning cultural programs through clubs and publicity halls.[72] Predictably, the youth league was also the most heavily mobilized during projects requiring labor. Ninety percent of labor mobilization for construction projects in Inje County was done through the youth league, prompting the party to comment that the league should try to increase its focus on raising the cultural standard and physical training of its members rather than just using them for hard labor.[73]

Indeed, the platform for the youth league began by emphasizing the importance of political education and the advancement of culture that was socially useful and productive. Its concept of culture was broad and holistic, including "science, art, literature, philosophy, and all knowledge suited to the Korean situation today that would play a large role in limitlessly developing the politics and economy of the people."[74] What it excluded was all colonial remnants such as "bureaucracy, formalism, individualism, narrow-minded nationalism, slave mentality, debasement of women, familism and other feudal remains." The colonial period was characterized as a time when "there was no need to respect their laws, no need to protect and save their assets, and no need to participate actively in their economic development."[75] But now that the state and all assets were in the hands of the people, a new sense of respect for state laws, care for social assets, and love of labor had to be fostered. Politics, economy, and culture were considered to be closely related, so that the political, economic, and cultural development of society had to proceed hand in hand. In North Korea, this meant pursuing a people's democracy, a self-reliant national economy, and a democratic national culture "so as not to repeat the humiliation of becoming colonial slaves to imperialism."[76]

Consequently, the youth league's platform called on its members to work for a "strong and independent democratic country" while standing in solidarity with the International Youth League in the spirit of internationalism. None of these were entirely unique to the youth league in comparison with other organizations, but Article 6 stood out by calling on its members to "cultivate a love of labor for the welfare and prosperity of the country."[77] According to the league, labor can take on different meanings depending on the social system: "labor is humiliating and base, deplorable and unfair when the essential means of production are in the hands of a minority privileged class and is unable to provide the worker with even the bare minimum standard of living," but when the essential means of production are in the hands of the people, "labor is respectable, honorable, courageous, and *heroic*."[78] Labor was touted as a creative social force in national development and in the happiness and prosperity of the people, raising the efficiency of production as a dynamic force in social development.

The renewed emphasis on valuing labor as socially productive rather than as something to be shunned as inferior and degrading mobilized students and young people to participate in all major labor-intensive projects, from the construction of dikes, levees, and roads to the collection of the agricultural tax-in-kind. These were "socially productive" and "socially creative" forms of participation in collective life that would forge a revolutionary heroic subjectivity as an expression of socialist modernity. Toward this end, one of the tasks of the league was to "working-classize" the overwhelming majority of peasant youth into worker youth. Poor peasants and slash-and-burn farmers unable to make ends meet were absorbed into the workforce by advertising the benefits of becoming a worker and the important role that workers played in the development of the country.[79] In May 1948, for example, two hundred slash-and-burn farmers and poor peasants from Inje County were scheduled to move from the county to be placed in various factories and labor units across the country.

Of course the love of labor did not preclude an emphasis on the importance of study. An article in *Ch'ŏngnyŏn saenghwal* (Youth Life), the organ of the Youth League, emphasized the importance of reading as part of everyday life.[80] After criticizing a time when books would gather dust sitting idle in publicity halls, the article praised as exemplary the new practice of getting to work an hour early in order to have time for reading. A local leader was likewise commended for turning his parlor (*sarangbang*) into a publicity hall for the youth in his village to use as a reading room. Consequently, setting up reading rooms and libraries became a major priority for the youth league, and local groups organized programs to foster reading, including a "Night of Literature," the translation of Russian texts, and reading circles. Such types of educational projects had a close affinity with schools as most teachers and students were members of the league in any case. A large part of the league's activities thus centered on providing leadership to students and teachers, making sure that teachers were meticulous in their work and that students were motivated to attend school and study diligently.[81] The youth league was instrumental in efforts to change the social dynamic within schools so that teachers would stop using physical punishment to make students obey and senior students would stop beating younger students to make them bow, as was typical under colonial rule.

Emulating the Young Pioneers of the Soviet Union from its salute to the red scarves worn around the neck, the youth league organized and actively promoted the **Children's League** (*Sonyŏndan*) for students between ages ten to fifteen. With a membership of 660,000 in 1948, the children's league organized about half of all eligible children.[82] Claiming that "collective life had become the members' everyday life," an internal children's league document explained that the weekly meeting was conducted with great gusto, opening with poetry and literary works composed by its own members before moving on to discuss study topics, ending with lively merriment and recreational activities.[83] Part of this collective life involved taking responsibility for the learning of others so that "the comrades who knew [the lesson] took care of the comrades who didn't." This kind of collective learning, which encouraged good students to help others rather than pursue their own individual achievement, was in contrast to the competitive individualistic learning that was characteristic of the colonial period and postliberation South Korea.[84] As students took an interest in school through the various extracurricular activities offered by the children's league, parents praised the league for improving their children's grades and overall behavior.[85] Breaking down previous gender roles, boys learned the importance of dance as part and parcel of physical training, in contrast to previous disdain for dance among male students. Boys participated actively in gymnastics (*ch'eyuk muyong*) and marches (*haengjin muyong*) as a way to cultivate collective discipline (*chiptanjŏk kyuyulsŏng*).[86]

Under the guidance of the youth league, the children's league also took part in all major public events, for example, making paper flowers to pin on voters during elections, drawing cartoons and posters for May Day celebrations, and holding concerts and plays to entertain villagers during labor mobilization projects. The children's league persistently organized activities on weekends, targeting children from Christian families in order to dissuade them from attending church. Organizational life was also fostered through recreational activities such as camping. Youth league members from Sŏnch'ŏn County in North P'yŏngan Province went camping for a week in July 1947. The final report listed three gains from the trip: greater confidence in the people's committee; an appreciation for collective life; and the realization that liberalism and individualism are obstacles to collective life.[87]

Meetings and Study Sessions

As we have seen from the activities of social organizations, part of living a collective life meant attending meetings and study sessions as one of the hallmarks of daily life. A female factory worker in her early twenties was potentially committed to attending multiple meetings at her occupational league, the women's league, the youth league, and the party, depending on her membership in each of these organizations. We can infer, from earlier criticisms against women's league leaders for running around, allegedly neglecting the home, that there was a "withering away of private life." The replacement of private life with a dramatic expansion in public life was an everyday reality through all the meetings and study sessions that people were obliged to attend with a mixture of external and internal pressures for social recognition and self-improvement.

Figure 4.2. People reading wall newspapers (n.p., n.d.). RG 242, SA 2005, box 7, item 9. Courtesy of the National Archives and Records Administration.

Nonetheless, the minutes of meetings in the countryside show challenges in the process of creating new spaces of discussion and debate. For example, a party cell consisting of twenty-two members—82 percent poor peasants and no women—held their meetings with about fifteen to twenty people at one of their homes, lasting between one to two hours.[88] The meetings began with one of the members, usually the cell leader, reporting on the agenda. Each item was followed by some cursory discussion, after which a decision was made. By and large, the discussion consisted of affirming party policies and outlining how those policies were to be implemented in their village. Party leaders continuously urged the members to speak up and express their opinions in order to ensure democratic procedures within the party. But the villagers were reluctant to criticize their neighbors due to "fraternalistic tendencies" and "only a few comrades were regularly designated to speak instead of taking in the opinions of all the party members in the debate."[89]

The party took great pains to foster lively and open discussion not only to ensure democratic procedures but also to promote creativity and independent thinking. Party cells were criticized for damaging the democratic practices of the party by relegating discussion to the same handful of people rather than including every member, thereby hampering the effective implementation of party decisions because the actual opinions of all members were not taken into account.[90] In order to address such challenges, a newspaper column entitled "How can discussion be conducted well?" tried to elucidate why people avoided speaking up.[91] They were afraid, it explained, of making a mistake and being criticized, thereby losing face. People were also reluctant to repeat what others had already said, and often assumed that they lacked the requisite education and preparation. The article suggested that such fears needed to be boldly overcome, that those who had difficulty speaking up should be guided and provided enough time to prepare in advance and allowed to speak first before those with better speaking skills. The article advised that people should be given the chance to express their opinions freely and should not be interrupted or unconditionally criticized without explanation, and that decisions should be reached only after sufficient discussion had taken place. In part due to these problems, education became a priority to increase the "political level" of the people whether through formal schooling or through study groups. This goal was framed in the language of enlightenment whereby political education was necessary to guarantee democracy.

Party cells at urban schools were not spared criticism despite their more frequent and lengthier meetings. The party cell at the Pyongyang Girls' High School met twice a month, with each meeting lasting anywhere from two and a half to seven hours and with some meetings ending as late as midnight.[92] Because it was made up of high school teachers, the level of discussion was much more sophisticated than the discussion in village cells. There were repeated criticism and self-criticism sessions, which often broke out into full-blown debates about what constituted individualism, the differences between supervision and surveillance in party work, and the dangers of bureaucracy in the hierarchical organization of the party. The party encouraged criticism and self-criticism as favored methods for discovering and correcting mistakes in party work. Through them, the party hoped to cultivate steadfast members who would preserve internal democracy while rooting out feudal and colonial remnants. In reaction to a 1949 memo drafted by the Central Committee of the Workers' Party to all its members, party branches at various levels in Inje County discussed the merits of criticism and self-criticism as "promoting communication and camaraderie between party leaders and members," rather than serving to "depreciate" their authority.[93] Whereas Japanese colonial rule was deemed culpable for the proliferation of "past feudal remnants of flattery and sycophancy" rampant among the people, one discussant astutely observed that "some party members have shunned the party's internal weapon of criticism for fear that criticism could create personal distance."[94]

Consequently, pamphlets on self-criticism with extensive quotations from Soviet and Chinese sources were distributed to party members in order to instill the importance of using such methods during meetings.[95]

In the remote parts of Inje County, however, political education continued to present problems. It took almost two weeks for daily newspapers to reach the area, and even when they reached their destination, only about two hundred copies were supplied to the region.[96] Study sessions therefore became an important means to relay current news as part of political education and ideological training. They were followed by recreation and entertainment to foster active attendance and participation. Members of the youth league often performed traditional Russian dances in pairs, holding hands, alarming an older generation that was not used to such contact with the opposite sex.[97]

Topics covered in the study groups included Korean history, accomplishments after liberation in North Korea, conditions in other communist countries, current affairs including both domestic and international events, and Marxist-Leninist theory in the context of Bolshevik history for the more advanced party members. A February 1948 curriculum for the Inje County PC covered a broad range of topics from contemporary history to practical administrative matters:[98]

1. Basic stages of development of human society (4 hours)
2. On the enactment of the provisional constitution (4 hours)
3. Historical significance of North Korean democratic reforms (5 hours)
4. People's Committee and People's Assembly (2 hours)
5. International and domestic conditions (3 hours)
6. How the Democratic Publicity Hall should be used (3 hours)
7. On the Nam Township irrigation project and electrical facilities (1 hour)
8. Practical work (5 hours)
   TOTAL: 27 hours

A total of 106 men and four women from the county participated in these sessions over the course of three days, for nine hours a day. The list of topics indicates a strong emphasis on North Korean achievements and their significance in Korean history.

The slack winter months were a good time to conduct study sessions in the countryside. Like the sessions that were conducted in February, the Inje County Women's League used the month of December to carry out study sessions every day, including on weekends.[99] Lasting for two weeks, the sessions focused on Korea, especially conditions in the north as compared to the south, with only a smattering of Marxist theory. Not surprisingly, peasant women found the sessions difficult, especially the sessions on the Soviet Union and international affairs.[100] (For the full curriculum, see the appendix to this book.) Indeed, handwritten reflections and evaluations on a three-day youth league study session show rudimentary writing skills, with some commenting that "the lecturer spoke too fast and his writing was not detailed enough" to understand.[101]

For party leaders, party schools focused specifically on the role of the party in leading the masses with a heavy dose of Soviet history as a historical model. A monthlong course for a group of party cell instructors involved eight hours of lectures and three hours of discussion per day![102] The daily schedule was as follows:

7:00 a.m.	Wake up
7:00–7:30	Exercise
7:30–7:40	Clean
7:40–8:00	Wash
8:00–8:40	Breakfast
8:40–9:00	Study preparation
9:00 a.m.–1:00 p.m.	Morning lecture
1:00–1:40	Lunch
1:40–2:00	Study preparation
2:00–6:00	Afternoon lecture
6:00–6:40	Dinner
6:40–8:00	Break
8:00–11:00	Discussion
11:00 p.m.–7:00 a.m.	Sleep

The list of study topics for the twenty-five days (with 184 hours total devoted to study) included similar lessons on Korea, but placed much greater emphasis on Bolshevik history as providing important lessons in the development of the party in North Korea. The history of the communist movement in the Soviet Union offered a model for how the North Korean Workers' Party should proceed, but it was not simply its political history that was exemplary for the future of North Korea as a socialist state. Many looked upon the Soviet Union as providing an alternative paradigm for the development of a new social and cultural life as indicated by the rapid increase in membership of the Korea-Soviet Cultural Association.

The **Korea–Soviet Cultural Association** (*Cho-sso munhwa hyŏphoe*) was formed in November 1945 in order to foster friendship and cultural exchange with the Soviet Union.[103] Although there were only 3,703 members in early 1947, the membership exploded to some 850,000 members by December 1948.[104] Although the Soviet occupation and its close diplomatic relationship with North Korea after the occupation certainly explain the impetus for the creation of such a group, the overwhelming interest in joining the association can be understood only within the context of the pervasive image of the Soviet Union as a place of "advanced culture (*sŏnjin munhwa*) that must be urgently digested to develop a truly democratic national culture."[105] The Soviet Union was perceived to be a superior country, a place to be emulated by "disseminating its democratic culture to the countryside."[106]

The local chapter in Inje County was composed mostly of men as women made up less than 10 percent (217) of the 2,782 members. The vast majority were Workers' Party members (2,471) from peasant backgrounds (2,253) in their twenties and thirties.[107] By December 1949, however, women's membership in the county was up to a quarter of the 5,182 members.[108] Moreover, forty-eight men and five women in the county were learning Russian twice a week for four hours. Photo exhibitions and films on Soviet culture and lectures on the Soviet role in Korea's independence and development were also organized across the county.[109]

By 1949, over one thousand photo exhibits had been presented in the county with a total of 95,910 attendees, showing them the "everyday life of Soviet farmers, especially the actual everyday life of the advanced Soviet people living in socialist society."[110] For a county of approximately thirty thousand people, many people would need to have attended the exhibits multiple times to add up to such a huge number of attendees. A year-end report for the following year counted 268,265 attendees for 2,506 lectures, discussions, and concerts, an average of almost nine events for every person in the county.[111] The high attendance rates are no surprise in light of the marvel with which people viewed the developments in the Soviet Union, attested to by viewers' comments that they "wish nothing else than to visit the Soviet Union."[112] Such reactions were not limited to peasants. The delegation of North Korean leaders to the Soviet Union in early 1949 that included learned men such as Paek Nam-un, who had studied in Tokyo during the colonial period, wrote a number of adulatory travelogues about their trip.[113]

Table 4.4. Korea–Soviet Cultural Association lectures in Inje County, 1948

Title	Number of locations	Total number of attendees	Percentage men	Percentage women
Soviet aid for the Korean people	11	429	90	10
Superiority of Soviet culture over the reactionary American culture	27	2,744	82	18
Soviet aid for the development of Korean national culture	8	473	95	5
Soviet foreign policy	5	257	79	21
Soviet aid for the development of Korean national culture	2	97	86	14
Soviet foreign policy	17	1,650	67	33
Soviet aid for the development of Korean national culture	2	184	97	3
Soviet people are the vanguard and guarantor of peace and democracy for the people of the world	3	110	96	4
Total	75	5,944	86.7	13.3

Source: North Korean Workers' Party Kangwŏn Province Inje County Standing Committee Meeting Minutes No. 32 (1948.12.31), NHCC, vol. 3, 50. Also in RG 242, SA 2007, box 6, item 1.55.

Table 4.5. Korea–Soviet Cultural Association photo exhibits in Inje County, 1948

Title	Number of items	Number of days	Number of attendees	Percentage men	Percentage women
Conditions in the Soviet Union	39	3	260	90.0	10.0
USSR	23	3	1,440	64.0	36.0
USSR and fascist atrocity	33	9	5,770	67.0	33.0
Soviet athletics, Soviet–German War	68	9	7,309	58.7	41.3
Soviet athletics, Soviet–German War	130	61	32,202	66.0	34.0
Korea–Soviet friendship	45	11	2,199	79.0	21.0
Soviet–German War, Soviet athletics	90	11	267	70.0	30.0
Soviet–German War, Soviet athletics	45	24	2,785	87.5	12.5
Soviet–German War, Soviet athletics	45	15	768	79.0	21.0
Total	518	146	55,350	72.3	27.7

Source: North Korean Workers' Party Kangwŏn Province Inje County Standing Committee Meeting Minutes No. 32 (1948.12.31), NHCC, vol. 3, 50. Also in RG 242, SA 2007, box 6, item 1.55.

Commemorative dates important to Soviet history were celebrated through the Korea-Soviet Cultural Association, including Lenin's birthday, the anniversary of Lenin's death, the founding of the Red Army, and Hitler's defeat, but the largest event was the anniversary of the October Revolution, which was celebrated in villages throughout the county, with 17,696 people attending twenty-eight different events in 1948. Most other events were held at only one location and attended mostly by office workers (*samuwŏn*), indicating that they were likely workplace events limited to much smaller numbers of people, as shown in table 4.6.

With the end of the Soviet occupation and withdrawal of troops in December 1948, the Soviets were no longer an overt presence, but Soviet culture continued to elicit inspiration for a new kind of collective life.

Silsi (實施) vs. Silhaeng (實行)

With so many organizations in service to a collective life, people were often confused about the precise differences between the people's committee, the party, and social organizations. When asked to explain the differences, a party member from the youth league answered incorrectly that "religious people cannot join the party whereas they can join a social organization."[114] When the publicity director from the people's committee was asked the same question, he too responded mistakenly that "the party is a political organ and the social organization an administrative one." Although inaccurate, the statements reflect the role that each of the institutions took on in the public eye and the conditions for membership in each of them. Religious people clearly had a harder time joining the Workers' Party although there were no prohibitions against their joining whereas social organizations were more open, administering many of the political programs decided on by the party. Broad policy goals were implemented on the ground by the PCs with the help of social organizations while the party worked to guarantee the success of government decisions through "political work," educating the public on the validity of such policies.

Party members were repeatedly warned not to dominate the PCs and to differentiate between the party and the government. Not only publicly but internally, the party made sure that its members understood the importance of distinguishing between different institutions so that party officials would not overreach their jurisdiction. For example, an internal party document explained that all levels of the government were elected

Table 4.6. Korea-Soviet Cultural Association commemorative events in Inje County, 1948

Event	Number of places	Attendance			Participant class background				
		Total	Male (%)	Female (%)	Worker (%)	Peasant (%)	Samuwŏn (%)	Student (%)	Misc.
Lenin's death	1	34	90	10	9		91		1
Formation of Red Army	14	2,182	81	19	4	82	9	4	1
Lenin's birthday	1	36	92	8	3		97		
Hitler's defeat	1	99	94	6	12	6	82		
Gorky's death	1	238	84	16		9	46	45	
October Revolution	**28**	**17,696**	**55.8**	**44.2**	**4**	**92.3**	**9**	**6**	**4**
Total	46	20,285	82.8	17.2	6.2	31.6	52.2	9.2	0.8

Source: North Korean Workers' Party Inje County Standing Committee Minutes No. 32 (1948.12.31), NHCC, vol. 3, 51.

by the people, and as such warranted support even when there were "impure elements" within the ranks.[115] Rather than monopolizing government power, party members were told "to carry out the mass line" so as to include the opinions of all political parties and social organizations. The party saw the independence and autonomy of people's committees as integral to the mass line that would unite the majority of people in support of the government.[116] The party was considered the vanguard and was to be explicitly separated from the state because "the party does not directly govern the state [since] the state represents all of the people as a single entity."[117]

The party was meant to lead politically and ideologically by formulating broad goals, but it was the task of the government, that is, the PCs, to specify how and under what terms these goals would be carried out, and the social organizations were there to mobilize society in support. Indeed, unlike other countries of the Soviet bloc, the leaders of the local party branch and the PC were rarely the same person, leading to power struggles between the dual lines of authority; as one PC chairperson complained, "the people are only afraid of the party cell leader's stick of discipline, and do not fear the tasks of the sovereign institution of the PC."[118] Such duplication of state and party structures was the result of employing two different concepts of mass sovereignty: socialism, which places sovereignty in the working class, and nationalism, which places sovereignty in the nation as a whole.[119] Priorities for the party and the government thus competed for hegemony, giving rise to tensions between party and government officials. They had two competing sets of strategies—one of class struggle under the direction of the party and another of creating a united front under the banner of the people's committees—which left party members and PC officials in contradictory positions.[120] For example, private businesses were legal as was hiring workers, but a party member could face serious sanctions for doing so because they were construed as exploitation within the framework of class struggle.

Nonetheless, the party, true to its mass line, tried its best to preserve the autonomy of the government. During a series of Workers' Party meetings in a local township, the PC chairman, Yi Chong-hae, was repeatedly admonished for various errors, from negligence of his duties due to drunkenness to the unfair distribution of food and land during the land reform.[121] Yet he was only reprimanded by the party and continued to serve as PC chairman for over two years. Yi even submitted his own resignation as an expression of true remorse, but the party refused to accept it because "Comrade Yi Chong-hae has been elected by the general will of all the township people." Even after the elections in 1947, this people's committee consisted of eight poor peasants, three workers, four landlords, and one petit bourgeoisie (*sosimin*) despite attempts by the party to root out landlords from the PCs.

The relationship between the party and the people's committees was thus a delicate one. This was further complicated by a system of dual accountability within the government through horizontal and vertical lines of authority. These were meant to prevent bureaucratic tendencies by making sure that local leaders were not simply subordinated to the central government but were accountable to their local constituencies as well.[122] For example, the Inje County Education Department was subordinated to the local PC horizontally and vertically to the national Ministry of Education in Pyongyang. The vertical connection guaranteed that all regions in the country had a coordinated educational policy, while horizontal ties allowed room for management at the local level in order to implement policies appropriate to local conditions. That was the intended effect. More often, however, local PCs held greater allegiance to the villages from which they had been elected. Local officials underreported the amount of land under cultivation in their districts to avoid greater taxes by the central government, leading to charges of regionalism (*chibangjuŭi*).[123] They repeatedly underestimated production figures during the inspection of agricultural crops in order to prevent local grains from leaving their region.[124] Local PCs tended to think of their immediate interests whereas party members followed party discipline from above in implementing national policies.

This is not to say that local officials always acted in the interest of the villagers. Despite warnings against too much mobilization of labor and collection of taxes, illegal taxes continued to be imposed on peasants in order to finance local administrative budgets. Peasants were taxed for a variety of projects from the organization of land cadastres to the issuance of identification cards, the maintenance of local government offices, and election expenses. Parents of school children were often charged extra fees for incidentals such as picnics and teachers' weddings.[125] Such practices were severely criticized by the party as contributing to the division between the government and the people. Orders were given to strictly enforce the law against any illegal imposition of taxes and to curb the practice of eating for free when higher officials visited local offices, making sure that these officials paid for their own meals. The party was highly critical of elitist government and party officials who used their positions for personal gain, calling them *"yangban-ized"* after the *yangban* elite that had ruled Chosŏn society.[126] Similar critiques surfaced again and again in internal documents, attacking "bureaucratism" (*kwallyojuŭi*) for alienating the masses. A list of its defining characteristics included "dictating orders from the top, enjoying ruling over others, and suppressing them without listening to superior orders; showing off and exaggerating one's own accomplishments while scolding and debasing those below; only looking to one's superiors without working on the task at hand, lacking any detailed plan or purpose."[127]

This brings us back to the epigraph with which this chapter began, which described the ideal relationship between the individual and the collective. As we have seen in the description of the various organizations and the organizational lives therein, not all groups were condoned. Factionalism was fiercely attacked and bureaucracy was deemed detrimental to organizational health. The kind of collective envisioned was a very specific form defined by socialist class politics and nationalist identity politics, straddling a hierarchical class order that privileged the lower classes while embracing a form of egalitarian socialist internationalism that combined internationalism with a strong dose of national pride. This emerging collective would take precedence over and above other collectives with which every individual must identify as conceptualized in the educational text that was introduced at the beginning of the chapter.

Contrasting two words that both mean "to implement," the text differentiated *silsi* from *silhaeng*, defining *silsi* as "mechanically putting into effect in obedience" while *silhaeng* required "the display of enthusiasm and the utmost creativity" to carry out the task at hand.[128] The first Sino-Korean character that is common to both words means to bear fruit, in this case akin to accomplishing something. On the other hand, the second Sino-Korean characters can mean quite different things. *Si* means to give or extend a favor whereas *haeng* means to go or travel. I have thus rendered *silsi* as "to put into effect" as in *give* effect, emphasizing the perfunctory nature of its meaning while translating *silhaeng* as "to carry out" in order to highlight the movement embedded in the idea of *going* someplace. Let us look at a passage that makes the distinction between the two words clear.

There is no contradiction between command and obedience in self-conscious discipline, and indeed, the two have an organic connection, influencing each other. There is a big contradiction between *silsi* and *silhaeng*, however, in mechanistic discipline because rather than self-consciously carrying out the orders of the commander, it is done by force of command. There is no independent action or creativity in this case, and the one carrying out the command does not completely understand the objective nor is there any benefit for the person carrying out the command. Moreover, when a command is put into effect by oppressive discipline, it can only be put into effect under specific conditions and oversight, and when the conditions change or there is no oversight, it may not be put into effect at all. However, under self-conscious discipline, the implementer begins by understanding the purpose and the task, carrying out and putting into effect the command, sparing no creativity and effort and struggling to the end. Therefore, whether there is a change in the conditions or whether there is oversight and pressure, the task that was begun will inexorably be accomplished.[129]

The text differentiates between "mechanistic discipline" (*kigyejŏk kyuyul*) and "self-conscious discipline" (*chagakchŏk kyuyul*) in order to show that the discipline required by a collective life need not contradict individual interests. When collective and individual interests are brought together, the individual serves the collective by fulfilling the collective goal through one's individual creativity and independent thinking, which ultimately benefits the individual too. Knowing this, the individual does all she or he can to serve the collective and there is no contradiction in serving the collective interest rather than one's own. However, those unaware of this organic connection only follow orders superficially, because of external pressure like a machine, with no spontaneity, benefiting neither the collective nor the individual.

Thus, to live a collective life meant "to believe in the power of the organization as the most effective way to carry out the tasks at hand . . . to consider it the greatest honor and limitless inspiration for those living an organizational life."[130] Self-conscious discipline without contradiction between individual and collective interests was understood to be "the harmonious union of absolute submission, independent creativity, careful self-awareness, and spontaneity." As we have seen throughout this chapter, the proliferation of organizations attempted to foster this "harmonious union" by bringing people together into a variety of collectives with their own organizational discourses and practices, including countless hours of meetings and study sessions with their share of conflicts and challenges.

Although North Korea's emphasis on the collective has often been indicted as Stalinist, North Korea never witnessed the kind of wholesale purging of its enemies, as under Stalin in the 1930s. Nor was North Korean politics based on terror so much as on a form of populism, embracing peasants and intellectuals as part of a broad coalition of working masses. However much an emphasis was placed on the role of the state, modeling the Soviet Union as the exemplar of state socialism, there was room left in the interstices of centralized power for local intervention between competing interests toward compromise, particularly in the formative years after liberation. The ever-expanding role of the state has been characteristic of all modern states, capitalist as much as socialist, and can hardly be considered the defining feature of state socialism alone. Although North Korea remained squarely within the state-centric model, people's committees and other local organizations were seen as integral in the exercise of self-governance, which would unite state and society in the same way that individual and collective interests could be harmonized.

In order to begin an organizational life as part of the collective, one had to submit an application that included a resume and a short autobiography to each organization. Whereas most, if not all, institutional practices such as these are apt to be understood today as forms of Foucauldian discipline—reviled by postmodernists as the plight of modernity—such disciplinary measures were ironically the very instruments by which modern subjects were produced, which enabled the struggle for human emancipation, whether from material want or colonial remnants. In other words, the difference between "mechanistic discipline" and "self-conscious discipline" may very well intimate the ambivalence in modern subjectivity that echoes the dialectic of what it means to be a person of this world as both a product and a producer. Although the idea of the modern subject as autonomous is taken for granted, the very concept of the "subject" paradoxically has two opposing meanings, denoting, on the one hand, someone placed under authority or control, determined by forces greater than oneself, and, on the other hand, synonymous with the idea of a self-determining agent.[131] It is the equivalent of the dialectic in the Marxist subject between a "class in itself" and a "class for itself." North Korea may have lacked a prototypical "class in itself," such as a large industrial working class, but it did not shy away from creating a "class for itself."

Initiating the organizational practices discussed in this chapter to forge a collective identity as a "class for itself" was the writing of resumes and autobiographies. They were the first steps toward the construction of new collectives as concrete identities with which individuals could identify by composing a story of how one's personal life fit into the larger revolutionary agenda. This is the subject of the next chapter.

5. Autobiographies

Narrating the Revolution

I have a communist worldview, and I have been active in the party
organization because a strong working people's party that is at the center
of the working class is necessary for the development of postliberation
Korea into a strong, wealthy democratic country.
KIM HO-CH'ŎL, 1948

Figure 5.1. Photo from Kim Ho-ch'ŏl's resume (1948). RG 242, SA
2005, box 8, item 15.2. Courtesy of the National Archives and Records
Administration.

Born on April 8, 1905, in the northern city of Hŭngnam, South
Hamgyŏng Province, Kim Ho-ch'ŏl was working in the North Korean
People's Committee, Bureau of Foreign Affairs (*Pukchosŏn inmin wiwŏnhoe
oemuguk*) when his resume and short autobiography were compiled on
June 14, 1948.[1] After detailing the hardships he faced while growing up
as a boy in colonial Korea, his autobiography described a fascinating journey that took him first to San Francisco in 1927 for a brief stay, then on
to Chicago where he enrolled as a student of English for four years at the

Lewis Institute, the present-day Illinois Institute of Technology. He was unable to finish his degree, however, as he was detained in 1932 for his involvement with the American Revolutionary Writers League and expelled from the country. He then made his way to Berlin where he was involved with the Red Aid movement for a month and with the International Red Aid in Moscow for six months, before finally returning to Korea in 1933.[2] Soon after his return, he was arrested and served a five-year prison term for attempting to organize a Red Aid group in Hŭngnam.

Although Kim's life is a remarkable example of socialist internationalism in action, it was not entirely uncommon for Koreans to have such transnational experiences; colonial rule pushed many to leave their homes in search of better opportunities. Countless other personnel dossiers included experiences in Manchuria, China, and Japan. What distinguished Kim's dossier was the presence of three distinct versions of his autobiography. They provide a rare opportunity not only to examine the development of narratives about the North Korean Revolution as a work in progress but, more important, how that process of narrating the revolution as one's own autobiography enabled North Koreans to see their lives within the context of larger social forces, and ultimately, in the most ideal of cases, to see themselves as revolutionaries who were instrumental in carrying the revolution forward. North Korea was not exceptional in mobilizing people in a transformative project by identifying them as the very subjects of history.[3] Although the precedence of Soviet experience was influential, the significance of these autobiographies lies in the possibility of understanding how North Koreans made use of autobiographical practices to merge their own individual life histories with the larger revolutionary project in North Korea.

Continuing the exploration of how individual and collective interests were negotiated and forged during the revolution in order to create a new social life, this chapter examines the everyday practices of filling out resumes and writing autobiographies as mechanisms by which such categories as "worker" (*nodong*) and "poor peasant" (*pinnong*) became salient identities for individuals as a revolutionary *class for itself* rather than merely a descriptive term while new uses were made of terms such as *samuwŏn* (office worker), which became a catch-all category for those that could not quite fit the worker or peasant class. Rather than juxtaposing the individual and the collective as oppositional categories, this chapter, like the last, illustrates in detail the process by which they were constituted dialectically. Individual autobiographies served to define concretely what aggregates such as worker and peasant signified while such collective identities offered a way to narrate and make sense of individual experiences.

The major themes found in common throughout the autobiographies demonstrate the extent to which the narrative form was the foundation on which particular life stories were "emplotted."[4] Nonetheless, the form itself must be historicized to show how new narrative forms were the product of modernity, not only in the proliferation of history as a particular kind of narrative form but also in the translation and publication of biographies and autobiographies throughout the colonial period.[5] Sharing common experiences of capitalist colonial modernity, many of the autobiographies included similar stories of economic hardship compounded by ethnic discrimination, which became one of the main themes by which to plot one's life story in the postcolonial period. Previous privileges under colonial rule that did not fit the standard narrative of the oppressed finding liberation now had to be explained or one would risk singling oneself out as reactionary. In the aftermath of colonial rule, such practices constituted a necessary moment of reflection and deliberation about the colonial past as a way forward.[6] If the autobiography, by its very nature, dealt with the past, it did not stop there. It was also an occasion for the formulation of one's future purpose as a way to envision how one's life fit in with the making of the North Korean Revolution. Returning to Kim Ho-ch'ŏl's autobiography, we begin by comparing his three autobiographies to show the development of a collective narrative of revolution, after which other examples of autobiographies are discussed to reveal common themes that figure prominently in their narration.

The Autobiography

The three versions of Kim's autobiography were written on separate sheets of paper in different styles of handwriting. The version written on the resume form itself, which I call the official version, was composed in vernacular Korean, written horizontally left to right, in fluid handwriting. The next version was written on rice paper, vertically right to left, in vernacular Korean in large block letters. Finally, the last version was written vertically, right to left, in mixed Sino-Korean script on yet another type of paper that was left over from the colonial period, as indicated by the imprint "*Shōwa*" (Emperor Hirohito was known as the Shōwa emperor) on the margins. The autobiographies were undated, making a definitive chronology of the three versions inconclusive. However, the last autobiography in the dossier was likely the first to be written. Not only was it composed in the mixed Sino-Korean script, a practice that was increasingly discouraged, but it was written on colonial-era paper. It also lacked any reference to the numerous positions Kim held in the postliberation period that he included in his other autobiographies. For these reasons, I refer to the earlier drafts as "first" and "second" autobiographies in the inferred chronological order, distinguishing them from the final official version.

According to the latter, Kim Ho-ch'ŏl's father had been a small merchant (*sosangin*) in the fishing town of Sŏhojin, who at the end of the Chŏson Dynasty had signed up with an American company to go to Hawaii with Kim's two elder brothers, Kim Ho-yŏn and Kim Ho-sik. In all likelihood, Kim's father and brothers were recruited to work in the sugar plantations of Hawaii during the first wave of Korean immigration to the United States.[7] Unlike the immigrants who settled in Hawaii, however, Kim's father returned to Korea and attempted to set up a commercial business, trading marine products, ginseng, and other items between Hawaii and Japan. The business failed, however, after accumulating a large debt for which the family had to give up their house and other assets. The family was left to live in a small thatched house where Kim was born as the fourth son. His father failed to acquire a job and his mother had to provide for the family by taking on domestic work for the head of a local Japanese school, in addition to needlework on the side. When Kim turned eight, the family moved to Tongjin Private School as caretakers of the school grounds, but Kim was not able to enroll there until he was thirteen. He finished his basic education by gathering firewood after school every day to help with family finances.

His third elder brother, Kim Ho-yŏl, was teaching at Ch'angsin School in Masan when in 1921 he became "the first Korean to go to Australia" to study at the University of Melbourne. However, he died five years later at the tender age of twenty-seven. When his eldest brother began teaching at Sungsil College in Pyongyang, Kim joined him there to attend Sungsil Middle School, graduating after five years to matriculate to a two-year program at the college in 1925. After graduation from college, Kim followed his eldest brother to the United States in 1927, leaving behind his sixty-five-year-old father and fifty-year-old mother to eke out a living by gathering firewood and other odd jobs. His second brother in the United States sent their parents a thousand dollars, improving their lot somewhat, but Kim was arrested shortly after returning to Korea in 1933 and sentenced to five years in prison for attempting to organize communist groups. In 1935, while he was in prison, his mother died. When he returned home after finishing his prison term in 1938, he found that his father, now almost eighty, was "half-blind, begging for food from the villagers, their house almost in ruins." His father died soon thereafter, on June 13, 1939. At this point in his narrative, Kim contemplated his father's political orientation: "My father had a rather progressive ideology because he had traveled early on to Japan, America, and the three oceans. When I was little, I remember my father teaching my older brothers about the history of American independence, Vietnam's loss of independence, and Korean history. Influenced by my brothers' patriotism, I wished to be a patriot myself."

Having completed the narrative about his family in the first two pages of his official autobiography, Kim went on to describe his own experiences as an adult in the remaining two pages. When he docked at the San Francisco harbor on May 31, 1927, he had twenty-five *chŏn* (four U.S. dollars, according to his second autobiography) in his pocket. His "exploitation at the hands of the Americans" began at the "world-famous" Hotel Virginia in Los Angeles where he worked from June to August 1927 before he moved on to Chicago.[8] While working in American, Chinese, and Korean restaurants and factories, he studied at the Lewis Institute from September 1927 until June 1932.[9] He joined the American Revolutionary Writers League in October 1929, focusing on the "black people's question" (*hŭgin munje*).[10] In March 1932, the authorities discovered that he had participated in the campaign to stop the execution of eight black youths, likely the Scottsboro Boys. He was arrested, held in Cook County Jail, and finally expelled from the country, presumably under laws that forbade immigrants from being members of certain radical organizations.[11] His official autobiography does not mention his stay in Berlin before going on to Moscow, although his resume clearly notes his Berlin sojourn as does his second autobiography.

Kim then visited Moscow in August 1932, returning to Korea in March 1933 with plans to organize a local Red Aid branch, a Korea-Soviet Friendship Association, and other leftist cultural groups, only to be arrested by the Japanese colonial authorities in November 1933 while planning to commemorate the October Revolution. He was to serve five years in prison as a "Hamhŭng Prison Revolutionary," as he described himself in his resume. He left prison "falsely promising to stop revolutionary activities and focus solely on his family life."[12] He justified his decision to get out of prison under false pretenses as motivated not by selfish interests but by larger goals: "The truth is that I was dominated with the desire to have really done something before I died rather than being attached to life." After his release on November 7, 1938, he tried to continue his political activities, but "the police kept a strict watch as [he] was the first person to serve a prison term with experience studying in the United States." He gave up organizing but while working at a bookstore run by his wife's family he tried to stay connected with the anti-imperialist movement in Hamhŭng through contacts with students and intellectuals.

On August 14, 1945, he heard news that Japan's surrender would be announced the next day, and began actively organizing with his comrades, establishing the South Hamgyŏng Province People's Committee Preparatory Committee on August 17. He was also involved in the provincial organization of the Communist Party with Chŏng Tal-hyŏn and O Ki-sŏp, two well-known communists in the area.[13] Kim was made a full party member on October 22, 1945, and simultaneously put in charge of the party cell in the Hamhŭng City People's Committee until March 1946, when he was demoted to probationary status for failing to provide witnesses to vouch for his activities in Moscow during his evaluation by Mu Chŏng and Hŏ Ka-i. Nonetheless, he was reinstated to full membership three months later, on June 23, 1946. Kim concludes his official autobiography with the statement in the chapter epigraph, declaring his communist worldview.

Although the details of Kim's individual life history are unique, the overall structure of his autobiography is not. In writing it, he clearly followed the directions printed in the margins of the official resume form, which instructed people to first describe their family's occupation, living conditions, and political stance between their date of birth and Korea's liberation on August 15. They were then to write their personal history from the age of seven and how their social life had changed after liberation, including personal relationships, names and occupations of friends, and motivation for these relationships. They were to conclude with details about their occupation and party affiliation after liberation, including that of parents and relatives. The instructions singled out national liberation on August 15, 1945, as a key marker in organizing the autobiography, calling for information about one's conduct during the colonial period and the effects of liberation before moving on to the postliberation period. Accordingly, the first two pages of Kim's official autobiography began by detailing his family's economic situation, elaborating on his parents' occupations and his father's "progressive ideology." He then went on to address his personal history with descriptions about his trips abroad and political activities before liberation, concluding with descriptions about the days leading up to liberation and the subsequent frenzy of organizational activities, including his admission into the Communist Party.

Autobiographies not written on the official resume form but on separate sheets of paper without the accompanying directions to guide them still followed the same general format. Instructions were hardly necessary with repeated practice as the guidelines were internalized in the very act of writing them. Indeed, the practice was refined through more meticulous instructions that required specific details from the colonial period, both negative and positive, including any affiliation with the colonial government, the imperial army, or other collaborating organizations, as well as participation in revolutionary organizations and any related criminal record, with reasons for arrest, dates of imprisonment, reasons for release, and political stance after release. Moreover, guarantors and corroborators were required to vouch for the authenticity of the personal history claimed by the autobiographer, and they were directed to write in vernacular Korean horizontally. Not only did the application form literally shape the content of the narrative by suggesting what to include, but quite visibly determined the linguistic landscape—what the written text would look like and what kinds of linguistic practices would be used.

Based on such evidence, one might suspect that the autobiographies were formulaic, with a standard narrative, and that they were difficult to distinguish one from another. Not only were the details unique to each account, however, but finding a way to craft one's autobiography was a process of trial and error that could either succeed or fail. Kim Ho-ch'ŏl's three separate autobiographies represent three different attempts to narrate the revolution in a way that could effectively insert one's individual history into that of the collective. The emerging guidelines for autobiographies gave them a concrete narrative form, beginning with colonial conditions rooted in family background, then marking the significance of liberation as a watershed moment, and finally concluding with postcolonial activities. The implicit logic within this form was the possibility of a heroic tale of liberation and continuing struggle for national construction after a time of hardship and misery. It was to be a story of trial, overcoming, and triumph in which people as agents take their destiny into their own hands rather than a world in which things happen to people. It was inherently a modern account. But placing one's life history in this narrative emplotment could not be taken for granted. Narrative strategies had to be learned and crafted in the multiple drafts of writing one's life history as exemplified by Kim's three autobiographies. In fact, earlier autobiographies attached to party applications do not contain narratives of life histories, but a simple listing of educational and professional experiences, reproducing the information in the resume. There is no plot, and the attempted autobiographies are only one to two pages long.[14] Likewise, for those whose life histories did not fit into the desired narrative form, the autobiographies remain mere chronologies, moving from one fact to the next without a narrative arc.

Not surprisingly, Kim's first draft, written in somewhat sloppy handwriting in mixed Sino-Korean script, is the shortest of the three, with the bare minimum of details to provide the chronology of his life, beginning with his father's business failure, working for the Japanese school headmaster, and starting school at the age of thirteen. There is very little detail about his brothers, and only a short sentence about his involvement with the communist movement while studying in the United States, before moving on to his imprisonment by the Japanese authorities. Although at first glance it seems to be the most unremarkable of the three, the defining element in the first autobiography is the insertion of moments of critical reflection, exemplified by the concluding statement:

> As someone who joined the national liberation movement, I tried endlessly to live according to my conscience and not engage in any cowardly acts (*pigŏphan apchaebi norŭt*) toward the end of their pilfering war. As a result, I did not do anything shameful to my subjective conscience. Trying to find the opportunity to work since liberation day, I have tried to contribute the little I can toward national construction thus far.

A bit earlier in the text, Kim had also made a critical assessment of his prison life, concluding that he failed to carry out an overt struggle against prison authorities under the pretext that he was hoping to carry on political activities after his release. Instead of reflecting a confident heroic revolutionary in a newly liberated Korea, the attitude bears a striking resemblance to the confessional of a colonized subject under interrogation, with a tone that is defensive, hesitant, and cautious.[15] Whereas other autobiographies also included such moments of self-criticism—a widespread communist practice, including in postliberation North Korea—most autobiographies that included self-criticism did so as a way to show how they had corrected their previous faults and mistakes.

Thus, in a complete turnabout, Kim's second autobiography contained multiple interjections absent from both the first draft and the official one that signaled a different strategy of narrative emplotment even while it maintained the same overall narrative structure. One of the distinguishing features of the second autobiography is the elaborate descriptions of his family. It begins earlier chronologically to include the end of the Chosŏn Dynasty. While traveling to and from Seoul for the civil service examination, his father became involved with the Tonghak Rebellion (1894–95) and his relatives were all massacred during the uprising.[16] His father was the only survivor. In this way, the family history began further back in time to include the pivotal event of the Tonghak Rebellion, celebrated in Korean historiography as the largest peasant uprising. North Korean historiography has been keen to appropriate this history as part of a Marxist historical development of class struggle. The question, then, is why this episode was left out of the official narrative. One possible explanation is that his father's ability to take the civil service examination marked his family's elite *yangban* status at a time when the social revolution in North Korea was attempting to rid society of such status distinctions as a legacy of the so-called feudal period of Korean history. Thus, as significant as the Tonghak Rebellion may have been in Korea's revolutionary history, Kim could not continue to evoke his family's involvement in the uprising without also implicating his family's *yangban* status. Thus, the official version left out an ambivalent family history that did not bear directly on Kim's own life history.

The second autobiography also has more details about his third brother, who was considered a "genius," graduating from Hamhŭng Yŏngsaeng Middle School and Kyŏngsŏng Yŏnhŭi College, "giving the family hope for a better future." We also learn that the caretaker work at the private school was arranged by the teachers and villagers out of pity for the family of such a gifted student. A comparable emphasis on this third brother, however, is entirely absent from the official autobiography. Although his early death in Australia may have made any elaboration in the official autobiography rather superfluous, the details provided in the second autobiography may have turned out to be too ambivalent about what success signified under colonial rule. As will become evident in other autobiographies, successful educational opportunities under colonial rule were looked upon with skepticism, either as a potential sign of collaboration with the colonial regime or as an indication of being part of a privileged social class with the resources to obtain higher education. Moreover, Yŏngsaeng School, as a private Christian institution, was quickly becoming a locus of civil unrest in postliberation North Korea, while Yŏnhŭi College (present-day Yonsei University in Seoul), also a private Christian school, was located in South Korea.

Potentially the most perplexing aspect of Kim's autobiographies is the lack of any descriptions of his activities in Berlin or Moscow in all three versions. Listed prominently in his resume among revolutionary activities undertaken during the colonial period, he stayed in Berlin between July 1 and August 10, 1932, as a propagandist with Red Aid.[17] From Berlin, he went to Moscow to continue his activities with the International Red Aid until returning to Korea in March 1933. While attempting to set up Red Aid branches in Hŭngnam, Hamhŭng, Wŏnsan, and Yangyang between March and October 1933, he was arrested by colonial authorities. So, why did he choose to leave these details out of his autobiographical narratives when they clearly attest to a revolutionary, and therefore desirable, personal history? According to his official autobiography, in March 1946 he was placed on probation in his party membership status for three months because he was unable to provide witnesses to vouch for his activities in Moscow. This may have been one factor in his reluctance to elaborate on his activities with Red Aid, but more significantly the instructions for the autobiography laid clear emphasis on national liberation as the primary event that was to organize the narrative. Thus, ambivalent stories of competing collectives—whether it was about the Tonghak, Christian schools, or the Red Aid—were left out so as not to leave the autobiography open to multiple interpretations.

Such a strategy is not altogether surprising when dealing with revolutionary periods that tend toward minimizing ambivalence in favor of dichotomies that create a dramatic opposition between progressive and reactionary forces. However, what truly sets the second autobiography apart from the official one is the sentimental narrative style. For example, after the failure of his father's business venture, he writes about the "many days the family went hungry, skipping dinner and breakfast." Kim goes on to describe how he would look on longingly at the food prepared for the headmaster's family, consuming the leftovers when they were done with their meal. He remembers how his mother shed tears at this situation, "groveling like dogs, which brought tears to [his] eyes upon reflection." Such stories of hunger and destitution are compounded by colonial subjugation. While he was in prison, his mother went to visit him in Hamhŭng Prison in November 1935, but the prison authorities would not allow her to see him. She returned home, heartbroken, and became ill; she died a few weeks later, on December 15, before his release. When he finally returned home, his father "could not recognize his own son because he was half-blind," and half of the house was crumbling, with little to no furniture, and "only a lone chest with mother's clothes and mine were left as if waiting for me to return." Kim's long description of his student days is most poignant:

> While the 70-odd students were studying and playing joyfully in the playground every day, I went out to the sea with a basket of fruit to sell to the fishermen and pier workers or I went to the mountains to gather firewood to help my mother. Whenever I passed the school playground with the wooden A-frame, my heart felt like it was going to burst. I would go to the mountain and sit on top a boulder, looking out at the East Sea, not once or twice cursing the world in which one cannot study without money. Even while living on school grounds, it was not until I turned 13 that I was able to attend Tongjin School. In March 1919, the year I turned 15, I [shouted] "Long Live Korean Independence" in front of the police station with other students. The cops beat me to death and my school teacher cursed me to death, saying "you think Korea will become independent just because the likes of you call out long live independence. . . ." I remember. I remember clearly. I remember how my mother was happy saying that Korea will be independent and then the police chief will be run off and we would be able to live in his house. I consoled my mother replying that this will definitely come to pass.

These entries unique to the second autobiography are laden with emotional language around specific episodes—mealtime, passing by the school yard, looking out at sea, participating in the March First Movement, the attempted prison visit, and the return home—presenting a different strategy from the official version, which stated his family hardships, matter-of-factly, with very little detail about his youth, schooling, or home life.

The emphasis on the March First Movement may have been left out ultimately due to criticisms about its pacifist nationalist character. However, the overall change in tone is most dramatically expressed in the conclusion:

> Because I studied in the United States, I have lived as a worker and I have directly seen with my own eyes the conditions in a capitalist society and the effects of the Depression, as opposed to those in the socialist Soviet Union. I have a communist worldview. I am proud in front of the future Korean generations. I consider it a boundless honor to have become one of the workers for the democratic construction [of Korea]

under the wise leadership of General Kim Il Sung. Long Live the Red Army that rescued me from the grips of the Japanese swords! Long live Chairman Kim Il Sung, the sun and great leader of our people, who has guided me to walk the righteous path without casting me away!

The second autobiography is emotive and poetic in a way that the others are not, with more embellishments about poverty, starvation, and suffering, ending with triumphant exclamations that would seem to be more appropriate at a rally.

Contrary to a linear model of narrative development toward greater detail and more elaborate accounts, the official version is shorter and to the point, with no references to the Soviet Union or the Great Leader. The final official version exhibited neither any of the hesitancy or caution shown in the first draft nor a sense that something had to be proven by displaying one's internal state of mind, as in the second version. The final autobiography was self-assured and steady, confident in its authorship and the author's place in the revolution. The metanarrative of revolution that emerged through this kind of mass autobiographical writing underscores the intimate connection between universal narratives and particular stories that dialectically give rise to each other. Individual autobiographies drew upon master narratives while they were in turn reinterpreted and reinforced by individual narratives. The building blocks of such narratives, that is, the skeletal form of the metanarrative, could be found in the resume.

The Resume

Signaling the increasing emphasis on a uniform national language, the resume form instructed applicants to complete it in their own handwriting in vernacular Korean, avoiding errors or gaps.[18] Earlier resumes, often filled out in Chinese or mixed Sino-Korean script, had been relatively simple.[19] One of the earliest resumes used to apply to join the youth league included a short list of eleven items: place of origin (*ponjŏk*), current address, name, sex, religion, family occupation and living conditions, personal property, educational and occupational history, special skills, organizational memberships, and history of political struggle.[20] Such resumes were decidedly less detailed, barely two pages long with no accompanying photo. As time went on, however, resumes became lengthier, retrieving more and more biographical information that functioned specifically to differentiate the time before and after liberation. By 1948, when Kim Ho-ch'ŏl's last known dossier was compiled, the standard resume included the following forty-two numbered items to be filled out across four pages with Liberation Day, August 15, acting as a key marker throughout the resume.[21] Class hardly stood out as the single most important element amid the long list of required information.

1. Place of occupation; position
2. Name; original name; nickname
3. Sex
4. Ethnicity, or nationality (*minjok*)
5. Birthdate
6. Place of origin (*ponjŏk*)
7. Place of birth
8. Current address
9. Parents' primary occupation before and after **August 15** and place or name of work
10. Parents' relation to land reform (confiscated land in *p'yŏng* [1 *p'yŏng* = 3.32 square meters]; distributed land)
11. Own relation to land reform (confiscated land in *p'yŏng*; distributed land)
12. Parents' assets before and after **August 15**
13. Own assets before and after **August 15**
14. Social composition (*sahoe sŏngbun*)
15. Family background (*kajŏng ch'ulsin*)
16. Party affiliation (date of membership; party card number; guarantors' name and position); name of party at time of joining
17. Other party and foreign party affiliations
18. Education level (last school graduated and degree earned)
19. Civil service before **August 15**
20. Accomplishments (publications or inventions)
21. Skills
22. Political school or lecture attended after **August 15**
23. Travel abroad (date; country; district; reasons for travel)
24. Detailed list of education, occupation, prison term, revolutionary activities, military service, and unemployment since 7 years of age (date; address; place; position)
25. Name and occupation of witnesses able to vouch for one's resume
26. Positions other than main occupation (date; institution; tasks; district)

27. Elected office in central, provincial, city, county, township, or village elections, including government institutions, party, and social organizations (date; place; position; responsibilities)
28. Foreign language (which language at what level)
29. Administrative sanctions or sanctions by party or social organization (date; type of mistake; type of sanction; sanctioning institution)
30. Administrative awards or awards by party or social organization (date; type of merit; type of award; awarding institution)
31. Participation in government or organizational positions before **August 15**, i.e., *Kungmin ch'ongryŏnmaeng; Taehwasuk; Hyŏphwahoe; Rokkiyŏnmaeng; Chisŏnghoe; Kyŏngbangdan; Pan'gongdan*; village head; district chief; etc.
32. Awards or prizes received before **August 15**
33. Participation in **liberation** movement or underground movement (date; region; organization; type of activity; name of leader)
34. Arrest, detention, prison term for participation in political movement (date; region; case name; reason for release)
35. Arrest, detention, prison term for reasons other than political movement
36. Military service, for or against **liberation** (date; name of unit; reason for participation)
37. Faith, name of religion, dates
38. Family relations, including live-in family, separated family, relatives (name all family members, including name, age, and party affiliation for those over 20 years of age; for relatives, list only those over 20 years old)
39. Friendship relations
40. Hobby
41. Date, name, signature
42. Name of resume handler, signature

As visible in the long list, it was important to differentiate the time before liberation from the time after liberation, not only in terms of class (items 9 through 15) but also in terms of political participation (items 31 through 36). Thus, the information included in the autobiography and in the full one-page list of experiences since age seven (item 24) had to be reiterated and duplicated under the appropriate headings further down the form according to positions, awards, political activities, military service, and prison terms served before liberation, providing yet another occasion for both the one filling in the resume and the one examining it to evaluate one's conduct as a colonial subject. Moreover, one's own occupation, wealth, and colonial experience were not sufficient indicators; the background of one's parents—before and after liberation—was just as important. Thus, "social composition" (*sahoe sŏngbun*, item 14) and "family background" (*kajŏng ch'ulsin*, item 15) were both important in determining one's overall social class. By contrast, earlier applications for party membership had required current occupational information only and did not require additional information about one's own wealth or that of one's parents.[22]

Similar developments can be traced in early Soviet history, where in the 1920s people were categorized into basic socioeconomic groups such as wage earner (*proletariat*) and property owner (*khoziaeva*) in the aftermath of a revolution that aimed to abolish social classes.[23] Rather than dwelling on social origins, the Soviet Union took the "dictatorship of the proletariat" to heart, recognizing citizenship and voting rights only for the "toilers" until 1936, when a new constitution restored constitutional rights to all citizens. In order to inscribe class struggle into social reality in the absence of traditional class markers, an agricultural society was "reclassed" into the proletariat, which included *kolkhoznik* (former peasant turned urban workers) and *batraks* (agricultural workers), against the *bourgeoisie*, which was largely made up of the intelligentsia as the most visible survivor of prerevolutionary elite status after the expropriation and emigration of most capitalists and landlords. Peasants were also reclassified into *bedniaki* (poor peasant), *seredniaki* (middle peasant), and *kulaks* (rich peasant), a strategy that was adopted in North Korea. However, the abolition of the previous internal passport system, criticized as a form of feudal oppression denoting status (*soslovie*, that is, noble, clergy, merchant, peasant), left no effective mechanism by which the new classes could be systematically identified.

Thus, in 1932 internal passports were restored, ostensibly to stem the tide of peasants descending on the towns to escape the famine-stricken countryside, but the change essentially reinstated the identification system, this time in the form of "social position" (*sotsial'noe polozhenie*) as a form of class identification that was ascriptive and hereditary. It was kept in place until 1974.[24] Such social positions were constituted by a combination of one's current social standing, social status before the revolution, and parents' status, often resulting in disagreements about which of the three was most important in determining social position. Genealogical pedigree that extended both into the past and the future, establishing a "social trajectory," became increasingly important in ferreting out class enemies. All Soviet state employees and party members in the 1930s filled out questionnaires about social identity, including class origins such as former status and parents' occupation, occupation before entering state employment, and current social status, to be included in personnel dossiers as part of Soviet record-keeping practices. In conjunction with such records, short autobiographies were compiled not only by party and state personnel but by members of educational institutions and other nonparty organs throughout Soviet society, engendering "the largest collective autobiographical project undertaken in modern history."[25]

Despite its obvious emulation of the Soviet model, North Korea did not exhibit the kind of anxiety shown by the Bolsheviks about class purity that regarded peasants and artisans with contempt as conservative forces.[26] Moreover, intellectuals were never branded as bourgeois and cast as class enemies in North Korea. Although Soviet influence was palpable in the resume, with similar classification systems and the inclusion of autobiographies, North Korean resumes and autobiographies emphasized *national* liberation as a turning point. This was not so much an internal conversion than an external transformation of material conditions with the end of colonial rule. True to the anticolonial mass line and united front adopted throughout the revolution, large numbers of peasants were incorporated into the Workers' Party and the intelligentsia was integrated into the revolution through the social category of *samuwŏn*, which embraced intellectuals, teachers, office workers, white-collar workers, managers, technicians, and the like. The term has some resemblance to the Soviet classification of "employee" (*sluzhashchie*), which included urban white-collar workers, the intelligentsia, and state elites, as well as middle peasants and artisans, but North Korea never witnessed anything close to the kind of denigration of intellectuals as happened in the Soviet Union under Stalin or in China during the Cultural Revolution. Kim Ho-ch'ŏl himself identified his own social class as *samuwŏn*, a conveniently ambiguous category that enabled large numbers of people with unclear backgrounds to join the revolution. Kim's family, after all, was considered part of the merchant class.

The identification of "social composition" in resumes in conjunction with autobiographical narratives about one's social upbringing generated a new system of social classification as new collective identities now took pride of place. There were multiple strategies to articulate a desirable social class beyond the simple categories used in the resumes. It was up to each autobiographer to effectively use his or her life history to present a positive class identity, as can be seen in the different strategies in Kim

Ho-ch'ŏl's three autobiographies. The chronology of one's life was set out in the resume, but the autobiography had to put these events into relationship with one another through the process of emplotment to produce a narrative that depicted one's life as meaningful within the larger revolutionary history. Whereas previous achievements such as education were potentially a sign of collaboration and ambiguous class identity, experiences of poverty and prison that would have been regarded with shame and disdain during the colonial period took on new heroic significance, helping to solidify tenuous peripheral identities such as Kim's as the fourth son of a failed merchant into stout central protagonists of revolution as a "Hamhŭng Prison Revolutionary." Even if one's family background did not present an entirely clear picture, as in Kim's case, whose father was a small merchant, aspects of one's colonial experience could be highlighted to articulate a class consciousness.

North Korea thus put colonial experience front and center as the most important criteria defining postcolonial social formations. Although family background was certainly important in articulating one's identity, it was not always decisive, and the autobiographies presented one arena in which to deploy multiple strategies in reconfiguring one's family status. Many complained of land dissipated by family illness or discord with parents as a way to distance oneself from one's family background, focusing on one's own hardships, particularly in the lack of resources to go to school, a strategy also used by Kim Ho-ch'ŏl. Receiving higher education under colonial rule was a sign of privilege, and the autobiographies showed a variety of strategies in explaining one's education to dissociate it from class privileges.

For example, Yi Yun-myŏng (b. January 11, 1926) of Hwanghae Province was the first son born to a family of teachers.[27] According to his autobiography, he was "influenced by his senior schoolmates with [leftist] tendencies" while in middle school, thereby garnering the ire of the teachers, and he was "indefinitely suspended from school for snubbing the Japanese teachers and assaulting a Japanese." His grades were good enough to get him into Keijō Imperial University, where he was in his second year at the time of liberation. Reflecting back on his student life, he wrote, "I was passionate in my previous life, but it was a life without theory, and though liberation came, I was not ideologically armed to struggle to serve the homeland and the people." He ends up leaving Seoul, returning to his hometown in the north because, although he "did not want to leave school," he felt that what he had "learned at school was reactionary." Ultimately, he parts ways with his entire family, explaining that "father had a different class position than I had. I became even more courageous in the struggle against my family. Finally in the summer of 1947, father moved to South Korea taking the whole family. I remained here by myself for the purity of my class position."

An evaluation included in his file described Yi's personality as "passionate, disliking mediocre things." The evaluator wrote: "He has a strong fighting spirit with a sense of responsibility. However, his shortcomings include a weak sense of review and preparatory work . . . seldom leav[ing] records of his work. . . . Although he is eager and self-motivated in his work, he has a tendency to show off to the masses. But he has ample leadership skills. His political consciousness is very high. His ideological consciousness is expressed firmly, but due to his family background, he must be kept under watch. In trying to find ideological fault in his work or everyday life, none can be discovered." Although his family background was a source of concern for his evaluators, he used his autobiography to express disillusionment with his colonial education as well as with the South Korean regime, most dramatically evidenced by his conscious break with his family in deciding to remain in the north alone. Thus, his position as a teacher at Sariwŏn High School was secured from the time he arrived in Hwanghae Province in 1947 until the time of his autobiographical writing in 1949.

Kil Song-hǔi, also known as Kil Sun-ja (b. October 9, 1905), from a middle peasant family from North P'yŏngan Province, offers an example of how a middle-aged woman managed to articulate her class consciousness in the process of composing her autobiography.[28] According to her narrative, her father had prohibited her from continuing her education beyond grade school. After consulting with her older brother, who had served a prison term for participating in the March First Movement, she left home to attend school in Pyongyang. She graduated to become a teacher, but there was much discrimination against Korean teachers. The resentment expressed in her writing was not limited to ethnic discrimination:

I was disgusted by the arrogant attitude of the bourgeois women, going about hands adorned in yellow and white gold, looking down upon female grade school teachers as working women without money or rights, and I could not suppress my rage and discontent at this rotten society. But because of economic difficulties, I had no choice but to barely maintain my livelihood by receiving a salary as a teacher at Hǔich'ŏn Normal School. . . . Still, I committed a great national sin for some ten years until August 15 in the wretched condition where I could not but force the innocent children to use Japanese language and worship at Shinto shrines whilst feeling guilty. But, as a result of the heroic struggle of the Soviet Army, the Japanese were run off and in a liberated homeland, under the wise leadership of General Kim Il Sung, the Gender Equality Law has shown the road ahead for women, and there is no comparing my happiness, working for the ideal of developing the hopeful children as champions of national construction in the democratic school where freedom and peace overflow today. With the fighting spirit of a revolutionary teacher in search of the path called forth by the homeland and shown by history, I resolve to fight courageously until the end, throwing this body into the democratic education demanded by the students and wanted by the people. . . . Although my role is small, I resolve over and again to courageously fight with all my heart, without cherishing my life, for the complete unification of the country under the Democratic People's Republic of Korea, overthrowing the Syngman Rhee and Kim Sŏng-su clique, uniting firmly around our wise leader Premier Kim Il Sung.

Like the previous example, Kil Song-hŭi reflected back on her twenty years as a teacher under colonial rule as a choice forced on her by economic necessity, expressing disdain for the kind of class and ethnic contempt she was exposed to as a primary school teacher. Liberation marked a key turning point, however, as she triumphantly described the striking changes that had taken place in the "liberated homeland," particularly for female teachers. After joining the Communist Party in 1946, she became the principal of the local school in Hŭich'ŏn in 1947. Thus, for her autobiography it mattered less that her occupation as a teacher under colonial rule could brand her as a collaborator than did the possibility of narrating her experience of class and ethnic conflict brought together under colonialism.

In contrast to such examples, those unable or unwilling to make strategic use of autobiographies because of their landlord status or history of collaboration with the colonial government wrote much shorter narratives, simply reiterating the information on the resume. Predictably, these dossiers had negative evaluations of their performance as "passive," "ideologically weak," and "unable to eradicate one's landlord-like nature" (chijujŏk kŭnsŏng).[29] Still, there were plenty of examples of those from landlord families who were able to join the Workers' Party.[30] Although not all dossiers lend themselves to a clear explanation of how compromised individuals gained entry into the party, strategies for reconfiguring one's family background may be gleaned in some examples of dossiers with well-documented evaluations that can be compared with the autobiography to see how information was manipulated and shaped to one's own advantage. Some did attempt to hide or lie about their family background, but evaluators seem to have been able to catch such instances without much difficulty, citing "petit bourgeois dispositions" in their "lack of experience with suffering" or evidence of advanced degrees from schools in Japan.[31] The examples below are more nuanced, showing the critical role autobiographies played in opening up a discursive space for the articulation of ideal backgrounds.

Han Sŏng-bong (b. November 29, 1919) of South P'yŏngan Province was a member of the Workers' Party and the director of the South P'yŏngan Province Teachers Training School when his dossier was compiled in 1949.[32] In his autobiography, he described his father as the third son of a poor peasant family who was able to work his way out of poverty, becoming the manager of a Japanese-owned rice mill. By the time he started school at the age of eight, his family was doing relatively well. But his father died in 1930, leaving the family with seven thousand *p'yŏng* (2.3 *chŏngbo* or hectares) of land. He convinced his mother to let him continue his schooling, enrolling in Keijō Higher Commercial School in 1938. While there, he began reading Marxist texts, noting that Friedrich Engels's *Anti-Dühring* (1877) had impressed him the most. After graduation in 1941, he obtained a teaching position at a private Korean school in China. But he found himself in conflict with a Japanese military official stationed there and left, returning home. Upon his return, he was placed under police surveillance for failing to adopt a Japanese name in compliance with the name change policy. He found work at a rice mill and was working there when he "welcomed liberation thanks to the decisive victory of the great Soviet Union," a common statement throughout many of the autobiographies. He continued his job at the rice mill until he was put in charge of the education section under the local people's committee between April 1946 and March 1949.

Although the only noticeable potential glitch in the narrative involves the confiscation of six thousand out of the seven thousand *p'yŏng* of his family's land during the land reform in 1946, Han's evaluation provides additional information regarding his family background, especially in connection to South Korea. According to the evaluation, his wife's family managed a small factory in Seoul, and before liberation had operated a tailor shop. However, his wife's two younger brothers, both in Seoul, were members of the South Korean Workers' Party, and his wife's paternal aunt had been active in the South Korean Women's League and was now an editor with the *Rodong sinmun* (Workers Daily), the primary newspaper and organ of the North Korean Workers' Party, published in Pyongyang.[33] The evaluation concluded that although six thousand *p'yŏng* of his mother's land had been confiscated and thus his family background was not ideal, he had a politically progressive ideology with much political experience after liberation. The evaluation acknowledged his potential as a loyal official with proper reeducation and organizational training.

Far more serious than both landlord status and connections to South Korea was the taint of collaboration. Kim Chu-hyŏng (b. December 30, 1922) of South Hamgyŏng Province was a Workers' Party member and teacher at Hamhŭng High School when he wrote his autobiography in January 1950.[34] His autobiography began: "When I was born, father's occupation was with the county government." Although he left unclear what position his father had held in the county, this fact alone was quite detrimental. But Kim attempted to reformulate his family background by describing the dire situation they faced. His eldest brother died early of illness in 1934, and his second brother drifted here and there between various construction sites as a laborer, working at the Hŭngnam People's Factory after liberation. Kim himself moved for a while with his father's multiple relocations, but after graduating from grade school he grew up under his maternal grandfather in Hamhŭng. The large family had a difficult time making ends meet on his father's meager salary, and his maternal grandparents took him in since they had no children after his mother. He, in turn, was looking after them in their old age after liberation. He closed the narrative about his family by explaining that his father quit his job in the county office in 1942, and worked as the director of the Hamhŭng Rubber Shoes Association until 1946. In such fashion, he minimized his father's position as a county officer in the colonial government while focusing on his brother's working class roots and the family's scant resources, which led his maternal grandparents to raise him, further distancing himself from his father.

As a strategy to explain his behavior, which must have come under criticism, he attributed his "irritable and self-centered" personality to his grandparents' "blind love." He wrote that he disliked "being around people and in the spotlight," was unable to express himself candidly, "secretly disagreeing with what others do and say, growing up as an antisocial youth" with a stutter problem. He concluded that he had developed an "abnormal" (*pijŏngsang*) personality as a result of his unusual upbringing under his grandparents. After graduating from high school in 1940, he went to Tokyo the next year to continue his schooling and was forcibly conscripted in January 1944. He was unable to return home until October 1945. He fell ill shortly thereafter until the spring of 1946, and was married in October of that year. Kim began teaching in February 1947 and joined the Workers' Party in June of the same year.

Despite his best efforts to obfuscate his family background, a letter of inquiry filed in Kim's dossier exposed his father (Kim Pyŏng-ho, age sixty) as having worked for almost twenty years in the county office under the Japanese, serving as the county magistrate in the last two years before liberation. Based on this information, the evaluator deduced that Kim was able to study in Japan and graduate from college as a result of his father's status, "never experiencing hardship." The evaluation equated his "irritable, impatient, and critical personality" with his identity as an intellectual, "unable to eradicate his dispositions as an intelligentsia although he tries very hard to do so." Despite the relatively positive evaluation about his abilities as a teacher with expertise in his field and respect from his peers, his promotion to the position of mathematics teacher for the Provincial Teachers School was denied by the Ministry of Education due to his father's history of collaboration.

The autobiography of another instructor, who was eventually terminated, shows that collaboration was not a simple matter but overlapped with other potential rivalries and family feuds, serving as a pretext to settle old scores. Han Ki-ch'ang (b. April 10, 1921), from a middle peasant family of North P'yŏngan Province, was a member of the Workers' Party although twelve thousand *p'yŏng* of his family's land had been confiscated during the land reform.[35] His autobiography attempted to rehabilitate his family history after they had been relocated as collaborators. He explained that his father's position as the district chief (*kujang*) in the last year of colonial rule was the result of a new rule banning those who did not speak Japanese from holding official positions, which forced the previous chief to relinquish his position and his father to reluctantly take over the job. According to Han, the previous chief mistakenly assumed that this was the result of his father's scheming to obtain the position. When a Japanese official came to town to appropriate grain because the village had failed to offer up adequate donations to the war effort, he stayed with the former chief, who informed on his father, telling the Japanese official that he was hiding grain. Angered by the allegations, Han's older brother retaliated with physical violence, injuring the chief. The next year, when Korea was liberated, the former chief became the chairman of the local peasant league and relocated Han's family, reportedly in revenge, threatening the villagers and taking advantage of the chaos of the immediate postliberation period.

His narrative not only attempted to depict his father's term of office as district chief as unwanted and unsolicited, but also as uncooperative toward the Japanese war effort, thereby challenging the taint of collaboration surrounding his family. However, an evaluation attached to his dossier indicated that his father had been the town head (*tongjang*) for some ten years under colonial rule prior to taking over the position of district chief in the last year of the Japanese occupation. Han made no mention of this fact in his autobiography—to be sure this was a fact best left hidden if at all possible. Moreover, he made certain to distance himself from his father by noting his separation from him when his father began to live with his concubine after liberation. Nonetheless, Han was terminated from his teaching position.

Although attempts were made to frame social composition to one's advantage and the autobiographies provided one medium by which to accomplish that task, the taint of collaboration denoted by official positions under the colonial government was difficult to erase, as shown in the latter cases. They offer a clear example of where the line was drawn in ferreting out counterrevolutionaries in North Korea, exposing the boundaries of the narrative form in articulating a collective narrative of liberation. Those whose family members had directly participated in the colonial apparatus would not be part of the collective narrative. Nonetheless, one ambiguous group given the room to maneuver were teachers from the colonial era, whose autobiographies show the process by which intellectuals were incorporated into the collective narrative of liberation through self-criticism.

The Collective Narrative

Many teachers' resumes included extensive experience as educators during the colonial period, but they were not cast out as collaborators. They were integrated into the revolution through a narrative of self-criticism. Certainly, the shortage of teachers meant that pragmatically they could not be ostracized at a time when one of the major goals of the revolution was to extend mass education. But equally, if not more, important was the understanding that the later years of colonial rule coerced many into serving the colonial apparatus, and it was up to the autobiographical narrative to atone for one's problematic past role in the imperial project. Because many intellectuals had been drawn to forms of cultural nationalism, this method also served to distance them from nationalist ideology, thereby implicitly critiquing the conservative nationalist movement as having failed to bring about independence for Korea.

Kim Chŏng-sŏng (b. January 20, 1919) was one such teacher from a poor peasant family in North P'yŏngan Province.[36] He studied with the renowned Quaker peace activist Ham Sŏk-hŏn at Osan School between April 1932 and March 1938, describing the experience as the most formative in his life. According to his autobiography, the school taught him to despise the Japanese (referring to them with the derogatory term, *woenom*) and love one's own nation (*minjok*), especially through Ham's clandestine lessons on Korean history, which expressed patriotic fervor and therefore had been banned by colonial authorities. Through these lessons, Kim became firmly aware that "I am Korean," even though as a teacher he had propagated the "education of slavery" under the Japanese. Expressing regret, Kim wrote:

Where did the ideology of nationalism I received at Osan go, even if narrow and limited, that I exclaimed *naisen ittai* [Korea and Japan as one body], urging the young students to become imperial subjects and stop using the Korean language. Greater crime than that was to shout with my own mouth that Korean youth should sacrifice their lives for His Majesty the Emperor, driving the young Korean youth to their deaths by urging them to join the military training schools. Excuses could be made that the pressure from the Japanese was severe and it was an inevitable thing in order to live under Japanese surveillance, but there is unbearable shame today after liberation to stand in front of the classroom as if someone without conscience, and I regret my past crimes.

By the time of this writing, his mentor Ham had already fled to the south in 1947, as had many of his friends, for which he lamented. Despite such social connections and his status as a teacher under colonial rule, he was awarded recognition as a model teacher twice in 1947 and 1948.

Another example is that of Kim Ki-hwal (b. November 5, 1930), who was from a family of teachers in North P'yŏngan Province.[37] Echoing a similar process of repentance upon liberation, he wrote, "I began to open my eyes to the barbaric slavery education (*yamanjŏk noye kyoyuk*) of the Japanese even if faintly. Even to me, who had thought that all Japanese actions were to bring us happiness, I realized that the draft and the volunteer system were all to serve the invasive war of the Japanese." The final freedom from the "chains of slavery" came with liberation from the "decisive role of the Soviet Army on August 15, 1945," he continued. As a result, he experienced a "180 degree ideological reform" after liberation toward "internationalist ideology" (*kukchejuŭi sasang*): "Nation (*minjok*) and nationalism (*minjokjuŭi*) are entirely different, and I have clearly learned that nationalism is most perverse (*akdok hada*) and that a rightfully democratic Korea can only be based on internationalism." Despite his family background, he was able to graduate from a teachers college in 1949 and, as someone with a "sound political ideology" and a "high theoretical standard," was immediately awarded a teaching position at a boys' middle school in Sariwŏn. Read together, the latter two autobiographies critique nationalism as an inadequate ideology of resistance against colonial rule, unable to bring about independence, which was ultimately credited to socialist internationalism.

These sentiments were reiterated by Yi In-jŏn (b. April 15, 1911), who was from a poor peasant family in North P'yŏngan Province that had received one thousand *p'yŏng* of land in the land reform. He was the curriculum director at the North P'yŏngan Province Teachers Training School when he wrote his autobiography in June 1949.[38] Having also attended the Osan School between 1919 and 1929, he lauded the school's anti-Japanese motto for resisting imperialism but concluded that such an ideology was ultimately based on a "narrow-minded nationalism" (*p'yŏnhyŏphan minjokjuŭi*).[39] He described his personality as melancholic because of hardships in his youth. He was unable to go to college because the family could not afford the monthly school fees. The only way he could continue his education was by going to a teachers school, a choice he was not happy to make. Because he had only attended Osan, a private Korean school, until that point, he was the only one of the thirteen Korean students at the teachers school who did not speak Japanese, and he faced derision from his teachers and fellow students.[40]

He described the six years of his life as a teacher before liberation as a "life of poverty and deformity," becoming a "faithful servile teacher of the Japanese" (*woenom ŭi ch'ungbok kyowŏn*). He justified his decision as one that had been motivated in part by the desire to "pour love upon the children." When liberation finally came, he "felt his body heavy with remorse," as his autobiography became a medium by which to contemplate his actions:

The Japanese emulated Germany, changing the name of primary schools (*sohakkyo*) to national schools (*kungmin hakkyo*), devoting everything to the war, and demanding that education serve the war as well. When I went to Pongsan National School, I implemented a program of education that aided their war. I promoted Shinto worship, emperor worship, and the use of the Japanese language, mobilizing students to assist the war, urging donations. I sincerely criticize myself for having faithfully served them as their servant, mortified at such actions. As someone who was neither able to host father's sixtieth birthday party (*hwan'gap chanch'i*) nor able to offer one packet of medicine as mother and younger sibling lay dying, I was utterly foolish in playing their servant in order to eat when I wallowed in such destitution.

Writing about the immediate aftermath of liberation, he criticized his lack of awareness of the "correct line for our nation to advance." In his own words, he "had no ideological system, only thinking simplistically without principle that we should forge our own path with our own hands. It was easy to mistakenly adopt nationalist ideology." Bringing the autobiography up to the present, Yi claimed that he was working hard to purge the remnants of Japanese imperialism, repenting for his crimes as an imperialist educator. He ended his autobiography by detailing his current efforts and sketching out his future intentions in a narrative of personal transformation:

> I am working hard to clear away any propensity for bureaucratic and self-absorbed tendencies, striving to stand in the position of the working people from beginning to end. In this way, my ideology will be completely reformed while fighting for the democratization of schools in order to erase my past crimes and contribute to the education for the unification of the homeland and the struggle for world peace.

Some attempted to paint a picture of ideological transformation so profound that a previous life of poverty or deprivation was not even necessary. Ri Wŏn-gap (b. March 1, 1923), who was from a middle peasant family from North P'yŏngan Province, was a teacher and a member of the Workers' Party even though fifteen thousand *p'yŏng* of his family's land had been confiscated during the land reform.[41] Unlike the previous autobiographies, he makes no mention of hardship under colonial rule, and indeed describes his colonial experience as one imbued with wonder and fascination at new experiences:

> Having only learned Chinese characters at a *sŏdang* [traditional academy], it was infinitely more fun to learn various subjects at school.

Learning Japanese was especially of interest to my young heart. . . . While receiving my school education in the countryside and gaining various modern rudimentary knowledge, I came to aspire to become a commendable person by becoming a teacher like the teachers that were educating me. . . . I was accepted into the Pyongyang Teachers School at age 17 (February 1939) after an examination. Nothing could be compared to my happiness at the time. I had applied and strived to reach my goal and it had been realized. This was after the so-called China Incident when the evil hand of the Japanese invasion of Asia was spreading. Despite these conditions, I was simply proud and happy about my acceptance into the school to become a teacher. At the time, I didn't know about Japan's war of invasion and militaristic policies in the homeland, thinking that Japan's policy regarding Korea was justified. Such ideas from my early youth developed further while studying at the teachers school. Thus, I was not able to gain any revolutionary ideology, instead supporting the educational policies of the Japanese imperialists, heading in an anti-democratic direction against the people, training our nation's children to become imperial subjects.

Liberation marked a major turning point, however, as he repented, "liberated today and reflecting back upon my pro-Japanese ideology, approving of their educational principles and policies as righteous, not understanding the deceptive realities, I feel so much remorse, mortified by my useless life." Having expressed his remorse, Ri continued to detail his transformation by describing his life after liberation:

On August 15, 1945, the day of liberation for our homeland and our nation finally came. With the heroic struggle of the Soviet Army, our nation was liberated from the yoke of Japan. After liberation, we didn't have the correct understanding of the Soviet Union, failing to treat them courteously after their advance into North Korea. Of course, one big reason was the lack of understanding of the Russian language. . . . Awakening from the deep sleep imposed by the Japanese, I have finally realized my past mistakes and the direction to be taken henceforth, actively educating the children to struggle for the new national construction of the Korean nation. During this time, I have come to know clearly the path forward for our Korean nation through the instructions from superiors, various meetings, newspapers and magazines published in North Korea.

Consequently, he was given the opportunity to enroll in the North Korean Russian Language School, through the nomination of the North P'yŏngan Province Education Department, between May 1946 and January 1947. He was provided with all essentials and basic necessities, including a scholarship of five hundred *won* per month. It was certainly not a bad arrangement as things could have been far worse for someone who had professed such ardent enthusiasm at colonial modernity.

These self-professed "180 degree" ideological reforms were made into tangible narratives of transformation through national liberation as a dramatic marker that offered the possibility of a clear before and after, delineated without ambiguity. Such striking alterations in outlook are generally difficult to claim without seeming disingenuous. But narratives of liberation that effectively merged individual histories with the nation focused very specifically on the appropriation of national liberation as an occasion for personal liberation, as best shown in the following example.

Ri Sang-wŏn (b. May 18, 1922), from a poor peasant family from North Hamgyŏng Province, was a high school teacher whose parents had received seventeen hundred *p'yŏng* of land during the land reform when he wrote his autobiography in 1949.[42] He explained that he had attempted to continue his education beyond grade school during the colonial period, but he could not meet the property requirements. Thus, he concluded, "before coming up against limitations in my own abilities, I was enraged at the detestable actions of those with money." But liberation marked a turning point:

> However, on August 15, 1945, the liberation of the homeland was achieved through the power of the heroic Soviet Army, and I returned home after putting things in order. Today I think back. What were my actions and that of my close friends? On September 1, 1945, I worked as a local instructor, bringing together students that had scattered after liberation when security could not be maintained, teaching them our vernacular script. . . . In March 1947, I obtained fruitful results in the elections as an election officer during the township and village committee elections. On April 5, 1947, I joined the Workers' Party, the vanguard of the working class. Between December 1946 and June 1947 for half a year, almost 30 *chŏngbo* of land was reclaimed, working as a committee member for the irrigation project in my hometown. At this time, I realized that people's sovereignty (*inmin chugwŏn*) was the correct policy. As a result, today after the completion of the project, when

I go home, the golden paddy field on the 1,700 *p'yŏng* of fertile land
distributed to us brings forth a new happiness. . . . In this fashion, I have
received double and triple the national benefits, convincing me that I
must firmly defend and secure these national benefits, continuing to
strive for its development.

There is no doubt here that Ri genuinely identifies with the collective narrative of revolution as his own individual narrative of liberation. Noting
all three pivotal events of the revolution covered in chapter 3 as personally
beneficial and transformative in his own life, Ri's autobiography narrates
the revolution not simply as a passive observer or recipient of its gains but
as its very protagonist. He taught the local youth how to read and write
even before the official launch of the literacy campaign; he successfully
organized the local elections in an exercise of popular sovereignty; and
he helped reclaim more land for cultivation and distribution after acquir-
ing his own land during the land reform. He therefore firmly identified
himself as a member of the collective vanguard, leading the revolution. He
was already an ardent supporter of the revolution, as is evident in his enthusiastic participation, but the process of writing his autobiography gave
him an opportunity to narrate and be proud of his achievements. It made
apparent his role in the revolution and its significance in his life, which
helped him reaffirm his commitment not only to those in the position of
evaluating him but more important to himself.

This chapter has examined autobiographies as a creative practice in the
construction of modern socialist subjects, but this is not to undermine the
equally disciplinary function of such practices. In addition to the standard resume, information was also compiled through surveillance reports
(*yojuŭiin k'adŭ*) and the collection of public opinion (*kunjung yŏron sujip*).
Moreover, the authority of autobiographical narratives faced challenges
presented by evaluation (*p'yŏngjŏngsŏ*) and inquiry (*ŭimunsŏ*) reports that
added yet another layer to the information provided in both the resumes
and autobiographies. Many dossiers included evaluations, which assessed
the applicants' biographies before and after liberation, including their family life and relations with family members, their personality as reflected
in public opinion and in relations with other people, their attitude toward work and study, and their level of political consciousness. Seen as
instrumental in shaping the minds of the next generation, teachers were
especially carefully evaluated, including additional assessments of their
managerial and lesson planning skills, their religious affiliations, and any

potential connections to South Korea.[43] If autobiographies presented a platform on which individuals could fashion an image of themselves in the best possible light that could successfully combine individual and collective narratives of liberation, this platform was not limitless but conditioned by specific rules and boundaries. Guidelines instructed authors how to compose their autobiographies, and outside evaluations confirmed or discredited the narratives set out in them.

Returning to the person with whom this chapter began, Kim Ho-ch'ŏl's dossier also included two evaluations by unknown authors, one dated August 24, 1948, and the other dated January 15, 1949. The first one contained details about his private life and family background not found in Kim's own writings, noting how he supported his wife and child with his own salary, because he was the only one to remain in North Korea from his father's family. His parents had died before liberation, and both of his older brothers had settled elsewhere during the colonial period: his eldest brother in Seoul as a merchant and his second brother in the United States after immigrating there. His wife's elder sister, a former reporter for *Tonga ilbo*—a daily newspaper based in Seoul—was reported missing, likely indicating that she had gone south. Although this was not favorable information for Kim, such facts were mitigated by his own party membership and that of his wife, his wife's brother, and his sister's husband.

The evaluation also included what other people thought of him and his relationship with his peers. In general, he was well regarded, enough so to be nominated to run for city representative. Extensive remarks about his personality and character concluded that Kim was not proud, but measured in carrying out his duties:

> He is somewhat passive in his actions, but he carries out the tasks given to him from the organization without a word of complaint and reports often to his supervisors. Although he is somewhat older in age, he does not treat younger officials with contempt. Although he is of merchant background, he is relatively progressive. Although improvement in his political level is expected, it is as yet weak. He participates diligently in his studies, but his stuttering and unnatural language could have adverse effects in leadership positions. Some also say that translation projects could be difficult with the level of English he acquired while in the United States.

The evaluator concluded that his abundant knowledge of other countries and his English language skills are suitable for his current position, but that he could use further educational development in the future.

The second evaluation, though less detailed, was far more positive, praising his family as having a revolutionary tradition with their involvement in the Tonghak Rebellion. He was regarded a model *samuwŏn* with "the fortitude to bear hardships. . . . He finishes all projects that he has taken up without complaint, is friendly with his comrades, and careful when exchanging opinions with them. He is calm and unpretentious (*ch'imch'ak hago sunbak hada*). His comrades and the people think well of him as he is not arrogant and one cannot see him get angry." Contrary to the first evaluation, this one concluded that "he displays good democratic spirit in his work with experience of struggle. He is fluent in English, and is diligent in his studies, firm in his ideology and political consciousness. He is a model worker, fulfilling his responsibility as an official in the construction of our country." Fortunately for Kim, the glowing second evaluation seems to have attenuated the reservations expressed in the first, and there appears to be little factual discrepancy between his autobiography and the evaluators' findings, securing his position within the collective.

The autobiography served to create purposive individuals not only discursively within the narrative as historical agents but also in practice in the very act of writing it, which required narrative emplotment, ascribing significance and causal connections between events. To write one's individual history within the framework of the collective narrative of colonial rule, liberation, and revolution was itself a political act of narrating the North Korean Revolution with liberation as a narrative apogee, merging national with personal transformation in that process. Certainly, there were autobiographies that credited the Soviet Red Army and General Kim Il Sung for liberating Korea, but most autobiographies did not contain such paeans. It was up to each autobiographer to attribute a particular causality to liberation as a turning point for the country and in their own life, thereby placing each individual in the position of genuine authorship rather than merely copying a predetermined format.

Creating a narrative takes a lot of work and is not a given. If information gathering was the only motive behind the mass writing of autobiographies, resumes would be sufficient. It hardly seems efficient to induce the mass writing of autobiographies when most of the necessary information was already included in the resumes and evaluations. What was the autobiography meant to accomplish through the collective narratives thus produced? In many ways, the purpose was quite similar to statements of purpose or personal essays required for college admissions or job applications today, through which applicants demonstrate their sense of purpose by providing a meaningful narrative of their personal history connected to larger social goals. Some details may be exaggerated and others may be left out, but independent of the content the very act of writing multiple drafts helps the author to make sense of the past and to plan the future. In the process, past events and episodes take on new meaning as conscious choices or inadvertent challenges to produce a historical subject with creativity, intentionality, and accountability.

Extended to society as a whole, mass autobiographical practice in North Korea was a collective exercise in writing the history of liberation, linking the individual's fate to that of the revolution. Hayden White points out that what makes narrative representation possible at all is the "need or impulse to rank events with respect to their significance for the culture or group that is writing its own history."[44] Likewise, autobiographical narratives in North Korea could be seen as the collective expression of the need to write the country's own history in the aftermath of colonial rule. As we have seen in the various examples presented throughout the chapter, the autobiographies in North Korea attempted to articulate revolutionary agents capable of great feats while narrating a new national collective into being. Being required to write them makes them no less powerful as a discursive device capable of imbuing the authors with individual pride, common purpose, and collective consciousness. Autobiographies were not simply disciplinary measures adopted by the state, but pedagogic practices that enabled the authors to shed their colonial identity and become a modern subject capable of making history.

Nonetheless, that process was one circumscribed by a kind of "violence by reduction" that condensed the complexity of individual life history and historical process into a neatly organized master narrative with an unwavering account.[45] Although the master narrative was not predetermined, the collective exercise of writing and reading autobiographies served to mold the boundaries of that narrative around a common denominator, and those that challenged the boundaries were not always successful. One such result was reflected in the dossier of Hŏ Ri-bok (b. April 6, 1910), a member of the Workers' Party from a poor peasant family of North Hamgyŏng Province.[46] A prolific writer and communist activist since the 1930s, he was highly engaged soon after liberation, serving as city mayor, minister of education for the county people's committee, and provincial PC representative until the first election in November

1946, after which he became director of the provincial PC staff training school and later an officer in the teachers and cultural workers occupation league. After authoring two texts on Korean history, which were deemed inappropriate, he was penalized by the party in October 1947 for publishing and distributing them without permission. Despite his extensive political experience and creative output, evaluators of his dossier recommended firing him from his position because he was not adequately prepared for his lessons. He was accused of regarding his teaching position as a way to make money, by appropriating public funds for personal consumption of food and drink. Contradicting themselves, the evaluators also acknowledged Hŏ's passion for his work, but he reportedly clashed with other teachers because of his arrogance. It is not clear whether these charges were fair or exaggerated in light of party censure. What is clear is that he disagreed with the sanctions imposed on him, and he used his autobiography to express his discontent. Countering that his local party branch pointed out his "political and organizational mistake for printing and distributing *Introduction to the Evolution of State and Society* and *History of Struggle for Korean Liberation*" almost a year after they had been published, he argued that the party "was theoretically incorrect." He thereby justified his rationale for not submitting to self-criticism, defiantly declaring, "my theory was correct."

The mass writing of autobiographies that had begun in the Soviet Union to cultivate modern subjects made intellectual self-examination a mass collective enterprise.[47] North Korea adopted the same practice as a common path toward socialist modernity, which would be constituted by modern socialist subjects, that is, the Socialist New Man. But, as is apparent from its gendered formulation, the universality claimed by the concept of the New Man was illusory, not only glossing over significant differences even among socialist subjects but also suppressing the potential for diversity in human experiences and the heterogeneity in their interpretations, as reflected in the last dossier. Whereas the emphasis on the collective narrative of colonialism, liberation, and revolution empowered many to share in the "collective effervescence" of building a new country, those like Hŏ Ri-bok who failed in their attempt to insert their lives into the grand narrative faced censure. With the available information, it is difficult to know what became of Hŏ—perhaps he was able to make his case and win his place in the collective narrative or perhaps he was expelled from the party. As a staunch communist since the colonial period, it is unlikely he fled to the south, an option that many others chose when faced with dwindling space for heterodox positions that were regarded unfavorably in the north. What is certain is that the process of creating a collective narrative entailed both inclusion *and* exclusion.

The next chapter shows how a program of gender equality that called for the inclusion of women on an unprecedented scale ultimately led to the blurring of boundaries between notions of femininity and masculinity.

6. Revolutionary Motherhood

Gendering the Revolution

Women today are struggling with all their passion and all their strength day and night for the creation of a new history of a democratic country. Today in the streets, men, women, the old, the young, everyone stops to listen to the women.
NAM HYŎN-SŎ, "WOMEN OF A NEW COUNTRY," JANUARY 1947

In Korea from ancient times, the master of the home was thought to refer to the husband . . . . We now realize that the master of the home must be the woman, that is, the wife or mother.
CHANG CHŎNG-SUK, "THE NEW HOME AND HOUSEWIFE," OCTOBER 1947

Figure 6.1. "Women's league organizing in liberated territory" (n.p., n.d.). RG 242, SA 2005, box 7, item 6. Courtesy of the National Archives and Records Administration.

All social revolutions in modern history have attempted to address the status of women as a critical element of social change, and North Korea was no different. Photographs from the time show firsthand how women were speaking out in public. Figure 6.1 is all the more striking because it was shot from behind the stage showing the back of the speaker facing the audience. What makes the image so powerful is the anonymity of the speaker, allowing anyone peering into the picture to stand in her place—to imagine what it would have been like to be standing on that stage. Despite evidence of women stepping out into the limelight, the photo also shows women wearing *hanbok*, the traditional Korean dress. Women in postliberation North Korea began participating in the public arena like never before, and yet women's agency was cast within the framework of the home, reinforcing what seem to be traditional roles as wives and mothers. How was "tradition" incorporated into a revolutionary program that purported to overthrow the old way of life? A clue may be found in the opening epigraphs. Women were to have an active role in the *new* country as *new* housewives in a *new* home. The significance of the new can hardly be overemphasized. The key to understanding the role of women in the North Korean Revolution is to grasp how traditional spaces such as the home and the roles therein were configured as "new."

Novel to North Korea was the way it dealt with traditional practices. On January 24, 1947, the North Korean government announced the Law to Eradicate Remnants of Feudal Practices, which consisted of four articles that all dealt with so-called feudal marriage practices.[1] Article 1 outlawed dowry exchange, stipulated up to a year of forced labor for anyone who gave money, animals, valuables, or labor to the parents or relatives of either parties of marriage. Even if no criminal penalty was imposed, those who exchanged dowries might have to pay a substantial fine. Article 2 upheld the principle of free choice in marriage and provided up to two years in prison for those who forced a woman into marriage or into maintaining a marriage, or who tempted and deceived a woman into marriage. Article 3 outlawed the practice of child marriage, imposing forced labor on those who married a person not yet of legal marriageable age (under seventeen for females and eighteen for males). Finally, Article 4 outlawed polygamy and stipulated a fine of up to two thousand *won* (approximately $50 at the time or $500 today) or forced labor for up to a year for those who practiced it.[2] Although these stipulations had been included in the Gender Equality Law passed six months before, in July 1946, traditional marriage practices proved tenacious, requiring further legislation specifically targeting polygamy, dowry exchange, and child and arranged marriages.

One such case, brought to court in 1947, involved a forty-one-year-old man, An Sŭng-un, with a son of fourteen (Chŏng-mo), and a forty-seven-year-old woman, Yi Yŏng-sun, with a daughter of eighteen (Kŭm-ok). They were charged with violating the Gender Equality Law by marrying their children under the legal marriage age.[3] When questioned by the prosecutor as to whether he knew about the Gender Equality Law, An responded that he did, but he had not known that it was such a serious offense. When asked why he arranged the marriage, he stated that he had been married at seventeen and sent off to his bride's house (ch'ŏgasari) for ten years before he was able to set up his own household, and thus he wanted to give his son the opportunity to marry "normally." Poor families with sons were at times obliged to send them off to the bride's house rather than bringing the bride home, as was customary. He went on to explain that he had also consented to the marriage because Yi's family was having a rough time, with nothing to eat, and she had come to him, proposing her daughter's hand in marriage. When asked whether he had forced his son to marry, his answer was symbolic of the traditional parent-child relationship in which children simply do as they are told: "He wasn't forced to get married. Chŏng-mo just married because I married him off, and he didn't say that he didn't want to get married."

When Yi was questioned in turn, she answered that she, too, knew that the marriage violated the Gender Equality Law, but, as she explained, three years earlier, in February 1944, Japanese colonial officers had come to recruit unmarried girls (possibly as "comfort women"), which led her to arrange with her neighbor An to have their children engaged to prevent her daughter from being taken away. When her harvest the previous year had failed due to floods, she had asked An twice for the marriage of their children, to which he finally agreed. She reasoned that since her daughter would eventually have to be married off anyway and was thus already "someone else's person" (nam ŭi saram in manch'i tŏ tulgŏt ŏpta), there was no point in keeping her further. Through the marriage, she had hoped to have her daughter fed and perhaps secure some help for herself. When asked whether she had inquired into her daughter's wishes, she replied, "When I asked my daughter, she said that she would marry perhaps because there was nothing to eat, and so I married her off." Since the case had been brought to court, the children had been separated and the daughter had returned to live with her mother. The prosecution demanded six months' imprisonment for both An and Yi, but they were given suspended sentences because "the defendants seem to have realized their mistakes."

This case and others like it illustrate how certain practices were condemned as "feudal." But no legislation or political campaign in North Korea ever denounced tradition or domesticity as in the Soviet Union when the private home was attacked as capitalist, leading to campaigns such as the "Down with Domestic Trash" in the late 1920s, while China condemned the family as the source of women's oppression during the 1960s

Cultural Revolution and the 1970s Anti-Confucian Campaign, aligning nationalism, feminism, and Marxism against tradition.[4] In North Korea, the family was not targeted as the source of women's oppression, but came to symbolize the Korean nation itself. As postcolonial studies have amply shown, women and the home in colonial contexts have often been privileged sites. Partha Chatterjee notably differentiated the "inner" cultural, spiritual identity from the "outer" material, technological prowess as two domains delineated by anticolonial nationalist writers in the development of Indian nationalism. The outer realm was the site of struggle for political power, while the inner domain provided the sovereign territory that gave birth to the nation as an imagined community.[5]

Although conventional histories of nationalism have privileged the public domain, the public and private comprised two sides of the same coin, both integral to the development of the nation. States with national sovereignty privileged the public sphere in its expression of sovereignty, whereas anticolonial nationalisms placed special weight on the "inner" realm—"not [as] a complementary but rather the original site on which the hegemonic project of nationalism was launched."[6] Domestic and feminine spaces were deemed outside of colonial purview, offering safe havens with greater potential for subversion. Indeed, women writers in colonial Korea managed to gain ground in publications as male writers were subjected to harsher surveillance and censorship; stories about "able" women and "disabled" men became prominent themes in colonial literature.[7]

Thus, contrary to conventional depictions of nationalism as masculine, the emerging form of North Korean nationalism blurred the boundaries between masculinity and femininity as women became embodiments of the nation. In the process, North Korea's relationship to the past became deeply ambivalent when the revolution aimed to overcome the past. The resulting compromise allowed North Korea's policy, adopting Marxist historiography, to target "feudal and colonial remnants" and "feudal relations" between men and women, but not tradition in toto. The Gender Equality Law outlawed concubinage, child marriage, and prostitution as feudal and colonial practices, but nowhere was there any reference to Confucian tradition or the family as a source of social ills. The family did not "wither away" under communism, as Engels had prescribed, but instead endured as the building block of North Korean communism.

Whereas the status of women in social revolutions often hinges on the extent to which they were "liberated," this chapter shifts the focus of investigation to the historical mechanisms by which feminine subjectivities were created and shaped rather than assuming that there was an authentic female subject to be liberated at all. What sets North Korea apart from other historical examples of social revolutions in handling the "woman question" lies in the contradictory deployment of tradition, shifting the meaning of motherhood and thereby the overall gender scheme as both women and men were to identify with mothers. In North Korea, motherhood became the primary trope by which to construct not only women's revolutionary subjectivity but that of all North Koreans, as everyone was extolled to emulate mothers as the most sacrificial model citizen. This is entirely different from representations of revolutionary brotherhood in the images of the masculine worker or peasant during the Bolshevik and Chinese Revolutions when women were extolled to become like men, never suggesting "even in the most utopian movements that men should learn from women."[8] By contrast, the figure of revolutionary mother became the quintessential icon of North Korean subjectivity, melding the old and the new. What requires explanation is precisely how motherhood was able to embody a revolutionary potential.

Untangling the woman question in North Korea in the late 1940s is enormously complicated by its position at the intersection of Japanese colonial rule and Soviet occupation, while bordering China's brewing revolution. North Korea combined these legacies in its own distinctive way to produce a singular example of socialist modernity that was inflected like no other by tradition. This chapter begins with a comparative examination of earlier references to motherhood before exploring just how North Korean women were mobilized as revolutionary mothers by looking at *Chosŏn yŏsŏng* (Korean Woman), the only women's journal published in North Korea in the immediate postliberation period.[9] It is clear from its earliest issues in 1946 that motherhood was being made to symbolize the revolutionary subject, not only for women but also for the rest of North Korean society, as the most unconditional form of sacrifice. This remaking of motherhood as a public persona would not have been possible without the colonial experience, which served to privilege women and the domestic sphere, laying the groundwork for Soviet influences to take root quite differently from other revolutions, including that of the Soviet Union itself.

"Wise Mother Good Wife"

Although Korea's long tradition of Confucianism is often touted as the main reason for the seeming persistence of traditional gender roles in the country, there is little explanation of why this should be the case in North Korea during a period of social upheaval aimed at discarding the past.[10] Sonia Ryang argues that it is not the legacy of Confucianism that is at the heart of the construction of women primarily as mothers, but rather the distinct cult of leadership and patriarchal discourses surrounding this phenomenon that replaces the category of "woman" with "motherhood," in which femininity is equated with maternity, "effacing the notion of gender altogether from the surface of the state politics."[11] Ryang concludes that "debate on the 'woman question' was almost non-existent," and that the legal measures for gender equality were pushed from the top down without the participation of North Korean women. But, of course, motherhood is hardly devoid of issues of gender. This chapter shows just how the "woman question" *did* in fact become a source of heated debate in North Korea in the postliberation period, involving North Korean women from all strata and revealing enormous challenges in the reconfiguration of gender relations.

It also bears remembering that "gender" is a relatively new term, and has no equivalent in Korean, as Ryang readily admits. Gender as a concept distinct from sex is rooted in twentieth-century Western feminist theory. As the concept traveled to East Asia, it was often translated as "sex difference" (*sŏngbyŏl*), conflating the distinction between sex and gender, which has led to the more recent transliteration as *chendŏ* in order to preserve the significance of social as opposed to biological difference. Gender as a category of social analysis is thus not so much "effaced" or cast into "oblivion" in North Korea, as Ryang suggests, but it has yet to become part of their lexicon. In regard to such phenomena, Heidi Hartmann has aptly differentiated the "woman question" from the "feminist question" by pointing out that most Marxist experiments have attempted to solve the woman question without dealing with the feminist one.[12] That is, women's participation in the social, economic, and political arenas was fostered without fundamentally questioning the social differentiation between women and men. Ultimately, Ryang's analysis equates North Korea's emphasis on family and motherhood with gender inequality without demonstrating how one leads to the other. However, North Korea was not alone in its use of motherhood, and a proper historical context will help situate the significance of motherhood in North Korea, not simply as a sign of women's oppression, but as part of the overall construction of gender.

Motherhood was a pervasive trope in the construction of women's identities throughout the world in the first half of the twentieth century, as it was increasingly subjected to state policy as part of the modernizing project. Throughout the nineteenth century, foundations were progressively laid on which the state could build its capacity for governmentality, among them the compilation of the census. With the effects of industrialization and mass warfare, particularly in the interwar period, states throughout the world began to associate national power with a large and disciplined population at the same time that fertility was declining due to urbanization and women's entry into industrial jobs. The consequence was a marked interest in state management of family life and reproduction, with heightened emphasis on motherhood and domesticity as ways to increase the population.[13] In Britain, for example, as the modernizing project came to be adopted by upper-class women in the construction of the ideal woman, motherhood became "mothercraft," by which lower-class women were trained to be modern wives and mothers with the appropriate scientific knowledge to set up a proper modern home.[14]

Likewise, Japan had embarked on full-scale industrialization beginning in 1868 with the Meiji Restoration, so that by the time it colonized Korea in 1910, the traditional extended family was fast being replaced by the nuclear middle-class family.[15] The need to create modern national subjects, disciplined and ready to answer the call of the state, whether as workers or soldiers, prompted ideologues to see women's education as integral to the training of proper mothers for the new generation. The construction of this foundation for a strong modern nation-state was to begin by exposing women to the "wise mother good wife" ideology. Contrary to the conventional understanding that the idea was derived from Confucianism, the role of "wise mother good wife" was a modern ideological construct for the education and mobilization of women in the period of modern state formation.[16]

Indeed, the modern formulation of the "wise mother good wife" stood in stark contrast to the Confucian tradition, which had prioritized filial piety, that is, the role of the daughter rather than the wife or mother. The parent-child relationship, which had taken precedence over the ruler-subject relationship under neo-Confucianism as practiced in Korea, was overturned by a new emphasis on the role of wife and mother. The "wise mother good wife," which was used in Japan as the embodiment of national essence and purity, became in the context of colonial Korea a way of molding women as subjects of the Japanese emperor, as loyal wife and nurturing mother to the Japanese Empire rather than to the family. The allegiance to the family clan, expressed through ancestor worship and filial piety, had to be broken by a future-oriented, forward-looking emphasis on the next generation that could cut the ties to the past rooted in family history. For this purpose, in the early 1900s biographies of French hero-ines Jean d'Arc and Madame Roland were translated and widely distrib-uted in vernacular Korean as examples of patriotic women that Korean women should emulate.[17] The "wise mother good wife" was, in effect, a key element in the making of a modern gendered citizenship that in-scribed women as at once mothers who nurture their children to become national subjects and as wives who, by taking care of the domestic hearth, enable men to participate as citizens of the nation-state. Women's repro-ductive roles made them eligible for national citizenship, fusing duties to the household to the nation-state.

By the mid-1930s, not only had the Soviet Union begun to rein in the liberal policies on marriage and divorce from the revolutionary pe-riod, but the Chinese Communist Party also began to change its policies, from viewing women as "new liberated women" to seeing them as "true revolutionary women," defined by filial piety, chastity, and motherhood.[18] For colonial Korea, however, the attempted fusion of family with national identity was tenuous at best precisely because of the contradiction between nationality and citizenship for the colonial subject. One's family member-ship, represented through the Korean surname, resulted in second-class status within the imperial order. By contrast, in Japan, the wartime mobi-lization of women as sacrificing mothers provided opportunities for Japa-nese women to become imperial citizens like men, enlarging their scope of participation in the economic and political arenas with greater voting rights and maternity benefits.[19] As almost sixteen million women were mobilized to join the Great Japan Women's Association, "more women participated actively in public life during World War II than at any time before or since."[20]

The brief popularity of New Women and Modern Girls in the 1920s gave way to the resurgence of the "wise mother good wife" as a way to mobilize women to become the rear guard in the imperial war effort.[21] The New Woman became an imported identity from the West with un-certain nationality and allegiance. Traditional women were the pure em-bodiments of the nation as opposed to the New Women who were deemed "sexually promiscuous, immoral, impure, individualistic, unproductive, and corrupt, easily swayed by outside forces."[22] Women were thus molded into an all-sacrificing mother, recruited into the war effort as protectors of the home front. In colonial Korea, too, the onset of total war mobiliza-tion breached the final barrier maintained by the traditional household as the family became the primary unit of mobilization in the National Spirit Total Mobilization Movement.[23]

In order to bring Korean women into the imperial fold, the colonial government launched extensive propaganda campaigns to switch the allegiance of Korean mothers from their families to the Japanese Empire. Countless Korean writers were mobilized to produce stories of motherly sacrifice. In a 1942 text, *Mother of a Military Nation (Kun'guk ŭi ŏmŏni)*, Pak T'ae-wŏn wrote:

> Has it occurred to you that the precious sons that you consider your own are in actuality not your own, but gratefully are the Imperial Majesty's precious sons. . . . They are sons that you are temporarily in charge of nurturing on behalf of the orders of the Majesty. Let's be sure to raise them unashamedly as future national soldiers, thereby offering them back to the Majesty in gratitude and glory when he calls. . . . You must learn from and model yourselves after Japanese mothers.[24]

But, try as they might, writers could not bypass the realities on the ground. Ch'oe Chŏng-hŭi's 1942 pro-Japanese short story, *Wild Chrysanthemums (Yagukch'o)*, still betrayed the difficulties the empire faced in recruiting voluntary Korean military conscripts because "always the mother's opposition is the greatest." This led to "bad behavior" or desertion by the few that made it into the volunteer corps. The story urged mothers to look beyond immediate family interests and their "blind love" for their sons toward a "larger and brilliant future" for the empire.[25] But Korean mothers could not be made to emulate Japanese mothers since their colonial subjection had by the 1940s become apparent through much-hated policies such as the forcible changing of Korean names into Japanese ones, regulations against using the Korean language, and mandatory worship at Shinto shrines that venerated Japanese ancestors. Nothing reveals the difference between colonial and postcolonial mobilization more than the difficulties faced by the colonial government in harnessing motherly duties as part of women's nationality. In effect, mothers resisted imperial demands as their families were exposed to the expropriation of foodstuffs and the forced conscription of family members as workers, soldiers, and "comfort women."

Such difficulties notwithstanding, women were organized into women's associations and encouraged to join women's work groups.[26] In order to facilitate women's entry into the workforce, domestic work was collectivized by organizing childcare centers and group kitchens, and, to reduce laundry, dark work clothes replaced the traditional white peasant attire. As in Japan, Patriotic Women's Associations (*Aeguk puinhoe*) were organized

across the peninsula and placed in charge of the home front: they provided medical care to soldiers, publicized the war effort, provided aid to
pregnant women, managed educational and correctional facilities, rescued
destitute children, prevented fires, organized mass rallies, distributed daily
necessities, and collected "patriotic" donations, in addition to more mundane tasks such as street cleaning and road repair.[27] The absence of men
due to mandatory conscription and the increasing shortage of labor freed
women from former patriarchal constraints, which enabled them to enter
the public arena, laying the foundation for the mobilization of women in
the postliberation period. The mass mobilization of women thus began
under colonial rule. Wartime mobilization provided many women with
their first experiences of being engaged by the modern state, however
reluctantly. This colonial legacy was appropriated and redeployed after
liberation for the mobilization of women, this time not as colonial subjects
but as national subjects in both North and South Korea. That North Korea
was able to successfully fuse women's domestic duties with women's roles
as modern national subjects had much to do with the extension of the family as a form of national identity, giving credence to the pervasive imagery
of the family in North Korean politics. Indeed, the country's leader, Kim
Il Sung, was soon to be referred to as ŏbŏi suryŏng, or "parently leader," a
leader who is both father and mother.

National Liberation as Women's Liberation

Colonial legacies were not limited to conservative ideas such as "wise
mother good wife," but also included the birth of socialist ideals. Growing
hardship in the first decade of colonial rule rendered the October Revolution of 1917 particularly compelling as an alternative model, intensified by
the failure of the March First Movement in 1919 to achieve independence
through peaceful means. The anticolonial movement took a radical turn
with the proliferation of socialist and communist ideas in the 1920s. Split-
ting away from the more moderate nationalists, socialist women organized
the Korean Women's Socialist League (Chosŏn yŏsŏng tonguhoe) in 1924 as
the first socialist women's organization in Korea.[28] For women who were
seeking alternatives to the conservative nationalist movement, the socialist
women's movement seemed to offer an approach that placed the majority of women at the heart of its program, combining national liberation
with the "liberation of propertyless women" as its primary objective. The
"propertyless" class was quite intentionally broad-based, including not

only peasants and workers but also intellectuals and students. The crux of their activities centered around publicizing women's issues through lectures, study groups, and gatherings on occasions such as International Women's Day on March 8.

In July 1927, the formation of Kŭnuhoe took the organization of women to the next level by bringing together nationalist and socialist women in a united front.[29] It called for an end to discrimination against women and to "feudal" practices such as early and arranged marriages while also advocating the protection of the rights of female peasants and workers. Its platform demanded:

1. Eradication of all social and legal discrimination against women
2. End of all feudal customs and superstition
3. Abolition of early marriage and establishment of free choice in marriage
4. Abolition of sale of women and licensed prostitution
5. Protection of economic interests for female peasants
6. Abolition of wage discrimination against female workers and institution of paid maternity leave
7. Abolition of night work and dangerous labor for female and child workers

When the socialists gained the upper hand within the group in 1929, four new items were added to the action plan, including the right to education, divorce, childcare, and health care. North Korea addressed these same issues through the Gender Equality Law and the Labor Law in 1946. Hŏ Chŏng-suk played a critical role as one of the main figures in both the Socialist League and the Kŭnuhoe, and she became one of the highest-ranking female leaders in the new North Korean government in the postliberation period, showing a degree of continuity among women activists.[30]

Members of the North Korean Democratic Women's League made concerted efforts to implement the new laws that improved the lives of women. Similar to the anticolonial movement, women's interests were framed in terms of founding a "wealthy and strong country." The platform adopted during the league's first congress in May 1946 called on members to focus on national construction, concentrating all their capacities on the establishment of a democratic republic in Korea by supporting the political program of the North Korean People's Committee. This included "struggling against the Japanese fascist elements and national traitors" as obstacles to the democratic construction of the country; cultivating Korean culture, politics, and economy; actively working to eradicate women's illiteracy; and striving to "overthrow feudal customs and superstition."[31] The league's activities reflected the focus on national construction: women were mobilized for construction projects and education campaigns, tax collection, gifts and donations for local orphanages and the security corps, tours to the countryside, and whatever else might be required in the building of a new country. The increasing role of women in national construction was formalized by two critical pieces of legislation that dealt specifically with the woman question.

Drafted and passed by the North Korean People's Committee, the Labor Law and the Law of Equal Rights for Men and Women (hereafter, the Gender Equality Law) laid out the basic framework by which women's roles would be defined in North Korean society as workers and mothers. The Labor Law, promulgated on June 24, 1946, included special stipulations for the protection of children and mothers, in addition to the basic clauses for an eight-hour workday, paid vacations, equal pay for equal work, and improvements in working conditions including health insurance. The clauses specific to women provided paid maternity leave for thirty-five days before, and forty-two days after, delivery; lighter work for expecting women beginning in the sixth month of pregnancy; and nursing breaks for thirty minutes twice a day for women with children under a year old.[32] It also prohibited pregnant and nursing women from working overtime at night. Maternity was carefully protected since women were expected to work while also embracing motherhood.

The same emphasis on the family can be seen in the Gender Equality Law, passed a month after the Labor Law, on July 30, 1946.[33] The full text of the law reads:

> Article 1: Women have equal rights to men economically, culturally, socially, and politically in all areas of life of the nation.
>
> Article 2: Women have the same rights as men to vote and be elected in the regional as well as the highest national organs.
>
> Article 3: Women have the same rights as men to workers rights, equal wages, social insurance, and education.
>
> Article 4: Women, like men, have the right to free marriage. Unfree and forced marriage without the consent of those marrying is prohibited.
>
> Article 5: When it becomes difficult to continue the married relationship, women have the same rights as men to free divorce.

The right to litigation to demand child support payments from the ex-husband is acknowledged, and such cases shall be processed at the People's Court.

Article 6: The legal marriageable age shall begin at seventeen for women and eighteen for men.

Article 7: Polygamy is a feudal practice from the Middle Ages and sales of women as wives or concubines are hereby prohibited as evil practices that violate women's rights. Licensed prostitution, private prostitution, and the *kisaeng* [female entertainer] system—*kisaeng* licenses and schools—are prohibited.

Article 8: Women have the same rights as men to inherit property and land, and women have the right to be given their share of property and land in case of divorce.

Article 9: All Japanese imperial laws and regulations pertaining to Korean women's rights are null and void as of the promulgation of this law. This law takes effect as of the day of promulgation.[34]

Articles 4 through 8 had to do with family law, regulating marriage and divorce, attesting to the centrality of the family in dealing with the woman question in North Korea.

More telling than the Gender Equality Law was the Regulations on the Implementation of the Gender Equality Law issued six weeks later, on September 14, 1946. Article 8 of the regulation stipulated that all marriages must be registered by submitting a marriage certificate to the appropriate local people's committee. Although the Gender Equality Law called for free marriage, marriages had to be registered, and nonregistered ones, including common law marriages, were not recognized. This is in sharp contrast with the Soviet Union between 1918 and 1944, when common law marriage was accorded the same status as registered marriage and children born out of wedlock were granted the same legal rights as "legitimate" children.[35] Couples could also divorce easily without the consent of both parties by simply registering the divorce with local authorities, hence the term "postcard" divorces.

By contrast, in North Korea, articles 10 through 22 of the regulation contained detailed procedures for divorce.[36] Although the right to divorce was acknowledged, one had to pass through various hurdles to obtain one. With the consent of both parties, divorce papers could simply be filed with the local people's committee, but if either party disagreed the couple had to file for legal divorce proceedings with the appropriate people's court. The court had to agree that there were legitimate grounds for divorce for it to be granted. There was also a fine of five thousand *won* for those filing for divorce more than twice, applying a financial burden to repeat divorces (although the fine could be waved at the court's discretion). By March 1956, divorce required legal proceedings even in cases of mutual consent.[37]

In light of what happened in the Soviet Union, North Korea was able to anticipate the ramifications of more radical policies. After describing the status of women in the Soviet Union in glowing terms, an article in *Chosŏn yŏsŏng* cautiously warned:

Lastly, let us look at the relationship between women and men in the Soviet Union. Immediately after the revolution, marriage and divorce were made simple, permitting freedom, in order to eradicate corrupt feudal practices. This does not guarantee women's freedom, however, but forces on women great physical blows such as abortions, or they have to take their baby to the orphanage. If they cannot do that, then, they must raise them on their own. Such licentious free marriage and divorce not only bring disorder upon a healthy society but also are great obstacles in increasing the population. Thus, gradually, conditions for divorce were strictly regulated, and even after divorce, men bore a great burden, thereby protecting women's interests. . . . Freedom without responsibility is nothing but indulgence. As the family is the unit of organization and family relations have great influence on a country and a society, it is necessary to establish a healthy family with proper relations between husband and wife. It is necessary to establish a bright yet pure, solemn yet free family of one husband and one wife. This we should learn from the Soviet Union.[38]

It so happened that the victims of liberal divorce policies were often women because men left their older wives for younger, "new" women, which had also occurred in the 1920s colonial Korea at the initial onset of discussions on free marriage and divorce. Such policies ended up hurting rather than liberating women, as one working-class Russian woman explained: "Women in the majority of cases are more backward, less skilled, and therefore less independent than men. . . . To marry, to bear children, to be enslaved by the kitchen, and then to be thrown aside by your husband—this is very painful for women. This is why I am against easy divorce."[39]

As a result, the Soviet Union introduced a new Family Edict in 1944 that restricted divorce by requiring court adjudication, and no longer recognized de facto marriages.[40] This lesson had been taken to heart by the time of North Korea's reforms in 1946, which never recognized de facto marriages or "postcard" divorces. Without a debate like those conducted in China or the Soviet Union about getting rid of the family as a feudal or bourgeois unit of production, North Korea brought together women's roles, as both mothers and workers, through two laws that held the family to be the basic unit of society—the Labor Law and the Gender Equality Law. And unlike the Soviet Union, where the existence of ethnic minorities would have precluded an emphasis on nationality, North Korean women were mobilized specifically around the idea of the nation as an extension of the family. True to Marxist internationalism, the first women's journal published by the Bolsheviks was the *Rabotnitsa* (Woman Worker), which was unveiled on International Women's Day in 1914.[41] By contrast, North Korea described its women first and foremost as Koreans, as indicated in the title of its first women's journal, *Chosŏn yŏsŏng* (Korean Woman).

Chosŏn Yŏsŏng

As the main publishing house within the North Korean Democratic Women's League, *Chosŏn yŏsŏngsa* was in charge of printing all materials for the education of women in postliberation North Korea. One of its primary responsibilities was the publication of the league's organ, *Chosŏn yŏsŏng*, whose first issue was published in September 1946.[42] The second issue did not appear until November, but from January 1947 the journal was issued monthly. Some twenty thousand copies were printed in 1946, increasing to ninety thousand in the next year.[43]

It is not entirely clear how the journal was distributed and to what extent women were exposed to its contents. In light of limited resources and high rates of illiteracy, rather than obtaining personal copies women likely shared copies through women's league meetings and study sessions, through local government and cultural centers. A November 1947 report on the work of the publishing house noted difficulties in collecting subscriptions from the regional league branches to recoup the two million *won* annual budget required for the publication of the journal.[44] To add to its revenue, each copy of the journal was priced at thirty *won*, as printed on its back cover, and included limited numbers of simple advertisements from small businesses such as beauty salons and tailor shops. There were regional variations in the reception of the journal. North and South Hamgyŏng Provinces—historically the seat of radical peasant movements—were the most diligent in submitting monies for the journal, contributing articles, and distributing the journal to readers. Kangwŏn Province, located along the 38th parallel and itself divided between the Soviet and American occupation zones, had the worst record, and South P'yŏngan Province let the copies "just pile on," showing little interest in the journal. An analysis of the journal's content during the previous year revealed that the editorial section comprised 16.4 percent, the home column 15.6 percent, educational materials 19.7 percent, literature and arts 21.5 percent, local news 11.2 percent, and miscellaneous items 12.5 percent. Based on these findings, the report was critical of the literary materials, which took up the most space, surpassing educational materials. It observed disapprovingly that the journal lacked a clear target audience, and failed to reach out to the majority of women workers and peasants. The coverage of local news was also deemed inadequate due to a shortage of regional reporters.

Despite such drawbacks, the journal covered a wide range of topics, from reports on the pace of economic development to tips on tending to various household chores. Written by staff writers in addition to contributions from readers, most issues consisted of eighty to one hundred pages, and included an editorial section, a column on homemaking, educational materials, a small section on news about the Soviet Union, and an arts and literature section. The opening editorial, comprised mostly of pronouncements on national policies, always came first, confirming the official nature of the publication. Educational materials varied from examples of model Soviet women to reading lessons and introductory articles about politics. The literature section included short stories, plays, essays, and poems, many of them sent in by readers. Depending on the issue, special sections celebrated anniversaries of liberation day, the promulgation of the Gender Equality Law, and other occasions that highlighted domestic and international news. By April 1948, the formal section on the Soviet Union was dropped except for occasional articles, anticipating the end of the Soviet occupation and the official establishment of the Democratic People's Republic of Korea in September of that year.

Topics that used to be addressed by reformers during the colonial period were reproduced in the homemaking column, including cooking recipes; tips on child-rearing and tailoring; basic medical knowledge, especially about women's reproductive health; and children's nutrition and hygiene. These had been popular topics in women's journals throughout the world in the construction of modern domesticity. During the 1920s and 1930s, each of the daily newspapers in Korea had carried columns devoted to the family and the home.[45] *Chosŏn ilbo*, for example, began in November 1924 to carry a column titled "Housewife" (*kajŏng puin*), which was serialized until July 1935. Another column called "Home" (*kajŏng*) was added in October 1931 and continued to appear until the newspaper closed its doors in August 1940.[46] Other newspapers followed with columns such as "Home Memo" (*kajŏng memo*), "Home Common Sense" (*kajŏng sangsik*), and "Home Trend" (*kajŏng siron*). Despite the overlap with earlier trends, what emerged as a new theme in *Chosŏn yŏsŏng* in postliberation North Korea was the blending of women's family duties as wives and mothers in the home with their new positions as workers outside the home.

As we saw earlier, motherhood was protected by law through the Labor Law and the Gender Equality Law. As women's labor was mobilized in the construction of a new society, women were called on to do it all. The following is an example of the daily schedule recommended for a wife and mother of a family of four that included the husband, a son of kindergarten age, and a one-year-old daughter.[47]

5:00 a.m.	Rise
5:00–7:00	Prepare breakfast; clean; eat breakfast
7:00–7:30	Clean up around the house; get ready for work; get son ready for school
7:30	Leave for work
12:00–2:00 p.m.	Feeding time (for daughter)
5:00	Off work
5:30–7:00	Prepare dinner; organize; simple laundry; eat dinner
7:00–9:00	Tend to children; sort out and mend clothes
9:00–10:30	Private time (study)
10:30 p.m.–5:00 a.m.	Sleep

Not only was the woman put in charge of all housework—cooking, cleaning, and childcare—but with this tight schedule, she was advised to take care of grocery shopping on the way home from work. Her only free time was from 9:00 to 10:30 p.m. and not enough time was allocated for a full night's sleep. Although the article acknowledged the difficulties that women faced in working, especially if their families were not appreciative of their new responsibilities, the burden of running the household still lay with them: "In whatever period, housework has been the responsibility of women. As long as everyone understands that women's liberation does not mean that women should abandon the home, this is also the responsibility of working women. . . . Children need the strength of their mothers the most. . . . In order to complete the economic plan for the democratic development of a wealthy and strong Korea, I ask the many mothers with families to take an active part within possible means or make the impossible possible through one's zeal."

So, how did women react to this? For all the official prodding, the difficulty of combining family duties with work and life outside the home continued to surface throughout articles that recorded the voices of average women in forums organized by the women's league.[48] Their uniform complaint was the lack of time to do everything. During a discussion about working women, on December 25, 1946, attended by a journalist, a teacher, a sales clerk, a hairdresser, and a representative of the women's league, the women were asked what their motives were in working outside the home, and what challenges they faced in balancing work and family.[49] They replied that they wanted to contribute to the economy as trailblazers for future career-minded women, and felt it necessary to be economically independent in order to achieve gender equality. They all agreed that women's situation had indeed improved after liberation due to government support and the enactment of the Gender Equality Law. They appreciated that there were so many more schools and that the distribution of basic necessities was carried out equally, even if insufficiently. The biggest problem, however, was the lack of time, as expressed in the following comments:

I never have enough time. Even if I do my best to work from early in the morning until late at night, I don't have enough time. I wish I had some time to spare. To be honest, I think that at this stage working women sacrifice a part of their family.

Because there is no spare time, everything naturally becomes simplified. Meals are eaten with only one dish, and clothing too, there is just one outfit. The most problematic is laundry, not to mention washing, and there's no time to mend the socks.

Asked whether husbands were understanding when the women were late coming home from work, women commented with laughter: "They understand, but they still seem to feel some kind of unspeakable displeasure. . . . Not displeasure, but perhaps anxiety is what they feel. . . . It's a big problem. Husband and wife both go to work, so why do I feel sorry and he doesn't; how do you solve this state of mind?" Women were upset about the lack of help from their husbands when it came to housework.

They pointed out their stubbornness, their ingrained habit of regarding men as being the sole breadwinner, and of having nothing to do with housework:

> It would be nice if they could help women a little more. Like when we were newlyweds, the husband would help the wife without being asked. . . . But the average man's pride doesn't seem to allow him to do so. . . . They think that it is a great disgrace for men to help their wives in the home, but this causes great harm to the children. Boys have to be taught to help around the house when they are young. We must absolutely stop educating girls and boys in different ways as it has been done until now.

More than anything, women wanted help with housework as a way of resolving the woman question. Some, like the woman just quoted, went so far as to advocate the equal socialization of boys and girls as a way to dissolve gender roles for future generations, in striking similarity to contemporary feminists. In another column entitled "A Word to the Gentlemen," one female factory worker reiterated the importance of actual practices over legal reforms, and urged women to step up while demanding men take up housework: "We should henceforth work hard and study diligently so as not to fall behind men in the least bit. If I were to demand something of men, there are many things, but more than anything, in terms of home life, instead of just making laws, they should think of women as equals, in their hearts, and it would be great if we could help each other with the housework."[50]

The mobilization of women into the workforce required a rethinking of women's roles as wives and mothers since they were now called upon to juggle both work and family. An article entitled "The Status of Women in History and Its Lessons" presented a forceful plea for men to adapt to women's changing roles, excoriating them to shape up:

> First, men themselves must greatly reflect upon themselves and change their understanding of women. Hoping for men's awakening, the following questions are put forth.
>
> **I. Are past customs of respecting men and debasing women liquidated?**
>   1. Are you happy when a son is born and disappointed when a daughter is born?

2. Do you discriminate between sons and daughters in sending them to school?

3. Do you demand too much labor from women in the house?

4. Do you want to be served by women?

5. Do you discriminate between men and women during meals?

II. Do men retain a sense of superiority?

1. Do you believe too much in the power of the fist?

2. Do you scorn the positive characteristics of women?

3. Do you respect your daughter's opinion on marriage?

4. Do you scorn the rise of women's roles?

5. Do you complain when women and men receive the same wage?

III. Do you take interest in women's liberation?

1. Do you feel that the number of girls' schools is insufficient?

2. Do you agree with the rise in women's status?

3. Do you help with the work of the Women's League?

With the slogan that "Those who have made women weak are the men of the privileged class," men should always ask themselves the above questions and try to rectify themselves while actively helping the women's movement, thereby negating the great English writer Shakespeare's insult on women, "Weak, thy name is woman," and sweeping such thoughts from men's heads.[51]

It is a remarkably radical manifesto, particularly in the context of a largely illiterate agrarian society. Women reacted to all the challenges they faced in combining work and family by insisting that men take up their share of responsibility. Rather than being simply mobilized from the top down, women were demanding that men also make the necessary changes in themselves to resolve the woman question. Although women contested notions about their "natural" place in the home and the division of domestic labor, such challenges were not always without ambiguity or a certain sense of guilt. Many women still believed that mothers held a crucial role in the home in taking care of the children.

During another roundtable organized by the women's league on August 13, 1947, women from the university, the prosecutor's office, and the women's league discussed the status of women with a factory worker, a journalist, a middle school teacher, and a homemaker. After reviewing all the progress that had been made over the past year, the journalist pointed out that

> in the past, living wasn't really living, so even though we knew we shouldn't, we took it out on the children, and so the children were naturally unhappy and just kept watch [so as not to get yelled at]. But now, we are so busy that there is no time for husbands and wives to fight or time to drink, and we read whenever there is a spare moment, so the children also naturally read more. From now on, children in Korea will also be quite happy and bright. But, because many mothers go out to work, children's health and care are neglected. There are more than a few such instances, but children try to be very understanding and also try to help out on their own. But, no matter what, it's probably not as good for the children as having their mothers always by their side.[52]

Because the family continued to be an important social unit, women's roles as mothers and wives never came under fire, and the woman question centered around how women's identities as mothers and wives had to be reconfigured now that women were working—on how women could combine work and family most effectively.

Between competing claims for women's labor power and women's complaints about the lack of time and cooperation from men, the resolution of the woman question came to reside in the role of motherhood that could fuse the old with the new. Rather than breaking down traditional gender roles, a sphere was carved out for women in which she reined supreme as "master of the home" (*kajŏng ŭi chuin*). The "new" home and "new" housewife was to be defined by her mastery over the domestic realm, as advocated in the quote with which this chapter began. The full quote reads:

> In Korea from ancient times, the master of the home was thought to refer to the husband, and women did nothing but help as demanded by the head of household who was the master of the home. However, that is an ideology born by a male-centric family system, and in reality, we now realize that the master of the home must be the woman, that is, the wife or mother. . . . There should be no trace left of the rotten idea of the past that "all a woman needs to do is bear children and do housework well." Today, even housewives should have great interest in society and politics, sensing joy and sadness on the state of the nation, world peace, and freedom, making contributions to them.[53]

Along with the powers of running the household, the article designated the most important areas of women's work as the household economy, domestic harmony, and the education of children. Motherhood, which under Confucian patriarchy had been understood as the duty to pass on the family name by producing sons, was reformulated as a form of social management through the supervision of home economics and the education of the next generation. The chairwoman of the women's league, Pak Chŏng-ae, echoed the important social duty that women performed as mothers by defining the "duty of motherhood" as "not only the basic nature of human beings but also an important indispensable social duty."[54]

The reconstitution of motherhood as a social duty was hardly new, and was quite consistent with trends throughout the world. Founded in November 1945 and representing women's organizations from forty countries including North Korea, the Women's International Democratic Federation called for the protection of motherhood in factories through the special treatment of pregnant and nursing women.[55] Likewise, the Soviet Union passed legislation protecting mothers in July 1946, giving aid to single mothers and women with large numbers of children. Women with more than ten children were honored as "Heroic Mothers," women with seven to nine were decorated as "Honorable Mothers," and those with five or six were awarded "Motherhood Medals."[56] Whereas the masculine industrial worker had been portrayed as the original hero of the Bolshevik Revolution in the first decade after the revolution, increasing hardships during the first Five-Year Plan (1928–32) required additional female workers and a greater sense of stability. Soviet political iconographers used motherhood not only to mobilize women but for a "sense of continuity offered by the maternal image, its suggestion of intimacy and solace . . . [for an] iconic conflation of mother and motherland, family and state serv[ing] to humanise and legitimise the party."[57] Such conflations have been commonplace in the modern era, and used in colonial Korea to mobilize women for the war effort through similar discourses of the sacrificing mother.

In itself, North Korea's emphasis on motherhood was not without precedent, but the decisive change that set North Korea on a different path was the extension of motherhood as the most exemplary form of selfless public service that *everyone*, not just women, should strive to emulate. Selfless, motherly sacrifice was extolled as a model virtue:

> I discover a model of such great sacrificing public service within the lives of women, and highly value such sacrificing public service from women. . . . *Everyone* mobilized for national foundation should learn a

great deal and take as a model such pure motherly sacrifice that is unconditional without earthly ambition or desire. Like the woman who
gladly endures and overcomes the greatest hardship for the joy of creating new life, our people should also fight and overcome all hardship and
persecution for the joy and hope of establishing our homeland.[58]

The article went on to explain that people should not pursue their own
selfish interests and well-being, but rather struggle for the good of all of
society. It urged women to gain economic independence not only for
themselves but for the nation, because without a self-reliant economy
there could be no national independence. Before identifying themselves as
women, women were to identify with the nation; the woman question was
equated with the national question. In the aftermath of colonial rule the
woman question was framed by the urgency of national construction and
the ambiguity of what tradition was supposed to mean in a revolutionary
postcolonial context—was it something to be overthrown or embraced?
The dilemma was resolved through the redeployment of motherhood as
the vehicle that encompassed both traditional gender roles and the new
revolutionary subject. Mothers became the ideal selfless public servant, a
model for all members of the nation to follow in the performance of their
social duty as citizens of a new country.

The technique, or form, of mobilization may not have been all that
different from other examples that appropriated motherhood as a mobilizing discourse, but circumstances had changed to make motherhood a
powerfully receptive icon, allowing a traditional role to become a revolutionary subject not only for women but for all North Koreans. What was
different was precisely the experience of the colonial period that enabled
the inscription of metaphors of the family in reference to the nation-state,
so that the state effectively became the family writ large and domesticity once again became the privileged domain. Who better to represent
the primary figure of revolutionary change in this domestic space than
women and mothers as the quintessential icon of the nation.

Mothers as Ideal Citizens

The resurgence of motherhood in North Korean political discourse has led
to charges that a form of nationalized patriarchy prevails in North Korea
with the leader as the patriarch ruling over the rest of society, "feminiz-
ing" the people who "play a stereotypical 'female' part in old-fashioned

romantic tales."[59] The interpretation misses the point, however, by looking through the same conventional bifurcated lens, dividing the world into fixed masculine and feminine forms rather than being sensitive to how they were in fact reconstituted. Portrayed as both father and mother, the leader in North Korea has more often been described as nurturing mother than disciplinary patriarch, with a particular emphasis on Kim Il Sung's mother, Kang Pan-sŏk, as a role model rather than his father. A nation-wide campaign to learn from her legacy was popularized in the 1960s with the publication of "Let's Follow and Learn from Madame Kang Pan-sŏk." According to the text, Kim Il Sung inherited his mother's ideology and character as a child, and on cold winter days when his mother returned after a long day of farm work, he would run out to greet her, warming her hands by blowing on them and reserving the warmest part of the room for her to sleep; if she fell ill, he would massage her hands and feet throughout the night without rest, nursing her back to health.[60]

Such imagery is much more feminine than masculine, and the imagery of maternal care and love has been extended into contemporary descriptions of military officers "loving their soldiers like their own children (ch'injasik) or younger siblings (ch'indongsaeng)," "preparing meals for them like their real parents (ch'inpumo)," "thereby arousing feelings of deep affection (aet'ŭt han chŏng) in the soldiers" for their commanding officers, quite unlike standard representations of the military as the epitome of masculinity.[61] Moreover, two out of the three epic revolutionary operas cast women as the main protagonist with the mother in the Sea of Blood as the most exemplary revolutionary hero.[62] Properly speaking, femininity and masculinity are not properties that can be "effaced" or engraved but performative characteristics that require a situated context to make sense. Although the leader is often depicted as a parent, North Koreans are not permanently feminized or infantilized as a result, but are called to become sacrificing revolutionaries as mothers, in the same way that people can simultaneously hold positions as parents and children.

Lest there be any doubt about the real changes in women's status, an essay from the April 1948 issue of Chosŏn yŏsŏng poignantly detailed the kinds of changes that were perceived to be new and far-reaching at the time. After visiting the small village of Omokdong, made up of forty-four poor peasant families, the writer described the ways in which women's attitudes were changing: "When I entered this village, the chairwoman of the women's league greeted me, readily putting forth her hand first. When had shaking hands without any awkwardness become a habit for women in their forties in such an isolated village? I was moved, firmly holding the heavy farm-worked hand." She went on to comment how "the discord between mother-in-law and daughter-in-law, the grievance of not bearing a son, the sighs of having a husband with a concubine, they had all disappeared two years ago, and now mother-in-law and daughter-in-law go to adult school arm-in-arm, and husbands and wives go to the market together."[63] Women standing up and speaking in public, shaking hands, and going to school were radical changes by the standards of the time. Stories about election day, for example, singled out women campaigning for voter turnout with a baby on their back, going to the polls despite being nine months pregnant, and postponing their wedding day in order to participate fully in the electoral process.[64] The women's league also compiled statistics on the number of women in various occupations as evidence of the expanded roles for women.

Despite the increasing numbers of women in other occupations, the vast majority of women, like men, were still peasants in a predominantly agrarian society. There were less than thirty-two thousand women

Table 6.1. Number of women by occupation, 1950

Occupation	Number of Women
Agriculture	532,429
People's Committee representative	11,509
Supreme People's Assembly	33
Elementary school teacher	4,732
Elementary school principal	42
Middle school teacher	522
Middle school principal	13
Technical school teacher	52
College student	17
Judge	53
Juror	1,363
Doctor	53
Pharmacist	23
Nurse	1,238
Midwife	185
Nurse's aide	2,237

Source: RG 242, SA 2009, box 3, item 150, "3.8 Kukche punyŏjŏl 39-chunyŏn pogo chegang" [Report on the 39th anniversary of March 8 International Women's Day], Central Committee of the North Korean Democratic Women's League (March 1950), 15–17.

working outside the agricultural sector, constituting less than 1 percent of the total female population. Under these circumstances, women were able to encompass roles both as reproducers and producers. Women's work as mothers and caretakers of rural households was validated as legitimate and valued work, so much so that women quit their jobs once they got married, presenting a problem in integrating women into the workforce well into the 1970s.[65]

As moderate as it may seem today, North Korean policies on women were still thought to be too radical by some. In order to alleviate fears that the breakdown in traditional customs would result in chaos and societal collapse, the article from which one of the opening epigraphs was taken tried to explain women's new expanded roles as part of what was necessary for national construction: "These days there are many women out and about in the streets day and night. But some people who don't understand may think that the women these days are crazy or that it is a state of anarchy, looking on with suspicious eyes. But that is not true. The women these days are not like the women of the past who sold their bodies. . . . Women today are struggling with all their passion and all their strength day and night for the creation of a new history of a democratic country. Today in the streets, men, women, the old, the young, everyone stops to listen to the women."[66] A few months later, as the women's league celebrated the one year anniversary of the passage of the Gender Equality Law, the cover of *Chosŏn yŏsŏng* featured the triumphant figure of the revolutionary mother, her hair gathered in a bun, indicating her married

Table 6.2. Number of employed women by sector, 1947

Type of Industry	Number of Employed Women
Textile	6,969
Chemical	4,109
Mining	2,093
Construction	1,246
Railway	857
Communication	763
Metal, foodstuffs, electrical, publishing	7,231
School, cultural institution, hospital	3,932
Political party, social organization, bank, managerial	4,618
Total	31,818

Source: Ri Kyŏng-hye, *Nyŏsŏng munje haegyŏl kyŏnghŏm* [Experience of solving the woman question] (Pyongyang: Sahoe kwahak ch'ulp'ansa, 1990), 60.

status. She is shown leading women toward liberation, not only in North Korea but in the south as well, denoted by her standing atop the chain that wraps around the southern zone of the Korean Peninsula.

In step with such changes, the *hojŏk*—the household registry system instituted under colonial rule that required a male head of household—was eliminated with the introduction of the citizen registration card on August 9, 1946, making obsolete patriarchal lines of descent.[67] South Korea was not to take such steps until 2005.[68] Nonetheless, the family was considered central, as Article 23 of the North Korean Constitution, enacted in 1948, stipulated: "Marriage and the family are under the protection of the state."[69] Still, the concept of the family was liberalized as parents were given equal rights and responsibilities over their children born out of wedlock. In lieu of the patriarchal family, the nuclear family became the basic "cell" (*sep'o*) of North Korean society, and practices that jeopardized this family unit, including sexual freedom and divorce, were discouraged.[70]

In the late 1940s, as North Korea grappled with the woman question, women in the Soviet Union were well on their way to being socially and economically integrated—they made up 40 percent of the labor force, 42 percent of technicians, and 43 percent of university students. Although the Soviet Union had been industrializing for several decades, motherhood continued to be an important part of women's identities and the state "guaranteed the conditions able to fulfill women's unique responsibility and pride as mothers."[71] By contrast, North Korean women were only just beginning to work in nonagricultural sectors outside the home. It would take another four decades before North Korean women made up half of the labor force. Appropriating the different ways motherhood had been employed throughout the first half of the century, North Korea began from its inception to rely on women to hold together the very fabric of society: sacrificing mothers would reproduce and educate future generations as model socialist subjects, while contributing to the developing economy as dedicated workers and citizens of a new socialist state. What was new was the emergence of a *collective* domesticity substantially different from the private domesticity situated in the bourgeois home with the individual woman as the homemaker. Collective domesticity transformed housekeeping into nation-building, whereby such efforts resonated not only with women but also with men as the state was equated with the family and every member of society was called on to make sacrifices as a mother should, and indeed would.

Friedrich Engels had provided a class analysis of women's oppression in *The Origins of the Family, Private Property, and the State*, attributing the oppression of women to the family when it became a unit of capital accumulation rather than of self-subsistence, as women became producers of heirs for men to pass down their wealth.[72] Adopting this perspective, many communist regimes have attempted to solve the woman question by dissolving households as units of private ownership, production, and accumulation. No longer bound to the biological and social role of reproduction in the household, women could now join the public sphere as political and economic agents equal to men. But this left open the question of who was to take care of the housework that had previously been done by women. The answer lay in the socialization, or collectivization, of housework through public canteens, public laundries, and childcare facilities. The assumption was that these institutions freed women to pursue a socially productive life outside the home.

North Korea was no exception, as it attempted to decrease the burden of housework on women. Childcare centers were set up for infants between the ages of one month to three years. The limited resources of the newly formed state did not allow for very many of these at first. In 1946, there was just one childcare center and sixty-four kindergartens.[73] By 1948, the 3.8 Childcare Center in Pyongyang, named after the March 8th International Women's Day, had a capacity for fifty infants between the ages of eight months to three years, outfitted with a playroom, bedroom, cafeteria, and bathroom, providing meals and snacks throughout the day. Regardless of the number of children left at the center, a mother paid 10 percent of her wages for the service.[74] By 1970, there were eighty-six hundred childcare centers and sixty-eight hundred kindergartens spread across the country.

Despite major strides enabling women to be economically independent and politically active, examples from *Chosŏn yŏsŏng* show that childcare and housework remained largely the duties of women. Even with the socialization of childcare, there were few real changes in the sexual division of labor, because gender roles within the family were simply reproduced in public institutions. Orphanages and childcare centers were run by women and the caretakers were often referred to as "mothers."[75] Moreover, gender segregation in labor sectors nullified the principle of equal pay for equal work, since women usually worked in occupations with lower pay, in the service and light industries, or in charge of primary school teaching and nursing. Men dominated the higher-paid occupations in mining and heavy industries, and took the jobs with the highest prestige, as managers, university professors, and doctors.[76] Although wages do not have the same effect on the quality of people's lives in socialist countries as they do in capitalist societies, since housing, education, health care, and food are free or heavily subsidized, such job segregation results not only in unequal pay but also in unequal status.

Ironically, communist leaders have had to rely on ideology to explain the continued problem of the woman question, because women's entry into the workforce has not led to a resolution. With the majority of the peasant population still uneducated, liberating policies did not always have liberating effects, as Ch'oe Yong-gŏn—former guerrilla, Kim Il Sung's comrade-in-arms, and chief of security in the Provisional People's Committee, later to become commander-in-chief of the People's Army—declared in 1946: "When Korea became independent, North Korea's democratic government liberated the women, but women did not know the true meaning of independence and democratic politics. . . . The problem of women's liberation in North Korea today is not with the sociopolitical system, but lies with the efforts of women themselves."[77] So, are we left in the incorrigible position of blaming women for their own oppression? Surely not; women, after all, have repeatedly questioned whether housework is to be their burden alone, and have challenged men to change the way they think about women and their own sense of superiority. But this challenge had limits.

In postcolonial North Korea, motherhood became the embodiment of the Korean nation, to be preserved as what was most Korean. Once seen as the hallmark of a traditional society that had to be eradicated for the sake of progress, women's roles as mothers came to be seen as distinctly Korean, something to be fostered. Although the colonial period is long over, the division of the peninsula, the Korean War, and the ensuing Cold War have all perpetuated a state of war, demanding continued sacrifice and the maintenance of the sacrificial mother as an iconic model. In North Korea, being a good mother was and still is equated with being a patriot and a public servant. Faced with the necessity of having to survive economically and politically, North Korea mobilized its people—including women—to work harder, sacrifice more, and unite as one people. In response to this call to give all to one's country, women and men gave what they could, empowered by their newfound country and proud of their membership in it. Motherhood, in this context, became the quintessential symbol of the ideal sacrificing citizen, not only for women but for everyone. Within this newly configured motherhood, expanded to signify more than the rearing of one's own children, to include the public domain as caretakers of society, women were both empowered and challenged to be part of the process of founding a new country.

However, the process was not without ambivalence. As shown in the women's reactions to demands made on them, they often felt overburdened and guilty for their lack of attention to their families, while at the same time questioning whether in fact they had to be defined by their place in the home. To the extent that women as mothers were elevated to the status of ideal citizens, they took center stage as revolutionary heroines. But insofar as women's identities were tied to motherhood, they did not have the power to define themselves outside of this very framework, which gave them a place and a voice in North Korean society. Agency, as Joan Scott has eloquently stated, is in all cases a negotiated outcome. Agents have always been circumscribed and "are not unified, autonomous individuals exercising free will, but rather subjects whose agency is created through situations and statuses conferred on them."[78] In North Korea, women's agency was created through their status as Mothers situated in the Home, a role which became an allegory for the ideal citizen in the homeland.[79]

7. "Liberated Space"

Remembering the Revolution

It was the end of the 36-year Japanese colonial life of slavery. . . . I too was swept up by the crowd, following them, shouting "*Manse!* [Long live] *Manse! Manse!* Long Live Korean Independence!" How can I express the explosion of that deep *han* [lament] and the instinctively and absolutely natural national ecstasy? I came back home after the whole day had waned.
KIM WŎN-JU (N.D.)

One day in early December 1945, I heard the best news upon my return to the homeland in ten years. That was the happy news that the nation's great sun General Kim Il Sung had called us. . . . The Great Leader kept me close to him, allowing me to work in the propaganda section of the party central organizing committee in order to raise me up as a full-fledged woman revolutionary.
HŎ CHŎNG-SUK, 1986

Figure 7.1. Prisoners leaving Sŏdaemun Prison in Seoul (August 16, 1945).

In figure 7.1 we see one of the most iconic images depicting Korea's liberation from colonial rule on August 15, 1945. It is ubiquitously displayed throughout South Korea in museum exhibits, school textbooks, and documentary materials, and reproduced widely on the Internet on both official sites as well as on private blogs. The picture, however, was taken the day *after* liberation when political prisoners were released from Sŏdaemun Prison.[1] That the photograph was taken on the 16th rather than the 15th does not diminish the sense of liberation, expressed in the raised hands of released prisoners cheering together with the crowd in celebration. Nonetheless, the more ambivalent mood of the 15th is sidelined, suppressing the trauma of colonialism as poignantly expressed by O Yŏng-jin in the second chapter.[2] Many reproductions of the photo also crop it at the foot of the standing men facing front, cutting out the one woman in the picture who is clearly looking toward the camera. It is the visual equivalent, her position just barely within the frame, of the way women have been largely silenced from narratives about liberation. Indeed, most photographs taken in the south in the immediate days following the announcement of Japan's surrender show few images of women at all, in stark contrast to North Korea's focus on women as seen in the last chapter.

Differences between the north and south in their treatment of liberation are also evident in divergent terminologies to refer to August 15, shifting between *haebang* (liberation), *kwangbok* (restoration), and *tongnip* (independence). In the south, "liberation" was increasingly associated with leftist politics, and "restoration" took on greater resonance when Syngman Rhee, a septuagenarian from the old guard with roots going back to the nineteenth century, became the first president of the new republic, inaugurating a separate southern state on August 15, 1948, exactly three years after liberation.[3] As a result, August 15 came to occupy contradictory meanings of liberation and division in South Korea, becoming an occasion for South Korean leaders to seek legitimation through symbolic events such as the demolition of the former colonial government building in 1995. In the north, where liberation opened the door to social revolution, "liberation" was the favored term, bringing together emancipation for the nation with liberation for the oppressed classes. Despite differing terminologies, August 15 as Korea's independence day is the only memorial day recognized in both the north and south today, becoming an occasion for bilateral talks as well as joint commemorative events in the spirit of reunification.

Perhaps because of the ambivalent meaning of liberation in the south, some South Korean scholars have elided the five-year postliberation period (1945–50) by subsuming it between 1937, with the outbreak of the second Sino-Japanese War, and the end of the Korean War in 1953 as part of a continuous state of war.[4] Although this kind of periodization highlights the state of unrest at the time, it erases liberation as a historical event that left an indelible mark on millions of people. Particularly for North Korea, the five-year period marked a definitive break with the past, with numerous reforms that involved mass participation at an unprecedented scale. Indeed, liberation within the context of the North Korean Revolution meant not only political independence but also embodied multiple meanings combining national liberation with class and women's liberation. The North Korea today that continues to suffer from the specter of the Korean War in both senses of that term—haunted both by the experience of war now past and by a possible return of the threat of war in the future—is in many ways a different one from the one that existed during those five years, and that period needs to be distinguished not only for what it was but also for what it could have been.

Liberation was undoubtedly marred by the ensuing civil war. But that is a perspective possible with the benefit of hindsight. Without knowledge of how history would unfold, liberation from colonial rule signified potential for a new beginning. Looking at the postliberation period through the lens of the subsequent war "silences the past" on various fronts, confirming Michel-Rolph Trouillot's point that "the presences and absences embodied in sources . . . are neither neutral nor natural. They are created. As such, they are not mere presences and absences, but *mentions* or *silences* of various kinds and degrees."[5] Not only does liberation become a nonevent in hindsight, but as evinced by the common characterization of the Korean War as a fratricidal war, women's place in the war and in the events leading up to that point get displaced by the very configuration of the conflict as one between brothers. Through oral histories and memoirs, this chapter unearths how stories and narratives about liberation are "mentioned" and simultaneously "silenced" by highlighting the differences in the experiences and memories of liberation between women and men of the north and south during the five years of liberation and revolution. Methodologically, this required sources beyond the traditional archive that have made up the bulk of the sources for the previous chapters. This final chapter also serves as a reminder that North Korea is situated within the history of liberation in Korea as a whole before the division was solidified and made so permanent.[6]

Predictably, narratives dealing with liberation were not uniform, and the discovery of gendered differences in them raised questions about the extent to which historical events and memories about them are themselves gendered. For instance, the presentation of individual life stories were often framed as microcosms of twentieth-century Korean history, categorized into periods of colonialism, division, war, reconstruction, and Cold War as overarching structures that periodized people's lives. Although these are conventional practices in the historiography of modern Korea, what does it mean for the same periodization to be applied in the organization of individual life stories? After all, the events embodied in each period place the nation-state as the primary subject of history: Korea was colonized, divided, fought over, and reconstructed. Certainly, individuals were affected and shaped by these events, but one could imagine using alternative chronologies that emphasize one's occupation, one's place of residence, or one's stage in life from childhood to parenthood.

As we shall see, the persistence of this national framework defined those narratives for which the nation-state was an overarching force whether in the north or south, fusing life story with national history. It should come as no surprise that men generally found this to be the easiest since they have been the primary subjects by which to delineate nationality, whether by protecting the nation through compulsory enlistment and military service or by passing on the nation's heritage through patriarchal lines of descent. By contrast, women's narratives were more ambiguous. In the north, where practices of mass autobiographical writing and collective life attempted to fuse individual life story with national history for all groups, including women, narratives were more uniform because such practices were meant to serve as homogenizing mechanisms. Nonetheless, women's life stories were punctuated by an uneasy relationship between life story and national history, especially acute for those, as in the south, without the institutional support needed to forge a strong collective memory.

The sources used in this chapter raise difficult questions about authorship and authenticity stemming from the complicated relationship between narrator, interviewer, editor, and publisher that determine what is included and what is left out of the final product, whether as published memoirs or transcripts of oral histories. Problems are compounded in the case of North Korean sources, if they can be found at all. Although Kim Il Sung left behind a multivolume memoir shortly before his death, individual memoirs are almost nonexistent except for those that deal with participation in Kim's anticolonial guerrilla struggle. Hŏ Chŏng-suk's *Minju kŏn'guk ŭi nanal e* (*Days in the Democratic Construction of the Country*), published in 1986, is a rare exception, but it revolves almost entirely around her interactions with Kim Il Sung. There is very little description of and reflection about her own life—an interesting detail in itself to which we will return. The increasing number of memoirs by North Korean defectors published today in South Korea and elsewhere are from a different generation and do not deal with the liberation period. As a result, whether speaking about the north or south, almost all narratives included in this chapter were published or gathered in South Korea, a reluctant yet unavoidable limitation in sources.

Working with oral histories and memoirs are thus fraught with pitfalls, but there are similar concerns in working with archival materials. In the end, we are always maneuvering within a symbolic web of meaning, and whether we are dealing with archives or memories, stories, much like archival materials, have to be interpreted and made meaningful. As Joan Scott so aptly put it, it is not enough to "make experience visible"; it is necessary to explain the inner workings of the mechanisms that give rise to the kind of experiences that *are* visible, because "experience is at once always already an interpretation *and* something that needs to be interpreted."[7] How, then, is the experience and memory of liberation generally interpreted?

Standard depictions of liberation exude a certain sense of "collective effervescence."[8] Many accounts begin with Japan's announcement of defeat in the Pacific War, bringing an end to its brutal thirty-five-year colonial rule. Koreans proceeded to celebrate, dancing and singing in the streets, and quickly burst into political activity to form an interim government in the spirit of true self-determination. Such descriptions characterize much of the scholarship dealing with this period, including this book. Indeed, it is the allure and excitement of the possibilities that were opened up by this "liberated space" (*haebang konggan*) that prompted modern historians to coin the term and study the period more closely. To be sure, times of instability accompanied by structural dislocations give rise to intense emotional excitement, which becomes a force in itself to exacerbate ruptures and creatively shape a new political order and social life.[9] But was this "liberated space" indeed liberating for everyone, and if so, in specifically which ways?[10] Did Korean women experience the postliberation period as a "liberated space" of revolution? The point here is to scrutinize the very process by which history is constructed as a homogeneous, often male, experience by exploring the historical ethnography of postliberation Korea in a way that is sensitive to the gendered dimensions of experience and memory.

In dealing with historical memory, Maurice Halbwachs is a useful starting point. He challenged Freudian conceptualizations of memory as essentially an individual asset by emphasizing that memory can function only within a collective context, and therefore memory must be seen as socially constructed.[11] Although he may have overstated the case, since memory can be intensely personal, his analysis of collective memory explains why different groups of people have different collective memories, often resulting in disputes not only over the reconstruction of the past but over present realities. Korean history has been no less fraught with contention, especially as the two Koreas continue to compete for legitimacy, and gendered differences in narratives of liberation underscore the importance of looking beyond standard narratives of any given historical event. I begin with the biographies of two men whose oral histories were collected in 2003.[12]

National History as Life Story

Ch'oe Sang-wŏn was born in 1923 in North Kyŏngsang Province, in the southeastern part of the Korean Peninsula, to a landed *yangban* family. After a period of study in Tokyo, he was forcibly drafted into the Japanese Imperial Army in January 1945. He tried to escape but was caught and held by the military police until liberation. Returning to his hometown in Kyŏngju after liberation, he found that his friends had already put him in charge of security in the local people's committee in light of his military experience and boxing skills. He soon took on additional responsibilities in the local peasant union, and was elected vice chair of the local youth league.

Increasing conflict with the American occupation forces over issues of self-governance and taxation culminated in the October Uprising of 1946, forcing Ch'oe underground along with other activists in the people's committees. After a year living in the mountains, he was arrested in October 1947 and sentenced to three years in prison. He was released after finishing his term, shortly before the start of the Korean War in 1950. He then moved to the southern port city of Pusan and lived with his brother until he was arrested again during the war in 1952. He escaped the fate of thousands of political prisoners who were killed in the south to prevent the potential augmentation of North Korean forces, when the charges against him were dismissed after some of his resourceful friends bribed the authorities. He continued to engage in various political activities for reunification after the war, serving another four-year prison term in 1972. I interviewed him five times in his home in March 2003, each time speaking for two to three hours.

By contrast, Kang Tam was born in 1933 in South Hamgyŏng Province in northeastern Korea to a poor peasant family. He attended school for the first time when mass education was extended to all children soon after liberation in North Korea. As poor tenant farmers, his family also received land during the land reform in March 1946. He was still a student when the Korean War broke out. His family survived the war by living in underground bunkers. After the war, he was active in the local youth league until joining the Korean People's Army in 1954. He gained admission into the Workers' Party in 1960, and finished his military service in 1961 after seven years as a marine. He then found employment on a fishing vessel. After a year, he went back to school for three years, graduating with a certificate in oceanic navigation. In 1965 he was recruited to navigate ships involved in intelligence operations in South Korean waters, but was captured at sea onboard the ship to South Korea.

Although he was convicted of espionage and given a life sentence in South Korea, North Korea considers these activities to be a form of political work for reunification, by sending agents with families and relatives in the south to facilitate contact with South Koreans. The ultimate purpose was to spark a mass uprising within South Korea for its own social revolution that would unite the two Koreas. Such a strategy was not as far-fetched as it might appear, because of the mass uprising in 1960 that brought down the First Republic under Syngman Rhee. The strategy was unsuccessful, but the "spies" that were sent south, and their families, bore the brunt of the failed policy. They were often executed or imprisoned for decades as long-term prisoners, tortured to "convert" and give up their ideologies, using methods from the colonial period. Their families were sent to prison for simply failing to report their own family members to the authorities. Even when they finished their relatively shorter prison terms, families and relatives were often socially ostracized as "reds" (*ppalgaengi*), unable to find jobs or places to live because they were continuously harassed by the police. As a result, long-term prisoners were often completely estranged from their families. Despite such hardships, many long-term prisoners continued to believe that their activities were justified in the face of national division for the sake of reunification. Kang Tam was released in a presidential amnesty in 1988, after having served twenty-four years in prison. He found employment in a construction company, and only in 2001 did he join other former political prisoners in reunification efforts. With the successes of the democracy movement in South Korea in the late 1980s, long-term political prisoners began to be released, and came together as part of the reunification movement since most of them had families in the north. I interviewed Kang at his home on two occasions, in May and July 2003, both times for two to three hours.

As evident from the brief synopses of their life stories, both men have suffered numerous years in prison and social alienation once outside prison. The Social Surveillance Law has required former political prisoners to report to local police authorities on a regular basis, including any travel plans within the country. It restricts them from traveling abroad and prohibits them from many political activities, including public protests. Although former prisoners have refused to abide by these requirements on the grounds that the law violates their fundamental rights to freedom of movement and expression, the authorities have enforced the letter of the law only sporadically and selectively. Nevertheless, sanctions against their political beliefs and activities undoubtedly influenced the kind of stories they were able to tell. They were also elderly while I was a relatively young, female Korean American graduate student at the time. I was often regarded as a distant relative from a foreign land—and from their perspective, a hostile one, since they were critical of American global power and its foreign policies, particularly toward Korea. They seemed to take the interview as an opportunity to teach me the "real" history of Korea, of the continuing legacy of resistance, of what it meant to be a "true" Korean. For example, Ch'oe would say, "this is the most important part; this is the most important to know clearly." They saw themselves as guides and teachers in my search for historical roots. My junior status was most obvious when, at the end of the interview, they would caution me not to forget my "roots" and find a nice Korean man to marry.

I was both comfortable and uneasy in this role. On the one hand, my fluency in Korean customs and language facilitated building up a rapport so that it became fairly easy to bond with them quickly. On the other hand, it was difficult to navigate the kind of demands and expectations placed on the relationship that went beyond the parameters of the interview. In some sense, this reflected the give-and-take of social relationships regulated by norms that govern any social interaction. Although I now have power over their words, I often felt that I was at their mercy during our time together as they were older male figures with stories that I hoped to learn from them. It is also possible that our roles of elder and junior prevented us from getting to issues that they felt were beyond the scope of this hierarchical relationship and their immediate goal of imparting their legacy to the next generation. Despite these limitations, the personal connection was important in bringing out their full stories.

It was striking the extent to which their narratives fit into the "collective effervescence" of the dominant discourse of liberation. For example, the opportunity to go to school after liberation stood out as a radically new experience for Kang in light of his previous life of poverty under colonial rule.

> Under the Japanese, the township seat was located in our village. If I just stepped outside the front door, there was a school that the Japanese had built only a few steps away. But, because our family was poor, we couldn't go to school. I had two older brothers and two older sisters. Without counting the younger ones, out of the four only the second brother was able to graduate from primary school. Because our family was poor, we made a living by tenant farming. In the summer, we rented some land and we also borrowed some infertile land, and in early spring mother would go out to the potato field and bring back these potatoes that looked like bird eggs to eat, and if that ran out, millet was planted a lot back then, and when the millet was ripening, bending its neck like this, we'd pick them, but we couldn't just eat it because it wasn't fully ripe. So, we'd steam it in an iron kettle, and it would ripen and we'd eat it. Then, a bit later, the rice starts to ripen in the fields, a bit before *ch'usŏk* (Korean Thanksgiving). But, the harvest wouldn't last until the next year, so we'd go to the mountains to forage for edible plants; we ate a lot of pine tree bark. You take the bark off a pine tree and strip what's inside, steam it and eat it. The wealthy eat this mixed with rice as a delicacy today, but kids just can't understand—you couldn't pass stool because you hadn't had enough to eat. But that's how it was for our generation.

After equating the Japanese colonial period with hunger and a lack of educational opportunities, Kang marked liberation with his admission into school:

> Then, liberation came, and Kim Il Sung came and declared the compulsory education system, so from the beginning all the students were unconditionally put under a compulsory education system. Then, from our generation alone, there were three students. The sister above me entered school into the fifth grade. I think I went into the fourth or third grade. Most everyone entered a couple of years below normal because they hadn't been in school. The sister right below me was supposed to go into the third grade according to her age, but entered the first grade. So, in one generation, there were three students. When you look at North Korean society at the time, it was a tremendous revolution.

New opportunities were not merely proclaimed as lofty revolutionary goals, but were visibly inscribed in everyday surroundings. The school changed its name from the Japanese, Kakusen National Citizens School (*Kakusen kokuritsu kokumin gakko*), to the Korean, Hakch'ŏn People's School (*Hakch'ŏn inmin hakkyo*), to reflect the dismantling of the colonial apparatus and the institution of mass education that finally opened its doors to all Koreans, including Kang and his siblings. It is no wonder that liberation served as a definitive marker in organizing Kang's life story.

Likewise, for Ch'oe, who had been forcibly drafted into the Japanese Imperial Army in January 1945, the experience of liberation was exhilarating:

> We weren't set free and discharged from the military base immediately on August 15, 1945. In the beginning, the Japanese were saying that this wasn't the end of the war but a temporary cease-fire. We started protesting, so we were finally discharged officially on the 17th or so. I went to Taegu Station and got on the train to Kyŏngju. There was a strange mood inside the train. Everyone had been hardened like frozen human beings inside a freezer, but they were now talking to each other happily even amongst strangers, kindly and affectionately. I don't know where it came from, but even though food was so hard to come by then, there were rice-cakes from somewhere and a stranger offered them to me saying, "Oh, you must try one of these." It's impossible to really express all the details of that time. [I thought to myself], this is what it is to live. Until then, Korean people had been living under strain, squashed under the Japanese gun and sword all the time for thirty-six years, almost forty years. Then, all that broke loose. So, in a word, it was an atmosphere of festivity. When I arrived at Kyŏngju Station on the train from Taegu Station, it was past seven or eight o'clock at night. I left the station and headed for my house. I was living in Kyŏngju City at the time. In a secluded place where no one could see, I pinched myself really hard here on my thigh. Is this a dream or is it real? When I pinched myself, it hurt. [I thought], ah, this isn't a dream, it's real. I was so happy.

Then Ch'oe seamlessly connected his life story with the years leading up to Japan's capitulation and liberation day as it might be told through the omniscient voice of historical texts. He traced the events leading up to August 15: from the 1941 Japanese bombing of Pearl Harbor, "when it seemed Japan would take over the world," to the 1943 Cairo Conference, which he saw as signaling the inevitable defeat of the Japanese at the hands of the Allied powers, to the formation of the Korean Independence League (*Kŏn'guk tongmaeng*, to be differentiated from the *Chosŏn tongnip tongmaeng*, also translated as Korean Independence League, formed in Yenan as the precursor to the New People's Party) in August 1944 in preparation for liberation. Then he described the day of liberation:

> August 15, there was liberation, and immediately the gates of Sŏdaemun Prison opened. When the gates opened, our comrades who had been fighting for independence all came out without one person being injured. As soon as they all came out, the signboard that appeared was the Committee for the Preparation of Korean Independence. . . . That signboard was posted all over the country.

Seoul's Sŏdaemun Prison had been notorious for housing many of the political prisoners jailed by Japanese authorities. Having been discharged by the military on the 17th far from Seoul, it is doubtful that Ch'oe would have personally witnessed the prison gates open on liberation day or prisoners being freed. Nonetheless, he made a personal connection to the legacy of the anticolonial movement by referring to the prisoners as "our comrades" (*uri tongjidŭl*), and associated himself with the national movement under the banner of the Committee for the Preparation of Korean Independence (CPKI):

> Beginning from that point, I worked with the CPKI. One of the biggest tasks was preserving the peace, and I was put in charge of the security corps (*ch'iandae*). In larger cities, security was important because at the time there was a shortage of food and materials. But, in the countryside where I was, everyone was self-sufficient by farming, so there wasn't much of that problem. The most important thing we did as part of CPKI was preserving peace and enlightening the citizens. So many people were illiterate. Since there were so few people who could read, the enlightenment movement was necessary. How we were liberated, by whose struggle, and what kind of country should we build. This is what CPKI did, and a step further, I don't remember the date, but a month or two after liberation, it changed to the People's Committee.

He connected his role in the local security corps with a sweeping view of what was going on nationally. What was missing was a more personal view.

There was a distinct absence of markers of domestic life in the stories of both men. Where were their families in these narratives? Did they get married or have children? Although such stories came up more readily during casual conversation, they did not make their way into the formal interview despite the fact that interviews were conducted in free form to allow the narrators to structure their own life stories with minimal intervention. Without probing, both men shared their family histories to a far greater degree off the record than during the formal interview. There were two instances during the interview when Ch'oe spoke about his wife. First, when Ch'oe was talking about the first few days after liberation, I asked, "Did you not have any family of your own at this time?" He simply responded by saying, "I did." I asked again, "Where?" to which he replied, "They were in Kyŏngju. The oldest [child] was about a year old when I came back after liberation. That one now lives in Seoul." He went on to explain that after liberation, he did not live with his family but stayed in town, supported by one of the wealthier members of the PC. When I asked how his wife and son were able to get by without him, he responded that they were staying with his wife's relatives. On a separate occasion, he recalled how his wife had been beaten so severely by the South Korean authorities when the people's committees came under attack that she lost consciousness after defecating and urinating on herself. He conjectured that it was due to these injuries that she eventually died of spleen cancer in 1960. That was the extent of Ch'oe's reference to his wife and children, and Kang made no mention of family at all.

The fact that both men were married to second wives may have played some part in hindering discussion of their complex family history. Although he made no mention of it, Ch'oe was married to Pak Sun-ja at the time of the interview. She had been a guerrilla fighter during the Korean War. In 1954, she was captured by South Korean authorities and imprisoned until 1965. Soon after her release, she was introduced to the widowed Ch'oe by a mutual friend and they married. They had two daughters of their own in addition to the six children from Ch'oe's first marriage. As for Kang Tam, he had been married in the north with a son and a daughter before being captured in the south. But after his release in South Korea, he had remarried, as he saw no prospect of returning to his wife and children in the north. Their second marriage may have prevented them from dwelling too much on their previous families, out of consideration for their current wives.

The relative silence about their immediate families was in stark contrast to their elaborate descriptions about the family in which they grew up. In fact, Ch'oe's narrative began with an extensive and detailed story about his family lineage that went back thirty-one generations. The focal point was one particular patriarch who had taken part in the fight against the Japanese Hideyoshi Invasion of 1592, thereby taking his family's nationalist credentials back four centuries. He told the story as if he had been there, with details about how the first battle had started in his hometown and how his ancestor had heroically come to its defense. By contrast, for Kang, who was raised in a poor peasant family and whose father had died when he was only nine years old, family lineage was not important. Kang began his life story with poverty and hardship due in part to his father's early death. His story was dominated by female figures as they became the head of household:

> My father died when I was nine years old, before liberation. So, life was even more difficult. If my father had been around, it would have been a bit better since he could go back and forth to Seoul and make money, bringing home some rice. Because my father died, everything fell on my mother. My mother was forty-four or forty-three when my father died. So, my mother lost her husband in her early forties, shouldering the whole household and the children. It's impossible to express in words all the hardship she lived through. Also, my [paternal] grandmother lived with us in our house. My grandfather had died earlier, and my grandmother lived a long time. That grandmother went through much hardship. In the spring, my grandmother would go to the mountain every day, scouring for herbs and plants, and also pine tree bark for us to eat. It was really rough for my grandmother. Yes, she helped my mother a great deal. My grandmother did most of the difficult things. When I was older, in the fifth grade and a bit more mature, I realized my mother was physically weak with a very bad stomach condition. My mother really suffered a great deal. . . . After liberation, 1945, '46, '47, it was still very difficult then. Things got better in 1948. The land reform was implemented in the north. So, all the landlords' lands were confiscated without compensation. For middle peasants, they left them enough land for their family to eat, and confiscated the rest. And they distributed it all to landless peasants, calculating how much land had been confiscated, how many families there were in the village, how big the family was, and so on. That's when life got better.

Stories about their childhood or ancestral family did not segue into stories about their own domestic lives, as national history became the primary vehicle for their life story. For Kang, too, national liberation served as a way to demarcate his previous life of poverty from improvement in conditions after liberation, even though the 1946 land reform did not noticeably improve conditions until 1948 due to the lack of a sufficient amount of farmland to distribute.

The men's narratives appropriated the larger themes of national history, at times going as far back as the sixteenth century. Their life stories were punctuated with events of national importance: the Hideyoshi Invasion, liberation day, the formation of the CPKI and people's committees, land reform, and compulsory mass education. This is no coincidence. One of the primary issues after liberation centered on just how to define the nation in a postcolonial context when the country was divided into two separate occupation zones. Competing sets of events came to be highlighted as a way to configure two distinct national subjects. In other words, specific historical events served as legitimating structures, lending meaning to one's experience and memory.

Indeed, the contrast in the descriptions of liberation day from those who had collaborated with colonial authorities is remarkable. Rather than liberation day as "liberated space," liberation is depicted as a nonevent. For example, retired educator Kim Sŏn's memory of liberation day was of "no one coming outside, and only staying home."[13] There was little excitement or elation in her short description. Asked how she had heard the news about liberation, she simply answered, "through the radio." Likewise, two Korean officers in the Japanese Imperial Army, Paek Nam-kwŏn and Pak Kyŏng-wŏn, had little to say about liberation day. Paek stated that he heard news of the surrender at noon on August 15, and heard rumors the next day that Korean officers in the Japanese Imperial Army would be killed as national traitors.[14] The choice of words here—"surrender" as opposed to "liberation"—is indicative of his position as a Japanese Imperial Army officer. Like Kim Sŏn, Pak also described refraining from moving about or meeting anyone, likely out of fear of retribution.[15]

Even those who had not overtly supported the colonial government experienced liberation day with ambivalence if they were in the company of the Japanese. Kim Sŏk-hyŏng, who later joined the North Korean Communist Party, becoming the local party chairman in his hometown in North P'yŏngan Province, described hearing news of liberation in his workplace at the local irrigation office, where there was an eerie silence after the fifteen-minute speech by the emperor conceding defeat. When one of the Korean workers walked over to the blackboard and wrote "Long Live Korean Independence" in big Chinese characters, there was still nothing but silence. Kim remembered somewhat apologetically, "No one clapped, although I clapped a little inside."[16] When celebrations began with days of festivities and the formation of local self-governing committees and security organizations, Kim, like Ch'oe, joined the security corps, disarming the Japanese and taking over Japanese property and administration. Despite attempts to curb violence, there were instances of spontaneous people's courts that wreaked vengeance on former collaborators, particularly those who had worked for the Japanese police.

Thus, all sides had a heavy stake in their claim to national history, even if only to escape persecution. Life stories served as a platform on which competing national histories battled for hegemony. Ch'oe, a long-time dissident in the south, and Kang, who was originally from the north, were outsiders to mainstream South Korean society, leading them to adopt dissident identities as part of the political opposition in the south.[17] Each of their narratives provided competing national histories to define the nation, in Kang's account as a liberated peasant and in Ch'oe's account as a persecuted revolutionary. In either case, it was a patently masculine account.

This way of organizing experience and memory was facilitated by their identification with a distinctive group: the political opposition. It is worth reiterating Halbwachs's point on collective memory, that "the individual calls recollections to mind by relying on the frameworks of social memory . . . [since] memory is a collective function."[18] Against severe political oppression, the opposition had created a countermemory that was at times just as hegemonic and dominant within its own ranks in order to produce an alternative narrative of national history. It often traced a linear history of mass resistance in modern Korean history, from the Tonghak Rebellion of the late nineteenth century to the armed independence movement during the colonial period, on to the people's committees after liberation, culminating in the democracy movement that eventually toppled the military dictatorship in the south.[19] Official North Korean historiography follows a similar linear development of nationalist class struggle, positioning the formation of the people's committees as direct precursors to the founding of the North Korean state.[20] The South Korean opposition was able to create an alternative national history that aligned with the north, perpetuating a homogeneous vision of empowerment through discursive and social practices of its own.

Publications and speaking engagements within opposition circles provided Ch'oe with ample opportunity to edit and polish his stories.[21] During our first meeting, Ch'oe handed me a one-page resume (yangnyŏk) with a short chronology of his life. It had been sequentially organized with events and activities deemed to be of historical significance. His narrative followed the chronology in his resume, and it served to structure and reinforce his memory, reminding him of what came next. The resume was not merely a list of positions he had held through the years, but included specific episodes, such as the "peasant cooperative tenant rights struggle," to highlight certain experiences while serving as security officer in the people's committee. In this incident, in June 1946 a tenant farmer had come looking for help when his landlord had attempted to throw him off the land after he had already prepared the field for planting. After Ch'oe helped the farmer finish planting in order to secure the tenant's rights over the land, as was customary, Ch'oe was thrown in jail for a month by local authorities. Activities for which he was persecuted, landing him in jail, were prominently listed so that the points of intersection with state authorities served as important markers in his life story.

By contrast, at the time of my interview Kang Tam had only recently joined the group of long-term prisoners, and thus he lacked a rehearsed narrative that was already organized in chronological order of importance. His life story jumped from one time period to another, flitting back and forth between the present and the past. He started the first interview by talking about where he was from, which led to an explanation of how North Korea had revised its administrative levels, abolishing the township (*myŏn*) in 1958.[22] A story about landlords leaving his hometown after the land reform in 1946 led to a story about some of his relatives who had left North Korea, whom he later met in the south after being released from prison in the 1980s. A story about an espionage case in his hometown in the north in the 1940s led to comparisons to his own espionage case in the south and brutal stories of torture while in prison in the 1970s. This prompted him to recall how much he had been beaten while his town was under South Korean occupation during the Korean War because he had relatives in the Korean People's Army and in the Workers' Party. The markers organizing his life story were not rigidly fixed, and his narrative jumped around both spatially and temporally.

Kang's reaction at the end of the first interview was telling. He claimed that we did not get to the "real story" because he kept telling the "wrong stories" (*ŏngttunghan yegi*). When I asked what the "real story" was, he chuckled and said that he did not know. But he seemed to offer a clue throughout the interview when he differentiated some stories as digressions (*yŏdam*). He used the term on three occasions to refer to a short reference to his family, a story about making fun of his teacher in his youth, and a story about getting into trouble for fighting while serving in the

military. Stories that did not have a direct relevance to national history
were considered digressions, irrelevant to understanding his life story. He
believed that the major markers in his life story should be liberation, war,
military service, his mission to the south, and prison—all parts of his life
that were directly connected to national history.[23]

For those who left North Korea within five years of liberation, memories of liberation and revolution are predictably quite different, although
no less preoccupied with national history. A renowned Quaker peace activist, Ham Sŏk-hŏn, offers an interesting parallel as someone who was
active in organizing the people's committees in the north before choosing to leave North Korea in 1947.[24] Born in Pakch'ŏn County in North
P'yŏngan Province in 1901, he was introduced to Christianity when he attended a Protestant school at the age of six, "naturally" adopting the faith.
Awakened to politics with the March First Movement, he was repeatedly
jailed throughout the colonial period for his anticolonial activities. Despite his political activism, Ham saw postliberation Korea as operating in a
vacuum, with no serious organization to mobilize Koreans and vulnerable
to manipulation by foreign powers.

Unlike Ch'oe and Kang, Ham saw the organization of the PCs as ad
hoc and temporary until exiled leaders could return from abroad: "People
[like myself] were pushed into work by the masses, who thought that
a government would be organized whether in China or America and
brought in, until which time we would be responsible for maintaining
security only provisionally. We couldn't think beyond that."[25] In his memoir, he went on to describe liberation day as he remembered it in a measured and passive tone:

> On liberation day, I heard the news while standing with a bucket of
> dung to fertilize the fields. . . . I felt an urge to go out. Rather than just
> doing what I could and standing back, I ended up going all the way to
> Sinŭiju, observing the meeting of the five provinces. . . . I can testify
> that the self-governing committees were the product of the humble
> people's desire for self-governance in the beginning. But, the people in
> it were seeped in old ideologies, too ignorant of political history. My
> thinking was also shallow, but even in my eyes liberation meant social
> change, not just a change in state power. In other words, all of social life
> was going to change from now on, history was going to start anew, but
> most of these people were limited to thinking that now that the Japa-
> nese had been run off after oppressing us, we can now run things in-
> tact with our hands. It was very ignorant. Landlords acted as landlords,

yangban acted as *yangban*, and that's how they wanted it. And most of these people were from the so-called propertied class. . . . So, there was no chance against the communists.[26]

Although admitting that the communists were the best organized force, he claimed that they had no popular support, based on his experience of dissent in the north around the Sinŭiju Incident.

The Sinŭiju Incident was the first instance of a violent crackdown on protests against communist hegemony over the PCs. At approximately noon on November 23, 1945, student protestors were gunned down by security forces in front of the North P'yŏngan provincial office building. As head of the education department in the province, Ham not only witnessed the event in which more than ten students were killed but was held responsible for the protests, beaten, and sent to prison for fifty days.[27] After his release, his land and home were confiscated. When pressured to become an informant on other Christians in the area, he fled, crossing the 38th parallel on March 17, 1947. Other demonstrations by anticommunists and Christians, especially against the trusteeship proposed by the Moscow Agreement at the end of 1945, gained momentum in 1946 with a coordinated series of demonstrations on the anniversary of the March First Movement. Reportedly, some three hundred students and twenty Christian pastors were arrested after anticommunist demonstrations in Pyongyang on March 1, 1946, leading one American intelligence report to conclude that "the nucleus of resistance to the Communist regime are the Church groups, long prominent in North Korea, and secret student societies. Resistance has been centered in the cities, notably P'YONGYANG, and has taken the form of school strikes, circulation of leaflets, demonstrations, and assassinations. The government has replied with arrests and imprisonments, investigations of student and church groups, and destruction of churches."[28] Limitations placed on freedom of speech, association, and religion were recurring complaints from those leaving the north, most of whom were Christians and landlords. Whereas leftists were persecuted in the south, Christians and landlords were increasingly harassed in the north.

O Yŏng-jin, another Christian from the Pyongyang area, left North Korea in November 1947 after being placed under surveillance and subjected to searches and harassment.[29] Born in 1916 to a Protestant minister, his father was vice-chair to Cho Man-sik in the Pyongyang CPKI after liberation. Although he identified himself as a liberal socialist during the colonial period, with a strong attraction to communist ideology, he bemoaned the discrepancy between theory and reality and the abuses of communism, labeling himself a "democrat" in the preface to his memoir published in the south. Upon hearing news of liberation, he was overcome by anxiety more than happiness, possessed by a vague sense of fear, as we saw in chapter 2. Even for someone who was from a solidly nationalist family, actively involved in anticolonial activities, there was deep ambivalence at the initial news.

Likewise for Ri Yŏng-hŭi in Unsan County in North P'yŏngan Province, where the sight of smoke from the burning of documents at the local police station signaled that something had happened, no one dreamed that it signified the end of colonial rule as the only radios were at the police station.[30] When news of liberation finally came a few days later, many villagers did not know what to make of it, and Ri writes that "it did not feel real" (silgam i naji ant'a). Rather than dancing and singing in the streets, people were confused and uncertain. Several students then organized a Korean language study group and a reading group, reading Jean-Jacques Rousseau's Emile and Adam Smith's Wealth of Nations. The students were arrested by the local security corps and released after five days with a warning that they were too young and the kind of ideology they were propagating was no longer appropriate.[31]

Thus not all memories of liberation were celebratory. For Ham and Ri, initial forays into "collective effervescence" led to disappointment whereas O's experience of liberation was tainted by traumatic memories of Soviet occupation that involved pillage and rape. Ragtag Soviet troops without adequate supplies relied on the spoils from the newly liberated population, particularly coveting wristwatches, fountain pens, and men's suits as symbols of modern life, and often taking photographs with these items.[32] Such actions led O to sense a kind of childlike purity and innocence among Soviet troops, but other, less-forgiving observers frowned on their lack of cleanliness and civility, for example, washing their faces by spitting on their hands and using their sack of bread as a pillow to sleep on or a cushion to sit on before the bread was consumed. O credits the "inferior" behavior of Soviet troops with providing Pyongyang residents with a sense of "superiority" that overcame the hegemony attributed to Western countries.

Once in Seoul, however, O noted the drastic difference in the treatment and status of the Japanese. He noted with disdain the American flag (rather than a Korean flag) atop the governor-general's building that had replaced the Japanese flag and the retention of former colonial personnel, whereas in Pyongyang the Japanese and their collaborators had been stripped of their positions and property. Many of them had to resort to the worst jobs, cleaning toilets and transporting trash, giving vengeful satisfaction to Pyongyang residents.[33] The most striking difference between the north and south after liberation in people's memories was the extent to which the south was increasingly engulfed in a state of chaos. When Ri Yŏng-hŭi, for example, returned to Seoul from the north to continue his studies, he found Seoul in a state of total anarchy and lawlessness. Inflation was out of control, and everyone was "out for himself." The "law of the jungle" prevailed, where only those who were shameless and had guile could survive. Ri recalled how many people from the north returned home as a result, again disillusioned, but this time about the south.[34] Although opinions were diverse and often contradictory, American intelligence also found evidence that "refugees coming to south Korea from Manchuria and some few from north Korea, wish to return there after seeing conditions (Housing and food prices) in south Korea."[35]

Regardless of whether the experience and memory of liberation consisted of disillusionment or "collective effervescence," male narratives deemed their life stories a worthy part of national history. The memoirs by Ham, O, and Ri were offered, for example, as an "autobiography," a "testimony," and a "passage," as reflected in the published titles, self-consciously inserting their lives within a national chronology for the historical record. Stories about domestic life had no place in these life stories, in which the nation defined most prominently who they were. National history was paramount and their life story was significant in so far as it was an extension of the nation. The national history so depicted was a decidedly masculine one, in which the male political subject became the quintessential embodiment of subjectivity in postliberation Korea, quite unlike the revolutionary mother offered as a model for the ideal citizen in North Korea. In this history, there was no female revolutionary or feminine agency that could answer the question, Did Korean women experience liberation as a "liberated space"? We must turn to women's narratives of their life stories to see whether an answer can be found.

Life Story as Women's History

To my chagrin, women—already a minority among those with experience of political involvement in the liberation period—flat out refused my requests for interviews, saying they had "done nothing" important enough to record. This reaction was interesting in itself because of the contrast from men about the way women viewed themselves. Whereas men often felt their stories had to be told and were eager when asked about their activities, women seemed embarrassed and reluctant. In the end, I was unable to conduct formal interviews with women, but they told stories in casual conversation that were corroborated by two valuable independent projects that coincided with my field research: a documentary film and an oral history project.[36]

These stories are supplemented by discussion of two memoirs. The first is by Kim Wŏn-ju (1907–95), a female journalist during the colonial period who became actively involved with the postliberation women's movement and eventually settled in North Korea in 1948.[37] The second is the already mentioned memoir by Hŏ Chŏng-suk (1908–91), who was an ardent socialist and feminist throughout the colonial period as a founding member of the Korean Women's Socialist League and the Kŭnuhoe in the 1920s. She joined the Korean communists in Yenan after taking refuge in China in the 1930s. Hŏ became the highest-ranking woman in the North Korean government after liberation, holding various posts in the cabinet, legislature, and the women's league throughout her life as minister of culture (1948), minister of justice (1957), chief of the Supreme Court (1959), vice-chair of the Korean Democratic Women's League (1965), and vice-chair of the Supreme People's Assembly (1972). The memoirs by Kim Wŏn-ju and Hŏ Chŏng-suk are rare examples of individual writing left by women involved in the politics of the postliberation period, north or south.

Whereas Kim was a reporter and Hŏ a partisan active in China before returning to Korea at the end of 1945, the other women whom I will profile were all guerrilla fighters in the south, taking up arms in support of the north during the Korean War. Although not all women took part in combat, more women fought in the front lines than stayed in the rearguard as political organizers or nurses and cooks. The ones who fought were often killed in battle, leaving few survivors to tell their stories.[38] The most famous of these sites of struggle was Chiri Mountain, but the fighting stretched across the T'aebaek and Halla Mountains, engulfing the vast mountainous terrain throughout the south. The genesis of this guerrilla movement began with the suppression of left-wing activities in the south under American occupation after the October Uprising in 1946. By the time separate elections were held in the south in May 1948, there were growing numbers of "mountain people" (*san saram*), as they were called.

The decisive turn to all-out guerrilla fighting began on Chejudo, an island off the southern coast of the Korean Peninsula that was fiercely protective of its autonomy and a stronghold for leftist politics. Many people refused to hold separate elections in the south that would perpetuate national division, and a mass rebellion broke out on the island.[39] The Sixth and Fourteenth Regiments of the newly created South Korean Army refused to put down the Cheju Uprising, instead staging a rebellion of their own and seizing control of the nearby towns of Yŏsu and Sunch'ŏn. So began a massive uprising that spread across the whole region, reinstating many of the people's committees that had been wiped out. The rebellion was crushed within a couple of weeks, and tens of thousands were arrested and imprisoned. However, many managed to flee into the mountains to make up the bulk of the guerrillas that continued to fight, some surviving until full-scale war broke out in June 1950. The profiled women joined the partisans after the outbreak of war although their political engagement often began earlier.

Born during the colonial period between 1924 and 1930, the women were from poor peasant families and were captured in 1952 during the Korean War, except for Pak Sun-ja, who was from a wealthy family and was captured in January 1954, some six months after the cease-fire.[40] They served prison terms ranging between eight years and thirteen years. They all married after their release, except Pyŏn Suk-hyŏn, who was married during the colonial period. A brief synopsis of each woman's biography follows.

1. Pak Sŏn-ae (older) and Pak Sun-ae are sisters, and were influenced by their father and brothers, who had been involved with the independence movement during the colonial period. They joined the guerrillas during the Korean War, and were captured by South Korean forces in January 1952. Pak Sŏn-ae served her full term, and was released in 1965. She then married another former partisan in a "companionate marriage," and had a daughter at age forty-two, but she was arrested again in 1975 and released in 1979.[41] Pak Sun-ae was released on parole in 1960, and also married a former partisan. Because he was originally from the north and did not have any relatives, they falsified the family registration records, hiding from the authorities and raising her sister's daughter until her release. They did not have any children of their own. Her husband died in 1979 due to injuries sustained during his guerrilla days.

2. Pak Sun-ja was born into a wealthy family. Influenced by her brothers and other relatives, she began her political activities before the Korean War. In the beginning of the war, she was active in the

Hadŏng County Women's League in South Kyŏngsang Province, joining the guerrillas once the north was in retreat. She was captured in January 1954 after the last guerrilla resistance ended in Chiri Mountain. She was released in 1965, and married Ch'oe Sang-wŏn. They had two daughters together, the first of whom was born with severe brain damage due to medical complications during birth.

3. Pyŏn Suk-hyŏn was born into a traditional family, unable to go to school or leave the house until she was seven or eight years old. The whole family moved to northern Manchuria when she was twenty, where she married at twenty-two in 1945. Liberation soon followed, and she moved to her husband's hometown, Sunch'ang, in North Chŏlla Province in southwestern Korea. Her husband was involved with the people's committee there, but with increasing suppression, the family split up, leaving her and her newborn son to bear the brunt of the police harassment. These ordeals opened her eyes to politics, and after her husband went to North Korea in 1947, she also joined the Communist Party. Shortly thereafter, there was a warrant out for her arrest, which forced her into hiding until the Korean War, when she became active in the local women's league. Once the North Korean forces retreated, she left her baby with her in-laws and joined the guerrillas, during which time she lost her right arm from frostbite. She was captured in February 1952 and released in 1960.

In contrast to these life stories, which had to be pieced together based on conversation, Kim Wŏn-ju's memoir was written chronologically, beginning with her childhood during the colonial period and ending with her participation in the North-South meeting of leaders in Pyongyang in April 1948.[42] Born into a poor peasant family, she was encouraged to succeed in school as a way to change her fate. She graduated from Pyongyang Girls' High School, considered one of the best schools in northwestern Korea in the 1920s. After a period of study in Japan, she began work as a writer for *Kaebyŏk* (Creation), a Korean nationalist journal in Seoul. Her meager salary was not enough to support her family, so she took a job writing for *Maeil sinbo*, the official organ of the Office of the Governor-General. In 1933, at the age of twenty-six, she married Sŏng Yu-kyŏng. Sŏng, who was from a wealthy *yangban* family, had left home to learn "new knowledge" in Seoul. A stint in Tokyo as a student exposed him to Marxism. She described him as "a progressive man who had experienced prison life twice after participating in the student movement. . . .

Although he was not able to assert himself in the struggle because of his class background and lifestyle, his class-consciousness and spirit of rebellion against the Japanese were much stronger than mine after living a life of poverty and oppression."[43] Though she considered him beyond her status, he had already married at the age of fourteen in an arranged marriage. His attempts to get a divorce came to naught as parental approval was required and his father was firmly against divorce as a disgrace to a *yangban* family. Despite family disapproval, Kim and Sŏng set up house together in 1933.

Choosing a married man for love and holding a job marked Kim Wŏn-ju as a classic New Woman, a term used during the 1920s and 1930s to refer to modern educated women who wore Western attire and held one of the new professional jobs. Opportunities open to women with a modern education were few and far between, however, and most urban women worked in factories and service jobs. Although New Women were viewed with a certain sense of awe and intrigue, they were also disdained for advocating free love, with many gaining ill-repute as a result of their relations with men. Indeed, Kim was critical of the negative stereotypes associated with New Women, and wary of being identified as one. Kim wrote quite cynically about marriage as a "fetter," seeing it as a practical means for survival and shelter rather than love. Kim almost seemed to regret her marriage altogether as she described the contempt from her in-laws toward her peasant background and the growing rift with her husband over "class differences," characterized by his stoic demeanor, picky food habits, and strict discipline in child rearing. This chapter in her life story comes to an abrupt end with the following statement: "I'll just relinquish everything, and sacrifice myself for the future happiness of my three children. It took thirteen years of such resignation. After thirteen years of marriage, August 15 liberation came."[44]

In comparison to men's accounts of liberation that unfolded in a decidedly national space, Kim's narrative of liberation began and ended in the domestic space of the home:

> August 15, 1945, they say the Japanese Emperor will be making an important broadcast. Everybody is running outside from each and every house, and there are sounds of men running in the alleys. I too ran out with my apron still on. . . . Everyone was running. People filled the wide street. As if the store had been set up for just this day, the radio shop placed a large radio on top a table in front of the store. It was eleven o'clock. There was a slow mumbling of a gloomy voice coming from the radio. Japanese Emperor Hirohito was speaking. One group close to the

radio suddenly shouted, "Japan surrendered!" All the people shouted at once, "*Manse! Manse!*" [Long live] And this wasn't enough for some as they jumped up and down, shaking those beside them, and embracing them. Suddenly the atmosphere changed into a cauldron of shouts of joy and happiness. It was the end of the thirty-six-year Japanese colonial life of slavery. . . . I too was swept up by the crowd, following them, shouting "*Manse!*". . . "*Manse! Manse!* Long Live Korean Independence!" How can I express the explosion of that deep *han* [lament] and the instinctively and absolutely natural national ecstasy? I came back home after the whole day had waned. . . . As soon as I stepped in the front gate, I threw myself as if falling flat on the wooden porch and cried out loud. Tears of joy! Tears of suffering, tears poured out that had been suppressed for tens of years in order to endure the pain. I carefully thought about what I had to do and the path I had to take. At first, I was bewildered. But, I knew exactly what it was that prevented my mother and me from overcoming unhappiness and suffering. It was because of feudal remnants. In order to prevent the reoccurrence of women's days past, in order to never again subject my loving daughters, poor nieces and the many other daughters to suffering, women must be liberated from feudal oppression and contempt.[45]

Liberation day opened a new chapter in Kim's memoir, not only marking a turning point in national history but in her own liberation as a woman. Having left the house still in her apron on the morning of August 15, she returned home later that day determined to work for women's liberation.

In some ways, the home that she had left that morning was not the home she returned to in the evening. The cathartic effect of stepping inside the front gate of the house and falling to the floor, crying tears of joy, enables a kind of overlay between the nation and the home. Liberation day was literally brought home in Kim's story, signaling the extent to which women may have experienced national liberation through the liberation of domestic space—an opportunity to reconfigure and reimagine an alternative domesticity. Along with the nation that had been regained, the home was also to be reclaimed and remade, free from "feudal" oppression. The years of mistreatment as a colonial subject were fused with "unhappiness and suffering" as a woman, so that national liberation was equated with women's liberation.

Consequently, Kim's very first venture after liberation was to seek out study groups. First, she attended the Korean Language School (*Han'gŭl kangsŭphoe*), finishing the course in two weeks, and then she enrolled in the Korean History School (*Chosŏn ryŏksa kangsŭpso*) for four months. Kim was desperate to find a way to participate in the remaking of society, and saw education as offering the opportunity to strengthen the nation toward national liberation as well as women's liberation: "Studying was a matter which would decide my fate; it was my duty as a daughter to resolve my mother's unfair treatment; and more generally, it was a weapon to destroy feudalism."[46] She was relieved that her husband was busy, leaving the house for days on end, because he would have disliked her "going out and about" and would have "meddled uselessly" if he knew.[47] But despite her attempts at participation in the weeks and months following liberation, she could not find her place. Space for her in the "collective effervescence" was limited. Certainly there were calls aplenty for women's liberation, women's right to vote, and an end to prostitution and sexual discrimination, but she found the women's meetings frustrating for their lack of clear direction and serious resolve. Simply put, women were out of the loop. It is telling that she had no other recourse but to join women's organizations rather than participating in the people's committee. Disillusioned with the bourgeois politics of the conservative women's organization, the Korean Women's Association (*Han'guk puinhoe*), whose members seemed more interested in advancing their individual reputations, she joined the leftist Korean Women's League (*Chosŏn punyŏ ch'ong tongmaeng*). In early 1946 she became the chief editor of their newspaper, *Punyŏ chosŏn* (Korean Woman—a different publication from the one in the north, using the more traditional term *punyŏ* that designates married women as opposed to *yŏsŏng*, the modern generic term for women used in the north). By April 1948, she had become the head of the education section of the women's league, and the memoir ends with her making the journey across the 38th parallel to the north to attend the North-South meeting of leaders in April 1948.[48]

Similar to Kim's experience, the roles available to partisan women upon liberation were limited in South Korea. Although Kim was fortunate to have had an education, most women did not have the same opportunities; the education of girls was not a priority for most families with limited resources during the colonial period. The lack of education curtailed the formation of wider social networks, and it was their male relatives, such as brothers and husbands, who were instrumental in introducing women to larger communities beyond their domestic realm. But with limited positions for women outside this space, they were placed in auxiliary roles. Pak Sun-ja, for example, was initiated into politics by running errands for her brothers. She explains that she went on most errands to organize secret meetings because she was the only woman, and therefore the least suspect.[49] When the Korean War began, she was put in charge of organizing the local women's league to feed the soldiers: "Because it was wartime, men took care of food supplies, and women did most of the cooking. There was a large field in Hadong. We made food from the greens in the fields to feed the People's Army."[50]

Pak Sŏn-ae had similar experiences but resisted having to adopt such secondary roles:

> Even in the mountains, people assume that it is naturally women who have to cook. Women think so too and naturally do it. I said no way because then we wouldn't be able to study. While it is study time for the men, we have to prepare food. So, I suggested forming groups of both men and women. Actually, most of them had suggested forming groups, but women ended up doing most of the work. But, when things like that happened, I really fought. I fought a lot. Of course it's a disadvantage for me. People would say that I'm not good, "That woman is doggedly tough (ŏkse ppajyŏtta)." [laughs] I'd hear stuff like that.[51]

Having been initiated into the political arena by their male relatives rather than by state policy, women lacked the organizational and institutional space that could support their participation once they had been brought in. They went from running errands for their brothers to cooking and cleaning for the partisans. Instead of being on center stage, women became supporting actors assisting the main stars, remaining more often than not on the fringes of the action.

In contrast to the north, local women's league branches also lacked state support. For example, Ch'oe Sang-wŏn's paternal aunt, who was in her fifties, was put in charge of the women's league, but when asked about the league's activities, he could not recall any:

> Yes, there was a women's section at the time. It was called punyŏ tong-maeng [women's league] then. Within the people's committee, the person in charge of the women's league was my aunt. I don't know her name, because I just called her komo, komo [paternal aunt]. My aunt was the chairperson. All those who had held some form of position came close to death several times. And, as I said before, over there by Kyŏngju and by Andong, they are very conservative. For women to come out and do something was still difficult. It's still like that!

At the time, since the center [in Seoul] had set up the women's league, we decided we should have a women's section in our township too, so my aunt held that responsibility. But in reality, there was no activity. I think—I'm not sure when it was, not 1945, but maybe '46 in the spring once—the wives of the officials [of the PC] gathered and had a picnic, and I think that maybe that was a gathering of the women's league.

Although there was awareness of the need to address women's issues, there was no state policy such as the Gender Equality Law around which the woman question could be taken up in the south. Indicative of women's status, particularly in the countryside, Ch'oe was unable to remember his aunt's name despite her official position, unlike the male relatives who he always referred to by name.

Nonetheless, issues of national liberation also took precedence for women, with Pak Sŏn-ae, for example, asserting that "women's rights were useless without a country," because "women were even more oppressed and mistreated when we had lost our country."[52] Participation in the national struggle was considered a form of personal liberation amounting to the liberation of women. Indeed, many partisan women described their time in the mountains as one of the most liberating experiences of their lives. Instead of being someone's wife or someone's daughter, they were able to dream of being revolutionaries, equal to their male comrades. Despite losing an arm during her guerrilla days, Pyŏn Suk-hyŏn was unequivocal about her life in the mountains, calling it "the most rewarding time in my whole life." She declared that she had "lived fruitfully," keeping her aspirations and doing "whatever I wanted."[53] Pak Sŏn-ae concurred: "There was nothing that was difficult for being a woman because we had lived under such oppression before. We were finally able to say anything, and do whatever we wanted. We are women, but also human."[54] Common to both women's sentiments is the sense of liberation at being able to do "whatever we wanted." They were no longer bound by duties and obligations associated with a traditional family, which determined what they could or could not do, whether in their natal family or with their in-laws. For the first time in their lives the women experienced a "liberated space" that was not defined by their place in the family.

Thus, the stories come full circle—the men's life stories appropriated national history as their own while women attempted to insert their life stories into national history by joining the national struggle, equating national liberation with women's liberation. But this endeavor was not

Figure 7.2. "Taejŏn partisans and People's Army" (n.d.). RG 242, SA 2009, box 9, item 74. Courtesy of the National Archives and Records Administration.

facilitated in the south, as demonstrated by the challenges women faced in finding established organizational spaces for their participation. As a result, women appropriated one of their core traditional identities, as mothers, to justify and validate their entry into the political arena through a form of revolutionary motherhood that had striking parallels with discourses in North Korea. Their firsthand accounts confirm the extent to which motherhood was not simply a rhetorical device but was experienced by women themselves as a new politicized identity.

Sometimes motherhood became a strategic identity used to carry out subversive activities: "Women had to take secret reports to communicate with so and so and tell them to be at such and such place by a certain time. Women would do such things really well. They'd go carrying a baby on their back, take laundry or some such thing, and that's how we met. Two or three would meet and talk about why we had to unite, raising consciousness."[55] Motherhood also became a source of political awakening, poignantly described by Pyŏn Suk-hyŏn:

When I got pregnant, I avowed that the ruling class had to be overthrown. For the future generation I had to go forth, but I couldn't leave because my baby was nursing and there was no place to entrust him. So

I just waited until he could be brought up without nursing. . . . Only if I left and joined the class struggle would class disappear and there would be a life of equality. I told my baby I was going to the kitchen to get some water, and then just left to join the comrades. As I left, I heard him cry, but I just left. I asked my parents-in-law to bring him up, and I just went into the mountains.[56]

Pyŏn transposed her concern for her own child to that of the whole "future generation"; her desire to create a better future for her son prompted her to leave him behind to join the partisan struggle. A skeptical reading of her story might question her motivations. Her story can be read as an attempt to justify her past actions, consciously or not, in order to alleviate her sense of guilt at leaving her baby. But her premeditated plans to leave render her almost coldly calculating and proud of her actions:

It's not that I didn't think about my son, but I didn't dwell on thinking that I wanted to see him. . . . I didn't worry about trivial things, about private things. That's how I lived. That's why I don't have *chŏng* [heart]. I didn't have the chance to give *chŏng* to my child, or to my husband. I only had a chance to give *chŏng* to my comrades. When my son was young, I consciously didn't give him any *chŏng*. Until he was four years old, I consciously didn't give him *chŏng*. If I gave *chŏng*, the child would feel it consciously, the mother's *chŏng*. Then, it would be hard for me to leave him. I decided not to give him *chŏng*, just hold it within myself. When he was asleep, I'd try grabbing his hand or rub my cheeks against his. That's how I raised him [until I left].[57]

Pyŏn had planned to join the partisans in the summer of 1946 when she first got pregnant, intentionally withholding affection toward her baby in preparation for her departure. When asked how she felt about the decision in retrospect, she responded:

As a mother, I was a heartless mother. The revolution would say that it was admirable, but as a mother, it was heartless. I don't know how it will be judged. [But] at that time, I did the right thing. . . . If I had stayed buried in my family, just raising my baby, I'd only know my husband, my child, and parents-in-law. But, now, I know all the comrades. And the young people that I know, I can give and receive love from them all. I gained all those people, sacrificing a few.[58]

Motherhood was taken from the private into the public realm to embrace not her own child but society at large and the future generations to come. The private indeed was the political as motherhood was transformed into a revolutionary identity.

Despite the heroic language of maternal agency in her story, however, Pyŏn was nonetheless forced to choose between her child and the revolution. Her view that the family is "private" and "trivial" stems from the dominant discourse that relegated the family to such status, forcing women to choose between the two, whereas the choice was never fraught with so much tension and conflict in men's stories.[59] Rather than critique such difference as unequal, Pyŏn advocated separate domains for women and men despite her belief in gender equality:

> No matter how much equality and freedom is called for, there are things that men have to do and things women have to do. Men can wash dishes and clean. But he can't breast-feed. He can't give birth. He can't make tasty side dishes. These are women's lot. Women should acknowledge them as her share and do them without a peep. . . . Outside she is a heroine. Inside the house she is a "wise mother good wife." She has all her rights. She does all her duties. This is how women should be.[60]

When asked whether this might not be too demanding for women, she conceded that it is more difficult for women than men, but that this cannot be helped. She self-reflexively wondered whether she was just too old-fashioned.

Women's participation in the partisan struggle enabled women to enjoy a form of "liberated space," leaving behind the home. Women felt empowered by their new identity as partisans despite severe political oppression, which only served to strengthen their identities as partisans rather than as women. But it was still their gender that was the source of brutal treatment when they were sexually tortured in prison. Moreover, the smaller number of female political prisoners meant that women, segregated from their male comrades, lacked the support that came from their collectivity, as Pak Sŏn-ae explained:

> The most difficult thing was that [women] were all imprisoned in one room, and there would be *ungsŏng ungsŏng* [low-level noise caused by a group of people talking]. There was no purpose. It only caused confusion. There would be division among the rank and file. A space had to be created for people to communicate. So, I concluded that an

organizational member must begin an organizational life even with just three people. If someone talks, then the rest should focus and listen.[61]

The capacity of male-dominated institutions to fully encompass women had limitations. Although women joined the partisan struggle and the later network of former partisans, a comparison of men's and women's narratives reveals a striking difference. Men's narratives failed to include their domestic life as important markers of their life stories whereas marriage and family structured women's lives, often constraining their choices, which ultimately led to the transformation of the very concept of motherhood to accommodate the tension between their partisan and gendered identities.

Pyŏn Suk-hyŏn's life story is a poignant example of how a traditional form of female identity represented by motherhood was transformed into a form of militant revolutionary as caretaker of future generations. Indeed, she was well aware of how traditional ideology can become a vehicle for new ideas and practices:

> Once a woman married, she had to die there at the in-laws. She couldn't run and leave, or remarry. That was ingrained in my head. That sort of will was linked to this political ideology. I hitched my thoughts to this ideology that if I die, I'd die here as a partisan. I wouldn't change. I mustn't change.[62]

Her life is yet another example of just how fluid the ideals of femininity and masculinity can be, especially during times of social change. Her traditional ideas about female chastity and monogamy were transformed into a militant motivation for the preservation of her ideological purity and loyalty without betraying her political cause.[63] Nonetheless, women's stories have not been part of the history of liberation as their life stories were marginalized at best as women's history.

A caveat must be added before concluding this section by discussing Hŏ Chŏng-suk's memoir published in North Korea. As evident in the title, *Days in the Democratic Construction of the Country*, her memoir puts national history front and center. This would seem to confirm the point from the previous chapter that the experience of liberation for women in North Korea was substantially different from the south, with strong state support for women's participation in national construction. As a result, there were numerous examples of women experiencing the revolution as a "liberated space," but how that period is memorialized in contemporary North Korea turned out to be quite different. As she tells us in her preface, Hŏ heard the news of Korea's liberation while "abroad" and upon her return to North Korea in December 1945 she "did not know how to navigate the sharp conflict between democratic and antidemocratic forces, the difficult economic situation, and all the different ideological claims."[64] There is no mention of where she was abroad and what she was doing there when, in fact, she was a guerrilla partisan in China, albeit not with Kim Il Sung's group in Manchuria, but in Yenan with Kim Tu-bong. That the so-called Yenan faction had been purged in the late 1950s, after the Korean War, required that her past also be expunged of any illicit information.

Rather than her own story of leadership, it was thanks to the Great Leader that she was able to fulfill her work without trouble. It was the Great Leader who single-handedly "led the revolution to establish the party, the country, and the military." Thus, she explains, the memoir was written for the historical record in order to show Kim Il Sung's wise leadership through her experiences while working closely beside him so that others might learn from *him*. True to her promise, the five-hundred-page book is not so much about her life as it is about her observations of *his* life between 1945 and 1958. She opens the book with her first meeting with Kim Il Sung, going on to describe how he meticulously supported her propaganda work with his careful edits and suggestions. He personally took an interest in her well-being, and guided her in the importance of a united front and the mass line. According to her narrative, liberation was achieved by Kim Il Sung and was cherished as a gift by the Korean people. In the north, in place of a contested national history, the story of Kim Il Sung has become paramount, becoming the framework by which to organize one's life story. Thus, women's stories, like that of Hŏ Chŏng-suk, are "silenced" in the north as well.

History and Memory

Marking the sixtieth anniversary of liberation, the year 2005 saw numerous scholarly publications, documentary projects, and commemorative events, reflecting back on August 15, 1945. The Korea Broadcasting Station in South Korea produced a four-part documentary, aired between August 9 and 12, on the "Memory of 8.15—How Do We Remember 8.15?" featuring "the unearthed memories of people too often overshadowed by official institutional history in order to retrace the period through the experiences and perspectives of ordinary people."[65] The project also led to a publication of a one-volume collection of oral histories gathered during the interview process. Forty individual stories were included out of some 150 interviews that were collected for the documentary. The short epilogue by the producers does not explain precisely how the stories were selected except to say that the project was motivated by the desire to highlight the life stories of average people and their everyday experiences during liberation. Ironically, most of the stories reproduced the standard framework of national history by invoking key political figures and events. It should come as no surprise, then, that of the forty individuals featured in the book only seven were women.

Women entered the "liberated space" of liberation and revolution to define it in their own ways, at times adopting the triumphant narrative of liberation in their own life stories. But there is ambivalence in their experiences and the memories associated with them. Pyŏn Suk-hyŏn's decision to join the partisans, leaving behind her son, recurs again and again in the telling of her life story. It is both a proud moment, as she says, "from the perspective of the revolution," and a haunting experience of abandoning her child. She is unable to bring these experiences together to critically assess the postliberation period, not simply as heroic but as shaping women's experiences in ways different from men.

Likewise, Kim Wŏn-ju's euphoric experience of liberation must be understood within the context of her thirteen years of marriage and child raising that set her running out into the streets in her apron on August 15, 1945. Whereas women were often dispersed and isolated in their homes, with limited spaces available for them outside the domestic space, men were able to use their organizational and institutional connections to imagine and inhabit a national space not only in the past but sustained into the present through the formation of collective memories. If, as Halbwachs noted, group formation becomes an important process in collective memory, then women often did not have independent organizations of their own for organizing and maintaining their collective memories, whether in the north or the south. Thus, parts of women's experiences may be lost, much as Kim's thirteen years went unmentioned in her memoir. The national framework of liberation and revolution has made women's experiences invisible in the same way that the woman in the opening photograph in this chapter has so often been cropped out of the frame. Despite growing awareness of the gendered dimensions of history, it seems we still need a "critique of history which has perpetuated silence of women's history and ignored 'personal' histories as inadequate evidence or product of those who are 'not quite' historians."[66]

A countermemory offered by the opposition served as one form of resistance to the disciplinary powers of an anticommunist historiography in South Korea. Its entry into public discourse became possible only in the late 1980s by the space opened up through the democracy movement in the south. Indeed, the memories uncovered in many subsequent oral history projects restored the voices of dissent that had been silenced during authoritarian rule. However, it is also the case that the "dominant memory is not monolithic nor is popular memory purely authentic."[67] Though countermemory and official history may seem to be in opposition, they nonetheless reinforce each other by sharing the nation as the basic framework by which to structure the past. In this process, some experiences lose their place because they are merely "private" and "personal," deemed outside the scope of a national history.

Such uses of history and memory for nationalist ends have led to critical thinking on the relationship between history and memory. Tessa Morris-Suzuki's distinction between "history as interpretation" and "history as identification" helps identify one reason why history and memory have been so problematically brought together, particularly with the rise of nationalism.[68] For her, history as interpretation is what the discipline of history generally aims to do in its search for causal connections among events, ideas, and institutions that have led to historical change. By contrast, history as identification invokes the past for a sense of belonging, involving imagination and empathy. This is how history is often popularized in mainstream society through museums, memorials, historical societies, and commemorative events. In other words, collective memory has more often been mobilized under the guise of history for a sense of belonging.

Presented this way, it is now clear why women's narratives were filled with ambivalence, whether it was the reluctance to be interviewed at all or narrative gaps in Kim Wŏn-ju's memoir or the lack of Hŏ Chŏng-suk's own life story in her memoir. The ambivalence results from the generalization of a particular (male) experience as a sweeping national history without conceding its particularity, whether it is Kim Il Sung's individual experience in the north or a more generic masculine one in the south. Rather than taking the history we know at face value, we can return to the opening photograph to ask: Who is that woman and what was she doing there? We could imagine the woman to be Kim Wŏn-ju and map her story onto the woman to imagine her there, *belonging* in that crowd, but much too often the woman is left out of the frame because her story is considered irrelevant in remembering and historicizing liberation.

In her study of working-class memory, Marianne Debouzy channeled Halbwachs by noting how difficult it was to form collective memory in the absence of organizations and institutions to order and make sense of experiences that were crucial to the formation of identity.[69] If it is true that the collective memory of the working class is cohesive by virtue of being politically organized and thus institutionalized in unions, collective action, and political parties, the life stories included here reaffirm the importance of institutions in the formation and retention of memories and identities, even more so for marginalized groups such as women.

The divergent collective memories between the north and the south pose powerful challenges for the future reconciliation of the two Koreas. This chapter has been concerned with inserting the experience of the anonymous woman in the photograph into the collective memory of liberation in order to create a more inclusive and diverse history of the postliberation period. Reconciliation between the north and the south, as well as between North Korea and the United States, will have to involve the sharing and understanding of their respective collective memories, in order to create a history that is not simply about stubbornly holding on to one's own sense of identification, but that is truly about interpretation in the awareness that all parties "belong" in this world.

Conclusion

Chajusong [autonomy], creativity and consciousness make man the most
superior and powerful being in the world, and induce him to approach
the world not fatalistically but revolutionarily, not passively but actively,
and to remodel the world not blindly but purposefully.
KIM JONG IL (1982)

From the first three seminal reforms that initiated a thoroughgoing
social revolution to the collective life enacted through multiple organizations, the North Korean Revolution was an attempt to institute a new
socialist everyday imbued with social meaning that would overturn the
alienation and subjugation experienced under capitalist colonial modernity. The result was a singular focus on the creation of autonomous
modern subjects, not just as empowered individuals (by way of writing
autobiographies, for example) but as part of the socialist collective that
fused individual and collective interests into one, leading to North Korea's
own distinct form of heroic subjectivity embodied in revolutionary motherhood. But liberation and revolution are remembered differently today,
especially in North Korea, where they are "violently reduced" to the accomplishments of Kim Il Sung alone.

North Korean history cannot be reduced to that of one man despite
attempts to do so, ironically by both propagandists and critics. Looking at
the everyday enables the placement of North Korea's history within the
larger history of modernity rather than treating it as an aberration or an
anomaly that is the antithesis of the modern. Indeed, improvements in
everyday life during the North Korean Revolution were measured by the
degree to which the countryside had caught up to modern ways of life
through statistics comparing before and after liberation in the number of
houses with tiled roofs as opposed to thatched roofs; the number of sewing machines, record players and radios; and the number of homes with
electricity.[1] In Kangwŏn Province, households with radios almost tripled,
from 854 before liberation to 2,570 two years after liberation. Electricity
was extended to 29,850 households from 16,513 households, and the number of homes with record players spiked to 869 from a mere 139 before
liberation. Thirty-three hundred households had newly purchased clocks,

2,315 homes had bought new armoires, and 1,181 households had acquired new sewing machines. With some 130,000 households in the province, improvements were far from reaching most people. However, they were the first steps toward a more hopeful future and the promise of a modern life. Already in 1949, per capita national income had more than doubled since 1945.[2]

By the 1970s, anthropologist Mun Woong Lee was able to document the qualitative changes in family structure and kinship relations, gender roles, education, and health care in an ethnographic study of rural North Korea.[3] Women worked, studied, and served in the military side by side with men; mothers-in-law took care of domestic chores while daughters-in-law worked outside the home; education was compulsory for ten years and provided free of charge; and medical care was also free. Kim Il Sung had proclaimed in 1964 that "the aim of building socialism and communism is, in the final analysis, to assure a happy life for the entire people and to satisfy more fully their steadily growing material and cultural needs."[4]

Advances in living conditions and economic indicators in the postwar reconstruction of North Korea surprised observers, who hailed it as "one of the greatest economic powers in Asia."[5] Yet the reference to "cultural needs" in Kim Il Sung's own speech highlights the importance of moving beyond quantitative measures to harness the creative potential of the everyday, as Arvatov had suggested, in the transition from capitalism to socialism. Caught between vacillating modernist paths, however, that could fall into reactionary forms from the heroic variant, the horizon of the possible for North Korea was ultimately limited by the Cold War as national security overshadowed other aspirations. The building of a "rich, strong, independent and sovereign state" and overcoming the "centuries-old backwardness and penury left over by colonial rule" became the final goals of a revolution that was accompanied by a bitter memory of loss of sovereignty, once again compromised by national division.[6] Revolutions must end as the radical changes are institutionalized and the everyday is once again habitualized. But for North Korea, the end came early with the Cold War.

Militarization and centralization of power went hand in hand as the peninsula headed for civil war. By October 1948 the founding of separate states in the north and south heightened tensions along the 38th parallel as North Korea moved to build up its "38 guard units" (38 kyŏngbidae) and the "self-defense forces" (chawidae) in order to thwart southern attacks.[7] Beginning in June 1949, the organization of border security and self-defense units became an agenda item at almost every party meeting in Inje County.[8] Supplementing the military and the police, these units were responsible for protecting factories, government offices, granaries, and the transportation and communication systems, and for taking villagers to safety should there be a southern attack. They were also given the right to inspect people's identification cards, take suspicious persons to the closest police station, and carry simple self-defense tools such as sickles, knives, and batons. Local commanders included leaders from the youth, women's, and peasant leagues.

Military training, particularly of youth league members and students, began in August 1949 with instructions in military strategy, weapons training, and aeronautics.[9] Such preparations were hardly an overreaction as the border threats were quite real. In July 1949, there was a large-scale attack by the so-called Tiger Unit (*horim pudae*) from the south that caused extensive damage to local villages, and on August 6, 1949, there was yet another skirmish in Nam Township.[10] As a result of these clashes in Inje County, forty people were killed, eighteen were kidnapped, twenty-two were injured, thirty-eight households with 156 people fled to the south, ninety-two farm animals were lost, 136 houses were burnt down, and 1,127 sacks of grain were destroyed.[11] In a counterattack, the Inje County self-defense forces occupied the southern half of Nam Township south of the 38th parallel for twelve days between August 6 and 20, 1949, mobilizing some 6,552 people until heavy rains disrupted the supply route and they had to retreat.[12] As a result, sixty-three people were killed and ninety-seven houses destroyed in the south while the north sustained twenty-five casualties with thirty-one houses burned or destroyed. For all practical purposes, the "liberated space" that had opened up in the years immediately after liberation had begun to close with the founding of two separate states in 1948 as both sides marched toward civil war.

Immediately after the fighting in Nam Township, the recruitment of self-defense corps members in Inje County was expanded. Before the fighting, it had been limited to the ages of eighteen to forty; now, it was open to those between the ages of sixteen and forty-five, thereby organizing almost all able-bodied residents into defense units.[13] The number of defense unit members increased to 8,295—5,130 men and 3,165 women— out of a county population of 33,722, mobilizing almost a quarter of the residents and over 70 percent of those eligible to join. Consequently, by 1950 an extensive security and surveillance network had been established. Every five households formed one surveillance unit, keeping an eye out for illegal lodgers and strangers from out of town, protecting local facilities and infrastructure, maintaining public health, and preventing fires.[14]

The units were organized and directed by the people's committees, not by the local police force, since their duties were broadly defined to include not only security but also monitoring sanitary conditions and the spread of infectious diseases. There were outbreaks of cholera in the first half of 1950, already a major problem in the south since 1946.[15] Being so close to the border, Inje County was exposed to the spread of epidemics from the south while being repeatedly subjected to instances of sabotage; the most serious cases involved looting and arson of important facilities such as factories and granaries. Indeed, many villages along the 38th parallel had to come up with strategies for defense even before directives from the central government, organizing firefighters and security guards for public facilities such as telephone lines, railways, and granaries. They were especially vigilant against unauthorized travelers. People with criminal records and those with family members who had fled to the south were most suspect; they were specifically placed under watch "in order to prevent beforehand any possible incidents."[16]

According to public opinion gathered by North Korean secret surveillance in 1950 before the start of the Korean War, peasants reacted to rising tensions with worries about daily survival. They were concerned about the bad harvest the previous year and wondered who would be left to till the land if people continued to leave for the factories and mines. Others in charge of defense wondered how long they had to continue guarding the area, with one complaining that he was "sick of it" (*kol i ap'ŭda*). After cattle were stolen and a guard kidnapped by infiltrators from the south on February 6, 1950, residents were disillusioned by the lack of response from the defense units, expressing skepticism about their competence and effectiveness. One peasant woman in her late forties complained that the guard units had no countermeasure despite the kidnapping, claiming she would join them "if they would be willing to go kill 'em."[17]

Physical confrontations were augmented by strategies to win the hearts and minds of the people. In 1949, there were repeated reports of South Korean planes dropping propaganda leaflets, trying to convince North Korean soldiers and defense units to join the south.[18] The leaflets offered free medical care for injured soldiers, arguing that they were not the enemy but that Kim Il Sung and his "cronies" were. "Why fight to the end just to have the Soviet Union as your homeland?" implored a leaflet as it promised safe passage to anyone who "returns to the bosom of the homeland" with the leaflet in hand. Many were not easily swayed, expressing disdain for and hostility toward the planes, wondering why the People's Army did not shoot them down. Others, however, were impressed with the planes and the kinds of resources that the south was able to mobilize, with one woman expressing concern that subsequent planes might drop bombs rather than leaflets and that it was "time to prepare to move into the mountains."

The woman's statement was ominous to say the least, but no one could have predicted the catastrophic war that was to take over three million lives, or 10 percent of the Korean population, over the course of a mere three years, making it the deadliest conflict in modern history outside of the two world wars. By 1952, there were "no more targets" left standing in the north, where, by war's end, American planes had dropped 635,000 tons of bombs and 32,557 tons of napalm, compared to 503,000 tons of bombs used in all of Asia and the Pacific during World War II.[19] While South Korea sustained 1,312,836 casualties, including 415,004 dead, North Korean casualties are estimated at two million, including a million civilians, which meant that the war had claimed, on average, at least one member from every family in the north.[20] The war left long-term physical and psychological damage that continues to shape North Korea's domestic and foreign policy down to the present day. Not only is it exceptionally guarded against the infiltration of foreign influence, whether in the form of tourists or the Internet, but it has one of the longest conscription stints in the world at ten years of mandatory military service for almost all males who meet physical and background requirements.[21] This may explain why men have increasingly come to dominate all levels of the social and political hierarchy in the postwar period despite the importance accorded to women before the war. With the war ending in an armistice rather than a peace treaty, North Koreans have been mobilized to continue preparing for a war that might resume at a moment's notice against a far superior power, the United States, which has not shied away from outright belligerence in the doctrine of preemptive strike. The Korean War has become the single most defining national experience, leaving North Koreans with a fiercely autarkic mentality as a form of internal cohesion against outside threats. The collective experience of suffering and trauma has left even less room for fluidity and experimentation in the everyday.

If the nineteenth century had already seen the "invention of traditions" in the West as a result of the loss of identity and historical continuity from the effects of modernity, then it is no surprise to find postcolonial societies such as North Korea redoubling their efforts to define a sense of identity in the aftermath of colonialism in the twentieth century.[22] Nationalism would come back with a vengeance in the process of decolonization. But, as betrayed by the reference to "cultural needs" in Kim Il Sung's speech, the problem of opening up the everyday to its full creative potential was embedded in any revolution that hoped to offer an alternative to capitalist modernity. How can the everyday fulfill its creative promise rather than reproducing the cycle of production and consumption under capitalism? The question is part and parcel of the foundational dilemma confronted by all social revolutions in the dialectic between destruction and construction. Once previous structures of oppression are destroyed, what should be built in their place? What should "autonomy" and "creativity" mean, for example, in concrete terms as cornerstones of Juche philosophy as noted in the epigraph?

Rather than fully opening up to the possibilities offered by such questions, however, the everyday was once again made to succumb to the exigencies of economic development and political stability in the aftermath of colonial rule and a civil war that became an international war, leaving behind the hopeful promise of a new everyday full of "productive and creative potentialities ... rich in potential subjectivity."[23] Socialism was largely defined in terms of material advancement, both as a way to "satisfy the centuries-old desires of the peasants" and to build a strong country that could keep foreign powers at bay, to never again revisit the experience of foreign domination and intervention. Like Lenin's depiction of communism as "soviets plus electrification," the "complete victory of socialism" was equated with production goals that would increase output in steel, electricity, and grain, represented in the North Korean national emblem.[24] To be sure, the socialist project was considered incomplete, because the "seizure of power by the working class is but the beginning of socialist revolution," but what was required for its completion continued to be couched in negative terms by old ideas and old structures that had to be obliterated: "In order to achieve the complete victory of socialism we must obliterate the distinctions between towns and the countryside and the class distinction between the workers and the peasants, reinforce the material and technical foundations of socialism, markedly improve the material and cultural standards of the people, smash the insidious manoeuvres [sic] of hostile classes and do away with the corrosive influence of old ideas once and for all."[25] The positive elements of the program to build the "material and technical foundations of socialism" and the "material and cultural standards of socialism" remained vague and limited. Once revolutionary aims were identified with material achievements, alternative possibilities for everyday life narrowed. Our age of abundance has shown that the problems of the human condition do not disappear when we are no longer hungry or cold, when our basic needs have been met. This explains the common rhetoric among revolutionary regimes of a never-ending *permanent* revolution. There can be no end to the cycle of feeding the masses, of defending the nation against external threats because these are life processes that can have no end.

Whether socialist or capitalist, the history of the long twentieth century has been about the unrelenting drive for modernization through industrialization that brings the two systems much closer together than commonly assumed.[26] For North Korea, like other socialist states, production instead of consumption became the paramount organizing principle. But socialist modernity was not supposed to be about production as an inherent good, but about the fulfillment of social needs neglected by capitalism. Socialism differentiated itself from capitalism precisely by linking economics to social and political questions. The socialist economy was meant to serve the collective interest of the people rather than people being put to work for economic growth. That was the rationale behind "scientific" socialism, which saw the material abundance created by a mature capitalism as the foundation for a historically "rational" transition to socialism. This would allow creativity to become the essence of the new socialist everyday rather than concerns about material welfare. But for all the abundance of capitalist production, "creative destruction" seems to be all that is left in its path so far.[27] Not only have the determinist assumptions in "scientific" socialism been proven to be rather unpredictable but "socialism in one country" (whether in Soviet Russia or North Korea) in the face of capitalist intervention has been shown to be impossible.

The novel revolutionary organs of self-governance in the form of people's committees as a platform for a new kind of everyday were in the end subsumed under centralized state power, resulting in the ossification of the everyday as a creative and revolutionary potential in North Korea. From its spontaneous beginnings, the people's committees had been the basis for the "conscious" exercise of "autonomy" and "creativity," which were to become the very elements of the Juche idea.[28] In fact, autonomous decision making and new creative outlets against bureaucracy have often been the aim for many of the cultural revolutions waged under socialist regimes, including the one in China. Kim Il Sung himself called for a "cultural revolution" by "raising the intellectual and cultural standards of the people" to become "the first in Asia to implement mandatory middle school education."[29] Greater educational and political opportunities were seen as foundations for people to be more autonomous and creative. Nonetheless, Article 50, Paragraph 6 of the new Constitution adopted in November 1948 gave the cabinet the power to overrule the people's committee.[30]

Their retreat was not a foregone conclusion, however. Even at the height of the Korean War, local people's committees were singled out as "a new organ of people's power."[31] In 1952, Kim Il Sung pointed out ways in which people's committees should be strengthened. He first blamed the remnants of colonial and feudal ideology for the lack of appreciation of what it meant to be leaders in the people's committees. Representatives began to act like colonial-era officials, "coercively ordering the people around" rather than motivating them and working on their behalf as their "loyal servants."[32] Examples of such abuses of power included people's committee chairs who had their land tilled by the people in their districts, or accepted monies from the people for their personal celebrations such as birthdays, or, just like colonial officials, exacted extra tax burdens from their constituents and confiscated grain by "looking in their rice jar and pantries."[33]

In order to combat such bureaucratic tendencies, Kim concluded that leaders of people's committees must maintain close relations with the people, taking stock of actual conditions on the ground and faithfully reflecting the people's opinions, rather than ignoring deficiencies and problems and rebuking criticism as obstacles to their own professional advancement. For example, planting was reported to have been successfully completed when it was not; an emphasis on the due date for the tax-in-kind prompted the harvest of grains before they were fully ripe; flooding went unreported; and officials demanded that peasants fill the tax quotas even if they had to buy the rice to do so.[34] Such conduct had ultimately led to the estrangement and disaffection of the masses. People's committee leaders were advised not to blame the peasants for being "underdeveloped," trying to do all the work themselves, but rather to delegate, engaging the participation of the majority of people. Most of all, city and county people's committee chairs were told to place the village people's committee at the center of all their work since they were the ones working directly with the people in the countryside and in the factories.[35] At the height of postwar reconstruction, people's committees were urged to become self-reliant, "creatively deciding what to do in accordance with local conditions" rather than "moving when pushed from the top, standing still without push, working like a machine by command, like puppets play."[36]

Despite the importance attributed to the people's committees, the 1972 constitutional revision folded the village people's committee into the cooperative farm management committee.[37] The most prominent form of direct democracy, which had sprung up after liberation to institute the bulk of the revolutionary reforms, took a back seat as politics was subsumed under economic management. Amid the urgency of postwar reconstruction, regional people's committees had already begun to take on the role of organizing production units shortly after the war. Although people's committees were considered "organs to maximally exhibit the people's democratic creativity and initiative in the construction of a socialist economy and culture," their most immediate roles prioritized "the suppression of anti-revolutionary forces" and "the protection of the homeland from imperialist aggression."[38] In 1959, while the people's committees retained their responsibilities to oversee local development of industry, agriculture, commerce, construction, education, and culture, the village chair was simultaneously made the chair of the cooperative farm management committee. This anticipated the merging of the village people's committees and the cooperative farm management committees in 1972. Socialist modernity was thus narrowly defined by the construction of a nation-state that had the power needed for self-determination, able to provide for its people and defend itself against any aggression that might threaten its independence.

Collective identities and practices that were once the basis for social change and a new everyday life increasingly became rigid systems of classification and regulation in North Korea in the face of a "cold" war that had erupted into actual war. The war's aftermath brought no resolution to the only country that remains divided by the Cold War. As the "post-" era dawned with the dissolution of the Soviet bloc and the rise of postmodernism, collective identities came under criticism as illusory at best and totalitarian at worst, whether in the various forms of nationalism or working-class politics. Collective identities have been discarded as "imaginary" partly because the individual as the basic unit of agency has such deep roots in liberal Enlightenment thought. But revolutions are nothing if not the result of collective imaginations. The question that remains open and crucial for those interested in social change as a process of emancipation is: What should the relationship between the individual and the collective be so as to allow space for individuality and yet preserve the empowerment that comes from belonging to a collective community?

This brings us to the paradox of modernity: no sooner did the idea of freedom and self-determination give birth to the modern self-defining subject than the power of human agency proved to be utterly destructive.[39] Belief in modern subjectivity unleashed totalitarian designs that took the human capacity for rational planning to its extreme conclusion. So, how can modern subjectivity, with its idea that emancipation can be achieved through human action, be sustained while preserving the open-endedness of spontaneous and unpredictable possibilities that refuse to be distilled into rigid forms of discipline and control in the name of rationality? Clarifying the relationship between the individual and the collective may serve as a reply. Although the liberal emphasis on individual freedom seems an antidote or the very opposite of totalitarianism, the paradox of modern subjectivity shows that it is in fact the very power accorded to individual agency that has enabled figures such as Kim Il Sung to believe in their power to shape the world. Thus, a true collective that brings together diverse interests through direct participation in self-governance serves to check any one individual ambition—not as a homogeneous or predetermined collective, as in traditional politics, but as an open-ended "multitude" with flexible and fluid boundaries.[40] Revolution is risky business, not only because the consequences of failure are severe but also because the consequences of success must leave open the possibility of the revolution being overturned by another revolution if is to remain true to itself. It is no wonder that most, if not all, revolutionary regimes have opted to close that window.

Capitalist colonial modernity in Korea homogenized the everyday in the interest of rational production for the most efficient use of time while offering little in the way of modern emancipation, whether as consumers or recognized political agents, for the great majority of people. In reaction, the people's committees waged a revolution, providing a medium by which a participatory politics could be instituted for a new collective everyday that was "public through and through" and geared toward the "needs of social practice," as Benjamin and Arvatov had optimistically observed in the aftermath of the first socialist revolution in Russia. Indeed, North Korean leaders took the Soviet Union as a shining example that was blazing the path toward a socialist modernity that they hoped to achieve for North Korea. Taking the Soviet experience to heart, a vanguard party was quickly established with social organizations connecting the people and the party as "transmission belts." Meetings and study sessions became a ubiquitous part of everyday life from the moment people submitted applications for membership with autobiographies that identified their writers as subjects of history, instituting a collective life that was enacted through the transformation of each individual life.

As a result, people no longer addressed each other in familial hierarchical terms but called each other comrade. Previous gathering spaces took on new social significance as colonial buildings were turned into communal rest homes, and communal wells became sites for teaching women to read. Collective labor was now valued as a socially meaningful activity for its own sake rather than for its efficacy or, worse, denigrated as demeaning. Individual and collective well-being were integrated as one through methods of criticism and self-criticism that were meant to foster communication and camaraderie. These practices share common roots in many socialist states, including the Soviet Union and China.

Still, the North Korean Revolution was its own singular experience of a more mass-based and yet more radical revolution that enabled unprecedented numbers of peasants to take up leadership positions through the first ever mass election held in Korea's history, and through a radical land reform that confiscated land without compensation, distributing it for free to the tillers. North Korea's experience of colonialism also influenced the way certain traditions would be valued as "national" characteristics to be incorporated anew into a distinctly North Korean socialist modernity. The adoption of motherhood as a generic form of revolutionary subjectivity to serve as a model for both women *and* men was one such example, strikingly distinct from other socialist ideals of revolutionary brotherhood. Similar forms of revolutionary motherhood could be found in contemporary discourses among women remembering the postliberation period in South Korea. But there were divergences between the way women and men remembered the time of "liberated space." Men's narratives used the nation as the framework through which to tell their life stories, whereas women's narratives spilled out beyond those boundaries and were thereby relegated to the margins, not as part of national history but as women's history.

In this book I have attempted to reach out to those margins, to bring attention to marginalized histories—the history of North Korea's experience of building socialist modernity, the history of villages undergoing revolutionary changes, the history of peasants becoming revolutionaries through new forms of everyday practices, and the history of women as constitutive of what liberation and revolution meant in practical terms. The continued division of the peninsula that heightens security imperatives at the expense of open discussion presents challenges navigating the politically contested understanding of the immediate postliberation period. The very difficulties in collecting oral histories are another reminder of the importance of recuperating a sense of "liberated space," both as Korea's concrete historical past and as a model for opening up to alternative possibilities beyond those caught in Cold War binaries.

Appendix

Sample Curricula

Sample Curriculum for Members of the Korean Workers' Party (1949)[1]

1. Korea after Liberation

1) The Soviet Union's decisive role in the war against Japan and Korea's liberation
2) Struggle between democracy and reaction in the solution to the Korea question
3) Political conditions in South Korea
4) The People's Committee is an organ of true people's political power
5) North Korea under people's political power and North Korea's democratic reforms
6) Historical significance of North Korea's democratic reforms
7) North Korea's democratic political parties and social organizations
8) The Korean people's and women's struggle for the construction of a united democratic country
9) Foundation of the central government of the Democratic People's Republic of Korea
10) Constitution of the Democratic People's Republic of Korea
11) Two-year people's economic development plan for the DPRK
12) One-year anniversary of the foundation of the DPRK

2. World Political Map

1) Overview of global geopolitics
2) Colonies and subject nations
3) Far East states and Near East states
4) Unites States of America
5) Great Britain

6) European states

7) Countries of people's democracy

8) Conclusion

3. Experience of Political Leadership of the Masses

1) World historical significance of the Soviet (Bolshevik) Communist Party's experience of leading the masses

2) Party doctrine

3) Experience of the Russian Marxists of working among the masses up to 1905

4) Bolshevik experience of working among the masses during the 1905 revolution

5) Bolshevik experience of leading the masses during the period of reaction

6) Experience of the Marxist Party during World War I

7) Experience of the Bolshevik Party during the preparatory period for the Great Socialist October Revolution and during the Revolution

8) Experience of the Bolshevik Party during the period of armed intervention and civil war

9) Experience of the Bolshevik Party during the period of struggle for the triumph of socialism in the Soviet Union

10) Experience of the Bolshevik Party during the period of the Great War for the Fatherland

11) What does the great experience of the Soviet Communist Party (Bolshevik) teach us?

4. Party Construction

1) Foundation of the North Korean Workers' Party

2) Second Party Congress of the North Korean Workers' Party

3) North Korean Workers' Party Platform

4) North Korean Workers' Party Rules

5. Current Politics

1) Recent international conditions

2) Aggressive policies of American imperialists toward Korea

3) Recent political conditions in North and South Korea

4) Recent conditions in China

5) Recent conditions in Japan

6. Methodological Problems on Leading Cell Study Groups
    1) How to increase the ideological standard of the study group
    2) How to conduct and direct the study group
    3) How should study group leaders prepare for lecture
    4) Exchange of experiences on leading study groups

Sample Curriculum for Members of the Women's League (1949)[2]

1. How did human society develop?
    1) How did human beings first come into the world?
    2) How did human beings first live in the world and how did they produce things?
    3) What is class, and who exploited whom?
    4) Did feudalism develop into capitalism?
    5) What is capitalism, who exploits whom under capitalist society, and why is it doomed?
    6) What is a progressive socialist society?

2. Korea after liberation
    1) The Soviet Union's decisive role in the war against Japan and Korea's liberation
    2) Struggle between democracy and reaction in the solution to the Korea question
    3) Political conditions in South Korea
    4) The People's Committee is an organ of true people's political power
    5) North Korea under people's political power and North Korea's democratic reforms
    6) Historical significance of North Korea's democratic reforms
    7) North Korea's democratic political parties and social organizations
    8) The Korean people's and women's struggle for the construction of a united democratic country
    9) Foundation of the central government of the Democratic People's Republic of Korea
    10) Constitution of the Democratic People's Republic of Korea
    11) Two-year people's economic development plan for the DPRK
    12) One-year anniversary of the foundation of the DPRK

3. Current political conditions
    1) Aggressive policies of American imperialists toward Korea
    2) Recent political conditions of South and North Korea

4. Women's movement
    1) Russian women's lives before the revolution
    2) Korean women's lives before liberation
    3) Women and children of a socialist country after the revolution
    4) Women and children of liberated Korea

Notes

Introduction

1. Department of Defense News Briefing Transcript (December 23, 2002), http://www.globalsecurity.org/military/library/news/2002/12/mil-021223-usia01.htm.

2. C. D. Elvidge et al., "Mapping of City Lights using DMSP Operational Linescan System Data," *Photogrammetric Engineering and Remote Sensing* 63 (1997): 727–34, cited in "Low Light Imaging of the Earth at Night," accessed April 17, 2012, http://dmsp.ngdc.noaa.gov/pres/low_light_120701/html/page4.html.

3. Accessed April 18, 2012, http://dmsp.ngdc.noaa.gov/pres/low_light_120701/html/page10.html.

4. Dwight Garner, "Carpet-Bombing Falsehoods about a War That's Little Understood," *New York Times*, July 21, 2010. http://www.nytimes.com/2010/07/22/books/22book.html.

5. "Dr. Evil" was a reference to Kim Jong Il in *Newsweek*'s January 13, 2003 issue in the cover story "North Korea's Dr. Evil: Is Kim Jong Il a Bigger Threat Than Saddam?" http://www.prnewswire.com/news-releases/newsweek-cover-north-koreas-dr-evil-73661467.html. "Axis of evil" was used by President George W. Bush in his State of the Union Address on January 29, 2002 to refer to Iran, Iraq, and North Korea. http://news.bbc.co.uk/2/hi/americas/1796034.stm. "Outpost of tyranny" was used by Secretary of State Condoleezza Rice in her prepared remarks before the Senate Foreign Relations Committee on January 18, 2005. http://news.bbc.co.uk/2/hi/americas/4186241.stm.

6. Chong-Sik Lee, "Politics in North Korea: Pre-Korean War Stage," in *North Korea Today*, ed. Robert A. Scalapino (New York: Frederick A. Praeger, 1963), 16.

7. Here I adopt Theda Skocpol's definition of social revolution as a "combination of thoroughgoing structural transformation and massive class upheavals." *States and Social Revolutions: A Comparative Analysis of France, Russia, and China* (New York: Cambridge University Press, 1979).

8. This literature is expansive, but useful are Andre Gunder Frank, *ReORIENT: Global Economy in the Asian Age* (Berkeley: University of California Press, 1998), and Kenneth Pomeranz, *The Great Divergence: China, Europe, and the Making of the Modern World Economy* (Princeton: Princeton University Press, 2001).

9. Immanuel Wallerstein, *The Capitalist World-Economy* (New York: Cambridge University Press, 1979), 133.

10. Joyce Appleby, Lynn Hunt, and Margaret Jacob, *Telling the Truth about History* (New York: W. W. Norton, 1994). The first uses of the term "modern" as synonymous with "now" began to appear in the late sixteenth century, leading to associations of modernity with the Enlightenment. However, the meaning of the term has evolved over the centuries, most recently gaining a positive connotation in the nineteenth century. Without denying the importance of

the changes that began with the Enlightenment in ushering in various aspects of what is commonly identified as modern, I share Raymond Williams's view that the nineteenth century saw the greatest changes, qualitatively changing the way people lived *within* the effects of modernity. See Raymond Williams, *The Politics of Modernism* (1989; New York: Verso, 2007), 31–33.

11. As political theory and movement, socialism has a long history that began in the early nineteenth century in reaction to the destructive effects of industrial capitalism. Since then, there have been many variants, from the early utopians to the syndicalists and reformists, but the socialism that gained the widest currency, including in Korea, was "scientific socialism" as expounded in the *Communist Manifesto* written by Karl Marx and Friedrich Engels in 1848. The latter was often referred to as "communism" in order to distinguish the Marxist variant of socialism from the utopian and reformist brands criticized by Marxists. See Daniel Bell, "Socialism," *International Encyclopedia of the Social Sciences* (1968), accessed August 25, 2012, available at http://www.encyclopedia.com/doc/1G2-3045001168.html.

12. Agnes Heller, *A Theory of Modernity* (Oxford: Blackwell, 1999), 5.

13. Anna Louise Strong, *In North Korea: First Eye-Witness Report* (New York: Soviet Russia Today, 1949), 11.

14. Ibid., 13, 19.

15. Andrei Lankov, *From Stalin to Kim Il Sung: Formation of North Korea 1945–1960* (New Brunswick, N.J.: Rutgers University Press, 2002), esp. chapter 1.

16. Erik van Ree, *Socialism in One Zone: Stalin's Policy in Korea, 1945–1947* (Oxford: Berg, 1989), 67–69, cited in Ryu Kil-chae, "Study of the People's Committees in State Building in North Korea, 1945–1947" [in Korean] (PhD diss., Korea University, 1995), 130.

17. Van Ree, *Socialism in One Zone*, 49–50, 91, 97.

18. Robert Scalapino and Chong-sik Lee, *Han'guk kongsanjuŭi undongsa 2* [History of Korean communism 2] (Seoul: Tolbaege, 1986), 424.

19. Bruce Cumings, *The Origins of the Korean War: Liberation and the Emergence of Separate Regimes, 1945–1947,* vol. 1 (Princeton: Princeton University Press, 1981), 138–39.

20. Lankov, *From Stalin to Kim Il Sung*, 4–5, 9

21. For a postwar example of socialist internationalism, see Rüdiger Frank, "Lessons from the Past: The First Wave of Developmental Assistance to North Korea and the German Reconstruction of Hamhŭng," *Pacific Focus* 23, no. 1 (April 2008): 46–74.

22. Bruce Cumings, for example, has done this by emphasizing the nationalist and corporatist roots of North Korean state formation. Bruce Cumings, "Corporatism in North Korea," *Journal of Korean Studies* 4.1 (1982): 269–94.

23. For examples of conflating the everyday and the ordinary, see Svetlana Boym, *Common Places: Mythologies of Everyday Life in Russia* (Cambridge: Harvard University Press, 1994), and Sheila Fitzpatrick, *Everyday Stalinism: Ordinary Life in Extraordinary Times; Soviet Russia in the 1930s* (New York: Oxford University Press, 2000). Although I share Fitzpatrick's concern for writing social and cultural histories of places that are often represented as if they are devoid of any authentic social or cultural experience, I problematize the way the everyday is taken for granted, particularly by studies of totalitarian regimes. Ironically, social histories that emerged within the milieu of the radical social movements of the 1960s with the explicit purpose of giving voice to the "voiceless," by showing how ordinary people could be agents and subjects of history in their everyday lives, were appropriated by studies of totalitarianism as a way to give voice to the "silenced."

24. Katheryn Weathersby, "Soviet Aims in Korea and the Origins of the Korean War, 1945–1950: New Evidence from the Russian Archives," Cold War International History Project, Woodrow Wilson International Center for Scholars, Working Paper 8 (1993), and Hak Soon Paik, "North Korean State Formation, 1945–1950" (PhD diss., University of Pennsylvania, 1993). For earlier examples, see van Ree, *Socialism in One Zone*, and U.S. Department of State, *North Korea: A Case Study in the Technique of Takeover* (Washington, D.C.: U.S. Government Printing Office, 1960)

25. The works of Dae-Sook Suh, *Kim Il Sung: The North Korean Leader* (New York: Columbia University Press, 1988), Lankov, *From Stalin to Kim Il Sung*, and Charles Armstrong, *The*

North Korean Revolution, 1945–1950 (Ithaca: Cornell University Press, 2003), are representative of this trend.

26. An Chong-ch'ŏl, *Kwangju chŏnnam chibang hyŏndaesa yŏn'gu* [Modern history of the Kwangju, South Chŏlla region: Focusing on the Committee for the Preparation of Korean Independence and the people's committees] (Seoul: Hanul, 1991); An So-yŏng, "Postliberation Organization and Activities of the People's Committees in North Kyŏngsang Region" [in Korean], in *Han'guk kŭnhyŏndae chiyŏk undongsa* [History of modern Korean regional movements], ed. Yŏksa munje yŏn'guso [Center for the study of historical issues] (Seoul: Yŏgang, 1993); Hŏ Ŭn, "Historical Background and Activities of the People's Committees in North Kyŏngsang Province" [in Korean], *Yŏksa yŏn'gu* [History research] 3 (1993); Kim Ch'ang-jin, "Activities of the People's Committees in 1945–46 and the Character of the American Military Government in the Kwangju Region" [in Korean], *Yŏksa pip'yŏng* [History criticism], Winter (1987); Kim Tong-man, "Organization and Activities of the Committee for the Preparation of Korean Independence and People's Committees in Cheju Region" [in Korean], *Yŏksa pip'yŏng* [History criticism] (1991); Sin Chong-dae, "The Formation and Dissolution of the People's Committees in Pusan, South Kyŏngsang Region" [in Korean], *Kyŏngnamdae han'guk kwa kukche chŏngch'i* [Kyŏngnam University Korea and international politics] (1992); Yi Il-chae, "Korean Communist Party and Labor Federation Activities and Guerrillas in the Taegu Area in the Immediate Postliberation Period" [in Korean], *Yŏksa pip'yŏng* [History criticism], Summer (1990). These studies were all published in the late 1980s and early 1990s, reflecting the burst of interest in the study and rewriting of postliberation history in South Korea in the aftermath of the 1987 democracy movement. Bruce Cumings's work is the most comprehensive study of the southern and northern PCs to date in either English or Korean. See especially chapters 8 and 9 of *Origins of the Korean War*, vol. 1.

27. Kim Yong-bok, "Organization and Activities of the North Korean People's Committees in the Immediate Postliberation Period" [in Korean], in *Haebang chŏnhusa ŭi insik* [Understanding pre- and postliberation history], ed. Kim Nam-sik (Seoul: Han'gilsa, 1989); Kim Kwang-un, "Formation of the Power-Structure and the Recruitment of Cadre in North Korea (August 1945–March 1947)" [in Korean] (PhD diss., Hanyang University, 1999); Ryu Kil-chae, "Study of the People's Committees"; Yi Chu-ch'ŏl, "A Study of the North Korean Workers' Party Members and Sub-Organizations" [in Korean] (PhD diss., Korea University, 1998).

28. For example, Yi Chu-ch'ŏl defines the most important feature of a socialist political system as one in which the state is ruled by a communist party. See Yi Chu-ch'ŏl, "Study of the North Korean Workers' Party Members," 3.

29. See the introduction in Michael Geyer and Sheila Fitzpatrick, eds., *Beyond Totalitarianism: Stalinism and Nazism Compared* (New York: Cambridge University Press, 2009).

30. Although no longer as relevant with the disappearance of the Second World of communist countries, debates about the degree to which the "actually existing socialist" states such as the Soviet Union and the Eastern European countries can truly be regarded as socialist abounded throughout the Cold War, leading some to claim that Stalinist Russia had "degenerated" from a workers' state to "state capitalism." For example, see Peter Binns, Tony Cliff, and Chris Harman, *Russia: From Workers' State to State Capitalism* (Chicago: Bookmarks, 1987). Certainly, the self-emancipation of the working class is a key tenet of socialism, but state ownership of the means of production cannot be equated with "state capitalism," as Rudolf Bahro has argued quite forcefully. See Rudolf Bahro, *The Alternative in Eastern Europe* (New York: Routledge, 1978). The shortcomings of "actually existing socialism" are fully laid out by Bahro, and need not be reiterated here.

31. For an example, see Bell, "Socialism."

32. Thomas Hosuck Kang, "North Korean Captured Records at the Washington National Records Center, Suitland, Maryland" (Library of Congress, 1975).

33. The captured documents are cited as Record Group [RG] 242, shipping advice [SA] number, box number, and item number, using the original shipping index when the materials were shipped to the United States from Korea. The NHCC volumes are cited with the original document title and date, the NHCC volume number, and page number.

34. Bruce Cumings, Dae-Sook Suh, Hak Soon Paik, and Charles Armstrong are among the few who have used the documents.

35. Only a limited number of sets for this collection are printed, and each set bears a unique identification number, including a warning that prohibits its reproduction and its viewing by unauthorized parties. In the event that the volumes are lost or are no longer needed, the reader is advised to contact the publisher. In spite of policies allowing the viewing of North Korean materials since liberalization in the late 1980s, South Korea continues to criminalize the viewing and use of North Korean materials through the National Security Law when deemed inappropriate by the government. Although scholars are usually exempt from such treatment, when I attempted to view these records during my Fulbright research trip in 2002–3, it took numerous phone calls on my behalf from the Fulbright Commission and negotiation with the National History Compilation Committee before I was granted permission. The irony was not lost on anyone when I pointed out that these records had been reproduced from the ones at the National Archives. In spite of such restrictions, students and researchers frequently borrow the material from the libraries and have them photocopied. Unfortunately, the documents reproduced by the NHCC do not include proper citations, making it difficult to locate the original. But, the NHCC reproductions do have the advantage of legibility because the original handwritten or blurry carbon-copied documents have been painstakingly typed. Among those I was able to locate for comparison, the reproductions did not contain any substantial disparities with the exception of some typographical errors. I have used the NHCC volumes primarily for the minutes of the meetings of the various organizations, citing the original document when located. However, the physical elements of the original documents—such as the kind of paper used, characteristics of the handwriting, technique of reproduction—are lost in the reproduced volumes.

36. Pierre Bourdieu, *The Logic of Practice*, trans. Richard Nice (Oxford: Polity Press, 1990), 56–57: "The *habitus* is a spontaneity without consciousness or will, opposed as much to the mechanical necessity of things without history in mechanistic theories as it is to the reflexive freedom of subjects 'without inertia' in rationalist theories. . . . This durably installed generative principle of regulated improvisations is a practical sense which reactivates the sense objectified in institutions. Produced by the work of inculcation and appropriation that is needed in order for objective structures, the products of collective history, to be reproduced in the form of the durable, adjusted dispositions that are the condition of their functioning, the *habitus*, which is constituted in the course of an individual history, imposing its particular logic on incorporation, and through which agents partake of the history objectified in institutions, is what makes it possible to inhabit institutions, to appropriate them practically, and so to keep them in activity, continuously pulling them from the state of dead letters, reviving the sense deposited in them, but at the same time imposing the revisions and transformations that reactivation entails."

1. Revolutions in the Everyday

1. Chu Chŏng-sun, "Yŏsŏng ŭi saenghwal hyŏngmyŏng" [Revolution in women's lives], *Chosŏn yŏsŏng* (April 1947), RG 242, SA 2005, box 2, item 34.

2. Se-Mi Oh, "Consuming the Modern: The Everyday in Colonial Seoul, 1915–1937" (PhD diss., Columbia University, 2008), chapter 3. Despite similarities, life reformists advocated a "revolution of the self" to cultivate a clear sense of self-identity. They highlighted individuality as the most important aspect to be developed rather than social conditions or a collective sense of class or nationality, which differentiates the movement fundamentally from both agrarian reformers and socialists. See especially Chang Paeksanin, "Ilsangsaenghwal ŭi hyŏngmyŏng" [Revolution of the everyday], *Tonggwang* (May 1925); Cho Chae-jo, "Modŏn namnyŏ wa saenghwal kaejo" [Modern men and women, and life reform], *Pyŏlgŏn'gon* (December 1928), both cited in Oh, "Consuming the Modern," 111–12.

3. Albert L. Park, "Visions of the Nation: Religion and Ideology in 1920s and 1930s Rural Korea" (PhD diss., University of Chicago, 2007). I say *limited* success because the missionary capacity to reach the Korean countryside had limitations. At its height in 1930, the YMCA had organized 165 cooperatives with some 3,548 members, still only a tiny fraction of almost twenty million peasants. YMCA, "Statistics and Information for the Calendar Year 1930" (Minneapolis: YMCA Archives, University of Minnesota), 3; Korean Young Men's Christian Associations, *Rural Program of the Young Men's Christian Association in Korea* (Seoul: National Council of the Young Men's Christian Association in Korea, 1932), 9, cited in Park. Moreover, the primary objective of the missionary-led agrarian movements to "regenerate" rural Korea was to "inculcate the living spirit of Jesus" and the "development of Christian character, Christian fellowship, and Christian service." See Induk Pak, "Work among Rural Women," *Korea Mission Field* (July 1933), 136, and Edith A. Kerr, "Regenerating Rural Korea," *Korea Mission Field* (April 1934), 70.

4. Gi-Wook Shin and Do-Hyun Han, "Colonial Corporatism: The Rural Revitalization Campaign, 1932–1940," in *Colonial Modernity in Korea*, ed. Gi-Wook Shin and Michael Robinson (Cambridge: Harvard University Press, 1999).

5. Lee Kyoung-ran, "Rural Society and Peasants' Life in Chosŏn during the Japanese Wartime Regime: With the Village-Society Network as the Central Figure" [in Korean], in *Ilche p'asijŭm chibae chŏngch'aek kwa minjung saenghwal* [Japanese Fascist Policy in Korea and Korean Life], ed. Pang Kie-chung (Seoul: Hyean, 2004).

6. For example, Brian Myers explains contemporary North Korea as a direct descendant of colonial-era Japanese fascism in B. R. Myers, *The Cleanest Race: How North Koreans See Themselves and Why It Matters* (Brooklyn: Melville House, 2010). For a typical example of Cold War literature, see U.S. Department of State, *North Korea: A Case Study in the Techniques of Takeover* (Washington, D.C.: Government Printing Office, 1961); and Robert A. Scalapino, ed., *North Korea Today* (New York: Praeger, 1963). For a more recent adaptation of the Cold War perspective into a neoliberal one, see Ralph Hassig and Kongdan Oh, *North Korea through the Looking Glass* (Washington, D.C.: Brookings Institution Press, 2000).

7. RG 242, SA 2006, box 16, item 23, "Youth League North P'yŏngan Province Sŏnch'ŏn County Nam Township Committee" (1948).

8. I have translated *hyŏnmak* from the text as "farmhand" but the exact meaning was difficult to trace. Because of the many grammatical and spelling mistakes, it is unclear whether the word was misspelled. It may be a derivative of *hyŏpmak* (夾膜), a separate dwelling place from the main house usually for a servant, or of *maksŏri,* which refers to someone who does rough work and hard labor in exchange for lodging, much like a servant. I thank professor Yu Se-jong and her colleagues, professors Yu Mun-sŏn and Cho T'ae-yŏng, for their help in tracking down these potential explanations.

9. "Pukchosŏn yŏsŏng ŭi saeroun saenghwal" [The new life of North Korean women]," *Chosŏn yŏsŏng* (September 1947), RG 242, SA 2005, box 2, item 34.

10. For a good overview, see Derek Schilling, "Everyday Life and the Challenge to History in Postwar France: Braudel, Lefebvre, Certeau," *Diacritics* 33, no. 1 (Spring 2003): 23–40.

11. Harry Harootunian, *Overcome by Modernity: History, Culture, and Community in Interwar Japan* (Princeton: Princeton University Press, 2000), xviii.

12. David Harvey shows just how far-reaching the changes in perceptions of time and space are to produce what he terms *time-space compressions.* See David Harvey, *The Condition of Postmodernity: An Enquiry into the Origins of Cultural Change* (Cambridge: Blackwell, 1990). Examples have all been taken from chapters 2 and 16, especially pages 28 and 264. Lefebvre also marks 1910 as a critical turning point: "Around 1910 a certain space was shattered. It was the space of common sense, of knowledge, of social practice, of political power, a space hitherto enshrined in everyday discourse, just as in abstract thought, as the environment of and channel for communication. . . . Euclidean and perspectivist space have disappeared as systems of reference, along with other former 'common places' such as town, history, paternity, the tonal system in music, traditional morality, and so forth. This was a truly crucial moment." Henri Lefebvre, *La production de l'espace* (Paris: Anthropos, 1974), quoted in Harvey, *Condition of Postmodernity,* 266.

13. Herman Lautensach, *Korea: A Geography Based on the Author's Travels and Literature* (Berlin: Springer-Verlag, 1988).

14. Im In-saeng, "Modŏnisŭm" [Modernism], *Pyŏlgŏn'gon* (January 1930), cited in Se-Mi Oh, "Consuming the Modern," 79.

15. Williams, *Politics of Modernism*, 40–41.

16. Partha Chatterjee, "The Nation in Heterogeneous Time," *Indian Economic and Social History Review* 38, no. 4 (December 2001): 399–400. To be fair, Chatterjee sets up this characterization of capitalist modernity (using Benedict Anderson and E. P. Thompson) in order to critique it as utopian. He is certainly right to point out that people do not live in empty homogeneous time and that the "real space of modern life is a heterotopia" (402). Nonetheless, empty homogeneous time is useful for understanding the *logic* behind capitalist modernity even if it is not always entirely successful in its operation.

17. Henri Lefebvre, *Everyday Life in the Modern World* (New York: Harper and Row, 1971), 33, 59–60.

18. Ben Highmore, "Introduction: Questioning Everyday Life," in *The Everyday Life Reader*, ed. Ben Highmore (New York: Routledge, 2002), 5.

19. Maurice Blanchot, "Everyday Speech," *Yale French Studies* no. 73 (1987): 12 (emphasis added).

20. Hannah Arendt, *On Revolution* (New York: Viking Press, 1963), 28.

21. Evgenii Bershtein, "'The Withering of Private Life': Walter Benjamin in Moscow," in *Everyday Life in Early Soviet Russia: Taking the Revolution Inside*, ed. Christina Kiaer and Eric Naiman (Bloomington: Indiana University Press, 2006), 221. See also Masha Lipman's descriptions of her grandparents' "revolutionary style" in the way they lived at home with "no dishes, no real furniture" because "it was all too bourgeois," in David Remnick, *Lenin's Tomb: The Last Days of the Soviet Empire* (New York: Vintage Books, 1984), 332, quoted in Katerina Clark, *Petersburg, Crucible of Cultural Revolution* (Cambridge: Harvard University Press, 1995) 1.

22. Walter Benjamin, *Moscow Diary*, ed. Gary Smith, trans. Richard Sieburth (Cambridge: Harvard University Press, 1986), 72 (emphasis added).

23. Ibid., 26, 85.

24. *Pravda* (June 13, 1928), 5, quoted in Peter Fritzsche and Jochen Hellbeck, "The New Man in Stalinist Russia and Nazi Germany," in *Beyond Totalitarianism: Stalinism and Nazism Compared*, ed. Michael Geyer and Sheila Fitzpatrick (New York: Cambridge University Press, 2009), 318. Pilgrimages from the West to observe the creation of a new socialist society were relatively common in the late 1920s and 1930s (321).

25. "Sotsialisticheskoe dvizhenie v Koree" [The socialist movement in Korea], *Kommunist Internatsional*, nos. 7–8 (1919), reproduced in English translation in Dae-Sook Suh, *Documents of Korean Communism 1918–1948* (Princeton: Princeton University Press, 1970), 47.

26. The discussion below is based on Oskar Anweiler, *The Soviets: The Russian Workers, Peasants, and Soldiers Councils, 1905–1921*, trans. Ruth Hein, 1st American ed. (New York: Pantheon Books, 1974), 51–54.

27. Ibid., 34–39. Unlike political parties, which were active underground due to their illegal status, the soviets were able to organize publicly, with their legitimacy and authority conferred by the free election of their deputies.

28. Ibid., 120.

29. Kiaer and Naiman, *Everyday Life in Early Soviet Russia*, 4.

30. Clark, *Petersburg, Crucible of Cultural Revolution*, 253.

31. Ibid., 51.

32. Christina Kiaer, *Imagine No Possessions: The Socialist Objects of Russian Constructivism* (Cambridge: MIT Press, 2005), 1. According to Kiaer, Trotsky saw *byt* as a kind of negative *habitus* from the past that could be an obstacle to the creation of a new form of social life. He saw it as something to be overcome and obliterated rather than a site of political action and social change as it was for Arvatov and other constructivists (54–60).

33. Ibid., 4.

34. For biographic detail, see Christina Kiaer, "Boris Arvatov's Socialist Objects," *October* 81 (Summer 1997): 105–18.

35. Boris Arvatov, "Everyday Life and the Culture of the Thing," trans. Christina Kiaer, *October* 81 (Summer 1997): 121 [originally published in Moscow, 1925].

36. Braudel had a similar conceptualization of the everyday as an embodiment of the material totality: "At the very deepest levels of material life, there is at work a complex order, to which the assumptions, tendencies and unconscious pressures of economies, societies and civilizations all contribute." Fernand Braudel, *The Structures of Everyday Life: The Limits of the Possible* (New York: Harper and Row, 1981), 333. He emphasized the totality of material life, laying bare the deeper structures at play. Rice, an everyday staple in Korea as across East Asia, is a case in point. As Braudel explains, rice is labor-intensive and resource-intensive to produce, which required state centralization for large irrigation projects and tight-knit communities in concentrated villages to pool labor and resources. A close relationship between town and country facilitated the distribution of rice to the towns, the largest of which was the capital with its concentrated powers of state administration. All this led to a dense concentration of population and strict discipline in traditional East Asian societies.

37. Arvatov, "Everyday Life and the Culture of the Thing," 122.

38. Ibid., 123–24 (emphasis in original).

39. Ibid., 125 (emphasis added).

40. Elizabeth Wood, *The Baba and the Comrade: Gender and Politics in Revolutionary Russia* (Bloomington: Indiana University Press, 1997), 197.

41. Ibid., 196.

42. Ibid., 194–205.

43. Boym, *Common Places*, 8, 35.

44. Wood, *Baba and the Comrade*, 195.

45. Kiaer and Naiman, *Everyday Life in Early Soviet Russia*, 5.

46. Choi Chatterjee, *Celebrating Women: Gender, Festival Culture, and Bolshevik Ideology, 1910–1939* (Pittsburgh: University of Pittsburgh Press, 2002), 106–13.

47. Whereas most Western historiography of the Soviet era sees the evolution of Soviet culture as a battle between avant-gardists (desire to transform) and the traditionalists (desire to hold back) ending with the triumph of the traditionalists, Katerina Clark explains that the opposition between the two was not as absolute as avant-gardist rhetoric claimed. In fact, the more fundamental dichotomy was between monumentalists and iconoclasts, representing the dilemma in any revolution between destruction and foundation. See the introduction in Clark, *Petersburg, Crucible of Cultural Revolution*.

48. Ibid., 27.

49. Roger Griffin, *Modernism and Fascism: The Sense of a Beginning under Mussolini and Hitler* (New York: Palgrave Macmillan, 2007), 141–48.

50. Mayfair Mei-hui Yang, "The Modernity of Power in the Chinese Socialist Order," *Cultural Anthropology* 3, no. 4 (November 1988): 420–21.

51. Ibid., 421.

52. Arif Dirlik, "The Ideological Foundations of the New Life Movement: A Study in Counterrevolution," *Journal of Asian Studies* 34, no. 4 (August 1975): 945–80.

53. John Bryan Starr, "The Commune in Chinese Communist Thought," in *Images of the Commune*, ed. James A. Leith (Montreal: McGill-Queen's University Press, 1978), 291.

54. "Outline of Views on the Question of Peaceful Coexistence," November 10, 1957, in "The Origin and Development of the Differences between the Leadership of the CPSU and Ourselves," Comment I on the Open Letter of the Central Committee of the CPSU of July 14, 1963, September 9, 1963 (Peking, 1963), quoted in ibid., 295.

55. Ibid., 292.

56. Chih-szu Cheng, "The Great Lessons of the Paris Commune: In Commemoration of Its 95th Anniversary," *Peking Review* 9, no. 16 (1966): 23.

57. Liu Guokai, *A Brief Analysis of the Cultural Revolution*, ed. Anita Chan (Armonk, N.Y.: M. E. Sharpe, 1987), 16.

58. Elizabeth J. Perry and Li Xun, *Proletarian Power: Shanghai in the Cultural Revolution* (Boulder: Westview Press, 1997), 11–12. Although the violence and paranoia exhibited during the Cultural Revolution is too often explained as another form of Stalinism or fascism and an inherent element within communist ideology, Lynn White astutely points out that "such violence is not unique in history," recalling other times when traditions were attacked and counterrevolutionaries killed in modern revolutions from the English to the French. See Lynn White, "The Cultural Revolution as an Unintended Result of Administrative Policies," in *New Perspectives on the Cultural Revolution*, ed. William Joseph, Christine Wong, and David Zweig (Cambridge: Harvard University Press, 1991), 102. For an example of the former position, see Andrew Walder, "Cultural Revolution Radicalism: Variations on a Stalinist Theme," in the same volume.

59. Leith, *Images of the Commune*, 301.

60. Perry and Li, *Proletarian Power*.

61. Ibid., 23.

62. Ibid., 146–47.

63. Ibid., 150.

64. "Decision of the Central Committee of the Chinese Communist Party concerning the Great Proletarian Cultural Revolution," *Peking Review* 9, no. 33 (1966).

65. Leith, *Images of the Commune*, 303.

66. Dongping Han, *The Unknown Cultural Revolution: Educational Reforms and Their Impact on China's Rural Development* (New York: Garland Publishing, 2000), 70. Although Han's study is somewhat controversial, it is based on a case study of Jimo County, Shandong Province, where his hometown is located, providing him with ample sources for interviews and official statistics. Although a reviewer found him "occasionally a bit romantic about the Cultural Revolution experience," some of his own experiences during the Cultural Revolution in Gao Village confirmed Han's findings, including evidence of improvements in education, irrigation infrastructure, social security, and health care. See Mobo Gao, "Review of *The Unknown Cultural Revolution: Educational Reforms and Their Impact on China's Rural Development*," *China Journal*, no. 47 (January 2002): 182–84.

67. *Morning Sun*, directed by Carma Hinton, Geremie Barmé, and Richard Gordon (Long Bow Group, 2003), DVD.

68. Liu, *Brief Analysis of the Cultural Revolution*, 140.

69. Ibid., 15.

70. Ibid., 139–40.

71. Ibid., 140–43.

72. David Zweig, "Agrarian Radicalism as a Rural Development Strategy, 1968–1978," in *New Perspectives on the Cultural Revolution*, ed. Joseph, Wong, and Zweig, 73–74. To be fair, Zweig's final assessment of the effect of the Cultural Revolution on rural development is negative, concluding that the restriction on private plots increased the gap between rich and poor peasants in some areas and that limits to horizontal interaction between villages under the guise of local self-sufficiency failed to take into account comparative advantages.

73. Lee Feigon, "The Cultural Revolution Revisited," in *Mao: A Reinterpretation* (Chicago: Ivan R. Dee, 2002), 171–72.

74. Sunyoung Park, "Everyday Life as Critique in Late Colonial Korea: Kim Namch'ŏn's Literary Experiments, 1934–43," *Journal of Asian Studies* 68, no. 3 (August 2009): 869. For a survey of Yu Hang-rim's work, see Kim Myŏng-sŏk, *Han'guk sosŏl kwa kŭndaejŏk ilsang ŭi kyŏnghŏm* [Korean fiction and the experience of modern everyday life] (Seoul: Saemi, 2002). Both Kim and Yu were originally from the Pyongyang area, and were active members in the North Korean Literature and Arts League. Kim was in the south at the time of liberation, defecting to the north in 1947.

75. Carter J. Eckert, Ki-baik Lee, Young Ick Lew, Michael Robinson, and Edward W. Wagner, *Korea Old and New: A History* (Cambridge: Harvard University Press, 1990), 315–18.

76. For example, Harvey explains the rise of nationalism as a reaction to the increasing uprootedness of modernity: "The ideological labour of inventing tradition became of great significance in the late nineteenth century precisely because this was an era when transformations in spatial and temporal practices implied a loss of identity with place and repeated radical breaks with any sense of historical continuity. . . The identity of place was reaffirmed in the midst of the growing abstractions of space." See Harvey, *Condition of Postmodernity*, 272.

77. *Donga ilbo* (February 11, 1933), quoted in Kang Man-gil, *Ilche sidae pinmin saenghwalsa yŏn'gu* [Study of poor people's everyday life during the colonial period] (Seoul: Ch'angjaksa, 1987), 221.

78. Chi Su-gŏl, *Ilche ha nongmin chohap undong yŏn'gu* [Study of the peasant union movement under Japanese colonial rule] (Seoul: Yŏksa pip'yŏngsa, 1993), 204, 266.

79. Cumings, *Origins of the Korean War*, vol. 1, 267.

80. Ibid., 270.

81. E. Grant Meade, *American Military Government in Korea* (New York: King's Crown Press, 1951), 56–71.

82. The excerpt is from a U.S. intelligence report that included English translations of North Korean pronouncements, documents, newspaper articles, and press reports. RG 554, box 65, "G-2 Reports: Data on North Korea Pertinent to South Korea" (folder 1).

83. RG 242, SA 2008, box 9, item 89, Paek Nam-un, *Ssoryŏn insang* [Impressions of the Soviet Union] (Pyongyang, 1950), reprinted in Paek Nam-un, *Ssoryŏn insang* [Impressions of the Soviet Union], ed. Pang Kie-chung (Seoul: Sŏnin, 2005), 80, 10. Paek (1894–1979) was introduced to Marxist thought during his study abroad in Tokyo and became one of the first Marxist scholars in colonial Korea. He was a professor at Yŏnhŭi College (now Yonsei University) between 1925 and 1938. Upon liberation, he was involved with various moderate leftist political groups until such activity was completely suppressed by the American military occupation. He left the south to participate in the North-South Leadership Conference in Pyongyang in April 1948, and settled in the north, holding important positions throughout his life as representative to the Supreme People's Assembly, minister of education, and president of the Science Academy. He was one of the key authors for the first Korean history textbook in the north, *Chosŏn minjok haebang tujaengsa* [History of Korean struggle for national liberation] (1949). For a succinct biography of Paek, see Pang's introduction.

84. Paek, *Ssoryŏn insang*, 127.

85. Ibid., 223, 264.

86. Ibid., 20.

87. RG 242, SA 2008, box 9, item 52, Chang Si-u, *Ssoryŏn ch'amgwan'gi* [Visit to the Soviet Union] (Pyongyang: Sangŏpsŏng minju sangŏpsa, 1950), 50–64.

88. Ibid., 85–86.

89. Ibid., 84, 87.

90. Paek, *Ssoryŏn insang*, 205.

91. Yu Seok-Hwan, "In/Outside of the Korean Peninsula: Narratives of Liberation" [in Korean], *Sangŏ hakpo* 29 (June 2010): 299.

92. Williams, *Politics of Modernism*, 76.

93. Rue Young-Ah, "Young-Kuk Yoo's Early Abstraction: Focused on the Influence of Constructivism during his Study in Japan" [in Korean] (master's thesis, Seoul National University, 2010), 4–5. Rue differentiates Russian constructivism, which influenced leftist Japanese intellectual circles in the 1920s during the period of Taishō democracy, from international constructivism, exemplified by Germany's Bauhaus school, which became the predominant strain of modernist influence in Japan beginning in the 1930s and had as its goal the standardization of all aspects of everyday life for total war mobilization. See Rue's chapter 2.

94. Harvey, *Condition of Postmodernity*, 33.

95. Williams, *Politics of Modernism*, 42–43.

2. Legacies

1. O Yŏng-jin, *Ssogunjŏng ha ŭi pukhan: Hana ŭi chŭngŏn* [North Korea under Soviet military occupation: A testimony] (1952; Seoul: Kukt'o t'ongilwŏn, 1983), 7; Panya Isaakovna Shavshyna, *1945-nyŏn namhan esŏ* [1945 in South Korea] (1974; Seoul: Hanul, 1996), 70.

2. Shavshyna, *1945-nyŏn namhan esŏ*, 74.

3. RG 554, Records of General HQ, Far East Command, Supreme Commander Allied Powers and United Nations Command, USAFIK XXIV Corps, G-2 Historical Section, box 65, "G-2 Reports and Miscellaneous Data on North Korea Pertinent to South Korea (folder 2 of 2)." Full translation of file containing handwritten originals of "Urgent Intelligence Reports" dated 25 Aug—1 Sep 45. (September 14, 1945)

4. Shavshyna, *1945-nyŏn namhan esŏ*, 72–73.

5. Cumings, *Origins*, vol. 1, 73.

6. Ryu Kil-chae, "A Study of the People's Committees," 69.

7. Interview with Ch'oe Sang-wŏn (March 2003). See chapter 7 of this book for details about the interview.

8. Cumings, *Origins*, vol. 1, 78.

9. Gi-Wook Shin, *Peasant Protest and Social Change in Colonial Korea* (Seattle: University of Washington Press, 1996), 152.

10. "National traitors" were defined as those who had collaborated with the Japanese, including but not limited to the royal family, government officials, prosecutors, judges, police officers, and members of pro-Japanese groups. See *Minutes of the National Congress of People's Committee Representatives* (Seoul: Chosŏn chŏngp'ansa, 1946), in *Collection of Modern Korean History Materials*, vol. 12 [in Korean] (Seoul: Tolbaege, 1986), 489.

11. An Chong-ch'ŏl, "A Study of Local Organizations of the Committee for the Preparation of Korean Independence and People's Committees in South Cholla" [in Korean] (PhD diss., Chŏnnam National University, 1990), 98–99, cited in Shin, *Peasant Protest*, 146. For a different view, that "peasants clearly needed leadership to emerge as a revolutionary force," see Chong-Sik Lee, *The Korean Workers' Party: A Short History* (Stanford: Hoover Institution Press, 1978), chapter 3.

12. Kim Nam-sik, *Materials on the South Korean Workers' Party*, vol. 2 [in Korean] (Seoul: Korea University Asia Research Institute, 1974), 158–59, cited in Shin, *Peasant Protest*, 146.

13. The U.S. occupation can be divided into three stages. The first stage was a brief period in September 1945 involving observation teams, which were sent to key regions for the purposes of gathering information. The second stage was a longer one in which tactical troops were sent to the provinces, in some places until December 1945. The final phase was the occupation by civil affairs teams trained to run a full military government. It was not until January 1946, when a full military government was in place, that a somewhat uniform policy was instituted in South Korea. See Cumings, *Origins*, vol. 1, 289–92.

14. As variables in determining the strength of the southern PCs, Cumings looked at the effects of population dislocation; rates of tenancy and landlordism; differences in geographic location; the presence or absence of modern transportation and communication facilities; the level of commercialization of agriculture; history of peasant activism, such as the presence of Red Peasant Unions under colonial rule; and finally the nature of the American occupation. (See ibid., chapter 8.) For the north, Kim Yong-bok and Ryu Kil-chae looked at the history of anti-Japanese struggle in the region; the ideological orientation of the PC leadership; differences in the relations of production among various regions; and the date of Soviet arrival. See Kim Yong-bok, "Organization and Activities of the North Korean People's Committees," and Ryu Kil-chae, "Study of the People's Committees."

15. RG 554, box 23, "Events and Conditions in North Korea."

16. Kim Kwang-un, "Formation of the Power-Structure and the Recruitment of Cadre in North Korea (August 1945–March 1947)" [in Korean] (PhD diss., Hanyang University, 1999), 23–26. For details on Soviet policy, see Ki Kwang-sŏ, "Soryŏn ŭi tae hanbando—pukhan

chŏngch'aek kwalyŏn kigu mit inmul punsŏk" [Analysis of Soviet policy, institutions, and personnel in North Korea], in *Hyŏndae pukhan yŏn'gu* [Study of contemporary North Korea] (Seoul: Kyŏngnam University Graduate School of North Korean Studies, 1998); Kim Seong-bo, "Soryŏn ŭi taehan chŏngch'aek kwa pukhan esŏ ŭi pundan chilsŏ hyŏngsŏng" [Soviet policy on Korea and the formation of the division system in North Korea, 1945–1946], in *Pundan 50-nyŏn kwa t'ongil sidae ŭi kwaje* [Fifty years of division and the problem of reunification] (Seoul: Yŏksa pip'yŏngsa, 1995); Chŏn Hyŏn-su, "Soryŏnkun ŭi pukhan chinju wa tae pukhan chŏngch'aek" [Soviet military occupation and its policies in North Korea], in *Han'guk tongnip undongsa yŏn'gu* [History of the Korean independence movement], vol. 9 (Seoul, 1995); and Pak Jae-kwŏn, "Haebang chikhu soryŏn ŭi tae pukhan chŏngch'aek" [Soviet policy on North Korea immediately after liberation], in *Haebang chŏnhusa ŭi insik* [Understanding pre- and postliberation history], vol. 5 (Seoul: Han'gilsa, 1989).

17. Donald N. Clark, *Living Dangerously in Korea: The Western Experience 1900–1950* (Norwalk, Conn.: Eastbridge, 2003), 121–25.

18. Ryu Kil-chae, "Study of the People's Committees," 78. For a firsthand account of Cho Man-sik's activities in the first month of liberation and the foundation of the CPKI in Pyongyang, see O Yŏng-jin, *Ssogunjŏng ha ŭi pukhan: Hana ŭi chŭngŏn*, chapter 2. According to O, residents were disappointed with the Pyongyang CPKI for its lack of power when repeated rumors circulated of imminent Japanese attack. He attributes its loss of popular support even before the Soviets appeared on the scene to their preoccupation with maintaining security and the status quo at the expense of fulfilling the people's need and desire for emotional and psychological release upon liberation (32–34).

19. O Yŏng-jin, *Ssogunjŏng ha ŭi pukhan: Hana ŭi chŭngŏn*, 76. O judges the PC under Cho to be powerless, contradicting his own testimony that the Soviets endorsed Cho's 3–7 distribution of fall harvests (70% to tenants and 30% to landlords) in the face of fierce communist opposition that called for tenants to keep 100% of the yield (79–80). Writing during the height of the Korean War, O at times reproduces conventional Cold War interpretations of Soviet conspiracy and control over affairs in North Korea that contradict his own explanation of events.

20. RG 554, box 65, "G-2 Reports and Data on North Korea pertinent on South Korea" (folder 2 of 2), Incl #3 to G-2 Summary #9 (4 Nov 45–11 Nov 45).

21. O Yŏng-jin, *Ssogunjŏng ha ŭi pukhan: Hana ŭi chŭngŏn*, 74–75. However, the author faults the Christian leaders for their inability to distinguish between socialism and Bolshevism, working with the communists and the Soviets to their ultimate detriment.

22. Armstrong, *North Korean Revolution,* 51; Kim Yong-bok, "Organization and Activities," 201.

23. Armstrong, *North Korean Revolution*, 53–54. Before the Civil Administration, local *komendatura* (military command) existed as Soviet military organs to coordinate the withdrawal of Japanese troops. See van Ree, *Socialism in One Zone*, 94–105, cited in Ryu Kil-chae, "Study of the People's Committees," 140. According to van Ree, there were initially 113 *komendatura*, which decreased to fifty-four by September 28, that continued to advise the local people's committees in 1945 before the Civil Administration was officially set up.

24. "Report of the Results of the Five Province People's Committee Meeting," Soviet North Korean Civil Administration Archives, box 433847, Folder 1, p. 1, and *Rodong sinmun* [Workers Daily] (September 19, 1946), cited in Kim Kwang-un, "Formation of the Power Structure," 45. There are later references in North Korean documents to this same bureau as the Six Provinces Administrative Bureau, but Kangwŏn Province may have been left out initially because it was divided by the 38th parallel and its provincial seat in Ch'unch'ŏn was south of the parallel.

25. RG 242, SA 2012, box 8, item 72, "Administrative Law of Korea" (no date).

26. Although there has been much debate on whether this constituted the founding of a separate state in the north, such considerations only make sense in hindsight, after the formation of two separate states in 1948. The provisional nature of the PPC was not only marked by the name itself, but the formation of the PPC was seen to offer a model for a unified Korean

government rather than the permanent division of the peninsula. See Ryu Kil-chae, "Study of the People's Committees," 186–96.

27. "Journal of Important Dates" [*Chungyo ilchi*], in *Collection of Modern Korean History Materials* [in Korean], vol. 12, 289–90, and RG 242, SA 2009, box 1, item 95, "Complete Collection of Laws and Regulations of North Korea" (November 1947), 8.

28. RG 242, SA 2005, box 2, item 89, "Minutes of the North Korean Province, City and County People's Committee Congress" (April 1947).

29. RG 242, SA 2012, box 8, item 72, "Administrative Law of Korea" (no date).

30. RG 242, SA 2006, box 15, item 32, "Social and State Institutions of the Democratic People's Republic of Korea" (February 1949), 45.

31. O Yŏng-jin, *Ssogunjŏng ha ŭi pukhan: Hana ŭi chŭngŏn*, 11–12.

32. Derek Sayer, *Capitalism and Modernity: An Excursus on Marx and Weber* (New York: Routledge, 1991), 59, 131.

33. Janice Kim, *To Live to Work: Factory Women in Colonial Korea, 1910–1945* (Palo Alto: Stanford University Press, 2009); Theodore Jun Yoo, *The Politics of Gender in Colonial Korea: Education, Labor, and Health, 1910–1945* (Berkeley: University of California Press, 2008).

34. Ken Kawashima, *The Proletarian Gamble: Korean Workers in Interwar Japan* (Durham: Duke University Press, 2009).

35. Between seven hundred and eight hundred thousand were conscripted as workers while another two hundred thousand were conscripted as soldiers. Sonia Ryang and John Lie, eds., *Diaspora without Homeland: Being Korean in Japan* (Berkeley: University of California Press, 2009).

36. Frederick Cooper has shown how "the concept of colonial modernity flattens history" since the "colonial question is not the modernity question, even if issues of modernity arise within colonial history." See Frederick Cooper, *Colonialism in Question: Theory, Knowledge, History* (Berkeley: University of California Press, 2005), 116–17. I share his critique, and reference the term here in order to challenge its pervasive use in describing the colonial period.

37. Inspired by Wilsonian principles of self-determination in the aftermath of World War I, the March First Movement was the first and largest mass uprising spawned during the colonial period. Between March and May 1919 it mobilized over a million Koreans to demand independence. Official Japanese counts estimated the number of casualties at 553 killed, 1,409 injured, and 12,522 arrested between March and December, while Koreans estimated over seventy-five hundred deaths, fifteen thousand injured, and over forty-five thousand arrests. See Carter J. Eckert et al., *Korea Old and New*, 276–81.

38. Andre Schmid, *Korea between Empires, 1895–1919* (New York: Columbia University Press, 2002); Park, "Visions of the Nation."

39. Kyeong-Hee Choi, "Impaired Body as Colonial Trope: Kang Kyŏng'ae's 'Underground Village'," *Public Culture* 13, no. 3 (Fall 2001): 431–58.

40. Similarly, Gi-Wook Shin and Michael Robinson frame the uniqueness of colonial modernity as one that "produced cosmopolitanism (a sense of shared universals) without political emancipation." See their introduction in *Colonial Modernity in Korea* (Cambridge: Harvard University Press, 1999), 11.

41. Chulwoo Lee, "Modernity, Legality, and Power in Korea under Japanese Rule," in ibid., 26.

42. Ibid., 30–31.

43. Andrew Gordon, *A Modern History of Japan: From Tokugawa Times to the Present* (New York: Oxford University Press, 2009), 91. For a copy of the Meiji Constitution, see Arthur Tiedemann, *Modern Japan: A Brief History* (New York: D. Van Nostrand Reinhold, 1962).

44. Chulwoo Lee, "Modernity, Legality, and Power," 32–33.

45. Lee Jong-min, "Colonial Disciplinary System in the Modern Prison under the Japanese Rule" [in Korean], in *Ilche ŭi singmin chibae wa ilsang saenghwal* [Everyday life of the Korean people under Japanese colonial rule] (Seoul: Hyean, 2004), 453.

46. Lee Sang-Euy, "The Production Increase Bureau in the Japanese Government-General in Korea and Its Industrialization Policies in the 1930s" [in Korean], in *Ilche ha kyŏngje*

chŏngch'aek kwa ilsang saenghwal [Economic policy and daily life in the colonial period] (Seoul: Hyean, 2008), 80.

47. Soon-Won Park, "Colonial Industrial Growth and the Emergence of the Korean Working Class," in *Colonial Modernity in Korea*, ed. Shin and Robinson, 135.

48. Woo Dae-Hyung, "Hisama Kenichi's Thoughts on Agrarian Problems in Colonial Korea" [in Korean], in *Ilche ha kyŏngje chŏngch'aek kwa ilsang saenghwal*. In a separate chapter in the same book, Woo also makes the point that despite advancements in agricultural technology, such as irrigation, use of fertilizer, and superior seeds, differential access to capital between landlords and poor peasants resulted in the monopolization of such advancements by landlords and rich peasants. See "The Introduction of New Rice Technology and Its Impact on Rural Structure in Colonial Korea" [in Korean] in the same volume.

49. Woo Dae-Hyung, "Hisama Kenichi's Thoughts," 25. Although rents varied widely, they could reach as high as four-fifths to nine-tenths of the harvest, deemed "the highest rents for leased land in the world." See Hoon K. Lee, *Land Utilization and Rural Economy in Korea* (Chicago: University of Chicago Press, 1936), 163.

50. Kim Dong-no, "Colonial Modernization and Change in Peasant Movements during the Japanese Colonial Period," *Han'guk sahoehak* [Korean sociology] 41, no. 1 (2007).

51. Chi Su-gŏl, *Ilche ha nongmin chohap undong yŏn'gu*, 119.

52. Gi-Wook Shin, *Peasant Protest*, chapters 5 and 6.

53. The Agricultural Lands Ordinance included protection for tenants, stipulating a minimum of three years for rent contracts, allowing the inheritance of contracts, and prohibiting the refusal of contract renewal without reason. See Gi-Wook Shin, "Rural Revitalization Campaign and Social Change in Colonial Korea: A Perspective of Colonial Corporatism" [in Korean], in *Ilche p'asijŭm chibae chŏngch'aek kwa minjung saenghwal*, ed. Pang Kie-chung, 338. Shin also notes the extent to which tenant farmers took advantage of this system—95% of applications for mediation were filed by tenant farmers, which in most cases (63.8%) were resolved within a month (340).

54. Hisama Kenichi, *Problems of Korean Agricultural Policy* [in Japanese] (1943), 6–8, quoted in Woo Dae-Hyung, "Hisama Kenichi's Thoughts," 36.

55. According to colonial records, between 1933 and 1939 disputes over tenant rights made up 80.9% of the total tenancy disputes whereas rent disputes made up only 17.4%. See Gi-Wook Shin, "Rural Revitalization Campaign and Social Change in Colonial Korea," 339.

56. Lee Kyoung-ran, "The Peasant's Everyday Life in Peasant Novels of the 1930s" [in Korean], in *Ilche ŭi singmin chibae wa ilsang saenghwal* [Everyday life of the Korean people under Japanese colonial rule] (Seoul: Hyean, 2004).

57. According to the 1930 census, most of the 1.16 million urban workers were "miscellaneous workers," including day laborers (40.4%) and housemaids or houseboys (27.6%). Factory and mine workers only made up 5.4% of urban workers. This would change during wartime mobilization as industrial workers became the largest group of nonagricultural workers by the 1940s. Soon-Won Park, "Colonial Industrial Growth," 134.

58. This was, for example, depicted in the novel *Mokhwa wa k'ong* [Cotton and beans] (1933) by Kwŏn Hwan. See Lee Kyoung-ran, "Peasant's Everyday Life in Peasant Novels," 420–28.

59. *Ture* emerged as an institution in the late seventeenth century among villages in large agricultural regions, bringing together the residents of the village, mostly tenant farmers, to plan and work together for the annual harvest. Yi Hae-jun, *Chosŏn sigi ch'ollak sahoesa* [Social history of villages in the Chosŏn period] (Seoul: Minjok munhwasa, 1996), 339. *Kye* was widely organized beginning in the mid-nineteenth century to pool resources in cases of emergencies such as illnesses and fires, or events that required large expenses such as funerals and weddings. Moneys for the *kye* were also collected for communal projects such as village rites; maintenance of communal wells, roads, and bridges; and the purchase of farm equipment. Kim Kyŏng-il, "A Study of Tonggye in Rural Society from late Chosŏn to Colonial Rule" [in Korean], *Han'guk hakpo* [Korea report] 10, no. 2 (1984).

60. Hisama Kenichi, *Problems of Korean Agricultural Policy*, 355, quoted in Woo Dae-Hyung, "Hisama Kenichi's Thoughts," 44. Shin has a slightly more positive assessment of the rural revitalization movement, citing colonial government records that show that 180,991 tenant households had acquired farmland through low-interest loans made by local financial cooperatives between 1932 and 1939. See Gi-Wook Shin, "Rural Revitalization Campaign," 344–45. However, the overall percentage of tenants who became owner-cultivators through government assistance was still incredibly small, making up only 0.8% of the total tenant and semi-tenant class; the purchased land amounted to only 0.5% of all rented land. See Gi-Wook Shin and Do-Hyun Han, "Colonial Corporatism: The Rural Revitalization Campaign, 1932–1940," in *Colonial Modernity in Korea*, ed. Shin and Robinson, 89.

61. Kim Kyoung-mee, "1940s 'Kokusi' Education for 'Kominka' under Japanese Colonial Rule" [in Korean], in *Ilche p'asijŭm chibae chŏngch'aek kwa minjung saenghwal*, ed. Pang Kie-chung, 147–48. Mandatory education under colonial rule was to be implemented in 1946, and thus never saw the light of day.

62. O Sŏng-ch'ŏl, *Singminji ch'odŭng kyoyuk ŭi hyŏngsŏng* [Formation of colonial primary education] (Seoul: Kyoyuk kwahaksa, 2000), 133, cited in ibid., 147.

63. Japanese settler children were sent to primary schools (*sohakkyo*) whereas Korean children were recruited into "normal schools" (*pot'ong hakkyo*) until the second Education Ordinance in 1938, which moved to unite the two. See Jun Uchida, "A Sentimental Journey: Mapping the Interior Frontier of Japanese Settlers in Colonial Korea," *Journal of Asian Studies* 70, no. 3 (August 2011): 706–29.

64. Kim Kyoung-mee, "Specific Disciplines at Public Elementary School under Early Japanese Rule," in *Ilche ŭi singmin chibaewa ilsang saenghwal*, 490–92.

65. Ibid., 495.

66. Ibid., 497.

67. An T'ae-yun, *Singmin chŏngch'i wa mosŏng: ch'ongdongwŏn ch'eje wa mosŏng ŭi hyŏnsil* [The politics of motherhood in colonial Korea] (P'aju: Han'guk haksul chŏngbo, 2006), 228; Kim Hye-kyŏng, *Singminji ha kŭndae kajok ŭi hyŏngsŏng kwa chendŏ* [The formation of the modern family and gender under colonial rule] (Seoul: Ch'angbi, 2006), 106.

68. Kim Kyoung-mee, "Specific Disciplines at Public Elementary School," 501. In 1905, there were as many as ten thousand private academies throughout Korea, whereas in 1906, after Korea became a Japanese protectorate, the Japanese had set up only twenty-two primary schools. By 1910, there were still only 101 primary schools with 16,946 students (489, 499).

69. Ibid., 512–15.

70. Ibid., 504.

71. Gi-Wook Shin and Do-Hyun Han, "Colonial Corporatism," 93.

72. Lee Kyoung-ran, "Rural Society and Peasants' Life in Chosŏn during the Japanese Wartime Regime," *Ilche p'asijŭm chibae chŏngch'aek kwa minjung saenghwal*, ed. Pang Kie-chung, 368.

73. Ibid., 398–99.

74. Yi Jong-min, "Residents Mobilization and Regulation of Everyday City Life during Wartime: Focus on the Patriotic Unit Campaign in Seoul" [in Korean], in *Ilche p'asijŭm chibae chŏngch'aek kwa minjung saenghwal*, ed. Pang Kie-chung, 443–44.

75. Lee Kyoung-ran, "Rural Society and Peasants' Life in Chosŏn during the Japanese Wartime Regime," 373.

76. Sun Jae-won, "Labour Mobilization and Worker's Life during Wartime" [in Korean], in *Ilche p'asijŭm chibae chŏngch'aek kwa minjung saenghwal*, ed. Pang Kie-chung, 463.

77. One hundred and eighty days of the calendar year were designated "dangerous," requiring special surveillance by the colonial police, many of which were anniversaries of revolutionary movements. Examples include November 7, October Revolution; January 9, Bloody Sunday; January 15, assassination of Rosa Luxemburg; January 21, Lenin's death; March 8, International Women's Day; March 14, Marx's death; March 18, Paris Commune; April 22, Lenin's birthday; May 1, May Day; May 4, China's May Fourth Movement; and May 5, Marx's birthday. See Shavshyna, *1945-nyŏn namhan esŏ*, 32–33.

78. Yi Jong-min, "Residents Mobilization and Regulation of Everyday City Life," 424–25.

79. Lee Kyoung-ran, "Rural Society and Peasants' Life in Chosŏn during the Japanese Wartime Regime," 369.

80. Ibid., 371.

81. Mizuno Naoki, "Late 1930s Thought Control Policies in Colonial Korea: 'Thought Purification Tactics' and Its Ideological Foundations in South and North Hamgyeong Provinces" [in Korean], in *Ilche p'asijŭm chibae chŏngch'aek kwa minjung saenghwal*, ed. Pang Kie-chung, 117–44.

82. Ibid., 138–39. In South Hamgyŏng Province near the Sino-Korean border, Kim Il Sung's anticolonial partisan struggle was reportedly widely known with Kim regarded as a hero. The ideological purification campaign there included specific instructions to instill aversion to Kim among its residents by emphasizing his young age, elementary education, and propensity for excessive delusions about Korean independence and the realization of communism (137).

83. Lee Sang-Euy, "The Korean 'Senior Workers' and Labor Discipline during the Japanese Occupation Era" [in Korean], in *Ilche ha kyŏngje chŏngch'aek kwa ilsang saenghwal*, 174.

84. Chulwoo Lee, "Modernity, Legality, and Power," 47–48.

85. Kim Kyoung-mee, "1940s 'Kokusi' Education for 'Kominka' under Japanese Colonial Rule," 153. Whereas the Korean language and history were part of the curriculum in the 1920s, the Primary School Ordinance of 1938 specified that the purpose of primary school education was the development of imperial subjects; it no longer included instruction in the Korean language and Korean history (155).

86. For a detailed discussion of Japanese and Korean historiography in colonial textbooks, see Kim Kyoung-mee, "1940s 'Kokusi' Education for 'Kominka' under Japanese Colonial Rule," in *Ilche p'asijŭm chibaejŏngch'aek kwa minjung saenghwal*, ed. Pang Kie-chung.

87. *Total Mobilization* (August 1939), 16, quoted in Yi Jong-min, "Residents Mobilization and Regulation of Everyday City Life," 417.

88. Lee Jun-sik, "Propaganda Policy and War Mobilization Ideology during the Japanese Fascist Period" [in Korean], in *Ilche p'asijŭm chibaejŏngch'aek kwa minjung saenghwal*, ed. Pang Kie-chung, 241. Nonetheless, according to colonial statistics the number of Koreans watching films increased steadily so that in 1942 there were over twenty-seven million movie theater visits. This averaged to one film per person per year in all of Korea, but moviegoers were likely concentrated in the urban areas (193, 244).

89. Yi Jong-min, "Residents Mobilization and Regulation of Everyday City Life," 426.

90. Ibid., 427–28.

91. Ibid., 429–31.

92. Shavshyna, *1945-nyŏn namhan esŏ*, 78, 81.

93. Wada Haruki, *Kim Il-sŏng kwa manju hangil chŏnjaeng* [Kim Il Sung and the anti-Japanese war in Manchuria], trans. Yi Chong-sŏk (Seoul: Ch'angjak kwa pip'yŏngsa, 1992); Hongkoo Han, "Wounded Nationalism: The Minsaengdan Incident and Kim Il Sung in Eastern Manchuria" (PhD diss., University of Washington, 1999), 29. Han provides various sources on estimates of the number of victims with Chinese estimates as low as 431 to local residents estimating up to three thousand. Although it's difficult to derive an exact figure, Han estimates that there were well over one thousand victims. Since Japanese sources place the number of party members at 465 and guerrilla fighters at 1,096, Han notes that there were more victims than the number of partisans in the area, including substantial numbers of local residents. As evidence of the absolute destructiveness of the purge, not only in terms of partisan lives but also in the total disintegration of mass support for the partisans, the number of members in local mass organizations dropped from over ten thousand in 1933 to less than a thousand by the following year (347–49).

94. See introduction in Hongkoo Han, "Wounded Nationalism." The remainder of the discussion relies on Han's introduction.

95. Chi Su-gŏl, *Ilche ha nongmin chohap undong yŏn'gu*, 118.

96. Hongkoo Han, "Wounded Nationalism," 15.

97. Ibid., 10.

98. Ibid., 11.

99. Ibid., 17. Chinese communists justified their suppression of Korea's own revolution for independence under the pretext that "victories for the revolutionary movements in large countries would automatically lead to victories for the revolutionary struggles or independence movements in the adjacent small countries" (354).

100. Ibid., 83.

101. Ibid., 330–34. See *Hangil ppaljjisan ch'amgaja dŭl ŭi hoesanggi* [Recollections of the participants in the anti-Japanese partisan war], 12 vols. (Pyongyang: Chosŏn rodongdang ch'ulp'ansa, 1959–69); *Hangil mujang t'ujaeng chŏnjŏkchi rŭl ch'ajasŏ* [In search of the battlegrounds of the anti-Japanese armed struggle] (Pyongyang: Chosŏn rodongdang ch'ulp'ansa, 1960); Kim Il Sung, *With the Century*, vol. 4 (Pyongyang: Foreign Language Publishing House, 1993), 307–30.

102. Dae-Sook Suh, *Kim Il Sung: The North Korean Leader* (New York: Columbia University Press, 1988), 34.

103. Ibid., 35. Although North Korean official historiography claims that Kim Il Sung was president of the Association, Suh doubts such claims. Regardless of who was president, the coordination between the guerrillas and the members of the Association leaves little room for doubt that there were extensive connections between them throughout the period of partisan struggle from 1936 to 1940.

104. Dae-Sook Suh, *Documents of Korean Communism 1918–1948*, 460–61. Even though Suh introduces the document as devoid of aspirations for a socialist revolution, "strongly anti-Japanese but not Communistic, patriotic but not proletarian, more terroristic than revolutionary" (435), elements such as the development of collective farms and the use of confiscated property in the relief of the unemployed seem to me quite clearly socialist inspired. The platform's target audience—"laborers, peasants, soldiers, youth, women, and all working masses"—also resonates with communist language. Moreover, the bylaws of the Association state that its aim is to organize "those who work in factories, schools, barracks, and shops," authorizing the organization of a branch when there are more than three members of the Association in a factory, enterprise, farm, military barracks, store, or village (463). This is the standard organizational method for communist party cells, reproduced in postliberation North Korea, as detailed in chapter 4. Although domestic communists also had similar platforms, there was little opportunity to implement them under the harsh climate of direct surveillance and crackdown by colonial authorities in Korea proper, leading to a sporadic underground movement. For an example of a platform from the Chŏnnam League of the Korean Communist Party dated May 1933, see Suh, *Documents of Korean Communism*, 171–76. For a sense of how much focus there was on preserving organizational secrecy, see 200–205.

105. Ibid., 456–57.

106. Kim Il Sung, *With the Century*, vol. 4, 70–71, cited in Hongkoo Han, "Wounded Nationalism," 355.

107. According to Japanese police records, Kim Il Sung was imprisoned briefly by the Soviets in October 1940 under suspicion of being a Japanese spy when he took refuge in the Soviet Union from the Japanese extermination campaign. Hongkoo Han, "Wounded Nationalism," 355.

108. Kim Il Sung, "On Eliminating Dogmatism and Formalism and Establishing Juche in Ideological Work," December 28, 1955, in Kim Il Sung, *Selected Works*, vol. 2 (Pyongyang: Foreign Language Publishing House, 1971), 593, cited in Hongkoo Han, "Wounded Nationalism," 356–57.

109. This is not to say that modernity does not have uneven and particularistic mechanisms of its own, from the segmentation of the labor force to the global hierarchy of national economies. The point is to highlight the underlying logic of capitalism and colonialism beyond their immediate effects.

110. Christopher R. Browning and Lewis H. Siegelbaum, "Frameworks for Social Engineering: Stalinist Schema of Identification and the Nazi Volksgemeinschaft," in *Beyond Totali-*

tarianism: Stalinism and Nazism Compared, ed. Michel Geyer and Sheila Fitzpatrick (New York: Cambridge University Press, 2009), 236.

111. According to Charles Armstrong, "The key term expressing the philosophical outlook in all areas of life in the DPRK [is] *juche*, often translated as 'self-reliance,' propagated in North Korea since the mid-1950's and enshrined in the DPRK Constitution as the 'guiding principle of politics' in 1972." Charles K. Armstrong, "'A Socialism of Our Style': North Korean Ideology in a Post-Communist Era," in *North Korean Foreign Relations in the Post–Cold War Era*, ed. Samuel S. Kim (New York: Oxford University Press, 1998), 33.

3. Three Reforms

1. RG 242, SA 2006, box 13, item 65, *Minutes of the National Congress of People's Committee Representatives* (November 1946).

2. North Korean Workers' Party Kangwŏn Province Inje County Standing Committee Meeting Minutes No. 31 (1948.12.12), NHCC, vol. 3, 24.

3. For a dissertation comparing Inje County before and after the Korean War, see Monica Hahn, "Transformation of System in the 'Re-taken Areas' during the Korean War—Focused on Inje-gun in Gangwon-do" [in Korean] (PhD diss., Catholic University of Korea, 2009).

4. See official Inje County website, accessed July 25, 2011, http://www.inje.go.kr/home/english/info/info_02.asp.

5. The South Hamgyŏng representative to the National People's Committee Representatives Congress in November 1945 claimed that half of the ten thousand political prisoners detained each year during the colonial period came from his province, which had been the most active region in the organization of peasants and workers throughout the colonial period. Upon liberation, an estimated one thousand political prisoners were released from the provincial capital of Hamhŭng. See *Minutes of the National Congress of People's Committee Representatives* (Seoul: Chosŏn chŏngp'ansa, 1946), in *Collection of Modern Korean History Materials*, vol. 12 (Seoul: Tolbaege, 1986), 488.

6. Two dissertations in Korean have specifically dealt with Inje County based on these records. See Yi Chu-ch'ŏl, "A Study of the North Korean Workers' Party Members and Sub-Organizations," and Monica Hahn, "Transformation of System in the 'Re-taken Areas' during the Korean War—Focused on Inje-gun in Gangwon-do." Yi examines the political system with the main emphasis on the Workers' Party, characterizing postliberation North Korea largely in terms of party control of state power with poor peasants and workers as its base of oligarchic power, while Hahn's focus is on the transformation of Inje County from a county in North Korea before the Korean War to one under South Korea after the war. Both are political histories and neither one deals with the social and cultural aspects of changes in North Korea. I see state and society as constitutive of each other, rather than oppositional, emphasizing the social and cultural elements as arguably the more significant aspects of the North Korean Revolution.

7. RG 242, SA 2009, box 3, item 103, "Survey of Two Years of Work in Each of the Provincial People's Committees" (1947.9).

8. *Minutes of the National Congress of People's Committee Representatives* (Seoul: Chosŏn chŏngp'ansa, 1946), 70, in *Collection of Modern Korean History Materials*, vol. 12, 489.

9. North Korean Workers' Party Kangwŏn Province Inje County Standing Committee Meeting Minutes No. 62 (1949.9.27), NHCC, vol. 3, 636–37.

10. North Korean Workers' Party Kangwŏn Province Inje County Standing Committee Meeting Minutes No. 16 (1948.7.6), NHCC, vol. 2, 375. Also in RG 242, SA 2007, box 6, item 1.60.

11. An exception may be Hwanghae Province, which had the largest concentration of farmland in the northern half of the peninsula and thereby the greatest number of tenant farmers. Its landlords offered the strongest resistance against the land reform in 1946. Still, almost

three-quarters of all wet fields were in the south while the north had two-thirds of all dry fields. See Andrew J. Grajdanzev, "Korea Divided," *Far Eastern Survey* 14, no. 20 (October 10, 1945): 282.

12. North Korean Workers' Party Kangwŏn Province Inje County Standing Committee Meeting Minutes No. 58 (1949.8.25), NHCC, vol. 3, 521.

13. Sakurai Hiroshi, "Kita Chosen nogyo no kikaika ni tsuite" [The mechanization of North Korean agriculture], *Ajia Keizai* 6 (November 1965): 72, cited in Mun Woong Lee, "Rural North Korea under Communism: A Study of Sociocultural Change," *Rice University Studies* 62, no. 1 (1976): 46.

14. "Inje County Report on the Situation of Labor Unions by Industry," (1946.6.11), NHCC, vol. 15, 13–14; "Inje County Table of Enterprises" (1946.7.30), NHCC, vol. 15, 57–59.

15. "Military and Skilled Personnel in Inje County," Inje County Workers' Party Labor Bureau (1946.10.29), NHCC, vol. 15, 62–73.

16. *Chŏngro* [Correct Path] (February 25, 1946), cited in Kim Kwang-un, "Formation of the Power-Structure and the Recruitment of Cadre," 159.

17. "Decisions of the North Korean Peasant League Congress," NHCC, vol. 7, 340–41, cited in Kim Kwang-un, "Formation of the Power-Structure and Recruitment of Cadre," 159. For further details about the proceedings, see Kim Seong-bo, "The Decision-Making Process and Implementation of the North Korean Land Reform," in *Landlords, Peasants and Intellectuals in Modern Korea*, ed. Pang Kie-chung and Michael Shin (Ithaca: Cornell East Asia Series, 2005), 227.

18. *The Historical Experience of the Agrarian Reform in Our Country* (Pyongyang: Foreign Language Publishing House, 1974), 47–48.

19. According to Gi-Wook Shin, a study of several districts in the seventeenth and eighteenth centuries showed that "about 10% of the landholders owned 40% to 50% of the registered land, while middle or poor peasants comprising about 60% of the rural population controlled only about 10% to 20%." When the population increased, and new technology along with crop specialization encouraged intensified labor use in the middle to later periods of the Chosŏn Dynasty, tenancy began to rise. While landlords were increasing their fortunes through usury and high rental rates, the rural poor were faced with underemployment and competition from the surplus of labor. See Gi-Wook Shin, *Peasant Protest and Social Change in Colonial Korea*, 22.

20. Ibid., 51. See also Yi Sun-kŭn, "Issues Regarding the Development of the Agricultural Industry in North Korea" [in Korean], *Inmin* [People], inaugural issue (1946), 68, cited in Yi Chu-ch'ŏl, "Study of the North Korean Workers' Party Members," 22. Before colonial rule, all land technically belonged to the Chosŏn state under the authority of the king.

21. *Pukchosŏn t'ongsin* [North Korea News] (August 1947), 3, cited in Yi Chu-ch'ŏl, "Study of the North Korean Workers' Party Members," 22.

22. RG 242, SA 2007, box 7, item 18, "North Korean Democratic National United Front Fights for Democratic Reforms" (July 1947), 15. Four percent equaled 156,367 households and 50 percent of land equaled 2,002,265 *chŏngbo* of land. According to a 1942 Japanese survey, landlords made up 3.3 percent of rural households but owned 60 percent of all agricultural land, and 80 percent of rural households were either partial tenants or landless. See Ko Sung-hyo, *Gendai Chosen no nogyo seisaku* [Agricultural policy in contemporary North Korea] (Kyoto: Minerva Shobo, 1971), 2, cited in Mun Woong Lee, "Rural North Korea under Communism," 17.

23. "A Starving Hell" [in Korean], *Tonga ilbo* [Far Eastern Daily], Seoul, March 24, 1932, quoted in Gi-Wook Shin, *Peasant Protest*, 69.

24. Gi-Wook Shin, *Peasant Protest*, 75–76, 85, 95–100. The tenancy system was predominant in the southern commercialized regions of the Korean Peninsula, creating somewhat different structural conditions between the north and south. Shin argues that small landowners with tax burdens and increased debt suffered more with the Depression, thus leading to their radicalization. Shin also notes that the geographic distribution of workers' radicalization did not correspond in any meaningful way with that of the peasants. He thus questions the causal connection conventionally made between poverty and radicalization.

25. *Historical Experience of the Agrarian Reform in Our Country*, 63–67; Kim Il Sung and H.D. Malaviya, *Theses on the Socialist Agrarian Question in Korea*, 1st ed. (New Delhi: Socialist Congressman Publications, 1970), 65; Mun Woong Lee, "Rural North Korea under Communism," 19.

26. One *chŏngbo* equals 2.45 acres.

27. Kim Seong-bo, *Nampukhan kyŏngje kujo ŭi kiwŏn kwa chŏn'gye: Pukhan nongŏp ch'eje ŭi hyŏngsŏng ŭl chungsimŭro* [Origins and development of the North and South Korean economic structure: On the formation of the North Korean agricultural system] (Seoul: Yŏksa pip'yŏngsa, 2000); Kim Seong-bo, "The Decision-Making Process and Implementation of the North Korean Land Reform," 207–40.

28. Kim Seong-bo, *Nampukhan kyŏngje kujo ŭi kiwŏn kwa chŏn'gye*, 207.

29. Ibid., 223. Kim also points to the shift toward a more radical position among Soviet policymakers when negotiations with the United States for a unified Korean government fell apart at the end of 1945 (215–17).

30. RG 242, SA 2013, box 2, item 242, Korean Peasant League Fourth Congress (1949.4.20).

31. Gi-Wook Shin, *Peasant Protest*, 174. See also Cumings, *Origins of the Korean War*, vol. 1, and Mun Woong Lee, "Rural North Korea under Communism."

32. Hildi Kang, *Family Lineage Records as a Resource for Korean History: A Case Study of Thirty-Nine Generations of the Sinch'ŏn Kang Family* (Lewiston, N.Y.: Edwin Mellen Press, 2007), 202.

33. "Decisions on the North Korean Land Reform Law" (March 7, 1946), NHCC, vol. 5, 232–33.

34. "Overview of the Land Reform and Future Tasks—Report by Kim Il Sung at the Sixth Enlarged Standing Central Committee Meeting of the North Korean Communist Party" (1946.8.13), in RG 242, SA 2012, box 8, item 88, Collection of Party Documents 1 (1946), 29.

35. Mun Woong Lee, "Rural North Korea under Communism," 19–20.

36. "Kangwŏn Province Inje County Workers' Party Agricultural Bureau" (1946.9), NHCC, vol. 18, 5.

37. *Historical Experience of the Agrarian Reform in Our Country*, 67–72.

38. Kim Il Sung, *Selected Works*, English ed., vol. 5, 335, cited in ibid., 74.

39. Ibid., 78.

40. RG 242, SA 2012, box 8, item 88, Collection of Party Documents 1 (1946), 33–34.

41. Kim Seong-bo, "Decision-Making Process and the Implementation of North Korean Land Reform," 233–34.

42. Monica Hahn, "Transformation of System in the 'Re-taken Areas'," 51, 54.

43. RG 242, SA 2012, box 8, item 88, Collection of Party Documents 1 (1946), 35.

44. John Washburn, "Russia Looks at Northern Korea," *Pacific Affairs* 20, no. 2 (1947): 152–60.

45. "Evaluation of the Land Reform and Future Projects," NHCC, vol. 1, 3 and 48, cited in Ryu Kil-chae, "Study of the People's Committees," 224 (see also 238, 262), and Kim Kwang-un, "Formation of the Power-Structure," 167.

46. RG 242, SA 2009, box 3, item 103, "Survey of Two Years of Work in Each of the Provincial People's Committees," (1947.9).

47. RG 242, SA 2008, box 9, item 72, North Korean Tax System (May 1947), 66. Also in "Decision on the Agricultural Tax-in-Kind," NHCC, vol. 5, 318–19. In May 1947, the agricultural tax-in-kind was revised to reflect different yields, stipulating 27 percent for rice paddies, 23 percent for dry fields, 25 percent for orchards, and 10 percent for slash-and-burn highlands (91). By comparison, individual income was taxed at 6 to 20 percent, with an average of 9 percent, and business income was taxed at 12 to 63 percent, with an average of 26 percent (55).

48. *Rodong sinmun* [Workers Daily] (November 21, 1946), cited in Kim Kwang-un, "Formation of the Power-Structure," 165.

49. Ibid., (November 25, 1946), cited in Kim Kwang-un, "Formation of the Power-Structure," 165.

50. RG 242, SA 2012, box 8, item 28, "Kangwŏn Province Ch'ŏrwŏn County Department of Interior Surveillance of Public Opinion" (January 3, 1950).

51. RG 242, SA 2006, box 16, item 36, "North P'yŏngan Province, Sŏnch'ŏn County, Sŏnch'ŏn Township People's Committee (Secret) Documents" (1949–50).

52. Decreed in December 1949 to demonstrate the superiority of collective management in the rural economy, full agricultural collectivization did not begin until after the Korean War. After the war, preferential treatment was given to cooperatives over individual farmers in order to persuade farmers to voluntarily join the cooperatives. The government gave every possible form of assistance to cooperatives, including renting farm machinery, reducing taxes, providing grain loans, supplying urban workers during peak season, and providing access to high quality seeds. By August 1958 the entire rural population of North Korea was organized into cooperatives, and many of them were reportedly enthusiastic about the process. The small-scale, labor-intensive farming practices throughout much of Korea, which included forms of collective harvesting and planting, facilitated collectivization. Still, decentralization was the operating principle as the county-level cooperative farm management committees took chief responsibility for managing production, and each farm was run self-sufficiently, with its own credit office, school, nursery, clubhouse, bathhouse, and even a cemetery in some cases. See Mun Woong Lee, "Rural North Korea under Communism," 25–29, 37, 43.

53. RG 242, SA 2007, box 6, item 9, "Various Documents," (1947).

54. Kim Il Sung, *Selected Works*, English ed., vol. 5, 341, cited in *Historical Experience of the Agrarian Reform in Our Country*, 53.

55. In March 1946, an estimated 34,670 North Koreans crossed the 38th parallel, while in April the number jumped to 50,450. The number dropped to 25,818 in May, steadily decreasing to 635 by the end of the year. Chosŏn ŭnhaeng chosabu, ed, *Chosŏn kyŏngje nyŏnbo* [Korean economy yearbook], vol. 1 (Seoul: Chosŏn ŭnhaeng, 1948), 9, cited in Mun Woong Lee, "Rural North Korea under Communism," 24.

56. The consumers union (*sobi chohap*) was officially organized on May 20, 1946, bringing together the ad hoc cooperatives that had formed immediately after liberation. Its function was to "struggle against profiteers" and to "connect consumption and production directly thereby improving the material and cultural life of the people." See RG 242, SA 2009, box 8, item 54.1, "Lecture Materials" (October 29, 1947). Workers were given priority in the distribution of goods through the consumers union. Then came teachers (exempting university professors), cultural workers, health workers, and urban *samuwŏn*. The final category included rural *samuwŏn* and college students. Individual producers such as peasants and merchants were not included among eligible groups for distribution because they had independent sources of income. Items for distribution included clothes, shoes, towels, and soap. See RG 242, SA 2013, box 1, item 1, "Regulations for the Distribution of Daily Necessities for Workers and *Samuwŏn*," North Korean Consumers Union, Kangwŏn Province, Munch'ŏn County Committee (1950), 4.

57. RG 242, SA 2010, box 2, item 76, "North Korean Workers' Party Hwanghae Province Public Opinion (Top Secret)" (1949). Another person, however, expressed frustration that the elections were limited to the north, and there was as yet no election covering the whole peninsula.

58. RG 242, SA 2005, box 5, item 43, "Overview of the North Korean Township and Village People's Committee Elections (Top Secret)," Central Election Committee (1947).

59. North Korean Workers' Party Kangwŏn Province Inje County Inje Township Second Cell Leaders Meeting Minutes (1946.10.15), NHCC, vol. 15, 603.

60. RG 242, SA 2009, box 3, item 138, "Election Publicity and Our Duty," North Korean Provisional People's Committee Publicity Bureau (1946.9), 10–11.

61. RG 242, SA 2007, box 7, item 18, "North Korean Democratic National United Front Fights for Democratic Reforms" (July 1947), 3; Armstrong, *North Korean Revolution*, 112.

62. RG 554, Records of General HQ, Far East Command, Supreme Commander Allied Powers and United Nations Command, USAFIK XXIV Corps, G-2 Historical Section, box 76 "Data on North Korea Pertinent to South Korea (Civilian)," (November 14, 1946).

63. RG 242, SA 2005, box 5, item 43, "Overview of the North Korean Township and Village People's Committee Elections (Top Secret)," Central Election Committee (1947), 28–30.

64. North Korean Workers' Party Kangwŏn Province Inje County Inje Township Cell Leaders Meeting Minutes (1947.2.27), NHCC, vol. 15, 619.

65. North Korean Workers' Party Kangwŏn Province Inje County Sŏhwa Township Enthusiast Congress Minutes (1947.2.16), NHCC, vol. 4, 600.

66. North Korean Workers' Party Kangwŏn Province Inje County Nam Township 6th Cell Leaders Meeting Minutes (1947.3.24), NHCC, vol. 15, 502. Also in RG 242, SA 2007, box 6, item 1.59.

67. Strong, *In North Korea: First Eye-Witness Report*, 19.

68. North Korean Workers' Party Inje County Nam Township Meeting No. 6 (1946.10.15), NHCC, vol. 15, 432–33.

69. "Democratic United Front Anju County Committee Important Documents" (1946.9), NHCC, vol. 18, 403–4.

70. North Korean Workers' Party Kangwŏn Province Inje County Sŏhwa Township Enthusiast Congress Minutes (1947.2.16), NHCC, vol. 4, 595.

71. RG 242, SA 2009, box 3, item 138, "Election Publicity and Our Duty," 24.

72. RG 242, SA 2005, box 3, item 43, "Overview of the North Korean Township and Village People's Committee Elections (Top Secret)," Central Election Committee (1947), 4. According to the same document, 4,387 people were denied the right to vote—575 for being pro-Japanese national traitors; 198 by court order; and 3,614 for being mentally ill (47).

73. Ibid., 68.

74. RG 242, SA 2005, box 5, item 43, "Overview of the North Korean Township and Village People's Committee Elections (Top Secret)," Central Election Committee (1947), 155–56.

75. Ibid., 160–67.

76. Ibid., 199–224.

77. Ibid., 202.

78. Ibid., 211, 223, 203–4, 201, 219.

79. RG 242, SA 2005, box 4, item 8, Various Documents North P'yŏngan Province Sŏnch'ŏn County Youth League (December 25, 1946).

80. RG 242, SA 2008, box 10, item 127, Yu Hang-rim, "Ansigil e taehayŏ" [Regarding the day of rest], *Kŏnsŏl* [Construction] 3 (February 15, 1947): 16–23. The article mistakenly cites chapter 3 of the Gospel of Mark.

81. Ibid., 17.

82. Hildi Kang, *Family Lineage Records as a Resource for Korean History*, 202–3.

83. Han'guk minjok munhwa yŏn'guso [Institute of Korean cultural studies], ed., *Naega kyŏkkŭn haebang kwa pundan* [My experience of liberation and division] (Seoul: Sŏnin, 2001), 150. According to oral history collected in this book, Syngman Rhee disregarded Christian concerns, stating that there were only fifty thousand Christians who actually attended church. South Korean surveys on the number of religious followers in North Korea in 1945 give 1.5 million members of the Ch'ŏndogyo, 375,000 Buddhists, 200,000 Protestants, and 57,000 Roman Catholics. See Ralph Hassig and Kongdan Oh, *The Hidden People of North Korea: Everyday Life in the Hermit Kingdom* (Lanham: Rowman and Littlefield, 2009), 188.

84. RG 242, SA 2005, box 5, item 43, "Overview of the North Korean Township and Village People's Committee Elections (Top Secret)," Central Election Committee (1947), 195.

85. North Korean Workers' Party Inje Township Cell Leaders Minutes (1947.2.27), NHCC, vol. 15, 624.

86. RG 242, SA 2007, box 6, item 7, "Various Documents," Inje County Election Committee (1947).

87. North Korean Workers' Party Kangwŏn Province Inje County Inje Township Enlarged Standing Committee Meeting Minutes (1947.2.11), NHCC, vol. 15, 467–68. An advocate of Korean independence through American support as a long-time resident in the United States, Syngman Rhee (1875–1965) was to become the first president of the Republic of Korea

in the south on its founding in August 1948. Also an independence fighter, Kim Ku (1876–1949) was imprisoned multiple times during the colonial period and charged with terrorist activities. Communists considered them both reactionary until Kim Ku visited Pyongyang in 1948 to attend the North-South meeting of leaders organized to prevent a separate election in the south that would in effect permanently divide the peninsula.

88. North Korean Workers' Party Kangwŏn Province Inje County Inje Township Meeting of Social Organizations and Political Parties Decision (1947.2.12), NHCC, vol. 15, 472.

89. North Korean Workers' Party Kangwŏn Province Inje County Nam Township 5th Cell Leaders Meeting Minutes (1947.2.14), NHCC, vol. 15, 493.

90. RG 242, SA 2005, box 2, item 89, "Minutes of the North Korean Province, City and County People's Committee Congress" (April 1947), Day 4, 57.

91. RG 242, SA 2006, box 15, item 32, "Social and State Institutions of the Democratic People's Republic of Korea" (February 1949), 33–35. The work of the Supreme People's Assembly also included the formulation of domestic and foreign policy, approval of the national budget and economic plan, and the formation of the Standing Committee of the Supreme People's Assembly to carry out its duties when in recess, because the Supreme People's Assembly met only twice a year. Consisting of a chair, two vice-chairs, a secretary, and seventeen committee members, the Standing Committee was meant to carry out the ongoing duties of the Assembly commonly associated with heads of state, overseeing the effective implementation of laws and the ratification of treaties. The Cabinet was constituted by a premier, vice-premier, and the heads of the various government departments as the highest executive body. It conducted diplomatic relations and foreign trade, and directed all domestic affairs, from the oversight of local government to national security (military), economy (currency, financial institutions), public health, and education (37–41).

92. RG 242, SA 2005, box 5, item 43, "Overview of the North Korean Township and Village People's Committee Elections (Top Secret)," Central Election Committee (1947), 76.

93. Ibid., 5, 112, 170.

94. Ibid., 119.

95. RG 242, SA 2005, box 5, item 43, "Overview of the North Korean Township and Village People's Committee Elections (Top Secret)," Central Election Committee (1947), 119–20.

96. RG 242, SA 2007, box 6, item 1.57, "Inje County Sŏhwa Township Party Meeting Minutes" (1948.11.28).

97. RG 242, SA 2007, box 7, item 18, "North Korean Democratic National United Front Fights for Democratic Reforms" (July 1947), 30.

98. "Decision to Maintain the Election Publicity Halls as Democratic Publicity Halls" (1946.11.8), NHCC, vol. 5, 66.

99. North Korean Workers' Party Inje County Standing Committee Minutes No. 28 (1948.11.23), NHCC, vol. 2, 698, 700. Similar meeting halls were organized by peasant unions active in the South Hamgyŏng region during the colonial period in the late 1920s and early 1930s. They were equipped with political pamphlets, newspapers, and books, including leftist Japanese journals such as "Marxism," "Internationale," "Red Star," and "Worker Peasant News" to "ideologically arm the union members." The walls of the halls were decorated with the photos of revolutionaries, political slogans, and recent news. They were reportedly the centers of daily agitation and underground activities for the young men and women of the peasant union. See Chi Su-gŏl, Ilche ha nongmin chohap undong yŏn'gu, 221.

100. North Korean Workers' Party Kangwŏn Province Inje County Standing Committee Meeting Minutes No. 6 (1948.3.30), NHCC, vol. 2, 133. Also in RG 242, SA 2007, box 6, item 1.66.

101. North Korean Workers' Party Kangwŏn Province Inje County Standing Committee Meeting Minutes No. 64 (1949.10.10), NHCC, vol. 3, 666. Also in RG 242, SA 2007, box 6, item 1.62.

102. Chosŏn chŏnsa [The complete history of Korea], vol. 23 (Pyongyang: Kwahak paekgwa sajŏn ch'ulp'ansa, 1979), 215, cited in Sonia Ryang, "Gender in Oblivion: Women in the

Democratic People's Republic of Korea (North Korea)," *Journal of Asian and African Studies* 35, no. 3 (2000): 329.

103. Soyŏn, "Nongch'on maengwŏn dŭl ŭi saenghwal esŏ" [The lives of rural league members], *Chosŏn yŏsŏng* (May 1947), RG 242, SA 2005, box 2, item 34.

104. RG 242, SA 2006, box 14, item 67, "Rules for Korean Schools of the Illiteracy Eradication Campaign" (no date).

105. North Korean Workers' Party Kangwŏn Province Inje County Youth League Cell 50th Meeting Minutes (1949.12.20), NHCC, vol. 4, 167–68. Also in RG 242, SA 2007, box 6, item 1.48.

106. North Korean Workers' Party Kangwŏn Province Inje County Peasant League Cell 53rd Meeting Minutes (1949.10.4), NHCC, vol. 4, 435. Also in RG 242, SA 2007, box 6, item 1.50.

107. North Korean Workers' Party Kangwŏn Province Inje County Standing Committee Meeting Minutes No. 28 (1948.11.23), NHCC, vol. 2, 690. Also in RG 242, SA 2007, box 6, item 1.55.

108. North Korean Workers' Party Kangwŏn Province Inje County Women's League Cell 22nd Meeting Minutes (1949.12.25), NHCC, vol. 4, 223. Also in RG 242, SA 2007, box 6, item 1.31.

109. North Korean Workers' Party Kangwŏn Province Inje County Standing Committee Meeting Minutes No. 4 (1948.3.10), NHCC, vol. 2, 103. Also in RG 242, SA 2007, box 6, item 1.66.

110. North Korean Workers' Party Kangwŏn Province Inje County Women's League Cell 34th Meeting Minutes (1949.12.22), NHCC, vol. 4, 279. Also in RG 242, SA 2007, box 6, item 1.31. See also North Korean Workers' Party Kangwŏn Province Inje County Peasant League Cell 9th Meeting Minutes (1947.12.3), NHCC, vol. 4, 297. Also in RG 242, SA 2007, box 6, item 1.50.

111. "Decision 133 on the Regulation and Implementation of the North Korean Education System" (December 18, 1946), NHCC, vol. 5, 670–72, cited in Kim Kwang-un, "Formation of the Power-Structure and the Recruitment of Cadre," 178.

112. RG 242, SA 2007, box 6, item 12.6, "Inje County People's Committee Decision No. 9: Overview of the 1948 People's Economic Plan and Decisions on the 1949–1950 Two-Year People's Economic Plan" (1949.3.29). Also in NHCC, vol. 18, 272. RG 242, SA 2007, box 6, item 1.9, North Korean Workers' Party Kangwŏn Province Inje County Committee Third Meeting Minutes (1948.8.20). RG 242, SA 2007, box 6, item 1.9, North Korean Workers' Party Kangwŏn Province Inje County Committee Fourth Meeting Minutes (1948.11.6).

113. RG 242, SA 2013, box 2, item 242, "Collection of North Korean Peasant League Fourth Congress Documents" (1949.4.20), 47–48.

114. RG 242, SA 2007, box 6, item 12.6, "Inje County People's Committee Decision No. 6: Overview of the Implementation of the General Budget of Inje County and Decisions on the 1949 General Budget" (1949.5.27). Also in NHCC, vol. 18, 252–53. There are indications of misprints on these figures as the percentages do not add up, but even taking into account these mistakes, it is clear that education made up the majority of the expenses.

115. RG 242, SA 2007, box 6, item 1.57, "Inje County Sŏhwa Township Party Meeting Minutes" (1948.3.26).

4. The Collective

1. RG 242, SA 2008, box 8, item 52, T'ae Sŏng-ju, "Problem of Educating Democratic Virtues," North Korean Teachers and Cultural Workers Occupation League (1949), 28, 33.

2. A. Kitobicha and B. Bolsop'ŭ, *1946-nyŏn pukchosŏn ŭi kaŭl: Ssoryŏn chakkadŭl ŭi haebang chikhu pukchosŏn pangmun'gi* [1946 North Korea's autumn: Soviet writers' visit to postliberation North Korea], trans. Ch'oe Hak-song (Seoul: Kŭlnurim, 2006), 158.

3. Armstrong, *North Korean Revolution*, 58. Yi Chu-ch'ŏl, "Study of the North Korean Workers' Party Members," 16. For a history of the Korean Communist Party, see Robert A. Scalapino and Chong-Sik Lee, *Communism in Korea*, 2 vols. (Berkeley: University of California Press, 1972), and Dae-Sook Suh, *The Korean Communist Movement, 1918–1948* (Princeton: Princeton University Press, 1967).

4. Armstrong, *North Korean Revolution*, 108.

5. The Korean Independence League (*Chosŏn tongnip tongmaeng*), which was formed in July 1942 in Yenan, was the precursor to the New People's Party, but its roots can be traced back further to 1938 when the Korean Righteous Army (*Chosŏn ŭiyongdae*) was formed in China as a fighting force for the liberation of Korea. See Sim Chi-yŏn, *Chosŏn sinmindang yŏn'gu* [Study of the Korean New People's Party] (Seoul: Tongnyŏk, 1988). Although the return of the leadership formed the bulk of the so-called "Yenan Faction" that could potentially have posed the strongest challenge to Kim Il Sung and his guerrillas, the majority of the soldiers stayed in China and continued fighting alongside the Chinese communists until the eventual triumph of the CCP in 1949. Cumings has argued that their combat experience was a crucial factor during the Korean War, and also explains the timing of the outbreak of the Korean War by pointing to the return of these Korean soldiers, who numbered in the tens of thousands at the end of 1949. See Bruce Cumings, *The Origins of the Korean War: The Roaring of the Cataract, 1947–1950*, vol. 2 (Princeton: Princeton University Press, 1992), chapter 11.

6. Minutes of the North Korean Workers' Party Founding Congress (August 1946), NHCC, vol. 1, 110; Minutes of the North Korean Workers' Party Second Congress (March 1948), NHCC, vol. 1, 422.

7. Minutes of the North Korean Workers' Party Second Congress (March 1948), NHCC, vol. 1, 296, 335. Based on Soviet sources, Ryu Kil-chae convincingly argues that the idea for the merger came from the Soviets as a way to deal with conflict among leftist groups in South Korea and the need for a united front against the repressive policies of the American occupation. See Ryu Kil-chae, "Study of the People's Committees," 248–54.

8. Minutes of the North Korean Workers' Party Second Congress (March 1948), NHCC, vol. 1, 471.

9. North Korean Workers' Party Kangwŏn Province Inje County Standing Committee Minutes, No. 34, 42, 57, in NHCC, vol. 3, 89, 282, 495.

10. *Rodong sinmun* [Workers Daily] (September 1, 1946), cited in Kim Kwang-un, "Formation of the Power-Structure," 212.

11. North Korean Workers' Party Kangwŏn Province Inje County Standing Committee Meeting Minutes No. 69 (1949.11.13), NHCC, vol. 3, 813. Also in RG 242, SA 2007, box 6, item 1.62.

12. North Korean Workers' Party Kangwŏn Province Inje County Standing Committee Meeting Minutes No. 34 (1949.1.11), NHCC, vol. 3, 93–97. Also in RG 242, SA 2007, box 6, item 1.43.

13. North Korean Workers' Party Inje County Enthusiast Congress (1946.6.22–23), NHCC, vol. 4, 526.

14. RG 242, SA 2006, box 15, item 51, "On the Issuance of the Single Party Membership Card (Top Secret)," North Korean Workers' Party Central Headquarters Organization Department (November 1946), 8–9. The review of members was carried out by a three-person review committee made up of the most diligent members in the county, which was sent to each cell to review all its members. They were not to exceed reviewing thirty people a day, and were not to disturb regular working hours (10–11).

15. RG 242, SA 2008, box 9, item 65, Reference Materials on the Platform and Regulations of the North Korean Workers' Party (March 1949), 38.

16. North Korean Workers' Party Kangwŏn Province Inje County Standing Committee Meeting Minutes No. 8 (1948.4.14), NHCC, vol. 2, 186. Also in RG 242, SA 2007, box 6, item 1.67.

17. RG 242, SA 2007, box 6, item 1.57, Inje County Sŏhwa Township Party Meeting Minutes, (1948.10.31); RG 242, SA 2007, box 6, item 1.56, Inje County Puk Township Party Committee Meeting Minutes, (1948.3.23).

18. RG 242, SA 2009, box 7, item 30.2, "Life of the Party," Korean Communist Party Chinnamp'o City Committee Publicity Bureau (1946.2.10).

19. Ibid.

20. North Korean Workers' Party Kangwŏn Province Inje County Standing Committee Meeting Minutes No. 20 (1948.8.14), NHCC, vol. 2, 461–62. Also in RG 242, SA 2007, box 6, item 1.60.

21. Ibid., 467–68.

22. North Korean Workers' Party Kangwŏn Province Inje County Standing Committee Meeting Minutes No. 35 (1949.1.28), NHCC, vol. 3, 134–37. Also in RG 242, SA 2007, box 6, item 1.43.

23. RG 242, SA 2007, box 6, item 1.56, Inje County Puk Township Party Committee Minutes (1948.12.28).

24. North Korean Workers' Party Kangwŏn Province Inje County Inje Township Enthusiast Congress Minutes (1947.2.4), NHCC, vol. 4, 691–94.

25. North Korean Workers' Party Inje County Standing Committee Minutes No. 35 (1949.1.28), NHCC, vol. 3, 134–37.

26. North Korean Workers' Party Inje County Enthusiast Congress (1946.6.22–23), NHCC, vol. 4, 530.

27. RG 242, SA 2007, box 6, item 1.41, North Korean Workers' Party Kangwŏn Province Inje County Puk Township Second Representative Meeting Minutes (1948.1.27). Also in NHCC, vol. 15, 527–8.

28. Democratic centralism as a political concept came into currency during the Russian Revolution when both Menshevik and Bolshevik factions of the Russian Social Democratic Workers' Party held conferences in 1905, calling on the party to be organized along the principle of democratic centralism by which decisions by higher ranking bodies would be binding on lower organs. It was to become the operating principle for communist parties throughout the communist bloc. For a historical overview of the concept, see Michael Waller, *Democratic Centralism: An Historical Commentary* (Manchester: Manchester University Press, 1981).

29. RG 242, SA 2009, box 7, item 30.2, "Life of the Party," Korean Communist Party Chinnamp'o City Committee Publicity Bureau (1946.2.10).

30. "On the Party's Standard of Cooperation with the Work of Social Organizations," Decision of the 10th Meeting of the Party Central Committee (October 13, 1947), cited in Kim Kwang-un, "Formation of the Power Structure," 121.

31. RG 242, SA 2012, box 5, item 145, Inje County Sŏhwa Township Simchŏk Village Peasant League (1949.1.15).

32. RG 242, SA 2009, box 3, item 75, Explanation of Youth League Platform and Regulations (June 1949), 50–51.

33. Ibid., 66–71.

34. Ibid., 72.

35. The party group in the county youth league was organized on March 25, the trade union on March 30, the women's league on April 12, and the peasant league on April 15, 1947, while the organizations themselves had been organized in 1946. See North Korean Workers' Party Kangwŏn Province Inje County Youth League Cell Founding Meeting Minutes (1947.3.25); Inje County Women's League Cell Founding Meeting Minutes (1947.4.12); Inje County Peasant League Cell Founding Meeting Minutes (1947.4.15) in NHCC, vols. 4 and 7, 168, 279.

36. Workers were not a major force in North Korea at this time. Trade unions in North Korea were combined to form the North Korean Occupation League with a membership of 380,000 of the 430,000 workers in 1947, which made up less than 10% of the adult population. See Armstrong, *North Korean Revolution*, 87–88. For a detailed history of the transformation of the North Korean Federation of Trade Unions (*Chosŏn nodong chohap p'yŏngŭihoe pukchosŏn ch'ongguk*) into the North Korean Occupation League (*Pukchosŏn chigŏp tongmaeng*) in May 1946 and internal conflicts over the nature of the trade union in North Korea after liberation, see Yea Dae-yeol, "Haebang ihu pukhan ŭi nodong chohap sŏnggyŏk kwa nodong chŏngch'aek

t'ŭkchil" [Controversy about the characteristics of trade unions and the traits of labor policy in North Korea after liberation in 1945], *Yŏksa wa hyŏnsil* [History and Reality] 70 (2008), and Kim Kwang-un, "Formation of the Power Structure," 111–14.

37. *Chŏngro* [Correct Path] (February 1, 1946), cited in Kim Kwang-un, "Formation of the Power Structure," 109. Like the Youth League, the date of the official founding of the Peasant League in January 1946 should not be seen as evidence of the lack of peasant organizations before this date. The league was preceded by the ad hoc organization of local peasant unions.

38. North Korean Workers' Party Kangwŏn Province Inje County Peasant League Cell 43rd Meeting Minutes (1949.4.1), NHCC, vol. 4, 396. Also in RG 242, SA 2007, box 6, item 1.50.

39. RG 242, SA 2013, box 2, item 242, Peasant League Fourth Congress (1949.4.20), 53, 66.

40. RG 242, SA 2007, box 6, item 1.9, North Korean Workers' Party Inje County Committee Meeting No. 4 (1948.11.6).

41. North Korean Workers' Party Kangwŏn Province Inje County Peasant League Cell 26th Meeting Minutes (1948.8.5), NHCC, vol. 4, 340. Also in RG 242, SA 2007, box 6, item 1.50.

42. North Korean Workers' Party Kangwŏn Province Inje County Peasant League Cell 40th Meeting Minutes (1949.3.1), NHCC, vol. 4, 381–83. Also in RG 242, SA 2007, box 6, item 1.50.

43. North Korean Workers' Party Kangwŏn Province Inje County Peasant League Cell 51st Meeting Minutes (1949.8.27), NHCC, vol. 4, 426. Also in RG 242, SA 2007, box 6, item 1.50.

44. Pak Hyŏn-sŏn, "Policy on Women during the Anti-imperialist Anti-feudal Democratic Revolution" [in Korean], in *Haebang chŏnhusa ŭi insik* [Understanding pre- and postliberation history], ed. Kim Nam-sik (Seoul: Han'gilsa, 1989), 427.

45. Hŏ Chŏng-suk, "Statement to the Democratic Women of the World," *Chosŏn yŏsŏng* (February 1947), 9–15. All *Chosŏn yŏsŏng* citations are from RG 242, SA 2005, box 2, item 34.

46. The population of women is sometimes given at six million. See Hŏ Chŏng-suk, *Segye minju yŏsŏng undong kwa chosŏn minju yŏsŏng undong* [World democratic women's movement and the Korean democratic women's movement] (Pyongyang: Kongyangsa, 1947), cited in Pak Hyŏn-sŏn, "Policy on Women," 434–35, which also correlates with the thirteen million total North Korean population figure given in *Chosŏn yŏsŏng* (June 1947). However, the most accurate figure for the total population seems closer to nine million. See RG 242, SA 2005, box 6, item 1, Department of Interior and Security documents (1946–48). Soviet occupation reports give 9,332,540 as the total population of North Korea (86.47% in rural areas and 13.53% in cities). See Kim Kwang-un, "Formation of the Power Structure," 101.

47. Pak Chŏng-ae, "1947-nyŏndo pukchosŏn minju yŏsŏng tongmaeng saŏp ch'onggyŏl" [North Korean Democratic Women's League overview of work for 1947], *Chosŏn yŏsŏng* (January 1948), 4–7.

48. North Korean Workers' Party Kangwŏn Province Inje County Women's League Cell 22nd Meeting Minutes (1948.11.25), NHCC, vol. 4, 224. Also in RG 242, SA 2007, box 6, item 1.52.

49. North Korean Workers' Party Kangwŏn Province Inje County Standing Committee Meeting Minutes No. 41 (1949.4.3), NHCC, vol. 3, 234. Also in RG 242, SA 2007, box 6, item 1.65.

50. North Korean Workers' Party Kangwŏn Province Inje County Women's League Cell 10th Meeting Minutes (1948.3.18), NHCC, vol. 4, 193. Also in RG 242, SA 2007, box 6, item 1.52.

51. North Korean Workers' Party Kangwŏn Province Inje County Women's League Cell 5th Meeting Minutes (1947.10.4), NHCC, vol. 4, 182. Also in RG 242, SA 2007, box 6, item 1.53. North Korean Workers' Party Kangwŏn Province Inje County Women's League Cell 6th Meeting Minutes (1947.11.12), NHCC, vol. 4, 184. Also in RG 242, SA 2007, box 6, item 1.53.

52. North Korean Workers' Party Kangwŏn Province Inje County Women's League Cell 23rd Meeting Minutes (1948.12.8), NHCC, vol. 4, 231. Also in RG 242, SA 2007, box 6, item 1.52.

53. North Korean Workers' Party Kangwŏn Province Inje County Nam Township 7th Cell Leaders Meeting Decisions (1947.3.14), NHCC, vol. 15, 510.

54. North Korean Workers' Party Kangwŏn Province Inje County Nam Township 8th Cell Leaders Meeting Minutes (1947.3.24), NHCC, vol. 15, 515. Also in RG 242, SA 2007, box 6, item 1.59.

55. North Korean Workers' Party Kangwŏn Province Inje County Standing Committee Meeting Minutes No. 33 (1949.1.3), NHCC, vol. 3, 68. Also in RG 242, SA 2007, box 6, item 1.43.

56. North Korean Workers' Party Inje County Standing Committee Minutes No. 41 (1949.4.3), NHCC, vol. 3, 231–35.

57. North Korean Workers' Party Kangwŏn Province Inje County Standing Committee Meeting Minutes No. 72 (1949.12.13), NHCC, vol. 3, 926. Also in RG 242, SA 2007, box 6, item 1.62.

58. North Korean Workers' Party Kangwŏn Province Inje County Nam Township Youth Party Member Enthusiast Congress (1947.12.22), NHCC, vol. 18, 36.

59. RG 242, SA 2009, box 3, item 75, Explanation of Youth League Platform and Regulations (June 1949), 49.

60. Ch'ŏngnyŏn [Youth] (October 23, 1946) and (October 28, 1946), cited in Kim Kwangun, "Formation of the Power Structure," 105. RG 242, SA 2009, box 4, item 178, North P'yŏngan Province, Sŏnch'ŏn County, Democratic Youth League Documents (1947).

Like the Workers' Party, the Youth League also carried out the reregistration of all its members in March and April of 1946, and again in February, July, and August of 1947, in order to purge its membership of "impure elements" (pulsun punja). For example, the membership of one local youth league chapter decreased from 164 to 101 members as a result of the purge. Six had been expelled, thirty-one had changed addresses, and twenty-six had passed the age limit. RG 242, SA 2005, box 4, item 26, and item 38, North P'yŏngan Province, Sŏnch'ŏn County, Democratic Youth League Local Group Reports (September 1948).

61. RG 242, SA 2007, box 6, item 1.56, Inje County Puk Township Party Committee Meeting Minutes (1948.12.28); North Korean Workers' Party Kangwŏn Province Inje County Standing Committee Minutes No. 16 (1948.7.6), NHCC, vol. 2, 377.

62. North Korean Workers' Party Kangwŏn Province Inje Standing Committee Minutes No. 16 (1948.7.6), NHCC, vol. 2, 362–63.

63. Minutes of the North Korean Workers' Party Second Congress (March 1948), NHCC, vol. 1, 408.

64. "On Strengthening the Number of Female Officers within the League," Decision of the Central Standing Committee of the North Korean Democratic Youth League (January 26, 1949), NHCC, vol. 25, 98, cited in Yi Chu-ch'ŏl, "Study of North Korean Workers' Party Members," 256. Still, only thirty-three women (1.6%) held official positions within the league above the township level, leaving much room for improvement.

65. RG 242, SA 2008, box 8, item 52, T'ae Sŏng-ju, "Problem of Educating Democratic Virtues," North Korean Teachers and Cultural Workers Occupation League (1949), 51.

66. RG 242, SA 2005, box 4, items 27 and 38, North P'yŏngan Province, Sŏnch'ŏn County, Democratic Youth League Local Group Reports (September 1948).

67. Chŏngro [Correct Path] (November 14, 1945), 2, cited in Kim Kwang-un, "Formation of the Power-Structure," 102–3.

68. See autobiographies of Kae Chin-sun in RG 242, SA 2006, box 12, item 4.1, North P'yŏngan Province Teachers' Training School (1949); Kim Man-kyu in RG 242, SA 2005, box 8, item 34, Part 4, Teachers Resumes (1949); Kim Ŏm-kyu in RG 242, SA 2006, box 12, item 4.2, Central Teachers' Training School Teachers Resumes (1949).

69. RG 242, SA 2006, box 12, item 20.2, North Hamgyŏng Province Teachers Resumes (September 1949).

70. For more on the Moscow Agreement, which gave the conservatives the first opportunity to paint themselves as patriots by opposing the trusteeship, see Cumings, *Origins of the Korean War*, vol. 1, chapter 7.

71. North Korean Workers' Party Kangwŏn Province Inje County Overview of Youth Work for 1947 (1947), NHCC, vol. 15, 626.

72. North Korean Workers' Party Kangwŏn Province Inje County Youth League Cell 27th Meeting Minutes (1948.8.28), NHCC, vol. 4, 63–66. Also in RG 242, SA 2007, box 6, item 1.40.

73. North Korean Workers' Party Kangwŏn Province Inje County Standing Committee Meeting Minutes No. 29 (1948.12.2), NHCC, vol. 2, 738. Also in RG 242, SA 2007, box 6, item 1.55.

74. RG 242, SA 2009, box 3, item 75, "Explanation of Youth League Platform and Regulations" (June 1949).

75. Ibid., 60.

76. Ibid., 6–7, 14.

77. Ibid., 21.

78. Ibid., 21–22 (emphasis added).

79. North Korean Workers' Party Kangwŏn Province Inje County Peasant League Cell 21st Meeting Minutes (1948.5.30), NHCC, vol. 4, 322–24. Also in RG 242, SA 2007, box 6, item 1.50.

80. RG 242, SA 2008, box 9, item 38, Ch'oe Yun-kyŏng, "Experience of Reading Instructions to the Youth," *Ch'ŏngnyŏn saenghwal* [Youth Life] (April 1950).

81. RG 242, SA 2007, box 8, item 78, Hyŏn Chŏng-min, "On the Work of the Social Organizations in Schools," *Haksaeng mun'go* [Student Text] (July 1949), 25–58; North Korean Workers' Party Kangwŏn Province Inje County Youth League Cell 30th Meeting Minutes (1948.10.10), NHCC, vol. 4, 70. Also in RG 242, SA 2007, box 6, item 1.40.

82. RG 242, SA 2005, box 4, item 31, North P'yŏngan Province, Sŏnch'ŏn County, Such'ŏng Township Children's League Documents (1948). For specific reference to the Young Pioneers (referred to as the *ppiyonel*), see RG 242, SA 2009, box 4, item 178, North P'yŏngan Province, Sŏnch'ŏn County North Korean Democratic Youth League Documents (1947).

83. RG 242, SA 2006, box 16, item 31, North P'yŏngan Province, Sŏnch'ŏn County, Children's League Reports (1948).

84. One of the teary-eyed complaints made by contemporary North Korean students after settling in South Korea is that the South Korean students refused to share notes. See *The Long Journey: To Know Is to Love!* Dir. Tae-jin Nam (Seoul: Setnet School, 2009), DVD. See also Jiyoung Song, *Human Rights Discourse in North Korea: Post-colonial, Marxist, and Confucian Perspectives* (New York: Routledge, 2011), 141.

85. RG 242, SA 2006, box 16, item 31, North P'yŏngan Province, Sŏnch'ŏn County, Children's League Reports (1948).

86. Ibid.

87. RG 242, SA 2005, box 4, item 8, Various Documents North P'yŏngan Province Sŏnch'ŏn County (August 10, 1947).

88. North Korean Workers' Party Kangwŏn Province Inje County Inje Township Puk Village Sangdap Cell Meeting Minutes (1949), NHCC, vol. 15, 653–706. Also in RG 242, SA 2007, box 6, item 1.36.

89. North Korean Workers' Party Kangwŏn Province Inje County Inje Township Puk Village Sangdap Cell Meeting Minutes (1949.3.5), NHCC, vol. 15, 662–63. Also in RG 242, SA 2007, box 6, item 1.36.

90. RG 242, SA 2007, box 6, item 1.49, North Korean Workers' Party Kangwŏn Province Inje County Inje Township Puk Village Chungdap Cell Meeting Minutes No. 25 (1949.3.4).

91. RG 242, SA 2009, box 6, item 57, Newspaper clipping in People's Army soldier's notebook (no date).

92. North Korean Workers' Party South P'yŏngan Province Pyongyang Girls' High School Provisional Party Cell Meeting Minutes (1948–49), NHCC, vol. 26, 105–490.

93. North Korean Workers' Party Kangwŏn Province Inje County Enthusiast Congress Minutes (1949.6.22–23), NHCC, vol. 4, 523. Also in RG 242, SA 2007, box 6, item 1.51.

94. North Korean Workers' Party Kangwŏn Province Nam Township Enthusiast Congress (1949.7.15), NHCC, vol. 4, 557.

95. RG 242, SA 2009, box 7, item 30.2, "Life of the Party," Korean Communist Party Chinnamp'o City Committee Publicity Bureau (1946.2.10). This includes extensive quotations from the 1927 Soviet 15th Party Congress. RG 242, SA 2009, box 7, item 27, "Leadership Method," Korean Communist Party Chinnamp'o City Committee Publicity Bureau (no date but probably early 1946). This one is composed entirely of excerpts from Chinese sources, including quotations from Mao Tse-tung, the Chinese Communist Party newspaper, and the CCP Central Committee's "Resolution on Leadership Method."

96. Kim Tae-woo, "Propaganda Campaign of the Rural Community in North Korea, 1948–1949: A Case Study of Injae-gun, Kangwon-do" [in Korean], Yŏksa wa hyŏnsil [History and Reality] 60 (2006): 112–13.

97. Ibid., 114.

98. North Korean Workers' Party Kangwŏn Province Inje County Standing Committee Meeting Minutes No. 3 (1948.2.29), NHCC, vol. 2, 57. Also in RG 242, SA 2007, box 6, item 1.66.

99. North Korean Workers' Party Kangwŏn Province Inje County Women's League Cell 33rd Meeting Minutes (1949.12.7), NHCC, vol. 4, 274–77. Also in RG 242, SA 2007, box 6, item 1.31.

100. North Korean Workers' Party Kangwŏn Province Inje County Women's League Cell 13th Meeting Minutes (1948.5.8), NHCC, vol. 4, 199. Also in RG 242, SA 2007, box 6, item 1.52.

101. RG 242, SA 2009, box 4, item 178, North P'yŏngan Province, Sŏnch'ŏn County, Democratic Youth League Documents (1947).

102. North Korean Workers' Party Kangwŏn Province Inje County Standing Committee Meeting Minutes No. 70 (1949.11.27), NHCC, vol. 3, 817–19. Also in RG 242, SA 2007, box 6, item 1.62. For the full curriculum, see the appendix to this book.

103. Armstrong, North Korean Revolution, 172–73.

104. Kim Tae-woo, "Propaganda Campaign of the Rural Community in North Korea," 129.

105. North Korean Workers' Party South P'yŏngan Province Pyongyang Girls' High School Provisional Party Cell 5th Meeting Minutes (1949.1.9), NHCC, vol. 26, 487–88.

106. North Korean Workers' Party Kangwŏn Province Inje County Standing Committee Meeting Minutes No. 12 (1948.5.28), NHCC, vol. 2, 283–84. Also in RG 242, SA 2007, box 6, item 1.67.

107. Ibid., 278.

108. North Korean Workers' Party Kangwŏn Province Inje County Standing Committee Meeting Minutes No. 71 (1949.12.10), NHCC, vol. 3, 893–94. Also in RG 242, SA 2007, box 6, item 1.62.

109. North Korean Workers' Party Kangwŏn Province Inje County Standing Committee Meeting Minutes No. 32 (1948.12.31), NHCC, vol. 3, 50. Also in RG 242, SA 2007, box 6, item 1.55.

110. North Korean Workers' Party Kangwŏn Province Inje County Standing Committee Meeting Minutes No. 71 (1949.12.10), NHCC, vol. 3, 893.

111. North Korean Workers' Party Kangwŏn Province Inje County Standing Committee Meeting Minutes No. 71 (1949.12.10), NHCC, vol. 3, 894.

112. Ibid.

113. RG 242, SA 2008, box 9, item 89, Paek Nam-un, *Ssoryŏn insang* [Impressions of the Soviet Union] (Pyongyang, 1950), reproduced in Paek Nam-un, *Ssoryŏn insang* [Impressions of the Soviet Union], ed. Pang Kie-chung (Seoul: Sŏnin, 2005), and RG 242, SA 2008, box 9, item 52, Chang Si-u, *Ssoryŏn ch'amgwan'gi* [Visit to the Soviet Union] (Pyongyang: Sangŏpsŏng minju sangŏpsa, 1950). See also RG 242, SA 2012, box 1, item 40, Han Sŏl-ya, *Repporŭttaju: Ssoryŏn ryŏhaenggi* [Reportage: Travelogue of the Soviet Union] (Pyongyang: Ministry of Education, 1948), for a travelogue based on an earlier trip by cultural workers.

114. North Korean Workers' Party Kangwŏn Province Inje County Standing Committee Meeting Minutes No. 39 (1949.3.14), NHCC, vol. 3, 189–90. Also in RG 242, SA 2007, box 6, item 1.43.

115. RG 242, SA 2012, box 8, item 88, "Collection of Party Documents 1 (1946)," 45.

116. Based on the same set of sources, Kim Chae-ung makes the argument that the independence of the PCs was in principle only and that in practice the party held ultimate power, overseeing and directing the PCs and the social organizations. See Kim Chae-ung, "Rural Governing System in Postliberation North Korea: Focusing on Kangwŏn Province, Inje County, 1946–1949" [in Korean], *Yŏksa wa hyŏnsil* [History and Reality] 60 (2006). However, all Marxist-Leninist states have resorted to party control of the government, in part justified by the "dictatorship of the proletariat." The point here is that there was awareness that the government needed to be independent, and indeed the records show that the party often complained that the PCs took matters into their own hands.

117. RG 242, SA 2008, box 9, item 65, Reference Materials on the Platform and Regulations of the North Korean Workers' Party (March 1949), 23.

118. North Korean Workers' Party Kangwŏn Province Inje County Standing Committee Meeting Minutes No. 34 (1949.1.11), NHCC, vol. 3, 83.

119. For a discussion of the differences between capitalist and socialist mass sovereignty, see Susan Buck-Morss, *Dreamworld and Catastrophe: The Passing of Mass Utopia in East and West* (Cambridge: MIT Press, 2000), chapter 1. I have revised her scheme somewhat to discuss nationalist and socialist sovereignty in this case. Buck-Morss explains these two types of sovereignty as the result of the utopian discourse of equality (the "people" as sovereign) born out of the French Revolution, unleashing "two catastrophic forms of modern political life, revolutionary terror and mass-conscripted, nationalist war" (32).

120. Kim Chae-ung, "Rural Governing System in Postliberation North Korea," 47–48, 55. Kim sees the impetus for class struggle, and thereby the authority of the party, strengthened over that of the PC in Inje County because of its location along the 38th parallel, but I illustrate how essential the PC was, as acknowledged by the party itself. Indeed, the proximity of the 38th parallel may have allowed counterrevolutionaries to leave North Korea for the south with relative ease.

121. RG 242, SA 2007, box 6, item 1.42, Inje County Puk Township Party Committee Meeting Minutes, (1947.3.15–1947.9.1).

122. RG 242, SA 2012, box 8, item 72, Administrative Law of Korea (no date), 73–74.

123. RG 242, SA 2007, box 6, item 9, Various Documents (1947).

124. RG 242, SA 2007, box 6, item 1.56, Puk Township Party Committee Minutes (1948.12.28).

125. North Korean Workers' Party Inje County Standing Committee Minutes No. 34 (1949.1.11), NHCC, vol. 3, 101–4.

126. RG 242, SA 2007, box 6, item 1.56, Puk Township Party Committee Minutes (1948.12.28).

127. RG 242, SA 2009, box 4, item 178, North P'yŏngan Province, Sŏnch'ŏn County, Democratic Youth League Documents (1947).

128. RG 242, SA 2008, box 8, item 52, T'ae Sŏng-ju, "Problem of Educating Democratic Virtues," North Korean Teachers and Cultural Workers Occupation League (1949), 161–63.

129. Ibid., 162.

130. Ibid., 163.

131. Paul Smith, *Discerning the Subject* (Minneapolis: University of Minnesota Press, 1988).

5. Autobiographies

1. RG 242, SA 2005, box 8, item 15.2, Resumes and Autobiographies of Graduates and Teachers of the Pyongyang Russian Language School (1948–49).

2. International Red Aid, or the International Organization of Relief for the Revolutionary Fighters (MOPR, according to the Russian acronym) was created in 1922 with the support of the Comintern in order to give support to the "captives of capitalism," that is, political prisoners in capitalist countries, so that "their families will not be left to their fate, and that material aid is promptly organized for their wives and children." See *Ten Years of International Red Aid in Resolutions and Documents, 1922–1932* (Executive Committee of the I.R.A., 1932), 14.

3. For a similar argument for Soviet Russia, see Jochen Hellbeck, "Speaking Out: Languages of Affirmation and Dissent in Stalinist Russia," *Kritika: Explorations in Russian and Eurasian History* 1, no. 1 (Winter 2000): 71–96, and Jochen Hellbeck, "Working, Struggling, Becoming: Stalin-era Autobiographical Texts," *Russian Review* 60 (July 2001): 340–59. Igal Halfin has looked at autobiographies written by students in the Soviet Union for admission into the party in the 1920s, comparing them to confessionals akin to a spiritual conversion from darkness to light. The North Korean autobiographies examined here are much more diverse, focusing on outward behavior during the colonial and postliberation periods. Confession and conversion may have been more salient models for Russia with its Russian Orthodox tradition. See Igal Halfin, "From Darkness to Light: Student Communist Autobiographies of the 1920s," *Jahrbucher fur Geschichte Osteuropas*, bk. 2 (1997): 210–36.

4. In using the term narrative, I borrow Hayden White's definition of narrative as a specific kind of discourse, possessing the structure of a story with a well-marked beginning, middle, and end, in addition to a central subject, a turning point, and an identifiable narrative voice. Hayden White, *The Content of the Form: Narrative Discourse and Historical Representation* (Baltimore: Johns Hopkins University Press, 1987). See especially chapter 2.

5. Although a history of the biographical and autobiographical genre in Korea is beyond the scope of this book, for a historiography of historical writing in Korea, see Henry Em, *The Great Enterprise: Sovereignty and Historiography in Modern Korea* (Durham: Duke University Press, 2013).

6. Without a comparable reckoning, South Korea has been plagued with the continuing legacies of the colonial period down to the present as evidenced by the repeated controversies over "pro-Japanese" figures (*ch'inilp'a*), most recently exemplified by the activities of the Investigative Commission on Pro-Japanese Collaborators (*Taehan minguk ch'inil panminjok haengwi chinsang kyumyŏng wiwŏnhoe*) set up in 2005 under President Roh Moo-hyun and disbanded in 2010. The commission identified hundreds of pro-Japanese collaborators, stripping their descendants of property and wealth gathered during the colonial period. As recently as March 2011, the Constitutional Court ruled that the actions of the commission were constitutional when the descendants filed suit against the seizure of property. See Park Si-soo, "Seizing Wealth of Pro-Japanese Collaborators Ruled Constitutional," *Korea Times*, March 31, 2011. http://www.koreatimes.co.kr/www/news/nation/2011/03/113_84250.html.

7. Ilpyong J. Kim, "A Century of Korean Immigration to the United States," in *Korean-Americans: Past, Present, and Future*, ed. Ilpyong J. Kim (New Jersey: Hollym International, 2004).

8. Hotel Virginia was actually located in Long Beach, California. It opened in April 1908, to become the social center of the area for many years, and closed in October 1932, unable to survive the stock market crash of 1929. The building was demolished after the March 1933 earthquake. See Los Angeles Public Library Images, Virginia Hotel, Long Beach (1924), http://photos.lapl.org/carlweb/jsp/FullRecord?databaseID=968&record=1&controlNumber=79891.

9. According to Kim's student records at Lewis, he was not enrolled at the school until January 1928. The records indicate that he was affiliated with the Moody Bible Institute in some

manner for about three months before his enrollment at Lewis. Kim likely left this information out on purpose, moving up the date of his enrollment at Lewis, in order to expunge his record of any religious affiliations. Ironically, he seems to have gotten better grades in French (receiving mostly Bs and an A) than in English (Cs, Ds, and Fs). See Illinois Institute of Technology Archives, Lewis Institute Student Records, box 302, Record Group 3.2 (1898–1940). I thank archivist Catherine Bruck for her assistance in locating Kim's records.

10. The American Revolutionary Writers League (*Miguk hŏngmyŏng chakka tongmaeng*) may have been a precursor organization to the League of American Writers, a Popular Front organization of American novelists, playwrights, poets, journalists, and literary critics founded in 1935, but I have been unable to track down the English name of this group. For information on the League of American Writers, see Michael Denning, *The Cultural Front: The Laboring of American Culture in the Twentieth Century* (New York: Verso, 1998). In his second autobiography, Kim described the League as a "revolutionary cultural movement under the direction of the American Communist Party and the Anti-Imperialist League (*panje tongmaeng*)." He also claimed to have organized a group of Koreans for the study of the social sciences (*chaemi chosŏnin sahoe kwahak yŏn'guhoe*) while studying in Chicago.

11. According to his student records, Lewis Institute sent Kim's transcript to immigration authorities on April 6, 1932. The Scottsboro Boys were nine black teenagers ranging in age from twelve to nineteen who were accused of raping two white girls. All but the twelve year old were convicted and sentenced to death. After multiple trials and retrials, three served prison terms. The case was widely criticized as an example of racism and a miscarriage of justice. See James A. Miller, *Remembering Scottsboro: The Legacy of the Infamous Trial* (Princeton: Princeton University Press, 2009).

12. Kim is signaling here that he was compelled to undergo conversion (*tenkō*), as was common practice with political prisoners in the last decade of colonial rule, often forced through torture. I thank Henry Em for pointing this out. See the section on total war mobilization in chapter 2 for further context.

13. Chŏng Tal-hyŏn and O Ki-sŏp were both domestic communists who had joined the Korean Communist Party during the colonial period, and were active in organizing workers. O spent time at the Communist University of the Toilers of the East in Moscow in the early 1930s, a school set up by the Comintern to train communist cadres from colonized regions. He was a founding member of the Communist Party branch in North Hamgyŏng Province after liberation, rising to top leadership posts in the North Korean Communist Party and the Provisional People's Committee as the minister of labor. They were both purged in the 1950s. See *Pukhan inmyŏng sajŏn* [Dictionary of North Korean figures] (Seoul: Pukhan yŏn'guso, 1996), 510.

14. RG 242, SA 2007, box 6, item 8, Inje County Deferred Party Applicants Documents (1947).

15. For an example of a confessional by an apostate, Kang Mun-su, in 1934, see Dae-Sook Suh, *Documents of Korean Communism*, 209–23.

16. The Tonghak Rebellion is known as the largest peasant rebellion in Korean history. It broke out in the last years of the nineteenth century in reaction to decades of economic hardship and political corruption, instigating the Sino-Japanese War. See Carter J. Eckert et al., *Korea Old and New*, 214–22.

17. Kim uses the term *hyŏngmyŏngja huwŏnhoe* or *mop'ŭl* to refer to Red Aid, which appears to be the transliteration of the Russian acronym MOPR—Mezhdunarodnoye Obshtchestvo Pomoshtchi Revolutzioneram. I thank Ross King for helping me decipher this reference.

18. Recognizing the multiple languages used in the aftermath of colonial rule with the mass return of Koreans from Japan, China, and the Soviet Union, some of the resumes also inquired about the applicants' "natural language" (*chayŏn yongŏ*). See RG 242, SA 2007, box 6, item 8, Inje County Deferred Party Applicants Documents (1947). In fact, some forms were printed in Chinese and Russian although most were completed in Korean. These forms seem to have been used in workplaces with Koreans born and raised in Russia or China, such as the Soviet-Korean Shipping Company that dealt with international trade and required foreign

language skills. See RG 242, SA 2005, box 6, item 11, Korea-Soviet Shipping Company, Ltd. Staff Records (1948–49).

19. This is not to say that there was a linear development of official forms. The various forms used throughout the postliberation period were not uniform. Earlier forms were often mixed in with new forms as they continued to be used in conjunction with updated versions, and different institutions required slightly different amounts of information.

20. RG 242, SA 2005, box 4, item 39, North P'yŏngan Province Sŏnch'ŏn County Democratic Youth League Records (1946).

21. Kim Ho-ch'ŏl's resume in RG 242, SA 2005 box 8 item 15.2 (boldface added).

22. RG 242, SA 2007, box 6, item 8, Inje County Deferred Party Applicants Documents (1947). These resumes did not include records of sanctions or awards before and after liberation; military experience; family relations and friendships; or hobbies. The party applications in this file also show that the township's decisions to admit the applicants into the party were held back by the supervising county for further evaluation, indicating top-down supervision of local party decisions.

23. Discussion of the Soviet example is based on Sheila Fitzpatrick, "Ascribing Class: The Construction of Social Identity in Soviet Russia," *Journal of Modern History* 65 (December 1993): 745–70.

24. Ibid, 763–64.

25. Hellbeck, "Working, Struggling, Becoming," 341. According to Hellbeck, the *avtobiografija* was the "most widespread type of formalized self-presentation in the Soviet system," consisting of "a short account of an individual's life, submitted in prose and presented orally, listing this person's educational and professional achievements, but in its core focusing on the formation of his or her personality" (342).

26. Fitzpatrick, "Ascribing Class," 751.

27. RG 242, SA 2005, box 8, item 5, Hwanghae Province Sariwŏn High School Teachers Resume (May 5, 1949).

28. RG 242, SA 2005, box 8, item 33, Part 2, North P'yŏngan Province Hŭich'ŏn Women's Middle School Principal Resume (September 9, 1949).

29. For example, see Kim Chung-ho's evaluation in RG 242, SA 2005, box 8, item 5, Hwanghae Province Sariwŏn High School Teachers Resume (1949). One hundred thousand *p'yŏng* of his family's land had been confiscated in the 1946 land reform. Whereas the land reform law used *chŏngbo* (approximately a hectare) as a measure of land unit, most resumes used *p'yŏng*, a much smaller unit of measurement. One *chŏngbo* equals three thousand *p'yŏng*, thus the five *chŏngbo* that was set as the limit after which land was confiscated during the land reform equals fifteen thousand *p'yŏng*.

30. RG 242, SA 2005, box 8, item 6, Sariwŏn City Middle School Teachers Resumes (1949). See file for Ri Po-ch'ŏl, whose family lost forty-five thousand *p'yŏng* of land, and Rim Hyŏng-jun, whose family lost twenty thousand *p'yŏng* of land, but still managed to join the party.

31. See Chŏn Yŏng-suk's file in RG 242, SA 2005, box 8, item 30, Part 4, Pyongyang Women's Teachers College (November 1949), and Ri Su-ch'ul's file in RG 242, SA 2005, box 8, item 34, Part 4, Teachers Resume (1949).

32. RG 242, SA 2006, box 12, item 2, Teachers Resume (May 11, 1949).

33. The paternal aunt, Kim Wŏn-ju, is discussed in detail in chapter 7.

34. RG 242, SA 2006, box 12, item 2, Teachers Resume (January 7, 1950).

35. RG 242, SA 2006, box 12, item 4.1, North P'yŏngan Province Teachers Training School Resumes (1949).

36. RG 242, SA 2005, box 8, item 30, Part 2, Teachers Resume (November 1949).

37. RG 242, SA 2005, box 8, item 5, Hwanghae Province Sariwŏn High School Teachers Resume (October 9, 1949).

38. RG 242, SA 2006, box 12, item 4.1, North P'yŏngan Province Teachers Training School Resumes (1949).

39. Han Ki-ch'ang, another Osan School student discussed in the previous section, took pride in the nationalism imparted to the students by the school founder, Yi Sŭng-hun: "Despite not knowing what it was, it was difficult not to be attracted to the study of the nation (*minjok*)." But he also concluded: "Thinking back now, it is utter nonsense to speak of pure nationalism as did Yi Kwang-su [renowned nationalist writer who ultimately collaborated with colonial policies], as if it didn't matter who ruled or who had economic power as long as we could speak our language. . . . Only internationalism can be victorious and narrow-minded nationalism must be denounced, realizing that a friendly relationship must be obtained with the great Soviet Union" (March 19, 1949).

40. It was also at this time that he stopped going to church against the wishes of his parents, eventually moving out because of their pressure to attend services, causing family discord. Although this was clearly a narrative strategy to distance himself from his Christian parents at a time when Christianity was not looked on favorably, the issue of religion was not a major theme in the autobiographies. I have therefore chosen to relegate it to a footnote here.

41. RG 242, SA 2006, box 12, item 4.1, North P'yŏngan Province Teachers Training School (1949).

42. RG 242, SA 2006, box 12, item 20.3, Hamgyŏng Province (September 1949).

43. RG 242, SA 2005, box 8, item 1, Hwanghae Province Ŭnyul County Ŭnyul Middle School (April–May 1949). All top administrators at this school had previous experience teaching during the colonial period. However, they not only continued to teach but were able to join the party and hold high positions, including those whose lands were confiscated during the land reform.

44. Hayden White, *Content of the Form*, 10.

45. Larry Lockridge, "The Ethics of Biography and Autobiography," in *Critical Ethics: Text, Theory and Responsibility*, ed. Dominic Rainsford and Tim Woods (New York: St. Martin's Press, 1999), 136.

46. RG 242, SA 2006, box 12, item 4.2, Central Education Staff Training Institute (December 1949).

47. Fritzsche and Hellbeck, "The New Man in Stalinist Russia and Nazi Germany," 340. Differentiating Stalinism from Nazism, Fritzsche and Hellbeck point out that the impetus for discipline in Nazi Germany's preoccupation with race and the physical body came from the desire to counter the unpredictable effects of time with the spatial security grounded in the concept of the particular *Volk*. In contrast, the universalist outlook in the Soviet New Man was based on the belief in the progress of history for humanity as a whole.

6. Revolutionary Motherhood

1. Pak Hyŏn-sŏn, "Policy on Women," 425.

2. The Bank of Chosŏn, set up under Japanese colonial rule, continued to issue currency after liberation until its reorganization as the Bank of Korea in June 1950, just before the outbreak of the Korean War. The two occupation zones maintained a unified currency system until North Korea broke away and established its central bank in December 1947 and issued a separate currency. The value of the new currency remained on par for the most part. After liberation in 1945, the exchange rate was pegged by the occupying powers at fifteen *won* to the dollar, devalued in July 1947 to fifty *won* to the dollar, and drastically devalued in October 1948 to 450 *won* to the dollar, after which the Korean *won* continued its precipitous decline due to unstable political conditions. See http://oldsite.nautilus.org/DPRKBriefingBook/economy/ROKMonetaryHistory.htm (accessed August 29, 2010). The calculations have been made based on a W40:$1 exchange rate and a consumer price index of 657.8 for the year 2010 and 66.9 for 1947 with the following equation: 1947 Price x (2010 CPI / 1947 CPI) = 2010 Price.

3. RG 242, SA 2010, box 5, item 4, Hwanghae Province P'yŏngsan County Prosecutor's Statement (March 18, 1947).

4. Christina Kelley Gilmartin, *Engendering the Chinese Revolution: Radical Women, Communist Politics, and Mass Movements in the 1920s* (Berkeley: University of California Press, 1995), 4–5. See also Kay Ann Johnson, *Women, the Family, and Peasant Revolution in China* (Chicago: University of Chicago Press, 1983), and Judith Stacey, *Patriarchy and Socialist Revolution in China* (Berkeley: University of California Press, 1983).

5. Partha Chatterjee, *The Nation and Its Fragments: Colonial and Postcolonial Histories* (Princeton: Princeton University Press, 1993). See especially chapters 1 and 6. For a somewhat different formulation of how the nation is more generally feminized, see Jean Bethke Elshtain, "Sovereignty, Identity, Sacrifice," in *Gendered States: Feminist (Re)Visions of International Relations Theory*, ed. V. Spike Peterson (Boulder: Lynne Rienner, 1992), 149: "The Sovereign may bear a masculinized face but the nation itself is feminized, a mother, a sweetheart, a lover . . . the nation is home and home is mother. No more than one chooses one's parents does one choose one's country, and this adds even greater force to the nature of political love."

6. Chatterjee, *Nation and Its Fragments*, 147.

7. Kyeong-Hee Choi, "Chendŏ yŏn'gu wa kŏmyŏl yŏn'gu ŭi kyoch'ajŏm esŏ" [At the intersection of gender research and censorship research], in *Ilche singminji sigi saero ilkki* [Rereading of the colonial period in Korea] (Seoul: Hyean, 2007); Kyeong-Hee Choi, "Impaired Body as Colonial Trope," 431–58.

8. Johnson, *Women, the Family, and Peasant*, 167.

9. Copies of *Chosŏn yŏsŏng* from the post–Korean War period of the 1950s, 1960s, and 1970s have been the primary source for past studies of North Korean women, leading to arguments that the construction of North Korean women as mothers did not begin until the postwar period with the cult of leadership and the exaltation of Kim Chŏng-suk (Kim Il Sung's wife) as the "Mother of the Revolution" and Kang Pan-sŏk (Kim Il Sung's mother) as the "Mother of Korea." See Sonia Ryang, "Gender in Oblivion," 323–49.

10. Past studies of North Korean women can be roughly broken down into three broad camps. The first sees the breakdown of the traditional patriarchal family through communist policies as having a negative effect on the uniquely Korean sense of morality and virtue. See Kim Nam-sik, "Inquiry into North Korea's Family System" [in Korean], *Kukt'o T'ongil* [National Reunification] 4, no. 5 (1974). Others are critical of North Korea's policies on women for their maintenance of patriarchal relations, exacerbated by what they call "totalitarian state patriarchy" through women's mobilization as workers as well as housewives, increasing the double burden on women. See Yun Mi-ryang, *Pukhan yŏsŏng chŏngch'aek* [North Korea's policy on women] (Seoul: Hanul, 1991); Yi On-juk, "Social Status and Social Participation of North Korean Women" [in Korean], *Pukhan yŏn'gu* [North Korea Research], (Fall 1990); Yi Tae-yŏng, "Policy on Women's Liberation and Patriarchy in North Korea" [in Korean], *Pukhan yŏn'gu* [North Korea Research] (Fall 1990); Chŏn Sang-in, *Changes in North Korean Family Policy* [in Korean] (Seoul: National Reunification Research Institute, 1993); Chŏn Suk-ja, "The Image of Women in North Korea: Focusing on its Revolutionary and Traditional Aspects" [in Korean], *Han'guk sahoehak* [Korean Sociology] 29 (Summer 1995); Hwang Yŏng-ju, "Revolutionary Warrior and Wise Mother Good Wife: North Korean Women and National Development" [in Korean], *Kukche munje nonch'ong* [Journal of International Relations] 11 (1999); Pak Yŏng-ja, "The Politics about Woman in North Korea: Forming as 'The Innovational Laborer-Revolutionary Mother'" [in Korean], *Sahoe kwahak yŏn'gu* [Social Science Research] 13, no. 1 (2005); and Sonia Ryang, "Gender in Oblivion." A third approach attempts to understand North Korean gender policies through standards set by the North Korean state, maintaining a critical stance while giving credit for some improvements in women's lives. For a representative example of this last position, see Kyung Ae Park, "Women and Revolution in North Korea," *Pacific Affairs* 65, no. 4 (Winter 1992–93): 527–45; Pak Hyŏn-sŏn, "Policy on Women"; Ch'oe Hong-ki, "Change and Continuity in the Transformation of the Postliberation North Korean Family System," [in Korean] *Pukhan yŏn'gu* [North Korea Research] 2, no. 2 (Summer 1991);

Kim Kwi-ok, "North Korean Women Yesterday and Today" [in Korean] in *Pukhan yŏsŏng dŭl ŭn ŏttŏk'e salgo issŭlkka* [How are North Korean women living], ed. Kim Kwi-ok (Seoul: Tangdae, 2000); Hwang Eun-ju, "A Study of Women's Political Socialization in North Korea: Focusing on the Chosŏn Democratic Women's Federation and *Chosŏn Yŏsŏng*" [in Korean] (master's thesis, Hanyang University, 1994).

11. Ryang, "Gender in Oblivion," 323.

12. Heidi Hartmann, "The Unhappy Marriage of Marxism and Feminism: Towards a More Progressive Union," in *Women and Revolution*, ed. Lydia Sargent (Cambridge: South Ends Press, 1981).

13. David L. Hoffmann, "Mothers in the Motherland: Stalinist Pronatalism in Its Pan-European Context," *Journal of Social History* 34, no. 1 (Fall 2000): 35–54.

14. Anna Davin, "Imperialism and Motherhood," *History Workshop Journal* 5, no. 1 (1978): 9–66.

15. Kawamoto Aya, "Ideology of Good Wife Wise Mother and the Theory of 'Women's Emancipation' in Japan" [in Korean], *Yoksa pip'yong* [History Criticism] 52 (Fall 2000): 353–63.

16. Hong Yang-hŭi, "Theory of Wise Mother Good Wife in Korea and the Making of the Colonial 'Citizen'" [in Korean], *Yoksa pip'yŏng* [History Criticism] 52 (Fall 2000): 364–74. For a slightly different view that combines the influences of Confucian patriarchy, Japanese colonialism, and Western Christianity, see Hyaeweol Choi, "'Wise Mother, Good Wife': A Transcultural Discursive Construct in Modern Korea," *Journal of Korean Studies* 14, no. 1 (Fall 2009): 1–34.

17. Yi Sang-kyŏng, "A Study of Korean Women's Mobilization and the Image of the 'Militaristic Mother' under the National General Mobilization System by Japanese Imperialism" [in Korean], *P'eminijŭm yŏn'gu* [Feminism Research] 2 (Dec. 2002): 211.

18. Hyun Ok Park, "Ideals of Liberation: Korean Women in Manchuria," in *Dangerous Women: Gender and Korean Nationalism*, ed. Elaine H. Kim and Chungmoo Choi (New York: Routledge, 1998), 229–48.

19. Ueno Chizuko, *Nationalism and Gender* (Melbourne: Trans Pacific Press, 2004).

20. Gregory Kasza, *The Conscription Society: Administered Mass Organizations* (New Haven: Yale University Press, 1995), 93.

21. Japan was also a source of Western feminist ideas. Works by Henrik Ibsen, Ellen Key, August Bebel, and Alexandra Kollontai were often translated first into Japanese and imported into Korea, leading to the rise of the New Woman in Korea. Although the idea of the New Woman remained fluid and ambiguous in its representation of modernity, New Women were generally associated with women who had a modern education in urban areas, and were advocates of free love, marriage, and divorce. Many of them filled the ranks of the new female intellectual class as journalists, writers, or artists. However, Kim Kyŏng-il makes the important point that their primary defining characteristic was not their educational background as such, but their situated identity in the opposition between tradition and modernity. For a good review of the various ways in which the New Woman has been defined, see Kim Kyŏng-il, "Tradition and Modernity in the Formation of Modern Korean Society: On the Ideas of Family and Women" [in Korean], *Sahoe wa yŏksa* [Society and History] 54 (December 1998): 23–25. The term Modern Girl seems to have had a more derogatory connotation associated with consumption, vanity, decadence, and indulgence. See Kwon Myoung-A, "The Gender Politics of Wartime Mobilization Regime in Korea," [in Korean] in *Ilche p'asijŭm chibae chŏngch'aek kwa minjung saenghwal*, ed. Pang Kie-chung.

22. Ibid., 310–11.

23. Ibid., 300–303.

24. Yi Sang-kyŏng, "A Study of Korean Women's Mobilization," 219.

25. Ibid., 206–7.

26. Lee Kyoung-ran, "Rural Society and Peasants' Life," 396–98.

27. Kwon Myoung-A, "Gender Politics of Wartime Mobilization," 304–5.

28. Cho Kyoung-mi, "Study of the 1920s Socialist Women's Organizations: Before the Foundation of Kŭnuhoe" [in Korean], *Sookmyung Women's University Korean Studies Research* 2 (1992): 65–90.

29. Kenneth M. Wells, "The Price of Legitimacy: Women and the Kŭnuhoe Movement, 1927–1931," in *Colonial Modernity in Korea*, ed. Shin and Robinson.

30. Kwon Soo-Hyun, "Reconstruction of Feminism in Heo Jeong-sook" [in Korean], *P'eminijŭm yŏn'gu* [Feminism Research] 10, no. 1 (2010): 247–83. See chapter 7 for more biographic detail and discussion of Hŏ Chŏng-suk.

31. *Chosŏn yŏsŏng* (September 1946), the inaugural issue. In the copy of the platform in the January 1947 issue, another item was added: "Urge women to protect the nation." All *Chosŏn yŏsŏng* citations are from RG 242, SA 2005, box 2, item 34.

32. These articles are 14 through 17 of the Labor Law. See Pak Hyŏn-sŏn, "Policy on Women," 416–18.

33. Kim Yun-dong, "The law on the equality of the sexes in North Korea," *Chosŏn yŏsŏng* (July 1947): 18–24.

34. The colonial government had outlawed polygamy and concubinage while providing freedom of divorce and remarriage for women in 1922, but there had been no real efforts to enforce this legislation. See Hyunah Yang, "Envisioning Feminist Jurisprudence in Korean Family Law at the Crossroads of Tradition/Modernity" (PhD diss., New School for Social Research, 1998), 42–43, 56. The reference in the Gender Equality Law to Japanese imperial laws would imply regulations that were detrimental to women such as the forced recruitment of "comfort women."

35. Wendy Zeva Goldman, "Women, the Family, and the New Revolutionary Order in the Soviet Union," in *Promissory Notes: Women in the Transition to Socialism*, ed. Sonia Kruks, Rayna Rapp, and Marilyn B. Young (New York: Monthly Review Press, 1989), 59–81.

36. Pak Hyŏn-sŏn, "Policy on Women," 422.

37. Yun Mi-ryang, *Pukhan yŏsŏng chŏngch'aek*, 75.

38. Hong Ch'i-ok, "Ssoryŏn yŏsŏng ŭi sahoejŏk chiwi" [Social status of Russian women], *Chosŏn yŏsŏng* (September 1946): 50–54.

39. Goldman, "Women, the Family, and the New Revolutionary Order," 74.

40. Wendy Z. Goldman, *Women, the State and Revolution: Soviet Family Policy and Social Life, 1917–1936* (New York: Cambridge University Press, 1993), 340.

41. Chatterjee, *Celebrating Women*, 30.

42. For a study of the journal from 1979 to 1992, see Hwang Eun-ju, "Women's Political Socialization in North Korea," 73, 100, 54–58. She argues that North Korean policies on women have emphasized women's role as mothers as a result of changes made in the organizational membership structure from the fourth congress of the women's league in 1971, which included all women, to the fifth congress in 1983, which included only housewives. She claims that there were no longer any articles in the journal dealing with women working in factories after 1981. Based on the journal contents and contemporary novels, she argues that North Korean women are not simply depicted in traditional submissive roles, as previous scholarship has described, but as "revolutionary mother, comrade wife, and respectful but principled daughter-in-law." Nonetheless, she agrees with previous assessments that North Korean women have a dual burden as workers outside the home and as housewives in the home.

43. Kim Un-chuk, "Chosŏn yŏsŏngsa saŏp e taehan pogo" [Report on the work of the Chosŏn yŏsŏng publishing company], *Chosŏn yŏsŏng* (November 1947): 40–42.

44. Ibid.

45. Kim Kyŏng-il, "Tradition and Modernity," 31n32.

46. The term *kajŏng* was a neologism that began to be used at the turn of the twentieth century to denote the modern home, incorporating the Sino-Korean characters for household or family lineage with another denoting garden or courtyard. The term can be translated to mean both home and family, but I have used home uniformly as being closer to the original meaning.

The issues involved in this change from the family conceived of as a household to being based on the physical space inhabited by the nuclear family are complex and beyond the scope of this chapter. See Yoon Sun Yang, "Nation in the Backyard: Yi Injik and the Rise of Korean New Fiction, 1906–1913" (PhD diss., University of Chicago, 2009).

47. Chu Chŏng-sun, "Chikchang'ŭl kajin chubu ŭi saenghwal sŏlgye" [Daily plan for housewives with jobs], *Chosŏn yŏsŏng* (September 1947): 29–32.

48. *Chosŏn yŏsŏng* (February and April 1947).

49. "Round-table discussion of working women," *Chosŏn yŏsŏng* (February 1947): 54–60.

50. An Ok-rye, "Namsŏng ege tŭrinŭn malssŭm" [A word to the gentlemen], *Chosŏn yŏsŏng* (September 1946): 95.

51. Yang P'yŏng-ji, "Yŏksasang yŏsŏng ŭi chiwiwa kŭ ŭi kwaŏp" [The status of women in history and its lessons], *Chosŏn yŏsŏng* (Jan. 1947): 17–20.

52. "8.15 Haebang 2-chunyŏn kinyŏm yŏsŏng chwadamhoe" [Roundtable discussion for the second-year anniversary of the August 15 liberation], *Chosŏn yŏsŏng* (August 1947): 24–30.

53. Chang Chŏng-suk, "Saeroun kajŏng kwa chubu" [The new home and housewife], *Chosŏn yŏsŏng* (October 1947): 33–36.

54. Pak Chŏng-ae, "The labor law and women," *Chosŏn yŏsŏng* (September 1946): 33–34.

55. Pak Hyŏn-sŏn, "Policy on Women," 437–38.

56. "Mosŏng e taehan ssobet'ŭ chŏngbu ŭi koryŏ" [Considerations of the Soviet government on mothers], *Chosŏn yŏsŏng* (October 1947): 21–22. North Korea's interest in increasing its population must have been particularly acute, because it had only half the size of South Korea's population at a time of increasing competition over which side was to attain hegemony and legitimacy as the sole representative government in Korea.

57. Elizabeth Waters, "The Modernisation of Russian Motherhood, 1917–1937," *Soviet Studies* 44, no. 1 (1992): 123–36.

58. An Ham-kwang, "Hŭisaengjŏk in ponggongsim: T'ŭkhi yŏsŏng ege chunŭn marŭl kyŏmhayŏ" [Sacrificial public service: Especially a word to women], *Chosŏn yŏsŏng* (March 1947): 14–18 (emphasis added).

59. Ryang, "Gender in Oblivion," 341.

60. *Kang Pan-sŏk nyŏsa rŭl ttara paeuja* [Let's follow and learn from Madame Kang Pan-sŏk] (Tokyo: Chosŏn ch'ŏngnyŏnsa, 1967), 45.

61. For references to parental love and respect between officers and soldiers, see "For a Military Power Prepared for Modern Warfare" [in Korean], in *Sŏn'gun T'aeyang Kim Jong Il Changgun* [Sun of Military First, General Kim Jong Il], vol. 3, chapter 9 (Pyongyang: Pyongyang ch'ulp'ansa, 2006), accessed August 15, 2012, http://ndfsk.dyndns.org/anecdotes/070927–1.htm.

62. Im Hŏn-yŏng, "Anti-Japanese revolutionary literature of North Korea" [in Korean], in *Pukhan ŭi munhak* [North Korean literature], ed. Kwŏn Yŏng-min (Seoul: Ŭlyu munhwasa, 1989).

63. Ku Po-hae, "Nongch'on purak Omokdong" [Rural village Omokdong], *Chosŏn yŏsŏng* (April 1948): 28–31.

64. Sin Ko-song, "Myŏn ri inminwiwŏn sŏn'gŏ e issŏsŏdo yŏsŏng dŭrŭn ssaunda" [Women fight for the elections of the township and village People's Committees], *Chosŏn yŏsŏng* (February 1947): 24–26.

65. Ri Kyŏng-hye, *Nyŏsŏng munje hyekyŏl kyŏnghŏm* [Experience of solving the woman question] (Pyongyang: Sahoe kwahak ch'ulp'ansa, 1990), 97.

66. Nam Hyŏn-sŏ, "Saenara ŭi yŏindŭl" [Women of a new country], *Chosŏn yŏsŏng* (January 1947): 33.

67. Yun Mi-ryang, *Pukhan yŏsŏng chŏngch'aek*, 76.

68. American occupation policy in the south maintained Japanese colonial law throughout the immediate postliberation period, and the first legislation on family law in South Korea in 1957 was based on the principle of "respect for tradition" and "good customs." By contrast, in North Korea the 1946 Gender Equality Law specifically targeted "feudal customs" as harmful

to women. The first Civil Law in South Korea specifically stated that "when there is no pertinent statute regarding the civil affair, the case shall observe the customary law." The "good customs" to be preserved included the registration of married women in the husband's family register, the husband's role as the head of the family, the children's succession of the father's surname, and the male succession of family headship, essentially maintaining all aspects of the patriarchal family that had been institutionalized under colonial rule. With the elimination of the household registry in North Korea, all of the above had been legally repealed. See Hyunah Yang, "Envisioning Feminist Jurisprudence," chapter 4.

69. The revised Socialist Constitution was enacted on December 27, 1972. Its article 63 states, "Marriage and family are protected by the State. The State pays great attention to consolidating the family, the cell of society." Yun Mi-ryang, *Pukhan yŏsŏng chŏngch'aek*, 81, 102.

70. Kim Il Sung stated that "our ideal is . . . a society where all people live united in harmony as one big family" in "The Duty of Mothers in the Education of Children (Speech at the National Meeting of Mothers, November 16, 1961)," in *On the Work of the Women's Union* (Pyongyang: Foreign Languages Publishing House, 1971), 4, quoted in Jon Halliday, "Women in North Korea: An Interview with the Korean Democratic Women's Union," *Bulletin of Concerned Asian Scholars* 17, no. 3 (1985): 46–56, 52n28.

71. Chang Kil-sŏng, "Ssoryŏn sahoejuŭi 10-wŏl hyŏngmyŏng kwa ssoryŏn yŏsŏng ŭi chiwi" [The Soviet Socialist October Revolution and the status of Soviet women], *Chosŏn yŏsŏng* (November 1947): 10–14.

72. Friedrich Engels, *The Origin of the Family, Private Property and the State: In the Light of the Researches of Lewis H. Morgan* (New York: International Publishers, 1972).

73. Pak Hyŏn-sŏn, "Policy on Women," 450.

74. Advertisement inside the front cover of the April 1948 issue of *Chosŏn yŏsŏng*.

75. Kim Sŏk-yang, "Yugawŏn pangmun'gi" [Visit to an orphanage], *Chosŏn yŏsŏng* (October 1947): 55–57.

76. Yun Mi-ryang, *Pukhan yŏsŏng chŏngch'aek*, 203.

77. Ch'oe Yong-gŏn, "Chosŏn yŏsŏng dŭl ege chŏngch'i munhwa kyoyang ŭl kanghwa hara" [Strengthen the political and cultural education of Korean women], *Chosŏn yŏsŏng* (September 1946): 9.

78. Joan W. Scott, "The Evidence of Experience," *Critical Inquiry* 17 (Summer 1991): 793.

79. I use the term "allegory" here to denote the tenuous grounds on which such symbolic gestures may take effect so that they are unstable and inconsistent, subject to relatively rapid changes. My use of allegory as "profoundly discontinuous, a matter of breaks and heterogeneities, of the multiple polysemia of the dream rather than the homogeneous representation of the symbol" follows Fredric Jameson's formula in "Third-World Literature in the Era of Multinational Capitalism," *Social Text*, no. 15 (Autumn 1986): 73.

7. "Liberated Space"

1. Sŏdaemun Prison, which opened in 1907 as Keijō Prison under colonial rule, was the first modern prison built in Korea. Modeled after the American and English prisons of the nineteenth century, which borrowed ideas from Jeremy Bentham's panopticon, it segregated prisoners into individual cells with constant and total surveillance from impenetrable watchtowers. It was expanded in 1933 to house political prisoners. See Lee Jong-min, "Colonial Disciplinary System." For a firsthand eyewitness account of the release of the prisoners, see Shavshyna, *1945-nyŏn namhan esŏ*, 72–73.

2. O Yŏng-jin, *Ssogunjŏng ha ŭi pukhan: Hana ŭi chŭngŏn*, 11–12.

3. Sin Chu-baek, "8.15 Reproduced, 8.15 Forgotten in History Textbooks" [in Korean], and Chŏng Kŭn-sik, "Memory of 8.15 in Memorial Halls and Memorial Days" [in Korean],

in *8.15 ŭi kiŏk kwa tongasiajŏk chip'yŏng* [Memory of 8.15 and East Asian prospects], ed. Chŏng Kŭn-sik and Sin Chu-baek (Seoul: Sŏnin, 2006).

4. Yun Hae-dong, *Singminji kŭndae ŭi p'aerŏdoksŭ* [Paradox of colonial modernity] (Seoul: Humanist Books, 2007), 43–46.

5. Michel-Rolph Trouillot, *Silencing the Past: Power and the Production of History* (Boston: Beacon Press, 1995); emphasis added. Trouillot explains the mechanism of silencing as "an active and transitive process: one 'silences' a fact or an individual as a silencer silences a gun. One engages in the practice of silencing. Mentions and silences are thus active, dialectical counterparts of which history is the synthesis" (48). While characterizing the process of silencing as neither natural nor neutral, Trouillot is also careful to note that "effective silencing does not require a conspiracy, not even a political consensus [because] its roots are structural" (106).

6. In this respect, Inje County would seem to offer a perfect location for contemporary oral histories as a site that was north of the 38th parallel after liberation, but south of the demilitarized zone after the Korean War. However, in the only study of contemporary Inje County to date, Monica Hahn makes clear that the vast majority of residents in the area today are staunch anticommunists, having moved to the area after the south took possession of the region after the war. At the end of the war, as much as 60%–70% of the native residents of the county fled to the north, having participated in the revolution in various capacities, and the county magistrates, mayors, and village heads that had served under colonial rule were reinstated. Only a very small minority of those who remained had lived through the five-year postliberation period in the north, and it continues to be taboo for them to speak about their experience without incriminating themselves as "communists," punishable under the National Security Law. See Monica Hahn, "Transformation of System in the 'Re-taken Areas,'" 193–210.

7. Scott, "Evidence of Experience," 797.

8. I use Émile Durkheim's notion of collective effervescence: "There are periods in history when, under the influence of some great collective shock, social interactions have become much more frequent and active. Men look for each other and assemble together more than ever. That general effervescence . . . is characteristic of revolutionary or creative periods." See Émile Durkheim, *The Elementary Forms of the Religious Life*, trans. Joseph Ward Swain (New York: Collier Books, 1961), 242, cited in Colin Barker, "Empowerment and Resistance: 'Collective Effervescence' and Other Accounts," in *Transforming Politics: Power and Resistance*, ed. Paul Bagguley and Jeff Hearn (London: St. Martin's Press, 1999), 12.

9. William Sewell, for example, emphasizes the importance of emotional excitement in revolutionary transformation: "High-pitched emotional excitement is a constitutive ingredient of many transformative actions. . . . Emotional tone of action can be an important sign of structural dislocation and rearticulation. . . . The resolution of structural dislocation—whether by restoring the ruptured articulation or by forging new ones—results in powerful emotional release that consolidates the rearticulation." William H. Sewell Jr., "Historical Events as Structural Transformations: Inventing Revolution at the Bastille," *Theory and Society* 25 (1996): 865.

10. Taking inspiration from Joan Kelly's question about whether women had a Renaissance, Gail Hershatter followed suit by asking whether women had a Chinese Revolution. My question follows theirs. See Gail Hershatter, "The Gender of Memory: Rural Women and Collectivization in 1950s China," paper presented in the colloquium series of the Program in Agrarian Studies, Yale University, 2006.

11. Maurice Halbwachs, *On Collective Memory*, trans. Lewis A. Coser (Chicago: University of Chicago Press, 1992).

12. During my Fulbright Fellowship in 2002–3, I conducted formal interviews with two men with experience of the postliberation period. In the process of seeking interview subjects, I also conversed informally with a group of former long-term political prisoners, most of whom had served more than ten years in prison on various charges, from allegations of espionage to being communist sympathizers. Lest all long-term prisoners be considered spies, it should be noted that there were those whose cases were fabricated, and also cases in which ordinary people living in the north with families in the south secretly crossed over the border to see their

families but were caught in the process. I was able to make their acquaintance through Minka-hyup, a human rights group in Seoul that works for the release of political prisoners. The National Security Law has been the instrument under which the majority of political prisoners have been imprisoned since its enactment in 1948. The best study of the National Security Law and its numerous cases throughout the years is by Park Won Soon, *Kukka poanbŏp yŏn'gu* [Study of the National Security Law], 3 vols. (Seoul: Yŏksa pip'yŏngsa, 1992). Those interviewed gave me their consent to disclose their full names. Despite potential risks, the interviews may have served as a form of political statement by which they can counter negative stereotypes about political prisoners, and by which they make their voices heard, defying intimidation from the authorities against speaking out. They may also serve to gain some level of social recognition.

13. Han'guk minjok munhwa yŏn'guso, *Naega kyŏkkŭn haebang kwa pundan* [My experience of liberation and division] (Seoul: Sŏnin, 2001), 137.

14. Ibid., 176.

15. Ibid., 226.

16. Yi Hyang-kyu, ed., *Nanŭn chosŏn nodongdangwŏnio: Kim Sŏk-hyŏng kusul charyojip* [I am a member of the Korean Workers' Party: Kim Sŏk-hyŏng's oral testimony] (Seoul: Sŏnin, 2001), 130.

17. A South Korean term to refer to the political opposition as a group, *chaeya*, literally means "out of power." The *chaeya* is not always easy to pinpoint because it is defined in the negative rather than through a set of goals or practices. It has generally been associated with the broad grassroots democracy movement in coalition with the student movement and the labor movement that opposed the military dictatorships from the 1960s into the 1980s until the June Uprising of 1987, which ushered in direct presidential elections, ending decades of authoritarian rule in South Korea. Although there are elements of a leftist politics incorporating working class agendas, I use the term "opposition" rather than the "left" to denote a broader coalition that has been more nationalist than strictly leftist in the traditional sense of the term.

18. Halbwachs, *On Collective Memory*, 182–83.

19. The opposition is no longer as easy to define because the successes of the democracy movement in the late 1980s has led to the dispersion of the movement into more specific issues, such as the environmental movement, the women's movement, the consumer movement, the peace movement, and others. To some extent, the tradition of the older movement lingers on through organizations that continue to exist and through activists who have gone on to work in new organizations with experiences of a more cohesive past.

20. See RG 242, SA 2007, box 10, item 62, *Haebang hu Chosŏn* [Korea after liberation] (Pyongyang: 1949); Ri Na-yŏng, *Chosŏn minjok haebang t'ujaengsa* [History of struggle for national liberation in Korea] (Pyongyang: Chosŏn rodongdang ch'ulp'ansa, 1958).

21. See Korean History Research Association Modern History Testimony Team, *Kkŭtnaji annŭn yŏjŏng* [Unfinished weary path] (Seoul: Taedong, 1996). The book is a collection of life stories from former long-term prisoners, including that of Ch'oe Sang-wŏn and his wife, Pak Sun-ja. Although based on interviews, the book is not a transcript of the interviews, but an edited version of their stories.

22. Kang either misspoke or was mistaken about when the change was made. The change was made in a decision passed by the Supreme People's Assembly in December 1952. Lee Kye-Man and Kang In-Ho, "An Analysis on the Local Government Institution's Structure and Its Form in North Korea" [in Korean], *Taehan chŏngch'ihak hoebo* [Bulletin of the Korea Political Science Association] 12, no. 3 (2005): 128.

23. In a similar gesture, Kim Sŏk-hyŏng used his age to date events in the preliberation period, but switched to the calendar year in dating the postliberation period, requesting the interviewer for a copy of a chronology of the main events by year so that he could systematically proceed, fitting his life story to national history. See Yi Hyang-kyu, *Nanŭn chosŏn nodongdangwŏnio,* 116. For other examples of memoirs and oral histories that narrate one's life story through national history, see Ko Sŏng-hwa, *Na ŭi pimangrok* [My memo: Patriot's way] (Seoul: Hanulsa, 2001); Sim Ji-yŏn, *Yŏksa nŭn nambuk ŭl mutchi annŭnda* [History does not ask

north or south] (Seoul: Sonamu, 2001); Sin Jun-yŏng, *Yi In-mo: Chŏn inmin'gun chonggun kija sugi* [Yi In-mo: A memoir by a former People's Army war correspondent] (Seoul: Wŏlgan mal, 1992); Kim Jin-kye, *Choguk: ŏnŭ pukchosŏn inmin ŭi sugi* [Homeland: A memoir by a North Korean] (Seoul: Hyŏnjang munhak, 1990); Pak Jin-mok, *Nae choguk nae sanha* [My homeland my mountains and rivers] (Seoul: 1976).

24. Ham Sŏk-hŏn, *Na ŭi chasŏjŏn* [My autobiography] (Seoul: Chaeil Publishing, 1979).

25. Ibid., 209.

26. Ibid., 211–13.

27. Ibid., 213–16. American intelligence at the time obtained varying reports on the incident. Student protestors ranging from four hundred to twenty-six hundred attacked the PC and the Communist Party headquarters with stones and clubs, leading to eight deaths at the scene, thirteen more dead at the hospital, and seventy wounded. See RG 554 Records of General HQ, Far East Command, Supreme Commander Allied Powers and United Nations Command, US-AFIK XXIV corps, G-2, Historical Section, box 65, "G-2 Reports and Data on North Korea Pertinent on South Korea," (folder 2 of 2). See also Ham Sŏk-hŏn, "The Sinŭiju Student Incident That I Experienced" [in Korean], *Ssial ŭi sori* [Sound of a seed], no. 6 (November 1971).

28. RG 554 Records of General HQ, Far East Command, Supreme Commander Allied Powers and United Nations Command, USAFIK XXIV corps, G-2, Historical Section, box 65, "G-2 Reports and Data on North Korea pertinent on South Korea," (folder 1 of 2), Department of Public Information (March 13, 1946).

29. His story was introduced briefly in chapter 2. He left with just his diary, personal notes, and an unfinished memoir that had been compiled in secret during his two years in the north. His memoir was published in the south during the Korean War in 1952. O Yŏng-jin, *Ssogunjŏng ha ŭi pukhan: Hana ŭi chŭngŏn*.

30. Ri Yŏng-hŭi, *Yŏkchŏng: Na ŭi ch'ŏngnyŏn sidae* [My passage of youth] (Seoul: Ch'angjak kwa pip'yŏng, 1988).

31. Ibid., 90–92.

32. O Yŏng-jin, *Ssogunjŏng ha ŭi pukhan,* chapter 4.

33. Ibid., 65–66.

34. Ri Yŏng-hŭi, *Yŏkchŏng,* 99.

35. RG 554 Records of General HQ, Far East Command, Supreme Commander Allied Powers and United Nations Command, USAFIK XXIV corps, G-2, Historical Section, box 65, "G-2 Reports and Data on North Korea Pertinent on South Korea," (folder 1 of 2), Foreign Affairs Section (February 22, 1946).

36. See Kim Jin-yŏl's documentary film released in 2004 under the title *Ich'ŏjin yŏjŏnsa* [Forgotten Women Warriors] (90 min.) and Choi Ki-ja, "Study on Women's Partisans' Oral Life History for a Feminist History" [in Korean] (master's thesis, Hanyang University, 2001). These projects were the first of their kind. Although there had been studies done on partisans, none had focused specifically on women. I am indebted to P'urŭn yŏngsang, a documentary film collective in Seoul, and especially to Kim Jin-yŏl from the collective for providing me with much help during my research trip in 2003 by introducing me to Ch'oe Sang-wŏn and Choi Ki-ja and giving me access to transcripts from her video footage.

37. The memoir is included in a much longer memoir by her daughter, Sŏng Hye-rang. She is sister to Sŏng Hye-rim, who was Kim Jong Il's mistress and bore him his first son, Kim Jŏng-nam. Sŏng Hye-rang became a writer after graduating from Kim Il Sung University, and later worked as Kim Jŏng-nam's live-in tutor from 1976 until her defection in 1996. She states in the postscript that she defected to a third country out of fear, and was still in hiding at the time of writing. She smuggled out her mother Kim Wŏn-ju's memoir when she left North Korea, including it at the beginning of her own memoir. She notes that her mother wrote the memoir in the 1970s. See Sŏng Hye-rang, *Tŭngnamujip* [Wisteria tree house] (Seoul: Chisik nara, 2000), 48. Although Sŏng Hye-rang's memoir has a sensational ring to it, especially in the later parts, Kim Wŏn-ju's memoir contains details about women's experience of the colonial and postliberation periods. Because it deals mostly with the colonial period and ends before the founding

of separate states in the north and south, there would seem to be little motivation for distortion or fabrication, although its authenticity cannot be verified.

38. An exception may be Chŏng Sun-dŏk (1933–2004), who was a famed female partisan as the last partisan to be captured in 1963. She lost the use of one of her legs due to a bullet wound, and served twenty-two years in prison. The story of female guerrillas first became widely known through a novel based on her life. See Chŏng Ch'ung-je, *Sillok Chŏng Sun-dŏk* [The true chronicle of Chŏng Sun-dŏk] (Seoul: Taejehak, 1989). The book was written by a male author, however, and there were many criticisms, especially from Chŏng herself, that the author had misrepresented her story. Feminist scholars have critiqued such works for portraying women as pure and naïve peasants who joined the fighting simply to avenge the death of their partisan husbands rather than political agents in their own right.

39. When negotiations between Moscow and Washington failed over how to set up a unified Korean government, the United States spearheaded the formation of the United Nations Temporary Commission on Korea (UNTCOK) to observe elections in Korea, which the North Koreans and the Soviets boycotted. Thus, separate elections were held in the south, inaugurating the Republic of Korea on August 15, 1948. For details, see Bruce Cumings, *Korea's Place in the Sun* (New York: W. W. Norton, 1997), 211–24.

40. All biographic detail and synopses of their lives come from Choi Ki-ja, "Study on Women's Partisans' Oral Life History."

41. Marriage between those who shared the same political ideology was called "companionate marriage" (*tongji kyŏrhon*) in order to differentiate it from romantic or arranged unions.

42. In reaction to the decision by the south to hold separate elections in May, South Korean political leaders were invited to Pyongyang to work toward peaceful reunification and avert national division. Almost all prominent figures attended with the exception of Syngman Rhee, who was to become the first president of South Korea. Some 545 representatives from forty-six political parties and organizations attended the meeting held from April 19 to 22, 1948. See Armstrong, *North Korean Revolution*, 216.

43. Sŏng Hye-rang, *Tŭngnamujip*, 77.

44. Ibid., 84.

45. Ibid., 85–86.

46. Ibid., 28–29.

47. Ibid., 88.

48. According to Sŏng Hye-rang's memoir, Kim decided to stay in the north after the meeting and the family was separated until the Korean War. In the north, Kim worked as the editor of the international section of *Rodong sinmun* (Workers Daily), the organ of the North Korean Workers' Party, from 1949 until 1960. Meanwhile, Kim's husband had been imprisoned in 1947 in Seoul and was set free once the north took Seoul in the first few days of the Korean War. Sŏng described her father as a victim caught up in her mother's drive for liberation: "Poor father! Mom, flag in hand, leading the women's liberation movement and equality for women and men. Father seemed like a victim" (182). According to Sŏng, despite her mother's poor peasant background, Kim was demoted in 1960 from *Rodong sinmun* to Pyongyang's local paper because her husband was from a wealthy family (293).

49. Korean History Research Association Modern History Testimony Team, *Kkŭtnaji annŭn yŏjŏng*, 220.

50. Ibid., 226.

51. Choi Ki-ja, "Study on Women's Partisans' Oral Life History," 50.

52. Ibid., 40.

53. Ibid., 49.

54. Ibid.

55. Ibid., 44.

56. Ibid., 46. She was reunited with her son after ten years when she was released from prison in 1960.

57. Kim Jin-yŏl transcript, September 30, 2002. *Chŏng* is a rather complicated term to translate. It is commonly translated as affection or bond, and is often associated with sentiments of endearment and fondness, but it is not necessarily limited to such positive connotations and includes many forms of attachment.

58. Ibid.

59. On September 1, 2000, sixty-three unconverted former long-term prisoners were returned to North Korea as part of the agreement resulting from the North-South summit meeting that year. Of them, only twenty were originally from the north, but the others decided to "return" to North Korea because they considered the north their "ideological homeland." Several of those who went north had family in the south that they left behind. Among them was Yun Hŭi-bo, who was Pak Sŏn-ae's husband. See Choi Ki-ja, "Study on Women's Partisans' Oral Life History," 82.

60. Kim Jin-yŏl transcript, September 30, 2002.

61. Choi Ki-ja, "Study on Women's Partisans' Oral Life History," 61.

62. Kim Jin-yŏl transcript, September 30, 2002.

63. It should be emphasized that the traditional patriarchal family in Korea regulated the behavior of men as well as women. Former partisan women were not the only ones who were shielded from further political oppression if they married an ordinary, apolitical man. Former political prisoners such as Kang Tam were also encouraged to marry and have a "normal" family as a way to "reform" their life away from politics, settle down, and take responsibility as the head of household rather than as a social revolutionary. See also Ch'oe Nam-kyu's life story in Korean History Research Association Modern History Testimony Team, *Kkŭtnaji annŭn yŏjŏng*, 75.

64. Hŏ Chŏng-suk, *Minju kŏn'guk ŭi nanal e* [Days in the democratic construction of the country] (Pyongyang: Chosŏn rodongdang ch'ulp'ansa, 1986), 1.

65. Mun Che-an et al., *8.15 ŭi kiŏk: Haebang konggan ŭi p'unggyŏng, 40-in ŭi yŏksa ch'ehŏm* [Memory of 8.15: Landscape of liberated space, 40 individuals historical experience] (P'aju: Han'gilsa, 2005), 411.

66. Julia Swindells, "Liberating the Subject? Autobiography and 'Women's History': A Reading of *The Diaries of Hannah Cullick*," in *Interpreting Women's Lives: Feminist Theory and Personal Narratives*, ed. Personal Narrative Group (Bloomington: Indiana University Press, 1989), 24.

67. Jeffrey K. Olick and Joyce Robbins, "Social Memory Studies: From 'Collective Memory' to the Historical Sociology of Mnemonic Practices," *Annual Review of Sociology* 24 (1998): 127.

68. Tessa Morris-Suzuki, *The Past within Us: Media, Memory, History* (New York: Verso, 2005), 22. For similarly useful distinctions between memory and history, see Daqing Yang, "The Challenges of the Nanjing Massacre: Reflections on Historical Inquiry," in *The Nanjing Massacre in History and Historiography*, ed. Joshua Fogel (Berkeley: University of California Press, 2000); and Michael Kammen, "Review: Carl Becker Redivivus: Or, Is Everyone Really a Historian?" *History and Theory* 39, no. 2 (May 2000).

69. Marianne Debouzy, "In Search of Working-Class Memory: Some Questions and a Tentative Assessment," in *Between Memory and History*, ed. Marie-Noelle Bourguet, Lucette Valensi, and Nathan Wachtel (New York: Harwood Academic Publishers, 1990).

Conclusion

1. RG 242, SA 2009, box 3, item 103, Survey of Two Years of Work in Each of the Provincial People's Committees (September 1947).

2. W. Rosenberg, "Economic Comparison of North and South Korea," *Journal of Contemporary Asia* 5, no. 2 (1975): 90; Joseph Chung, *The North Korean Economy: Structure and Development* (Stanford: Hoover Institution Press, 1974), 146, quoted in Aidan Foster-Carter, "North

Korea: Development and Self-Reliance: A Critical Appraisal," *Bulletin of Concerned Asian Scholars* 9, no. 1 (January–March 1977): 46.

3. Mun Woong Lee, "Rural North Korea under Communism."

4. *Theses on the Socialist Rural Question in Our Country* adopted at the Eighth Plenary meeting of the Fourth Central Committee of the Workers' Party of Korea (February 25, 1964), in Kim Il Sung, *Revolution and Socialist Construction in Korea: Selected Writings of Kim Il Sung*, 1st ed. (New York: International Publishers, 1971), 57.

5. For North Korea as "one of the greatest economic powers in Asia," see Philippe Pons, *Le Monde* (July 1, 1974), quoted in Foster-Carter, "North Korea: Development and Self-Reliance," 49. In fact, references to the East Asian "miracle" began *not* with South Korea but with North Korea. See Joan Robinson, "Korean Miracle," *Monthly Review* (January 1965): 541–49.

6. *The Present Situation and the Tasks of Our Party*, report at the Conference of the Workers' Party of Korea (October 5, 1966), in Kim Il Sung, *Revolution and Socialist Construction in Korea*, 125.

7. North Korean Workers' Party Kangwŏn Province Inje County Executive Committee Meeting Minutes No. 25 (1948.10.21), NHCC, vol. 2, 632. Also in RG 242, SA 2007, box 6, item 1.55.

8. North Korean Workers' Party Kangwŏn Province Inje County Executive Committee Meeting Minutes No. 48 (1949.6.8), NHCC, vol. 3, 348. Also in RG 242, SA 2007, box 6, item 1.65.

9. North Korean Workers' Party Kangwŏn Province Inje County Executive Committee Meeting Minutes No. 54 (1949.7.21), NHCC, vol. 3, 527, 845–50. Also in RG 242, SA 2007, box 6, item 1.19.

10. North Korean Workers' Party Kangwŏn Province Inje Executive Committee Minutes No. 58 (1949.8.25), NHCC, vol. 3, 528; North Korean Workers' Party Kangwŏn Province Inje County Executive Committee Minutes No. 71 (1949.12.10), NHCC, vol. 3, 879.

11. North Korean Workers' Party Kangwŏn Province Inje County Executive Committee Meeting Minutes No. 73 (1949.12.27), NHCC, vol. 3, 936–40. Also in RG 242, SA 2007, box 6, item 1.62.

12. North Korean Workers' Party Kangwŏn Province Inje Executive Committee Minutes No. 58 (1949.8.25), NHCC, vol. 3, 528–36.

13. North Korean Workers' Party Kangwŏn Province Inje County Executive Committee Meeting Minutes No. 54 (1949.7.21), NHCC, vol. 3, 421, 534–35. Also in RG 242, SA 2007, box 6, item 1.19.

14. "Inje County Internal Affairs Bureau Document No. 1–4: Summary of Police Station Work (Secret)" (1950.6), NHCC, vol. 18, 310.

15. "On the Implementation of the Summer Cleaning," Puk Township Police Chief (1950.6.9), NHCC, vol. 18, 327–28.

16. RG 242, SA 2012, box 8, item 28, Kangwŏn Province Ch'ŏrwŏn County Department of Interior (1950).

17. RG 242, SA 2012, box 8, item 28, Kangwŏn Province Ch'ŏrwŏn County Department of Interior (1950).

18. RG 242, SA 2010, box 2, item 76, North Korean Workers' Party Hwanghae Province (Top Secret) (1949).

19. Head of Bomber Command in the Far East, General O'Donnell, quoted in Foster-Carter, "North Korea: Development and Self-Reliance," 47; Charles Armstrong, "The Destruction and Reconstruction of North Korea, 1950–1960," *Asia-Pacific Journal* 8, issue 51.2 (December 20, 2010).

20. Bruce Cumings, *The Korean War: A History* (New York: Modern Library, 2010), 35, 63.

21. Although conscription terms were codified at three to four years in 1958, actual service terms reportedly extended up to eight years. The ten-year service requirement became law in 1993. See *2009 Pukhan kaeyo* [2009 overview of North Korea] (Seoul: T'ongil yŏn'guwŏn, 2009), 97.

22. Eric Hobsbawm and Terence Ranger, eds., *The Invention of Tradition* (New York: Cambridge University Press, 1992).

23. Lefebvre, *Everyday Life in the Modern World*, 33.

24. Genaro Carnero Checa, *Korea: Rice and Steel* (Pyongyang: Foreign Languages Publishing House, 1977), 99. According to the book's editor's note, Checa was a Peruvian journalist, who wrote the book based on his numerous visits to North Korea and meetings with Kim Il Sung. Such writings by Third World figures were not uncommon among official North Korean publications, especially during the 1960s and 1970s, as they served to enhance North Korea's leadership in the Non-Aligned Movement while boosting North Korea's standing both domestically and internationally during the period when North Korea outpaced its southern counterpart by most measures. As an official North Korean publication, Checa's writing represented North Korean state policy despite its foreign authorship.

25. Ibid, 159–60.

26. Buck-Morss, *Dreamworld and Catastrophe*.

27. I use David Harvey's definition of creative destruction: "Creative destruction is embedded within the circulation of capital itself. Innovation exacerbates instability, insecurity, and in the end, becomes the prime force pushing capitalism into periodic paroxysms of crisis. . . . The struggle to maintain profitability sends capitalists racing off to explore all kinds of other possibilities. New product lines are opened up, and that means the creation of new wants and needs. Capitalists are forced to redouble their efforts to create new needs in others. . . . The result is to exacerbate insecurity and instability, as masses of capital and workers shift from one line of production to another, leaving whole sectors devastated." Harvey, *Condition of Postmodernity*, 105–6.

28. The emphasis on consciousness and creativity is hardly putting Marx on his head because as Raymond Williams observed regarding the denigration of culture as superstructure by orthodox Marxists, "what has then happened is that consciousness has been separated from the 'sphere of social being,' characteristically in the form of abstracting 'the superstructure from the base'." See Raymond Williams, "Beyond Actually Existing Socialism," *New Left Review*, no. 120 (March–April 1980): 6.

29. Kim Il Sung, "Si kun inmin wiwŏnhoe ŭi tangmyŏn han myŏkkaji kwaŏp e taehayŏ" [On the tasks confronting city and county people's committees] (speech delivered August 9, 1958), in *Kim Il Sung chŏjakjip* [The collected works of Kim Il Sung], vol. 12 (Pyongyang: Chosŏn rodongdang ch'ulpansa, 1981), 409–10.

30. RG 242, SA 2010, box 3, item 45, "Chosŏn minjujuŭi inmin konghwaguk hŏnbŏp" [Constitution of the Democratic People's Republic of Korea] (1948).

31. RG 242, SA 2012, box 8, item 47, Kim Il Sung, *Hyŏn kyedan e issŏsŏ chibang chŏnggwŏn kigwan dŭl ŭi immu wa yŏkhal* [Duty and role of local government organs in the present stage] (Pyongyang: Kungrip ch'ulp'ansa, 1952).

32. Ibid., 18–19.

33. Ibid., 20–21.

34. Ibid., 24–25.

35. Ibid., 42.

36. *Kim Il Sung chŏjakjip*, 414, 417.

37. Lee Kye-Man and Kang In-Ho, "An Analysis on the Local Government Institution's Structure," 128. The status and power of provincial and county people's committees were restored in the 1998 constitutional revision, which also restored the separation of powers between the people's committee chair and party secretary by mandating that the positions be held by different people. It is unclear how the reforms in 1998 have changed local governance, but reverting back to elements of the 1948 constitution could be read as a move to restore some of the local autonomy and revolutionary momentum from its early days in the aftermath of the devastating famine that led to the breakdown of the public distribution system and the centralized government. See ibid., 134–36.

38. Yun Chong-sŏp, "The Status and Function of Local Government Organs in the Present Stage of Socialist Construction" [in Korean], in *8.15 haebang 15-chunyŏn kinyŏm ronmunjip*

[Papers on the fifteenth anniversary of August 15 liberation] (Pyongyang: Kim Il Sung chong-hap taehak, 1960), 55–57.

39. Michael Halberstam, *Totalitarianism and the Modern Conception of Politics* (New Haven: Yale University Press, 1999).

40. I use Michael Hardt and Antonio Negri's conceptualization of the multitude: "New figures of struggle and new subjectivities are produced in the conjuncture of events, in the universal nomadism, in the general mixture and miscegenation of individuals and populations, and in the technological metamorphoses of the imperial biopolitical machine. These new figures and subjectivities are produced because, although the struggles are indeed antisystemic, they are not posed *merely against* the imperial system—they are not simply negative forces. They also express, nourish, and develop positively their own constituent projects; they work toward the liberation of living labor, creating constellations of powerful singularities. This constituent aspect of the movement of the multitude, in its myriad faces, is really the positive terrain of the historical construction of Empire." Michael Hardt and Antonio Negri, *Empire* (Cambridge: Harvard University Press, 2000), 61.

Appendix

1. North Korean Workers' Party Kangwŏn Province Inje County Standing Committee Meeting Minutes No. 70 (1949.11.27), NHCC, vol. 3, 817–19. Also in RG 242, SA 2007, box 6, item 1.62.

2. North Korean Workers' Party Kangwŏn Province Inje County Women's League Cell 33rd Meeting Minutes (1949.12.7), NHCC, vol. 4, 274–77. Also in RG 242, SA 2007, box 6, item 1.31.

Index